SPENSER STUDIES

V

SPENSER STUDIES
A Renaissance Poetry Annual
V

EDITED BY

Patrick Cullen AND *Thomas P. Roche, Jr.*

AMS PRESS, INC.
NEW YORK, N.Y.

SPENSER STUDIES:
A RENAISSANCE POETRY ANNUAL

edited by Patrick Cullen and Thomas P. Roche, Jr.

is published annually by AMS Press, Inc. as a forum for Spenser scholarship and criticism and related Renaissance subjects. Manuscripts ordinarily should be from 3,000 to 10,000 words in length, should include an abstract of 100–175 words, should conform to the *MLA Style Sheet,* and should be submitted *in duplicate.* They will be returned only if sufficient postage is enclosed (overseas contributors should enclose international reply coupons). Manuscripts and editorial correspondence should be addressed to Thomas P. Roche, Jr., Department of English, Princeton University, Princeton, N.J. 08544.

ISSN 0195-9468
Volume V, ISBN 0-404-19205-X

Contents

The damsel Abessa first appears walking ahead of Una in the wilderness, bearing a pot of water on her shoulders. This water-pot is one of many allusions to Genesis 21, all of which indicate that the damsel is Hagar, the bond-woman whose expulsion by Abraham was allegorized by Paul (in Galatians 4) as the spiritually reborn Christian's casting out of the rule of the law, the Old Covenant. To begin with, Abessa suggests the Jewish faith before the advent of Christianity; but having faced Una and fled, she represents the Jews in their failure to convert and recalls the fallen *Synagoga* of the medieval *Ecclesia-Synagoga* motif. Arriving in Corceca's house, Abessa suggests aspects of the Roman Church; the sequence of her roles implies that the contemporary Roman Church is heir to the vices of Judaism. Una's lion, whose mildness is not recognized by the terrified Abessa, seems to be a symbol of Christ, "the lion of the tribe of Juda." His initial fierceness is God's just anger, replaced with mercy through the incarnation.

Spenser's emerging conception of the status of his Faeryland, as he attempts to delineate the relationship between history and poetry, fact and fiction, helps explain his growing disillusionment in the last books of *The Faerie Queene.* The major issues at stake are revealed in two specific sections of the poem where Spenser sets together two versions of a similar story: the paired chronicles Arthur and Guyon read in the House of Alma (the disruptive

British history and the idealized Faeryland history) and the paired stories of union in Book IV (the harmonious wedding of the Thames and the Medway, and the more problematic uniting of Marinell and Florimell). Spenser endeavors to clear a space for his Faeryland where there are no pretensions to correspondence with actual experience and where, therefore, he can freely invent his ideal landscape; yet he also acknowledges a close association between his created world and the actual world that demands that he confront the unstable, disruptive nature of his fiction and its own remoteness from the ideal. The last books of *The Faerie Queene,* then, cannot simply be said to reflect Spenser's growing awareness that the actual world is antagonistic to his ideal Faeryland, for the poet sees congruence more than conflict between Faeryland and actuality. The poet does not just come to terms with the fallen state of the world—something he has always been aware of—but also comes to terms with the status of his own fiction, which subscribes to the actual and reveals his inability to create and sustain a golden world in poetry.

Triamond, Agape, and the Fates: Neoplatonic Cosmology in Spenser's Legend of Friendship

DAVID W. BURCHMORE

45

The three sons of Agape have been said variously to represent the harmony of the "three worlds" united by love, the unity of man's tripartite soul; or the "threefold power" of love. All of these meanings are compatible and their combination in a single figure is sanctioned by the systems of triadic correspondence elaborated by syncretistic Renaissance Neoplatonists. The three Fates, who grant Agape's request to join her sons' lives, were also said to correspond with the three worlds or with the three parts of the world soul. In acceding to Agape's wish, they are performing the cosmic function assigned them by the philosophers, uniting the three parts of man's soul as well as the parts of the universe through the influence of love. The description of the Fates "all sitting round about / The direfull distaffe standing in the mid" is borrowed from Plato's *Republic,* and is also placed at the exact numerological midpoint of the first third of the book. It is balanced by the figure of Amoret "in the midst" of the Temple of Venus at the center of the last third. The midpoint of the central third is occupied by the Cave of Lust. The placement of these three figures (Agape, Amoret, and Lust) embodies in the structure of the book the tripartite division of love (divine, human, and bestial) which is its subject.

'Deuicefull Sights': Spenser's Emblematic Practice in *The Faerie Queene*, V. 1–3

R. J. MANNING

65

Critics have dismissed the first three cantos of Book Five as rebarbative, as a "false start," or even as "largely irrelevant" to the Legend of Justice. While Spenser indicates that these cantos form an independent structural unit within the book as a whole, he also asserts that these cantos "agree" with his present treatise, and their purpose is "true vertue to aduaunce." The methods he employs are consistent with his practice elsewhere: he inserts into his narrative the traditional emblems of the book's titular virtue: in Canto One, the headless Lady is an ancient hieroglyph of Justice, while the knight's broken sword was used to symbolize over-rigorous severity; Canto Two deals with economic abuses, and contains the emblem of "handless Justice," while the Giant's broken scales show the damaging effects of corrupting avarice; Canto Three introduces the sun and the bridle, attributes of Nemesis, who restrains the emotional excesses of pride and anger which threaten the right administration of Justice. These cantos thus form an exemplary statement of the virtue of Justice. Indeed, Spenser goes further, and displays the preeminence of Justice over the other Moral virtues. Justice is allied with Wisdom in Canto One, with Fortitude in Canto Two, and Temperance in Canto Three, Justice always characterizing the most perfect expression of each virtue.

Minims and Grace Notes: Spenser's Acidalian Vision and Sixteenth-Century Music

SETH WEINER

91

In a celebrated but misunderstood instance of musical wordplay, Spenser refers to the Acidalian vision in Book VI, Canto X of *The Faerie Queene* as a *minim*. Treatises on practical music in Spenser's time defined *minim* as the note on which the musical beat was based. Spenser's use of the term wittily implies that the Acidalian vision, inspired by a simple country lass rather than by Gloriana, is at once a mere trifle and an episode of first importance—a truancy but also the vital beat or pulse informing the whole poem. The beat, again according to contemporary musical treatises, could be subdivided by two or by three, thereby producing what was known as *imperfect time* or *perfect time*, also called *minim time*. Spenser's vision consists of the *three* classical Graces moving about *one* country lass, a dance suggestive of *perfect*, or *minim time*. Accordingly, the relationship of the Graces to the lass, and of the whole inner cluster of figures to the outer ring of one-hundred maidens, can be described numerologically in terms of a series of ingenious triadic unfoldings and infoldings. The triads all point toward common-places of Pythagorean cosmology that complement the iconography of the Grace's dance as explained by art historians—namely, that it concerns the unfolding of inward courtesy, private and deep in the soul's inner sanctum, into the civilities and shared decencies that make society an ongoing concern. Spenser is telling us, in effect, that the music of the universe resonates in *minim time* with the music of civilized institutions. The final portion of this essay applies the last stated idea to the vexed question of the choreography of the dance and suggests (citing precedents in Renaissance art) that the Graces are all facing outward. This configuration fulfills all the usual requirements of the Senecan and Servian models for the good civil life and also suggests the process of triadic unfolding and infolding. It thus corroborates what the art historians have taught us in terms of the other sister art, music.

The Old Theology: Spenser's Dame Nature and the Transfiguration

HAROLD L. WEATHERBY

113

When in "The Mutabilitie Cantos" Spenser identifies Nature with the "God of Nature" and then draws an analogy between Nature and the transfigured Christ, he raises questions of interpretation which deserve better answers than they have hitherto received. Though the numerous sources conventionally cited for these passages (from Pythagoras to Chaucer) may have influenced Spenser's conception, they do not provide adequate precedents for identifying Nature with the specifically Christian God nor for comparing her beauty with that of Christ in the Transfiguration. Precedents are, however, to be found in the Greek Church Fathers. In the theology of Athanasius, of the Cappadocians, and of John of Damascus, the theosis of man and, through man, of the rest of Nature is a recurrent motif. Several classical statements of this doctrine were available in the sixteenth century in recently published continental editions of the Fathers. Most notable among these is a 1577 Parisian edition of St. John of Damascus's *opera* which includes his treatise on the Transfiguration—a homily which recapitulates the earlier Eastern teaching on the subject and makes a detailed connection between the deification of Nature and the manifestation of that deification on Mt. Tabor. Furthermore John of Damascus links to the Transfiguration another motif clearly visible in "The Mutabilitie Cantos"—the eschatological expectation of the end of time and change. In St. John's discourse, as in Spenser's poem, the epiphany of a divinized Nature prompts the expectation of a time "when no more change shall be."

The dedicatory sonnets present one of the 1590 *Faerie Queene*'s few editorial problems, since the two impressions print two quite different series, the first with only ten sonnets, the second with the full seventeen. Editors and bibliographers have assumed that the order is confused because it did not really matter. On the contrary, the sonnets are arranged in exact accordance with the heraldic rules for precedence. The strictness and importance of the rules can be gaged by the fact that the printer took the trouble and expense to add the omitted seven sonnets by inserting a four page cancel instead of simply tacking them on to the end of the first series.

The prevailing sense of marital "jocundity" that critics have found in *Epithalamion* has tended to overshadow elements of the poem that are less markedly joyful. Spenser's poetic celebrant sings only to himself in the opening stanzas and identifies himself with the elegiac tradition of Orpheus. The bride whom he later addresses is a mysteriously silent and passive figure, removed from the poet in being and in time as well as in virtue. The wedding day that is the poem's occasion is colored by experiences of "payne and sorrow," resignation and loss, that are not clearly and decisively eclipsed by the joys of matrimony. Spenser found expressive opportunities in his poetical marriage gift to Elizabeth Boyle that led him to explore a range of both secular and religious ambiguities in the theme of marriage. These ambiguities pervade not only *Epithalamion* itself but the Anacreontic songs at the end of the *Amoretti* and, along with the joyous tone that so many readers have noted, give to *Epithalamion* its unusual complexity and fullness.

Stephen Hawes's *Pastime of Pleasure* (1509) offers a theory and practice of aureation which distinguish him from earlier, fifteenth-century Chaucerians and which link him to continental Humanist thought. Hawes's interest in the relationship of himself to his reader articulates itself in several ways: in the narrative presentation of Grande Amoure as a reader of engraved texts and gilded pictures; in the poet's digressions on his own literary posterity through printed books; and in the poem's allegorical presentations of Fame. Aureate diction is thus not merely ornamental; rather, in its immutability and purity, it can serve as the ideal vehicle for the preservation of printed literature and for the expression of courtly ideals. Hawes takes the technical language of Ciceronian faculty psychology and mnemonic theory, combines it with the imagery of printing, and develops a language of "impression" which metaphorically can express concepts of poetic inspiration. These elements combine to provide Hawes with a vocabulary of replication and preservation, and they serve to associate his poem with several developments of late fifteenth-century continental thought: the "place logic" of educational theorists; the ethos of public life and literary fame; the new sense of textual integrity defined by editors of the classics.

Spenser's 'Emblematic' Imagery: A Study of Emblematics

MASON TUNG

185

There are two reasons why Spenser's images often appear "emblematic." One is that both Spenser and the emblematists draw from the same sources, *e.g.,* natural history, Aesop's fables, proverbial lore, and mythology. Consequently, parallels between Spenser's images and emblem books are the result not of direct borrowing but of drawing from the same sources, some of which are "emblematized," making it easier to establish coincidental resemblances. The other reason is that poetics and emblematics share many rhetorical concerns, such as the mixing of *dulci* and *utile, ut pictura poesis,* the ideal of expressing similitude with vividness (*enargeia* and *energeia*), the revealing of the intelligible in the visible, and the doctrines of imitation and representation. Spenser achieves the "emblematic" mode, not necessarily by borrowing from emblem books, but by realizing some of the common rhetorical ideals, especially those of imitation and *energeia* propounded by Aristotle. A case in point is in his treatment of the Graces' dance in Book VI of *The Faerie Queene.* The popular and traditional dance of the three Graces has been transformed into a unique image that not only meets all of Spenser's particular allegorical needs, but also fulfills the many rhetorical goals that are common to both poetics and emblematics.

Autobiographical Elements in Sidney's
Astrophil and Stella

THOMAS P. ROCHE, JR.

209

This essay is an addendum to my "*Astrophil and Stella*: A Radical Reading," *Spenser Studies* III, in which I tried to establish a distance between Sidney as artist and his fictional spokesman Astrophil. In this essay I try to account for the obvious references to Sidney's name, arms, and family (title, sonnets 83, 30, 70, 65), to the Devereux arms (sonnet 13), to Lord Rich (sonnets 9, 24, 35, 37) and Gifford's reportage of Sidney's dying comment of a "vanitie" that separated him from Christ: "It was my Ladie Rich." I argue that the "Vanitie" is not autobiographical but literary convention analogous to the retraction of Chaucer, citing as proof the imitations of Sidney's sequence by Barnabe Barnes, Henry Constable, Alexander Craig, and the elegies in Spenser's *Astrophel* volume.

Sidney's Portrayal of Mounted Combat with Lances

E. MALCOLM PARKINSON

231

In his revised *Arcadia,* Sidney vividly portrays jousting, covering the entire sequence of events from the moment the horses move forward until the knights slow their steeds after a clash. Sidney depicts combat with lances from multiple viewpoints: of the knights, the unskilled spectator, and the skilled spectator. In doing so, he reveals the complexities encountered by the combatants and the onlookers in determining precisely what occurred when two knights clashed. These complexities not only indicate that certain knights, such as Lelius, who may represent Sir Henry Lee, could run rigged courses to deceive onlookers at a tournament, but also continue a significant theme in the *Arcadia*, the difference between appearance and reality.

Sidney's verisimilar anatomies of jousts and of running at the ring show the technical skill of the accomplished knight and so explain why Amphialus, for example, deserves his reputation as a formidable combatant in the lists. Moreover, since it was so unusual for a practicing jouster to write about jousting with such sustained authenticity of detail, the *Arcadia* forms an outstanding complement to formal records and heraldic descriptions of the Accession Day Tilts, held during Elizabeth's reign, by revealing some of the psychology and tactics of knights in tournaments.

'The Gardin of Proserpina This Hight': Ruskin's Application of Spenser and Horizons of Reception

JEFFREY L. SPEAR

If, as H. R. Jauss argues, the life of a literary work is not intrinsic but an interaction between the work and its readers, then literary criticism is less a progress toward definitive readings than the record of historically conditioned meanings as revelatory of readers as of their chosen texts. The "outdated" readings that so often serve as foils for the latest ones thus reveal not the history of error but the historical horizons of earlier periods and become clues to understanding them. Sympathetic understanding of Ruskin on Spenser requires recognition of the historical and linguistic distance between our world and Ruskin's, a distance as real, if less extreme, than that between the sixteenth and the nineteenth or twentieth centuries. Read in an evangelical context, Ruskin emerges as a belated figure in a Protestant tradition in which Spenser figures as both poet and teacher. While his reading of Spenser anticipates modern iconographic studies, it also questions the aesthetic bias underlying our secular interpretations of such episodes as the destruction of the Bower of Bliss. Finally, Ruskin's reading of Spenser provides an insight into his own mythopoetic criticism of Victorian society and the works of J. M. W. Turner in *Modern Painters*.

Illustrations

Index

Contents of Previous Volumes

Preface

I N THIS THE FIFTH VOLUME of *Spenser Studies*, the first to
be produced *ab ovo* by AMS Press, we thought it fitting to
thank AMS for rescuing this annual from an early demise and to
restate our editorial policy. That we began this undertaking
without funds and without any staff was an act of foolhardiness
born of a naïve faith in the scholarly quality of those working
on Spenser and poetry of the English Renaissance. That we
have achieved a Volume V is a miracle justifying that naïve
faith. For the first two volumes we would not accept articles
from the editors or the editorial board, which practically swept
the cupboard bare of established scribbling Spenserians, but
fortunately through serious attention to papers read at conventions such as the Modern Language Association and the Spenser
section of the Medieval Conference at Kalamazoo, we were able
to gather excellent papers, often by young scholars who had not
published previously. The success of these volumes encourages
us to continue our policy of not seeking out established names
or of commissioning articles or of inducing articles by an-
nouncing topics for subsequent volumes. Those who were
accepted on the grounds of this policy may feel pleased by its
liberality; those rejected, who often had to wait far too long for
rejection, will not be pleased, and to these scholars we can only
offer apologies from the staff of two with many hats to wear
and to encourage them to send us what next they do, with a
promise of a reply within three months.

Several reviews have remarked on the eclectic nature of our
articles, and this is not chance but policy. We have no axe to
grind, although we have a predilection toward what used to be
called "historical criticism," by which we mean criticism growing out of a knowledge about the English Renaissance in fields
that illuminate poetic technique: what did they know that we
have forgotten that will help us to read Spenser and his contemporaries better? This is a very wide injunction, and we hope
that it will encourage many scholars to submit their articles to
us.

We will not accept articles on drama, on Milton, on Herbert or other seventeenth-century poets, unless they bear in some important way on the problems of Spenser and poetic theory of the English Renaissance in the sixteenth century.

The articles in this volume exemplify our policy, which is nothing more than a policy of excellence and need. Kathryn Walls, David Burchmore, R. J. Manning, Seth Weiner, Harold Weatherby present new evidence on biblical, Neoplatonic, iconographical, musicological, theological backgrounds to readings of particular portions of Spenser's poem. Carol Stillman's, the shortest piece in this volume, presents what we all should have known before, the reason for the ordering of the Dedicatory Sonnets to Spenser's poem, a thesis that has not been stated before. Jacqueline Miller and Douglas Anderson present readings of *Faerie Queene,* 2.11 and *Epithalamion* that challenge or amplify currently accepted readings of those parts of Spenser's work. The articles not specifically on Spenser range from Seth Lerer's brilliant treatment of Stephen Hawes to Jeffrey Spear's splendid reassessment of John Ruskin's reading of Spenser. Thomas Roche contributes an appendage to his article on Sidney in the previous volume. Malcolm Parkinson's article on Sidney's knowledge of arms in the *Arcadia,* breaks our rule of publishing only articles on poetry, but its excellence and significance for our knowledge of Renaissance studies made it mandatory, as well as Mason Tung's enormously learned piece on emblematic imagery.

Volume VI is already in preparation, and we would welcome submissions for that volume and the succeeding four volumes, for which we are already contracted. Length is not a question unless it goes beyond our initial stipulated limit of 10,000 words. We might also remind you that our initial difficulties came from lack of library sales. It would be to our mutual benefit if you would see that your library subscribes.

SPENSER STUDIES

V

I

KATHRYN WALLS

Abessa and the Lion: *The Faerie Queene*, I.3. 1-12

*T*HE ABANDONED Una, accompanied only by the lion, journeys in search of the Redcrosse Knight for a long time without seeing even a sign of anyone else until she finds and follows a track made by human feet and sees, walking slowly ahead of her, a damsel carrying a pot of water. Catching up with her, Una calls out, asking for directions. When the two women actually face each other, Una is disappointed; the damsel does not speak (for she is a deaf mute), and her only reaction is to take flight. She throws down her pitcher and runs.

This is a strange and elusive episode. Abessa's lack of initiative, her baffling silence and her neutrality (she is at this point neither hoped-for friend nor outright enemy) make her lack definition. Her flight means that Una must continue almost as before, so that the meeting is, on the face of it, an anti-climax. But the passage is, on the other hand, full of narrative movement and emotional intensity. It is, in a word, dramatic, and its drama together with its enigmatic character creates an expectation of special significance. What does the confrontation of Una and Abessa represent?

In the next phase of the action, the significance of Abessa is clear, and commentators seem to have felt that there is, therefore, no real question to answer. Stanzas 10–12 are generally seen as a narrative ploy, or as a kind of overture hinting at themes which remain to be fully developed. Some of the resonance of the imagery has been perceived, but it is always discussed in relation to the following episode, in which the cottage inhabited by Abessa and her mother very quickly turns out to be Roman Catholicism providing a temporary and inhospitable residence for religious truth[1] Corceca exhibits ignorant superstitious devotion, while Abessa herself, whore of Kirkrapine and recipient of his stolen goods, suggests the corrupt Roman clergy, enriched by wrongful taxation of the churches abroad. The booty itself indicates idolatry, and altogether Abessa begins to look like a twin of the similarly-named Duessa (who is establishing a hold over Redcrosse at this very time). In stanza 18, when all these points have emerged, we find out for the first time that the "damsel" is called *Abessa*. While the name is susceptible to more sophisticated interpretations,[2] the most obvious association, through *abbey*, is with monasticism. Abessa, therefore, at the point at which she is named, clearly does represent aspects of the Roman Catholic Church.

But this would not, I think, strike us from stanzas 10–12 alone. I would argue that the damsel has a different (albeit related) significance before she reaches her mother's cottage. My argument rests principally upon the biblical allusions which are threaded through these preliminary stanzas. But it is worth noting that even at the literal level stanza 12 marks a transition, bringing both Abessa—as yet anonymous—and Una from "deserts wyde" (10.1) into a claustrophobic interior, where day gives way to night (15.1) and action almost ceases.

The most concrete defining feature of the damsel is the "pot of water" which she bears "on her shoulders sad" (10.9). This detail is given particular emphasis when the damsel, seeing the lion "With suddaine feare her pitcher downe she threw" (11.6). This pitcher seems to present itself as a key to the allegory. Commentators from Upton on have suggested that it is an allusion to the woman of Samaria (because she was going to draw water when she met Christ, John 4), but they have not gone very far to explain the function of this association in terms of the immediate context. Kellogg and Steele, for example, point out that the Samaritan woman was "an adultress and an idolater," but they see the allusion as a foreshadowing of the next episode, in which adultery is explicit and idolatry virtually so.[3] There are, as we shall see, more interesting reasons for an allusion to the woman of Samaria here, but there are other possibilities to consider—as Upton himself recognized: "Our poet paints according to the simplicity of ancient customs and manners, and his painting is therefore the more natural and pleasing. See Genesis 24.15,45: 'Rebecca came out with her pitcher upon her shoulder.' So likewise the woman of Samaria, John 4.7. And the very same natural picture we have in Homer."[4] As Upton intuitively perceived, the image is archetypal. There is another woman in Genesis (not mentioned by Upton) who carries a water-vessel, and who resembles Abessa quite strikingly in several other respects too. That woman is, of course, Hagar. Her story is strange and sad. An Egyptian slave, she was given to Abraham by his aged and apparently sterile wife Sarah, and bore him a son, Ishmael. She was twice forced to flee into the wilderness, the second time because Sarah observed Ishmael mocking her own miraculously-conceived son, Isaac:

> Wherefore she said unto Abraham, Cast out this bond-woman and her son: for the son of this bondwoman shall not be heir with my son, even with Isaac. . . .
> And Abraham rose up early in the morning, and took bread, and a bottle of water, and gave it unto Hagar, putting it on her shoulder, and the child, and sent her away: and she departed, and wandered in the wilderness of Beersheba.
>
> (Genesis 21.10,14)

Una is travelling through "deserts wyde" when she meets Abessa (10.1), apparently therefore an inhabitant of "the wilderness." But it is the bottle of water which Hagar carries, and carries on her shoulder, that links her most graphically with Abessa. This bottle figures in numerous paintings of the dismissal of Hagar,[5] and it is crucial to her story. When her water is used up, Hagar puts Ishmael under a shrub to die, and goes a distance away from him to weep (Genesis 21.15–16). Illustrations of this incident suggest Abessa even more strongly than the biblical story, for they typically show an abandoned water-bottle[6]—probably because it is to figure in the divine rescue of Ishmael. God responds to Ishmael's plight, and his angel encourages Hagar (17–18). Then "God opened her eyes, and she saw a well of water; and she went, and filled the bottle with water, and gave the lad a drink" (19). At this point, of course, Hagar's action is the reverse of Abessa's, since Abessa abandoned her pitcher for good. But Abessa's flight is paralleled in Hagar's story earlier on when, being pregnant, Hagar first attracted Sarah's resentment: "And when Sarai dealt hardly with her, she fled from her face" (Genesis 16.6). The phrase is repeated when, having met an angel by a fountain in the wilderness, Hagar explains "I flee from the face of my mistress Sarai" (8). Spenser reiterates that Abessa "fled" ("fled away" 11.7; "Full fast she fled" 12.1). What is more, her flight, like Hagar's, is associated with a "face." Although her terror is first (and finally) explained by reference to the lion by Una's side, an alternative explanation lies in the penultimate lines of stanza 11:

> Till seeing by her side the Lyon stand,
> With suddaine feare her pitcher downe she threw,
> And fled away: for neuer in that land
> Face of faire Ladie she before did vew,
> And that dread Lyons looke her cast in deadly hew.
>   (11.5–9)

Spenser's inclusion of this seemingly superfluous reason has troubled some commentators,[7] and it does create a somewhat clumsy effect. In view of this we might—having recognized the awkward line as one strand in a whole web of allusions to Hagar—suspect that Spenser was more concerned to recall Hagar's reaction to Sarah than he was to create a smooth and consistent literal surface. Although neither Genesis 16 nor Genesis 22 actually mentions Hagar's fear (leaving us to infer it from events), "fearing" (cf. "suddaine feare," above) is given as the meaning of Hagar's name in a sixteenth-century English concordance.[8]

It is not hard to explain why Spenser should have introduced a damsel resembling Hagar into his Book of Holiness. In a well-known and extremely influential passage in the Epistle to the Galatians, Paul interpreted the story of Hagar allegorically:

> Tell me, ye that desire to be under the law, do ye not hear the law?
> For it is written, that Abraham had two sons, the one by a bondmaid, the other by a freewoman.
> But he who was of the bondwoman was born after the flesh; but he of the freewoman was by promise.
> Which things are an allegory: for these are the two covenants; the one from the mount Sinai, which gendereth to bondage, which is Agar.
> For this Agar is mount Sinai in Arabia, and answereth to

Jerusalem which now is, and is in bondage with her children.

But Jerusalem which is above is free, which is the mother of us all.

For it is written, Rejoice, thou barren that bearest not; break forth and cry, thou that travailest not: for the desolate hath many more children than she which hath an husband.

Now we, brethren, as Isaac was, are the children of promise.

But as then he that was born after the flesh persecuted him that was born after the Spirit, even so it is now.

Nevertheless what saith the scripture? Cast out the bondwoman and her son: for the son of the bondwoman shall not be heir with the son of the freewoman.

So then, brethren, we are not children of the bond-woman, but of the free.

(Galatians 4.21–31)

This passage was always important as an authoritative example of allegory, and it was particularly important to Protestants as an endorsement of the doctrine of justification by faith. The Despair canto is saturated with references to Galatians (among other related Pauline writings), as Nohrnberg has shown,[9] and the broader relevance to Book I of Paul's theme of spiritual rebirth and his imagery of rival women, mountains, and the heavenly city scarcely needs demonstration.

In view of Paul's authority, a reference to Hagar almost inevitably suggests Galatians. And Spenser does seem to have Galatians in mind in canto iii, even though his allusions to it lack the concentration and the extended unmistakable verbal echoes of his allusions to Genesis, and are in a general way less pronounced. There is a possible allusion to Paul's interpretation of Hagar in the "mountaine hore" (10.6) around which Abessa had taken her path ("this Agar is mount Sinai in Arabia"), and there are glimpses of Paul's comparison in the stanzas which frame our episode; Una is described as having been "desolate" (until joined by the lion, 9.1), while Abessa has a mate (though not a "husband") in Kirkrapine. Looking much further ahead, we can see that the as yet unhappy Una is destined ultimately,

like the barren freewoman, Sarah, to "rejoice," when in canto
xii she "to the Redcrosse knight / betrouthed is with ioy"—
there are five references to "ioy" and "reioycing" in the first
four stanzas of this final canto. There may also be a subtle
adjustment of Genesis towards Galatians in the way Spenser,
like Paul, concentrates on two women, omitting Abraham who
is, of course, pivotal in the Old Testament story.[10] Paul's
comparison provided one starting point for the long-lived and
rich tradition of the portrayal of Church and Synagogue as two
women, one triumphant, the other broken—one a queen and
the other a deposed queen. Spenser's pair of women are natural
heiresses of this tradition.[11]

But although anyone recognizing Hagar in Abessa might be
expected to recall Galatians also, the Old Testament story
stands out more vividly in Spenser's narrative (also a *story*) than
Paul's allegory and the subsequent tradition of *Ecclesia-Synagoga*
tableaux—at least to begin with, until Una catches up with the
damsel. Why should Spenser give priority, as it were, to
Genesis? The answer lies, I think, in its relative complexity.
Hagar is a sympathetic figure. Since she was brought to Abraham by Sarah in the first place, Sarah's resentment (while
understandable) seems unfair, and Hagar's consequent expulsion an event which is at least tinged with sadness. It is hard to
tell whether Spenser and his contemporaries—schooled in their
interpretation of the Bible by Paul and the fathers—would have
been troubled by this element of pathos.[12] But even without the
"human level," the story of Hagar is more complicated than
Galatians 4 would lead us to expect. Having commanded her
expulsion, God rescues Hagar from the extremity of her suffering, and addresses to her a promise for her son Ishmael: "I will
make him a great nation" (Genesis 21.18). In response to this
part of the story, even Calvin, to whom Paul's thinking was
especially crucial, was able to contemplate reversing the terms
of Paul's analogy—seeing Ishmael's preservation as a hint "at
the calling of the Gentiles" who were to become "the spiritual
offspring of Abraham."[13] There is a positive side to Hagar,
which Paul's neat dichotomies cannot take into account. To
Spenser, however, this side is relevant. For a while his Abessa
is, like Hagar, a figure with a positive part to play in God's plan.

To explain: Paul, as we have seen, identified Hagar with "the
Jerusalem that now is," the Jewish faith in the Christian era.

Spenser's damsel is certainly *Synagoga* (Jewish belief and the Jewish law, enshrined in the Pentateuch in particular, and in the Old Testament generally), but she does not become the "Jerusalem that *now* is"until she confronts Una in stanza 11. At first, as she walks ahead of Una ("slow footing her before" 10.8) she seems to represent the Jewish faith in Old Testament times, the forerunner of the Church. Una's catching up with Abessa must refer to the advent of the Christian Church, which is naturally a crisis for the Synagogue. The only right thing for the Synagogue to do at this juncture is to pay homage to the Church, willingly relinquishing its own separate identity. Failing to do so, the damsel steps (almost literally) out of an innocent ignorance into one which is willful. It is, I think, in order to include the pre-Christian history of *Synagoga* that Spenser has preferred to make the damsel more immediately reminiscent of the sympathetic Hagar, giving a kind of secondary role to Paul's interpretation. It is when she proves unable to hear Una's voice (11.4) that the damsel begins to suggest the Jews in their deafness (a Pauline metaphor)[14] to the Christian message, and when the two women face each other (this has happened by line five, when Abessa sees the lion), they begin to recall the medieval *Ecclesia-Synagoga* motif, in which the image of *Synagoga* as the forerunner of the Christian church (veiled truth) is also *Synagoga* in the Christian era, opposed to *Ecclesia*, blind to the truth of the gospel, and vanquished. In fleeing, Abessa literally turns her back on Una—not of course for the first time, but for the first time culpably. Her flight indicates the proverbial obstinacy of the Jews in their failure to convert, but it also shows—more profoundly—the inevitable fate of the Jewish faith (or rather, the Jewish faith in its former role as the truest religion) at the appearance of Christianity; it must, as Paul put it, "vanish away" (Hebrews 8.13), for there cannot be two true faiths—truth is one, *Una*. Spenser's reference to Abessa's "deadly hew" (11.9) and description of her running "as if her life vpon the wager lay" (12.2) are not there principally to heighten the drama, or even, more significantly, to give emphasis to the fear which characterizes those lacking in Christian faith (although they do, of course, accomplish these things)—their chief function is to state this crucial point. We see that Abessa yearns and strives for the impossible—escape to a world into which Una has not arrived. She does so because (and this is

the allegorical point) it was only in such a world that the Jewish
faith could have a separate yet irreproachable existence.

There is of course a third phase in the damsel's history, which
begins when she reaches the cottage and her mother. I have
emphasized the independence of stanzas 10–12 from the anti-
Catholic satire of stanzas 13ff., but that independence is not
absolute. The two passages are closely linked as a sequence of
events—largely through the figure of Abessa herself—and this
continuity has, as one would expect, allegorical significance. It
is generally recognized that Spenser's attack on Catholicism in
stanzas 13ff. emphasizes what Protestants saw as a reversion to
the legalism and ceremonial of Judaism.[15] Once Abessa on her
first appearance is understood to be *Synagoga*, this point comes
very much into the foreground; the sequence of Abessa's roles
(perhaps as much as her behavior in 13ff.) expresses the Protestant conviction that the Roman Catholic Church was deaf to the
truth, and in this and in its emphases upon works and ceremonial, was playing the part of the post-Christian *Synagoga*.
Expressing this general idea, John Foxe called the Catholic
Church the "Synagogue of the world."[16] An engraving in the
1583 edition of his *Acts and Monuments* shows Pope Clement
beneath the foot of Henry VIII, with appropriately modified
attributes of *Synagoga*; his undignified sprawl is an exaggeration
of the fainting stance of the *Synagoga* of medieval painting and
sculpture, and like her he has a falling crown (in his case a triple
crown) and a staff which, although it is not broken, is clearly
useless.[17] In this engraving, as in Spenser's allegory, the post-
Reformation Catholic Church is a close relation of the post-
Christian *Synagoga*.

I would like to return now to Abessa's former and intermediate identity when, once Una has caught up with her in stanza
11, she becomes *Synagoga* juxtaposed with *Ecclesia*. When we
look closely at Spenser's figures we see that, while they recall
the medieval tradition, they are also in some ways exceptional.
Spenser must have been familiar with the *Ecclesia-Synagoga*
motif[18] from many sources and, as Rosemond Tuve has so
beautifully demonstrated from a number of examples,[19] Spenser's memory was particularly receptive of such visual images.

There is a lovely fifteenth-century example in Rochester
Cathedral which Spenser—as secretary to the Bishop of Rochester in 1578—must have known well. Stone carvings of *Ecclesia*

and *Synagoga* flank the doorway leading from inside the Cathedral to the Chapter House. These carvings make a convenient exemplar of the whole tradition: the Rochester *Ecclesia* wears a crown, and carries in her right hand a cross-topped staff, in her left a church building.[20] *Synagoga* is blindfolded, her crown is falling, and the staff in her left hand is broken, while the tablets of the law in her right hand are upturned, presumably about to slip from her grasp. Virtually everything to do with *Synagoga* is on its way down; her sinuous posture indicates that her whole body is about to fall, in the direction of the crown she has already lost, and the tablets and staff which she is in the process of losing. (While not every representation of *Ecclesia* and *Synagoga* is identical in all these respects, the Rochester pair is thoroughly conventional.)

Spenser recalls the convention in two main ways. Firstly and most obviously, he juxtaposes two women, as we have already noted. Secondly, he has Abessa throw her waterpot to the ground, so that it reflects the general tendency of *Synagoga* and her attributes. Although the tablets feature most commonly in (or slipping from) the hand of the medieval *Synagoga* figure, an upturned chalice occasionally appears in their place—and blasphemous Jews were sometimes shown with broken chalices at their feet.[21] These overturned and dropped vessels are quite reminiscent of Abessa's pot. Even more so is the stoppered vessel in the hand of *Synagoga* carved on the Norman font in the village church of Southrop, although this apparently unique detail is something of a mystery.[22] And, while an absolutely identical ancestor for Abessa's waterpot cannot be found in carvings or paintings of *Synagoga* (with the possible exception, of course, of this latter example), patristic commentators did make a repeated connection between waterpots and the theme of the old dispensation making way for the new, as D. W. Robertson, Jr.—explaining the Wife of Bath's apparently peculiar fascination with both the marriage at Cana and the Samaritan woman—has pointed out.[23] We recall that at Cana Christ ordered "six waterpots of stone, [set] after the manner of the purifying of the Jews" (John 2.6) to be filled with the water which he transformed into wine. Augustine explained that this water is like Christ who is hidden in the Old Testament, while the wine is Christ revealed in the New.[24] He discussed the woman of Samaria in similar terms; the water she first seeks is fleshly pleasure, as opposed to the grace which she receives from Christ.[25] His emphasis here is on conversion, the individual's experience of the coming of the new dispensation.

Augustine was a much-read author in the Reformation, and Spenser is likely to have known his commentaries. But his interpretations are hardly fanciful. Quite similar ideas must occur to any intelligent reader of John's gospel, since it does self-consciously proclaim the new dispensation (and John's reference to "the purifying of the Jews" is surely pointed). Putting all this material beside the allusion (through waterpot) to Hagar, one can see that a waterpot is appropriate in the hand of Abessa as *Synagoga*. But we cannot, I think, say that it is an *obvious* iconographic clue, in the way that, for example, falling tablets would have been—because it comes from verbal rather than visual sources or from sources which, though graphic, are relatively obscure. When it comes to the mainstream tradition, Spenser (in the choice, disposition, and stance of his figures) has drawn upon its subtle dramatic potential, rather than its much more obvious iconographic content. One can guess that this has to do with his wish to represent first of all the pre-Christian *Synagoga*, the Old Testament awaiting fulfillment by the New; the usual properties of the medieval figure make for a largely negative definition, more appropriate to *Synagoga* persisting as a separate religion in Christian times. The familiar *Ecclesia-Synagoga* images do appear, but Spenser mutes their relationship to the confrontation between Una and Abessa. Either the image itself is toned down (Una is "daughter of a king," iii.2.5, and a "royall virgin," 5.4—but she does not wear a crown; Abessa cannot hear—but she is not blindfolded), or it is attached to an allied character (Abessa's mother is blind; Una's champion wears a cross; Fidelia carries both a book and a cup "with wine and water fild vp to the hight," x.13.3, like many *Ecclesia*s).[26] Such images—some close and some quite distant from iii.11—do create a resonance for the moment in which Una and Abessa become *Ecclesia* with *Synagoga*, but Spenser has guaranteed himself room to move.

There is another unusual feature of Spenser's treatment of Una and Abessa—a feature which in its final impact is rather like the one we have just considered, in that it encourages us to think of the good history of *Synagoga* as well as the bad. Spenser's first description of Una in i.4 mentions four things in

particular—her ass, her veil, her sadness, and her lamb. Of
these four attributes only the lamb is unambiguously—in so far
as any image can be unambiguous—an image of Christianity;
the rest are very commonly associated with *Synagoga*. (I am
not, of course, trying to argue that these symbols are not also
appropriate to the Church in this fallen world.) The veil is
related to the blindfold (*Synagoga* as Old Testament hides the
truth, as well as being blind to it); *Synagoga* (in paintings rather
than sculpture) is often mounted upon an ass, in contrast with
Ecclesia on her gospel-headed beast;[27] and *Synagoga* has a characteristic sadness which, like her fallen crown, goes back to the
cry of Jerusalem in Lamentations 5.16: "The joy of our heart is
ceased. . . . The crown is fallen from our head." All of these
attributes are emphasized at the beginning of canto iii when the
"forsaken wofull" (3.2) Una, having (like the Israelites) "as in
exile / In wildernesse and wastfull deserts strayd"[28] (3.3–4),
alights from her "vnhastie beast" (4.2) and unveils (4.4–5). The
ass (which Spenser clearly feels no necessity to keep in the
picture at all times) is mentioned twice—in 4.2 and again in 8.8.
Given the scope of Book I (from the fall to the Apocalypse), it is
natural enough that Una should stand for true religion before
the birth of Christ (in other words, *Synagoga* as the Law which
Christ was to fulfill) as well as for the Christian Church.
Nevertheless, it is interesting that it is at the very point at which
Abessa is introduced that Una's likeness to *Synagoga* is so
pronounced. In other ways as well, Spenser creates an identity
between Una and Abessa. Una travels slowly (on "vnhastie
beast," 4.2) while the damsel is described as "*slow* footing her
before" (10.8), and Una's *sadness* in stanza 9 (line 4) is echoed by
the damsel's in the immediately following stanza. Staring at
Una in terror, Abessa might be compared with a child seeing
itself in the mirror for the first time. The similarities between
these largely antithetical figures create a small challenge for the
reader. It does, of course, make sense that the damsel and Una
should reflect each other. In a way, they are parts of the same
entity. Abessa had never seen a face like Una's before because
she herself, as *Synagoga*, had been the only true religion. She
now beholds someone whom she is to see as her rival, but who
is also in a sense her daughter, or her future. Una as the
Christian Church takes its roots in Judaism, and brings its
insights to maturity. One can elaborate on the same theme from

Una's point of view. When Una looked at the damsel's back, she was seeing her past self—the part of her that, as we say, "went first." Augustine formulated the notion which lies at the heart of Spenser's identification of the two women: "The Old Testament is nothing but the New covered with a veil, and the New nothing but the Old unveiled."[29] When Una unveils herself in stanza 4, she conforms perfectly with both definitions.

To conclude this investigation of Abessa, I want to return to our starting point, the pot of water—and to the suggestion that it is an allusion to the woman of Samaria. Since the Samaritan does not carry her waterpot "on her shoulders" (the fact that she carries a waterpot at all is only implicit in John 4); since the pot is only one of a number of allusions to Hagar's story in canto iii; and since an allusion to Hagar makes perfect sense of Abessa, bringing to light the richness and depth of Spenser's allegory in stanzas 10–12, we might be inclined to dispense with the notion that Spenser is particularly concerned to make us think of John 4 at all. But closer examination of the role of the Samaritan woman reveals that there is a probable allusion to her in stanza 11, and also that she is strongly relevant to Spenser's subject as I have been defining it (*not*, however, because she has led an immoral life). The point at which the Samaritan woman is most like Abessa—the only point at which her waterpot is actually mentioned—comes at the end of her encounter with Christ: "The woman then left her waterpot, and went her way into the city, and saith to the men, Come see a man, which told me all things that ever I did: is not this the Christ? Then they went out of the city, and came unto him" (John 4.28–30). Her action is clearly exemplary; recognizing Christ, she goes to bring others to him, thus becoming an evangelist.

In elaborating upon this point, both Chrystostom and Augustine stressed the abandonment of the pot; marking the moment of change, it became a symbol of conversion. "Observe her zeal and wisdom" urged Chrystostom, "For what the Apostles did, that after her ability did this woman also. They when they were called, left their nets; she of her own accord, without the command of any, leaves her waterpot, and winged by joy performs the office of Evangelists."[30] Similarly Augustine: "'The woman then left her waterpot.' Having heard, 'I that speak with thee am He,' and having received Christ the Lord into her heart, what could she do but now leave her waterpot, and run to preach the gospel? She cast out lust, and hastened to proclaim the truth. Let them who would preach the gospel learn; let them throw away their waterpot at the well. . . . She threw away her waterpot then, which was no longer of use, but a burden to her, such was her avidity to be satisfied with that water."[31] Even Calvin, who had little taste for allegory, saw the abandonment of the pot as a symptom of Christian zeal: "It is a sign of haste that she leaves her waterpot when she returns to the city. And it is the nature of faith that we want to bring others to share eternal life with us when we have become partakers of it."[32] Abessa, seeing Una and her lion, and dropping her pot in order to retreat more quickly into the familiarity and seeming safety of her mother's narrow cottage, merely parodies the Samaritan's outgoing response to Christ.[33] The Samaritan is what Abessa might have become—in other words, she is like the Church whose evangelical function she performs.

Since Spenser seems to have been alluding to Hagar and the Samaritan woman in close sequence (perhaps even in the same breath), it is interesting to note that the association of these characters is not without precedent. Rabanus Maurus makes it by implication in his commentary on Genesis. He begins by interpreting Hagar negatively, in the light of Galatians 4 (her *utrem aquae*, which he sees as a leathern bottle, is associated with the now invalid purification of the Jews, and the flesh of the old man).[34] But once she has seen the fountain, Hagar becomes those Jews who convert to Christianity. Elaborating on this, Rabanus paraphrases Christ's words to the Samaritan: "I am the fountain of living water; Let him who thirsts come and drink."[35]

It is baptism that marks conversion, and the theme of baptism is therefore close to all of the New Testament passages to which Spenser alludes—to the early chapters of John, Galatians 4 (and even, according to medieval hindsight, to the story of Hagar).[36] Surely John the Baptist was present in Spenser's incorrigibly associative mind[37] when he created his water-carrying damsel? John the Baptist is, naturally, often depicted holding some sort of vessel—and he touches on the preoccupations of canto iii in several other ways also. John's gospel virtually begins with John the Baptist; after his elaboration on

the "Word . . . made flesh" (1.14), the Evangelist quotes the
Baptist's declaration concerning Christ:

> . . . This was he of whom I spake, He that cometh after
> me is preferred before me: for he was before me. . . .
> For the law was given by Moses, but grace and truth
> came by Jesus Christ.
>
> (John 1.15, 17)[38]

Here is the sense of antithesis between law and gospel which
Una and Abessa as *Ecclesia* and *Synagoga* convey. Here also is an
emphasis on time (involving a latent metaphor of space) which
is present—or rather, developed—in Spenser's allegory; Una
follows in the path of Abessa, just as Christ followed John the
Baptist, the last Jewish prophet. Even the conscious paradox of
John's statement is communicated by Spenser since, although
from Abessa's point of view Una is a newcomer, Una has
"gone before" in the reader's experience of the poem. According to Matthew 3.11, 13–15, John was the first Jew to acknowledge Christ—in his preaching, and then dramatically, in their
only recorded meeting together, when John obeyed Christ's
command to baptize him in the Jordan. According to Luke,
John greeted Christ before either he or Christ was even born,
leaping "for joy" in Elisabeth's womb, "when Elisabeth heard
the salutation of Mary" (1.41).[39] Calvin explained that John the
Baptist stood "between the law and the gospel, holding an
intermediate office related to both."[40] Something between a
prophet and an evangelist, John—like the Samaritan woman—
indicates a role that Abessa as *Synagoga* conspicuously fails to
adopt.

The flight of Abessa has been taken as an example of Spenser's allegory at its most elementary—a "flat equational sign."[41]
But the damsel's headlong rush takes her through fifteen centuries, and it is richly significant. In the first place, it confirms that
she has lost the dignity which once belonged to her as the
embodiment of the faith of the prophets. Secondly, it casts her
in the invidious role of those who, although they have been
privileged by revelation, avoid the truth—the obstinate Jews
and finally the Roman Church in Tudor times. These phases of
Abessa's existence seem to carry with them three different
points of view: two similar women following each other at the

same (slow) pace on the same path are an image of continuity, reflecting a tolerant, historical perspective.[42] Facing each other, with Abessa on the verge of withdrawal, the two women become the medieval *Ecclesia-Synagoga* motif, which embodies the self-confidence of Reformation Christianity. In the end, as they dwell uneasily together in a cramped and corrupt home, they are the true and false Churches of the years leading up to and including the Reformation—and the point of view is zealously Protestant.[43]

Abessa's fear of the lion, like everything else about her, tends to be understood in relation to her clearly Roman Catholic phase, in which the lion's slaughter of Kirkrapine seems to represent Henry's dissolution of the monasteries; corrupt Catholicism trembles before a royal power which has put itself at the service of the true Church. But, as Thomas P. Roche has noted, the significance of the lion "is still a vexed question."[44] It may be that, like Abessa, the lion has a less topical significance, at least on his first appearance. Indeed, critics have tended to identify the lion of stanzas 4–9 less specifically, as strength, justice, or passion—but the figure of Henry is not too far away. Such interpretations scarcely acknowledge the paradoxes upon which Spenser insists in his initial account of the lion.

There is, firstly, an emphasis on vengefulness; we are told of "bloudie rage" (5.8) and "furious forse" (5.9). This cannot be savagery for its own sake, since the lion is equated with "auenging wrong" ("O how can beautie maister the most strong / And simple truth subdue auenging wrong?" (6.4–5). Nor can what Una describes as "hungry rage" be simply a bestial urge to eat Una, because "pittie" is its antithesis (8.4–5), and pity is more aptly opposed to anger (just anger, at that) than to a kind of unfocussed savagery. The lion's submission to Una involves the abandonment of outrage, not just the suppression of a bestial nature.

There is another striking and perhaps puzzling feature of the description of the lion. At first, Una and the lion are a dramatically contrasting pair, but gradually they become interchangeable. First the lion is vengeful, Una wronged ("wronged innocence," 6.3). (Even in this aggressor–victim relationship there is a suggestion of similarity, since to be vengeful involves having been wronged.) Then Una weeps "in great compassion" for the lion (6.8), and goes on to praise the same response in him, his "pittie" for her (7.5). When she speaks of her "sad estate" (7.5) the lion responds with sadness of his own ("sad to see . . ." 8.3). Una is "royall" (5.4) and a "virgin borne of heauenly brood" (8.7), and she comes to celebrate the lion's similarly kingly nature—as "Lord of euerie beast in field" (7.1), possessed of "princely puissance" (7.2). Each reflects the other's stance too; Una's first long look at the lion ("when she had marked long," 6.7) is matched by the lion's contemplation of her ("vpon her gazing stood," 8.4).

These things fall into place when we reflect that the change in the lion's nature corresponds exactly to the transformation of God's relationship to men celebrated by the New Testament. To begin with, the lion is like the just and angry God of the Old Testament (his "gaping mouth" [5.5] suggests Hell mouth through which those who have offended him must pass), but when he comes close to Una he becomes the merciful God of the New, Christ as proclaimed by the gospel. The "saluage blood" that he first seeks (5.3) will be replaced in time by his own (a possible reason for Una's tears of compassion). Una is like him just as the Church reflects Christ to the world. Altogether, stanzas 4–9 suggest the incarnation, through which Christ "being in the form of God . . . took upon himself the form of a servant, and was made in the likeness of men . . . humbled himself, and became obedient unto death . . . ." (Philippians 2.6–8). "Seruice," humility and obedience are all characteristics displayed by the transformed lion (9.7–9). This, and Una's pity for him, combine to suggest that he is Isaiah's prophecied "suffering servant." Una's encounter with him is full of details which recall the Annunciation.

Una, as a "royall virgin" displaying "heauenly grace" (5.4; 4.9) is like Mary. When the lion rushes at her she is unveiled, but also "farre from all mens sight" (4.4). This special privacy suggests the meeting between Mary and God's angelic ambassador, a moment of secret revelation—both of Mary (as a kind of bride) before God, and of God to Mary alone. The exclusion of specifically "mortall eye" from Una's unveiling (4.9) seems to hint slyly that the lion (since he most certainly sees it) represents an immortal being. Although Una plays the part of the human recipient of revelation, she also suggests God and Gabriel. Like God at the Annunciation, she unveils herself for the first time; she has an "angels face" (4.6); and her face is twice compared with heaven (4.7; 4.9). Although its relationship to Spenser's poetry is perhaps more oblique than the term "allusion" would suggest, the Magnificat, addressed by Mary to her cousin Elisabeth immediately after the Annunciation, may have provided the themes and terms of much of this part of the allegory:

> For he that is mighty hath done to me great things; and holy is his name.
> And his mercy is on them that fear him from generation to generation.
> He has shewed strength with his arm; he hath scattered the proud in the imagination of their hearts.
> He hath put down the mighty from their seats, and exalted them of low degree.
>
> (Luke 1.49–52)

Una's speech shares Mary's sense of wonder, and stresses the same paradox:

> The Lyon Lord of euerie beast in field,
> Quoth she, his princely puissance doth abate,
> And mightie proud to humble weake does yield
>
> (7.1–3)

While Mary speaks of human reversals achieved by God, Una stresses the analogous change undergone by a symbol of (as it seems to me) God himself, the lion as "Lord." This change lies behind the Magnificat, even though it is not addressed directly by Mary.

In his tameness, the lion has become like the "milke white lambe" which Una led in i.4.9.[45] His affinities with the lions of romance have been well recognized,[46] and in submitting to a virgin he is also like his heraldic partner, the lion-tailed unicorn[47]—and the image of the unicorn with a virgin had become by the late middle ages a symbol of the Annunciation.[48] Quotations from bestiaries and the like cannot, alone, prove anything about Spenser's intentions. But given the suggestions embedded in the texture of the poetry, it is worth noting that an association between the lion and Christ as God incarnate is traditional. According to the *Physiologus*: "[The lion's] first attribute is this. When he goes about the mountains and in his wanderings the scent of the hunter is borne to him, then he brushes away his footprints with his tail, so that the hunter may not find his cavern by following his track and do him harm. So has our Saviour—the strong conquering lion of the tribe of Judah, of the root of David—sent from the eternal Father— hidden his holy footsteps, that is, his divinity. With the angels he became an angel . . . with mankind a man, until he bowed himself and came to the mother Mary, whereby he redeemed the wandering race of men."[49] Gertrud Schiller has explained that the late medieval image of Mary standing on a lion is a symbol of the Incarnation—the lion alluding to the Messianic prophecy of Genesis 49.9ff. (which is taken up by Revelation 5.5: ". . . behold, the Lion of the tribe of Juda, the Root of David, hath prevailed to open the book") and thus to the royal descent of Christ implied by Gabriel in his address to Mary (Luke 1.32).[50] Spenser's contemporary, John Dixon, was quite ready to see that a lion might be a symbol of Christ. Although it is only Redcrosse (when referred to by Una as "my Lyon," 7.5) who is precisely identified with "Criste the sone of dauid" in Dixon's commentary, the "ramping Lyon" of 5.2 is clearly connected, being glossed "the tribe of Juda and rote of dauid."[51]

All this provides a more profound explanation for Abessa's fear in stanza 11. Abessa is afraid because she does not know the lion's true nature (as the story itself implies). She sees a just God, the bloodthirsty lion of stanza 5, while the true Christian Church knows and proclaims "the meekness (Vulgate *mansuetudinem*, "tameness") and gentleness of Christ" (2 Corinthians 10.1)—the "Lyon mylde" of the argument.

Since this interpretation of the lion virtually reverses the accepted emphasis on his essential inferiority to both Una and her former companion Redcrosse (he has even been explained as a "mere beast"),[52] it raises further questions about the lion's destruction of Kirkrapine, the episode which provides the strongest basis for the presently prevailing view. It is true that if the lion's submissiveness is Christ's mildness, it connects rather problematically with his actions in stanzas 19–20, which parallel those of a none-too-mild earthly king. While one cannot dismiss the associations with Henry[53] (and the lion may surely be allowed to represent both earthly and heavenly power, if Redcrosse can embrace the roles of Adam, Christ, and England), one might also think of Christ's one angry and violent action, the expulsion of the money-changers from the temple turned (like Corceca's cottage) "an house of merchandise"—an action which is described, significantly, in John 2.13–17, among the other chapters of John's gospel which are concerned with Christ's announcements and demonstrations of his identity at the beginning of his mission.

To return to our present subject: the confrontation of *Ecclesia* and *Synagoga* is usually associated with the crucifixion, when Christ's blood "seals" the New Covenant. The two figures are often depicted on either side of the cross, *Ecclesia* sometimes collecting in her chalice the blood from Christ's right side.[54] The redemption of fallen man is, of course, the subject of Book I, and there are constant allusions to the Crucifixion by which that redemption is accomplished, culminating in an extended allegory of the Crucifixion in canto xi. But here in this early canto Spenser chooses to draw on the earliest chapters of the gospels—the very hinge of the Bible, where the Old Testament quite literally gives way to the New. His image of the transition between the two Covenants—the meeting of Una and Abessa in stanzas 11–12—is the climax of a series of allusions to the early years of Christ's ministry and to the essential mystery of the Incarnation itself. There is a tradition behind this association of themes. As Gertrud Schiller has pointed out, medieval paintings of the Annunciation tend to incorporate symbols of the whole pattern of redemption—among them *Ecclesia* and *Synagoga*.[55] These were often represented by Gothic and Romanesque (or Byzantine) buildings respectively, so that a typical Annunciation might be set within a Gothic building against a background featuring a Romanesque temple. There is a sixteenth-century Flemish painting now in the Fitzwilliam Museum[56] which shows the same sense of the Annunciation as marking the end of the old dispensation, but through an image which comes somewhat closer to Spenser's Abessa as *Synagoga*; the angel's greeting is set in front of a dark stone doorway at the apex of which is a carving of Moses, holding the tablets of the law.

Looking back at the first twelve stanzas of canto iii, one may appreciate their coherence. The unveiling of Una, the change in the lion and the meeting between the women are all images of the same thing, the end of the Old Law. But we may also discern a significant sequence of events. Beginning with the Annunciation, Spenser makes a strong association between Una and Mary "with child of the Holy Ghost" (Matt. 1.18). This allows us to recognize a further allusion in the stanzas which lie between Una's first encounter with the lion, and her meeting with Abessa. After the Annunciation, Mary travels "into the hill country" (Luke 1.39) on the way to the home of her cousin Elisabeth. Medieval painters typically set Mary's meeting with Elisabeth, not inside a house, but outdoors—with a hill rising between the two women (presumably in order to indicate the journey at the same time as the visit itself).[57] It is hard not to see Una's journey and meeting as an allusion to the Annunciation-Visitation/Salutation sequence—especially since subtle allusions to the Magnificat have already stirred some reminiscence of Mary with Elisabeth, and the relevance to Spenser's theme of Elisabeth's as yet unborn son John the Baptist is clear. The parallel works in a parodic way, of course. Just as John's greeting of Christ was followed by rejection from most, so the positive image of Elisabeth quickly fades—or rather, stands only as a comment on those who turned their backs, those who are represented by Abessa as the medieval *Synagoga* figure. Once Una has met Abessa, and Abessa's identity as Hagar-*Synagoga* is clear, Una's association with Mary (which might have embarrassed Protestants) becomes less important than her identity as *Ecclesia*. I do not say "Sarah-*Ecclesia*" because Una's association with Sarah seems to exist only by implication, lacking a specific and independent basis. And yet—again in admiration of the coherence achieved by Spenser—one notes that Sarah's conception of Isaac (the beginning of Hagar's troubles) is a type of the Annunciation to Mary.[58]

There are many fountains and wells in the Bible, many water-vessels, many water-drawers, and many pairs of women.[59] Following Paul and the fathers, Spenser seems to have been highly sensitive to these patterns—patterns which enrich by association each single figure. His Hagar, therefore, is not plucked "cleanly," as it were, from Genesis. But, while Paul's "bondwoman" and the medieval *Synagoga* figure stand together on one side (reprobate), and Elisabeth, John, and the Samaritan on the other (exemplary), only Hagar is enigmatic enough to stand on both—suggesting not only *Synagoga* in two different phases, but also (if we take Rabanus Maurus and Calvin seriously) conversion and baptism. It is an indication of the great delicacy with which Spenser weighs and places each of his biblical allusions that Hagar, among a number of possible and probable relevant candidates, stands out as the clearest, most sustained, and most certain figure behind Abessa in stanzas 10–12.

Victoria University of Wellington

APPENDIX

Abishag

Given Abessa's connection with *Synagoga*, it is just possible that in naming her Spenser was (among other things) recalling *Abishag*, whose story is told in 1 Kings 1.1–4, 2.13–25. Abishag was the "fair damsel" (1 Kings 1.3) who was brought to give warmth to King David in his old age, when his clothes no longer warmed him. Abishag "cherished the king, and ministered to him: but the king knew her not" (1.4). After David's death, Solomon having succeeded to the throne according to David's will, Adonijah (Solomon's elder half-brother, who had hoped for the crown) asked Bathsheba to put before Solomon a request for Abishag as wife. Solomon interpreted this as a symbol of intent to rebel and seize power: "And King Solomon answered and said unto his mother, And why dost thou ask Abishag the Shunamite for Adonijah? ask for him the kingdom also; For he is mine elder brother . . ." (2.22). Because he had the temerity to ask for the former king's companion, Adonijah was killed at Solomon's command.

Connections between the biblical Abishag and Abessa are scarcely striking. But it is interesting to find strong associations made between Abishag and *Synagoga* in the *Bibles Moralisées*—obsessed as they were by the *Synagoga-Ecclesia* theme. The story appears in the first (Oxford) section of the divided Latin manuscript edited by Laborde:[60] The roundel which shows Abishag ushered (by a Jew on either side of her) in to the reclining king is glossed by a picture of Christ in glory, acknowledged from both sides by groups of Jews (distinguished as such by their pointed hats). The text associates the clothes which failed to warm the dying king with the Jews at Christ's death, and Abishag who does warm him with the Jews (in their acknowledgment of Christ) on the Day of Judgment. The French version edited by Reiner Hausser[61] handles this point slightly differently: the Jews who have brought Abishag to David (again two) stand together apart from her, while she sits with the reclining David's feet in her lap, warming them with her hands. The matching roundel shows Christ enthroned between Jews who turn away from him (on our left) and the personification *Synagoga*, who clasps his hand with her hands (on our right, directly beneath Abishag). Again the text associates David's coldness and worthless clothing with his death and the Jews, but his unconsummated relationship with Abishag is compared with

Christ's limited relationship with the Jews—he was "warmed" by *Synagoga*, although he engendered nothing by her. Here Abishag is taken to represent the Jews of the Old Testament, rather than the Jews at the end of time.

Earlier commentaries follow quite different lines; Adamus Scotus compares the relationship between Abishag and David with the chaste relationship between Mary and Joseph,[62] and Rabanus Maurus (also emphasizing that David's relationship with her was not carnal), interpreted Abishag as a personification of spiritual wisdom.[63] Rabanus does, however, connect the subsequent story of Adonijah with the subject of Judaism; in his desire for Abishag, according to Rabanus, Adonijah shows the desire to corrupt true spiritual wisdom with the observance of the ceremonies of the law.[64] In the *Bibles Moralisées*[65] Adonijah's fate is interpreted as the ultimate fate of evil-doers; Solomon presides over the killing of the man who would have subverted David's will (by attacking Solomon's kingship), and the resurrected Christ presides over the killing of those who have acted against the will of His Father in heaven—the victims are (predictably, in these anti-Semitic works) depicted as Jews.

It seems certain that, had Spenser encountered any such interpretation, he would have been interested in it. And, if he was remembering Abishag in naming Abessa, he may have remembered Adonijah also—in the fate of Abessa's corrupting and corrupted lover in the "cruell clawes" (19.8) of a beast who is Christ as well as a king.

NOTES

1. Hamilton, for example, notes that the mountain of 10.6 suggests "that upon which Moses received the law, by which covenant Abessa and Corceca still conduct their lives." This is, of course, a valuable point, but the "still" does direct our thoughts forward to stanzas 13ff. See A. C. Hamilton, ed., *The Faerie Queene* (London: Longman, 1977), p. 57.

2. I make my own suggestion in the Appendix above.

3. "The rest of this passage shows that the woman was both an adultress and an idolater." See Robert Kellogg and Oliver Steele, eds., *Books I and II of the Faerie Queene* (New York: Odyssey Press, 1965), p. 106.

4. Quoted in E. A. Greenlaw, F. M. Padelford, C. G. Osgood *et al.*, eds., Edmund Spenser, *Works: A Variorum Edition*, 11 vols. (Baltimore: Johns Hopkins University Press, 1923–49), I, 207.

5. Striking sixteenth-century examples include the painting by Jan Mostaert in which Hagar arches her left arm over her head to support the bottle on her right shoulder (1525, Netherlands Art Institute, no. 7811); and an engraving by Marten de Vos in the *Thesaurus Sacrarum Historiarum* (Antwerp, 1585, II, no. 4) in which Hagar's bottle is slung over her left shoulder. In both of these pictures, Sarah (type of the Church) is present, watching from her house in the background. I owe my acquaintance with these pictures to the Photographic Collection of the Warburg Institute.

6. This subject occupies part of the background of the Marten de Vos engraving discussed above (n.5), in which the bottle lies on the ground between a reclining Isaac and a kneeling Hagar. The bottle is extremely prominent in a twelfth-century illumination in MS Munich Stadbibl., Clm. 1459 (fol. iv), which depicts the angel showing Hagar the fountain. Hagar, Ishmael, and the angel (from left to right) are framed by the abandoned bottle (as big as Ishmael) on the left, and the restoring fountain on the right. Reproduced in Albert Boeckler, *Die Regensburg-Prüfeninger Buchmalerei des XII. und XIII. Jahrhunderts* (Munich, 1924), Abb. 31; and also in Adelheid Heiman, "Jeremiah and his Girdle," *Journal of the Warburg and Courtauld Institutes,* 25 (1962), 1–8, Pl. 3a.

7. Notably Warton: "She had never seen a lady before, which certainly was no reason why she should fly from the lion." Quoted in Greenlaw, ed., *Works,* I, 208.

8. *Two right profitable and fruitfull Concordances Collected by R.F.H.* (London: Christopher Barker, 1578); see "Hagar."

9. James Nohrnberg, *The Analogy of the Faerie Queene* (Princeton, N.J.: Princeton University Press, 1976), pp. 151–155. Nohrnberg also emphasizes the law-gospel antithesis in his illuminating discussion of Book I (his second chapter), and he compares both Duessa and Ignaro—but not Abessa—with Synagoga. See pp. 277 n.481; 346. Hagar is briefly mentioned ("like Hagar, Duessa is also exiled into the wilderness," p. 246) but not in connection with Abessa.

10. Paul puts his audience in the place of Abraham, the man called upon to make a choice. Spenser may be doing the same thing, although the lion— bonded as he is to Una—may touch very lightly on Sarah's husband. See below pp. 17ff.

11. There is, of course, a large literature on this subject, and it becomes impossible to disentangle individual contributions. My broad picture of the tradition is derived from: Emile Mâle, *The Gothic Image,* trans. from 3rd ed. by Dora Nussey (1913; rpt. New York: Harper, 1958) pp. 133ff., 170, 188, 190ff.; Margaret Schlauch, "The Allegory of Church and Synagogue," *Speculum,* 14 (1939), 448–464; M. D. Anderson, *The Imagery of British Churches* (London: John Murray, 1955), pp. 75–95; Lewis Edwards, "Some English Examples of the Medieval Representation of Church and Synagogue," *Transactions of the Jewish Historical Society of England,* 18 (1958), 63–75; Adolf Katzenellenbogen, *The Scriptural Programs of Chartres Cathedral* (Baltimore: Johns Hopkins University Press, 1959), pp. 59ff, 69–73; Bernhard Blumenkranz, "La Répresentation de Synagoga dans les Bibles moralisées françaises du XIIIe au XV siècle," *Proceedings of the Israel Academy of Sciences and Humanities,* 2 (1970); Luba Eleen, *The Illustration of the Pauline Epistles in French and English Bibles of the Twelfth and Thirteenth Centuries* (Oxford: Clarendon Press, 1982).

12. While it is abundantly clear that Spenser was familiar with the medieval tradition of biblical interpretation, there does seem to have been a new interest in Old Testament characters as human beings in the sixteenth century. Calvin is well-known for his insistence on the literal meaning of the Bible in his *Commentaries,* and this priority is quite evident in his discussion of Abraham's

life in the *Institutes* (II.x). The Geneva Bible virtually ignores Galatians in glossing Genesis 21.14 (the expulsion of Hagar): "True faith recounceth all naturall affections to obey Gods commandment."

13. Trans. T. H. L. Parker, in *Calvin's Commentaries: The Epistles of Paul*, eds. David W. Torrance and Thomas F. Torrance (London: Oliver & Boyd, 1965), p. 85. Calvin does go on to acknowledge Paul's interpretation.

14. Romans 11.8: "God hath given them the spirit of slumber, eyes that they should not see, and ears that they should not hear. . . ."

15. The Geneva Bible describes the Galatians as people who "of Painims began to bee Christians, but by false Apostles were turned backeward to beginne anewe the Iewish ceremonies, and so in stead of going forward toward Christ, they *ranne backward* from him" (note to Galatians 4.9, my italics). There is an implicit connection between the ceremonious Galatians and the corrupt Roman Church.

16. *The Acts and Monuments of John Foxe*, ed. George Townsend, 8 vols. (London, 1843–1849), I, xix. Calvin also identified Rome with the "Synagogue of Satan." See *Calvin's Commentaries: The Epistles of Paul*, p. 88.

17. Frontispiece to *The Acts and Monuments*, II (London: John Day, 1583).

18. See above n.11.

19. See in particular two essays in *Essays: Spenser, Herbert, Milton* (Princeton, N.J.: Princeton University Press, 1970); "Spenser and Medieval Mazers" (pp. 102–111), and "Spenser and Some Pictorial Conventions" (pp. 112–138).

20. *Ecclesia* has been damaged and restored, but apparently to her original form. See Edwards, 66–67.

21. See Edwards, 68–74. For the figure of *Synagoga* holding an inverted chalice on the reliquary of St. Eleutherius at Tournai, see J. Warichéz, *La Cathédrale de Tournai* (1930), Pl. 154; and for blasphemous Jews see the fifteenth-century woodcuts from the *Oraison Dominicale* reproduced in E. Dutuit, *Manuel de l'Amateur d'estampes* (Paris, 1884), Pls. 33 and 36. Edwards refers to both of these sources.

22. *Cf.* photographs in Anderson (Pl. 3) and Edwards (Pl. 3). Anderson does not discuss the vessel. Edwards compares it with the overturned chalices just mentioned, providing some useful examples. But in contrast to these, the Southrop vessel is held firmly upright, and is unmistakeably stoppered. (The word *Synagoga* is actually carved above this figure.)

23. D. W. Robertson, Jr., *A Preface to Chaucer* (Princeton, N.J.: Princeton University Press, 1962), pp. 317–331. Robertson refers to the *Glossa Ordinaria* (*P. L.* 114, cols. 364, 371ff.). Thomas P. Roche, Jr. and C. Patrick O'Donnell, Jr. usefully refer to Robertson in their note on 10.9, although they mention only the flesh-spirit opposition found by Robertson, not the (albeit analogous) law-gospel antithesis. See Thomas P. Roche, Jr. and C. Patrick O'Donnell, Jr. eds., *The Faerie Queene* (Harmondsworth: Penguin, 1978), p. 1083.

24. "Lege libros omnes propheticos, non intellecto Christo, quam tam insipidum et fatuum invenies? Intellige ibi Christum, non solum sapit quod legis, sed etiam inebriat; mutans mentem a corpore, ut praeterita obliviscens, in ea quae ante sunt extendaris." *P.L.* 35, col. 1159.

25. "Et enim aqua in puteo, voluptus saeculi est in profunditate tenebrosa: Hinc eam hauriunt homines hydria cupiditatem" *P.L.* 35, col. 1515.

26. There is a good example of this in a crucifixion in the *Hortus Deliciarum of Herrad of Hohenbourg* (2 vols.) ed. Rosalie Greene *et al.* (Vol. 36 in *Studies of the Warburg Institute*, ed. J. B. Trapp), I. Pl. 93 — a reconstruction from a nineteenth-century tracing of the now-lost medieval original. *Ecclesia* and *Synagoga* stand opposed to each other on either side of the cross, beneath depictions of the rent veil of the temple. Fidelia might be contrasted with Duessa, who abandons her cup (and crown) much like *Synagoga* in viii.25. In one significant action, Duessa and Abessa are both associated with Hagar — both are described as having "fled away" (compare viii.25.6 with iii.11.7).

27. As John M. Steadman has shown, the ass may also symbolize "the ministry—the vehicle of the orthodox doctrine," and so be "one of the signs . . . of the True Church." See "Una and the Clergy: The Ass Symbol in *The Faerie Queene*," *Journal of the Warburg and Courtauld Institutes*, 21 (1958), 134–137. Steadman also suggests that "Spenser may have intended an additional reference to the 'white asses' of Judges v. 10 . . . the *doctores* of the tribes of Israel, on whose doctrine the Hebrew people reposed" (pp. 135–136). The "Animale synagoge asinus stultus et laxus," as the ass upon which Synagogue is seated is described in the *Hortus Deliciarum* picture mentioned above (n. 26), must be a relation, in spite of its ugliness and opposition to the gospel. The *Glossa* quotes Isidore on Genesis 22.3: "Asinus insentatem stultitiam Judaeorum significat, quae portabat omnia sacramenta et nesciebat" (*P.L.* 113, col. 138). The ass seems more disturbing as a property of *Ecclesia* when *Synagoga* is present, sharply distinguished from the Church, than it does in canto vi, which Steadman illuminates.

28. It is possible that Spenser is preserving a distinction between appearance (however significant) and real identity—"*as* in exile. . . ."

29. *City of God*, XVI, xxxvi. Quoted by Mâle, p. 136.

30. Trans. William B. Erdmans, in *A Select Library of the Nicene and Post-Nicene Fathers of the Christian Church*, ed. Philip Schaff, XIV (Michigan, 1956), p. 118.

31. Trans. John Gibb, in *The Works of Aurelius Augustine*, ed. Marcus Dods, 15 vols. (Edinburgh: T. & T. Clark, 1872–1934), X (1908), 226. *Cf. P.L.* 35, cols. 1520–21.

32. Trans. T. H. L. Parker, *Calvin's Commentaries: The Gospel According to St. John*, David W. Torrance and Thomas F. Torrance, eds. (London: Oliver & Boyd, 1959), pp. 103–104.

33. John's setting of the encounter between Christ and the Samaritan recalls the meeting of Abraham's servant Eleazor with Rebecca at the well (Genesis 24.15ff.), the meeting which determined Rebecca's marriage to Isaac. This may be intentional, since Paul had already seen Rebecca (in her barrenness and miraculous conception) as a mother of the "children of the promise," like her mother-in-law Sarah (Romans 9.1–12). Spenser also may have Rebecca in mind (as Upton suggested, see n.4 above), as a type of the Church, one who (to use Paul's distinction) *is* Israel—joined to God by faith—and not merely (like Abessa once she has turned away) "of Israel" (Romans 9.6).

34. "Uter vero aquae, qui defecit, Judaica purificatio significatur defectura,

siva doctrina eorum carnalis in pelle mortua clausa, id est, in carne veteris hominis praevaricationis sententia damnata, quae nec refrigerium praestat, nec satiat sitim, sed aestu tepida vomitum facit" (*P.L.* 107, col. 564).

35. "*Ego sum fons aquae vivae; qui sitit veniat et bibat*" (*ibid.*, col. 564).

36. This is implicit in the commentary of Rabanus. An inscription on the twelfth-century manuscript illumination of Hagar at the fountain (see above n. 6) explicitly identifies the fountain with baptism.

37. Rosemond Tuve has written of the "mingling in Spenser's mind . . . of suggestions from things actually seen with suggestions imaged in the mind when reading" (*Essays*, "Spenser and Medieval Mazers," p. 102), and of a Spenser "not so much consciously imitative as sensitively retentive of images which, stamped in his mind by actual sight, were enriched by association and by his use of literary sources" ("Spenser and Some Pictorial Conventions," p. 138).

38. Quoted by Nohrnberg (*Analogy*, p. 189) in a discussion of the relationship between Seth as "a prototype for Redcrosse" (p. 188) and the circularity of the chronology implied by Book I.

39. If, as I argue pp. 18ff. stanzas 4–9 allude to the Annunciation, the Salutation—sequel to the Annunciation—is particularly relevant here.

40. Trans. Ford Lewis Battles, *Institutes of the Christian Religion* (2 vols.) in *The Library of Christian Classics*, XX–XXI, ed. John T. McNeill (London: SCM Press, 1961), II, 427. Calvin refers to Christ's statement that "The Law and the Prophets were until John" (Luke 16.16; Matt. 11.13).

41. Rosemary Freeman, *The Faerie Queene: A Companion for Readers* (London: Chatto & Windus, 1948; rpt. 1970), p. 71.

42. This relates interestingly to the whole question of "syncretism" in the *Faerie Queene*, discussed by James E. Phillips in "Spenser's Syncretistic Religious Imagery," *ELH*, 36 (1969), 110–130. See also D. P. Walker, "The *Prisca Theologia* in France," *Journal of the Warburg and Courtauld Institutes*, 17 (1954), 204–259. It may also be associated with a new sympathy for Jews which emerged (if sporadically) with Protestantism. See Salo Wittmayer Baron, *A Social and Religious History of the Jews*, XIII (New York: Columbia University Press, 1969), pp. 159ff., 217ff., 292. David S. Katz documents an interest in Judaism and sympathy for Jews in late sixteenth-century England in *Philo-Semitism and the Readmission of the Jews to England 1603–1655* (Oxford: Clarendon Press, 1982).

43. John Foxe's play *Christus Triumphans* (1556) provides an analogue for this development in three stages in the character of *Ecclesia*, who (to quote the play's modern editor) "represents at various times the pre-Christian Church, the early post-Christian Church, and finally the English Church." See John Hazel Smith, ed., *Two Latin Comedies by John Foxe the Martyrologist* (Ithaca, N.Y.: Cornell University Press, 1973), p. 38.

44. Roche, ed., *The Faerie Queene*, p. 1082. Roche gives a convenient summary of views on the lion.

45. Dr. Robert Easting has drawn my attention to a Middle English lyric which states the paradox in similar terms:

> Lullay, lullay, litel child,
> Thou that were so sterne and wild

Now art become meke and mild
To saven that was forlore.

See *A Selection of Religious Lyrics*, ed. Douglas Gray (Oxford: Clarendon Press, 1975), p. 13.

46. See Greenlaw, ed., *Works*, I, 365ff. Among the analogues given, the one from the Percival story in the *Morte d'Arthur* is particularly relevant. After he has gone to sleep beside his friendly lion, Percival dreams that he meets two ladies, one seated on a lion, the other on a serpent. In the morning a soothsayer explains that the lady on the lion stood for the Church, and the lady on the serpent for the old law. See Appendix IV, p. 398.

47. C. Boutell, rev. C. W. Scott-Giles, *Boutell's Heraldry* (London: Frederick Warne, 1954), p. 81.

48. See Gertrud Schiller, *Iconography of Christian Art*, 2 vols., trans. Janet Seligman (London: Lund Humphries, 1971), I, pp. 52–53.

49. Trans. James Carlill, in *The Epic of the Beast, consisting of English Translations of the History of Reynard the Fox and Physiologus*, ed. William Rose (London: Routledge, 1925), pp. 186–187.

50. *Iconography of Christian Art*, I, p. 22.

51. Dixon's reference to Revelation 5.5 at the end of his gloss on Redcrosse as Una's lion provides the point of connection. See *The First Commentary on the "Faerie Queene,"* ed. Graham Hough (privately printed, 1964), p. 5.

52. Mark Rose, *Spenser's Art* (Cambridge, Mass.: Harvard University Press, 1975), p. 42.

53. The lion's death at the hands of Sans Loy (stanza 42) poses a similar problem. Hamilton explains that "The Lion's fierceness is overcome by—that is, it leads to—lawlessness" (*The Faerie Queene*, p. 63). In so far as the lion is described as "saluage" (42.2) this makes sense, and it allows for the association between the lion and Henry VIII. But the fact that the lordly-hearted ("Lordly hart," 42.8) lion dies in noble self-sacrifice invites us to continue associating him with Christ. The contrast between these possible significances is extreme, even disturbing, but it is not uncharacteristic of Spenser, whose first Book interweaves and superimposes historical and spiritual allegories, with their respective themes of England's glory and individual holiness (which is shown, moreover, to be made up largely of humility).

54. As in the *Hortus Deliciarum* crucifixion mentioned above, n. 26.

55. *Iconography of Christian Art*, I, p. 49.

56. No. 98. This painting also displays the contrast between darkness and the light emanating from the angel which is common in paintings of the Annunciation. Schiller sees this as an image of "Christian belief as contrasted with Jewish unbelief" (I, p. 49). One thinks of the "secret shadow" (4.4) in which Una reveals her brightness (6–9). *Cf.* the imagery of Calvin: "In the precepts of the law, God is but the rewarder of perfect righteousness, which all of us lack, and conversely, the severe judge of evil deeds. But in Christ his face shines, full of grace and gentleness, even upon us poor and unworthy sinners." Trans. Battles, *Institutes*, 2, p. 357.

57. *Cf.* Schiller, I, figs. 111, 133.

58. *Ibid.*, p. 41.

59. The "tender-eyed" (explained in the Geneva Bible as "bleare-eyed")

Leah and her "beautiful" sister Rachel (Genesis 29.17), for example, were interpreted as *Ecclesia* and *Synagoga*. See Blumenkranz, 74. Rachel is like both Sarah and Rebecca in her barren-ness, and like Rebecca in that her future husband met her by a well (Genesis 29.2ff.). But Spenser does not recall her specifically.

60. A. de Laborde, *La Bible moralisée illustrée*, 4 vols. (Paris, 1911–28), I, Pl. 161.

61. R. Hausser, ed., *Bible Moralisée: Faksimile-ausgabe in originalformat des Codex Vindobonensis 2554*, 2 vols., Facsimile XL in Codices Selecti (Paris: Club du Livre, 1973), I, 113.

62. *P.L.* 198, cols. 231, 311–314.

63. *P.L.* 109, cols. 123–125.

64. *Ibid.*, cols. 125–126.

65. Laborde, Pl. 162, Hausser, p. 115.

JACQUELINE T. MILLER

The Status of Faeryland: Spenser's "Vniust Possession"

*I*N THE House of Alma, Arthur's reading of the *"Briton moni-ments"* is juxtaposed to Guyon's reading of the *"Antiquitie of Faerie* lond." This is a crucial scene, for here, in this early moment of *The Faerie Queene*, Spenser attempts to define and defend the status of his Faeryland, in the process attempting to define the relationship between fact and fiction, history and poetry. Yet it is also here, as the poet defends his creation, that he establishes the conditions of its disintegration.[1]

The discrepancies between the British history and the ac-count of Faeryland's past have been duly noted by critics: the *Briton Moniments*, sixty-five stanzas long, is a history full of violence, betrayal, upheavals, and interruptions in the line of succession; the *Antiquitie of Faerie lond*, only seven stanzas long, presents a peaceful, harmonious history with an unbroken line of succession to the throne. The differences between the two histories have been likened to the differences between the real and the ideal, history and poetry, fact and fiction, life and literature; the two chronicles have been called "contradictory" and "utterly irreconcilable."[2] Yet a crucial aspect of the histories is ignored when critics set about giving a general description to each. For although the British history is full of disorder and violence, it begins relatively quietly: the land is "all desolate," unsought even by merchants out for profit. Granted, it is a "saluage wildernesse," occupied, we soon learn, by a "saluage nation" of "hideous Giants" who "Polluted this same gentle soyle"; but the real history of Britain does not begin until the arrival of the first British ruler, Brutus—a man who gains his rightful title through orderly inheritance ("anciently deriu'd / From royall stocke of old *Assaracs* line") and who rightfully and justly reclaims the land from that hideous, plundering race: "And them of their vniust possession depriu'd."[3] British history commences, then, with a lawful act of re-possession by a man who lawfully derives his existence, title, and power from the line of succession: only afterwards do the incidents of upheaval and rebellion occur.

On the other hand, the history of Faeryland, however peacefully it proceeds, begins disruptively with an act of "unjust possession." The first thing Guyon reads about is the creation of the Faeries themselves:

> It told, how first *Prometheus* did create
> A man, of many partes from beasts deriued,
> And then stole fire from heauen, to animate
> His worke, for which he was by *Ioue* depriued
> Of life him selfe, and hart-strings of an Ægle riued.
>
> (II.x.70)

The Promethean legend is here presented to account for the creation of "all Elfin kind," a race whose very existence derives from a stolen gift that, to borrow a phrase from Denis Donoghue's study of the "Promethean imagination," has its "origin in violence, risk, and guilt," and that implicates its recipients in the original crime of theft.[4] Prometheus's action, defiant and blasphemous, animates the Elfin clan, giving them life, but a life that is inherently contentious, usurped, and unauthorized, an existence reaped as the spoils from an act of theft: only afterwards does the orderly progression of events unfold.

If, then, Faeryland is the world of fiction, of imagination, then fiction and the imagination exist only in opposition to a higher order and have at their source a rebellious, defiant quality. In fact, these qualities *define* the act of creation that can produce the triumphant vision of the truly virtuous, orderly life—a vision that is essentially (like the Promethean fire) an unauthorized possession.

This Faeryland also seems defined by its difference from the world of human experience about which Arthur reads, a world that it is clearly most unlike. I do not deny the claims of other critics that the Faeryland chronicle is quite distinct from the British one. In fact, I think the obvious differences are courted and made explicit by the poet (it is not insignificant that Guyon and Arthur each read alone, neither of them seeing what the other one so avidly peruses, neither of them sharing with the other the substance of his text). By so insisting that the stories are separable, the poet guarantees himself and his Faeryland a space to inhabit where there are no pretensions to (and hence no demands for) correspondence to the structure of actual experience—where, therefore, he can freely invent his ideal moral landscape. His invented world is obviously not fact, clearly unverifiable by the standard criteria of authenticity; and this is made clear by the discrepancies between it and the account that precedes it.

But it is with the over-reductive distinctions made by those critics that I disagree, because there is a more complex side to them that even my description above obscures. The relationship between human experience and the fiction *is* one of explicit contrast, but not one that can be characterized by general harmonious/disruptive, peaceful/violent categories subsumed by a simple ideal/real dichotomy. Because of the dual nature of both stories (their curious beginnings that do not fit the general content), the contrasts suggest dynamic alternation, not static opposition.

The two worlds are, in fact, mirror images of each other: the first with an orderly beginning, followed by disruption, rebellion, and usurpation; the second starting with an act of defiance and usurpation, and then proceeding peacefully, without disruption. Their exact contrasts imply that they are reciprocal states, and together they signify a continuum on which they both exist: harmony dissolves into disharmony, disharmony evolves into harmony; the ideal and the real can slip into each other. Therefore, although they now occupy different positions on this scale, we cannot conclude that these two histories are totally disjoint, that they are "utterly irreconcilable" views that can only be juxtaposed, never integrated. The similarities and the dynamics evoked by the two-fold nature of the contrasts indicate, on the one hand, that the ideal state is potentially realizable, that it is an actual possibility.

On the other hand, however (a more disturbing hand), they present the Faeryland vision as ultimately unattainable, predicting that it will recede, become remote, disintegrate. For this continuum suggests what is never directly expressed here: that the ideal vision of peace is not eternal; it is not as disassociable from reality as it may first appear, and thus it, too, may eventually dissolve into discord. In fact, the brevity of the account itself, compared to the lengthy British chronicle it follows, may imply that its vision cannot be sustained for very long. It is as if the origin of that stolen gift of Faeryland life never relinquishes its hold; the force of that defiant, unauthorized act always exerts itself and will continually be felt, will always be a part of the harmony that it both provides and defies. And the harmony will always contain elements of the discordant and troublesome reality that it inverts and needs as a foil. The only true act of creation described in both histories is the one that begets the Elfin race, an act of creation that is inherently usurped and disruptive but that also allows for the ideal to be formed *out* of the disturbing reality—an ideal, however, that is short-lived, that is born from disruption and carries it within itself.

If there is, then, a rift between the two histories, it is a rift between a fictional creation (obtained at great cost and risk) of an idealized version of human history and a more accurate description of that history—an ideal not simply set against the world, but an ideal *of* that world, sharing several of its attributes, presenting, briefly, a complementary picture of it.[5] They are, in short, two sides of the same coin. The disturbing elements of this relationship are kept in the background here: Spenser concentrates on the positive—Faeryland *does* figure forth the ideal—and he emphasizes the beatific *product* of creation rather than its less sanctified source. He capitalizes on the positive function of the contrasts that allow Faeryland to be constructed, and on the positive value of the reciprocity those contrasts imply: in Faeryland, it is possible to embrace the ideal order, to capture it and hold it up as a version of the world of human endeavors. But although this passage is, for the most part, optimistic about the poet's (as well as man's) access to that vision, its less attractive qualities—the negative implications of Faeryland's dependence on the human world as a counterpoint, of the dynamic relationship this necessitates, of the characteristics Faeryland must then share with actual human existence, and of the potentially debilitating nature of the act that generates it—are unmistakably and inescapably present.

The darker side of this concept—the difficult, unstable, disruptive nature of the Faeryland harmony—moves more into the foreground in a later passage that likewise sets together two versions of a similar story. At the beginning of Canto xi of Book IV, the narrator returns, after a lengthy absence, to the story of Florimell and Marinell, commenting uncharacteristically on his own activity, berating himself for (characteristically) leaving parts of his story unfinished.[6] He has "Left a fayre Ladie languishing in payne"; he has "doen such wrong, / To let faire *Florimell* in bands remayne" (IV.xi.1). But this self-castigation is misdirected, for the narrator next tells us that the crucial question for which even he has no answer is whether or not the story can or will be completed: it is out of his hands now, he adds, and only an unpredictable power more mighty than his as author can redeem the situation. After the grand introduction of promised resolutions, he can only lamely express his pity for Florimell:

> From which vnlesse some heauenly powre her free
> By miracle, not yet appearing playne,
> She lenger yet is like captiu'd to bee:
> That euen to thinke thereof, it inly pitties mee.
> (IV.xi.1)

The situation, in fact, seems rather dismal and hopeless. Florimell is held captive by "Vnlouely *Proteus*," who hopes "thereby her to his bent to draw"; she is imprisoned in a "dongeon deepe and blind," "cruelly" chained, dwelling with "horror" (xi.2–4), and, even worse, she continues to refuse Proteus out of unrequited love for someone who himself shows no signs of relenting: "all this was for love of *Marinell*, / Who her despysd" (xi.5).

Although the narrator has begun this canto with the stated intention of returning to redeem Florimell's plight after a period of unconscionable neglect and delay, all he can do, at first, is describe her situation, offer his sympathy, and then leave her once more. This time he leaves her not to pursue the story of other Faeryland characters, but to move to a more naturalistic and mythological setting, and to describe the wedding of the Thames and the Medway. A bit of the history of their courtship is provided first: the Thames had tried to woo the Medway "to his bed," "But the proud Nymph would for no worldly meed, / Nor no entreatie to his loue be led; / Till now at last relenting, she to him was wed" (xi.8). Initially, there are two parallels set up here to the story of Florimell: Proteus's as yet unsuccessful attempt to win Florimell, and Florimell's as yet unfulfilled relationship with Marinell. But the details of the troublesome courtship between the Thames and the Medway are only briefly hinted at and then are left behind; the major emphasis is given to the celebration of their union. The wedding feast is held, not surprisingly, in "*Proteus* house"; the story proceeds quite smoothly: it is all ceremony, a ritualized pageant, a procession in which

> All which long sundred, doe at last accord
> To ioyne in one, ere to the sea they come,
> So flowing all from one, all one at last become.
>   (IV.xi.43)

The union is achieved naturally; original harmony is restored easily, gracefully, without effort or trouble.

The *narrator's* job, as he presents it, has been relatively easy as well. To relate the story properly and as completely as possible, he has requested the help of the "records of antiquitie," which "no wit of man may comen neare," appealing to the Muse to whom those records "appeare" (xi.10). The story of this natural union is grounded in sanctioned texts to which men ordinarily have no access; aided by the revelation of them, he is granted through the intercession of the Muse (though it does not resolve all his difficulties), the narrator, now self-proclaimed spectator and transcriber, recounts ("reherses") the procession and records the harmonious marriage.[7]

This incident of undisturbed union—or reunion—clearly stands in opposition to the more troublesome, as yet unresolved, and still potentially unresolvable story of Florimell and Marinell, for which there is, apparently, no recourse to these or similar sources and none of their sanction; and it is to this more problematic episode that the narrator next forces himself to return. In the last stanza of Canto xi, the last stanza devoted to the rivers, we are told of one of the guests present at the banquet—Cymoent (or, as she is called here, Cymodoce), Marinell's mother. But the narrator, having taken a rather circuitous route to reach the end of the Florimell and Marinell episode, is weary, as is his Muse ("her selfe now tyred has" [xi.53]), and—to refresh himself after his previous endeavor and to prepare himself for the more difficult one that lies ahead—he pauses now to catch his breath, passing to the next canto to fully re-enter the world of the characters who inhabit his Faeryland. There we discover that Marinell has accompanied his mother to the wedding, to "learne and see / The manner of the Gods when they at banquet be" (xii.3). This perhaps suggests that, although no "antique" account of his story exists, the Thames and Medway story of ideal union can serve as a model for his activities, but we soon learn that Marinell, being "halfe-mortall" (unlike his sea-nymph mother, he is not "devoyd of mortall slime" [III.iv.35]), cannot participate in the ceremony; he too is a spectator of this scene and ultimately does not have complete and free access to it: "He might not with immortall food be fed, / Ne with th'eternall Gods to bancket come" (xii.4).[8] Marinell's situation, imposed upon him by his mortal nature—by his origins—now mirrors the narrator's in relation to Florimell; for when, as he wanders around "*Proteus* house," he hears Florimell's complaints and learns of her plight, he finds himself equally helpless, equally unable to do anything to aid her. His resistance to her vanishes, but he is completely impotent; he can only, like the narrator in Canto xi,

> . . . inly wish, that in his powre it weare
> Her to redress: but since he meanes found none
> He could no more but her great misery bemone.
> (IV.xii.12)

And now he shares the poet's sense of responsibility, to which he responds with a similar style of self-castigation: after trying to devise plans to save Florimell, he realizes that they are all futile, and

> At last when as not meanes he could inuent,
> Backe to him selfe he gan returne the blame,
> That was the author of her punishment.
> (IV.xii.16)

And Cymoent, returning to her son to discover him near death because of all this, is also unequal to the task; she even has difficulty discerning what the problem *is*. Apollo finally reveals the details to her; then, knowing that any appeal to Proteus

("the root and worker of her woe") will be in vain, she appeals
to "King *Neptune*," who, we learn, supersedes Proteus's authority—an authority that has, till now, been unquestioned,
though vile. In fact, we learn that Proteus's power over Florimell is a temporary fiction; the control he has been claiming and
executing is not really his. As Cymoent explains to Neptune,
Proteus has acquired Florimell by an act of "unjust possession"—

> For that a waift, the which by fortune came
> Upon your seas, he claym'd as propertie:
> And yet nor his, nor his in equitie,
> But yours the waift by high prerogatiue—
> (IV.xii.31)

and it is therefore fragile, unstable, incomplete, unauthorized.
To be sure, his rights of possession are now quickly dispelled,
the thing unjustly possessed now quickly retrieved. For Neptune "streight his warrant made, / Under the Sea-gods seale
autenticall, / Commaunding *Proteus* straight t'enlarge the
mayd" (xii.32), and Proteus, though "grieved to restore the
pledge he did possesse," knows that the game is over, and
"durst he not the warrant to withstand" (xii.32–33). Florimell is
freed and delivered to Marinell. But even this union is incomplete; the divine fiat of Neptune (the miracle hoped for by the
narrator in the beginning of Canto xi) does not resolve all
difficulties. There is no marriage, and no celebration; the narrator still cannot bring the story to its completion, a story that, he
concludes, "to another place I leave to be perfected" (xii.35).

The relationship between Faeryland[9] and the natural world in
Book IV is almost the exact opposite of the relationship between the Faery domain and the human world presented in the
chronicles Guyon and Arthur read in Book II. There, the Faery
domain is for the most part peaceful and orderly, with its peace
and order naturally obtained through lawful succession; the
disruptive essence of that domain is only briefly suggested.
Human history, on the other hand, is mostly disruptive and
difficult. Here, Faeryland is full of usurpations, betrayals, and
disorder, while natural history, despite a troublesome beginning (the courtship) that is only hinted at, proceeds peacefully
and gracefully, without interruptions. This reinforces the no-

tion of the continuum that, I suggested, contains the idealized vision created in Faeryland and its disturbing reality as enacted by man, for now Faeryland reveals, as its main attributes, all the negative features formerly found in human history, and the ideal is outside of its sphere. In fact, Faeryland and the human world have been conflated here: for if Marinell cannot fully partake of the ideal world of the rivers because he is *half*-mortal, then full mortals would, one supposes, like the narrator, have similar, if not even more severe restraints imposed upon them.

The possibility that Faeryland—now practically identified with the world of mortals—can embody the idealized vision is subverted; like Proteus's power to acquire and retain his unlawful possession, Faeryland's potential—as exhibited in Book II—to truly possess its stolen gift of ideal life is revealed as an illusion, and is overruled.[10] The consequences of that initial act of creation have been realized; the thing created, unauthorized, has been recalled. The ideal is now portrayed as existing outside the world of human endeavors and also—because they are now seen as identical—beyond the reach of the poet's fiction, beyond the scope of his created world. The narrator, it seems, is confronting his inability to capture that ideal state, which now stands in ironic contrast to—and as inaccessible to—man and, more particularly, the poet and his fiction. The ideal cannot be legitimately and fully located in the fictional world he creates, which is now recognized as a world that resembles, rather than reverses, the actual world; it remains remote, in the world of nature, a final vision of peace and harmony ultimately denied to man and his fictions, to ordinary humans as well as to poets.

The process implied by the continuum has occurred; the ideal of Faeryland has receded. The poet has no authority to create in his imagined world the perfected vision; his text instead closely adheres to the actuality he so wishes to transcend. Like Marinell, who can watch the harmony of the gods but can never enact it or incorporate it into his own life, the poet can read about and record harmony, but cannot enact it or model his Faeryland on it. The known world is his model; it structures his text. The golden world that can be evoked in Faeryland can be no more permanently inscribed than the ideal visions that any mortals (or, for that matter, faeries) who inhabit it can ever see or achieve: no more enduring than Red Cross Knight's vision on the Hill of Contemplation, no less fleeting than

Arthur's vision of Gloriana in his dream.[11] In the Faeryland created by a poet who is tied to—and bound by the limitations of—actual experience, ideals can be glimpsed but not finally embodied, momentarily grasped but never fully possessed or enacted.

It has not gone unnoticed that in the last three books of *The Faerie Queene*, there is a growing degree of self-consciousness and disillusionment as the poet despairs about the efficacy of his poetry; the narrative begins to attend explicitly to its own composition and to the issue of writing itself. The problem, as it is presented by most critics, is that the poet becomes increasingly aware that the actual world is antagonistic to his Faeryland, and he comes to realize that his poetry cannot deal with this corrupt contemporary reality. Roger Sale's analysis is the most topical: he explains that in response to political developments in England and Ireland, "Faerie Land has collapsed."[12] Harry Berger's explanation is even more representative: according to him, beginning with Book IV, "Faery comes into sharp conflict with the demands of the actual world"; there is a "growing loss of faith in history. . . . The poet cannot find the traditional and expected patterns of order in the chaotic world that surrounds him"; and "the poet is no longer certain about the ability of his imaginary forms to deal with the facts of social existence."[13]

The problem with these statements is that they neglect a major source of the poet's anxiety. To claim that either newly developed conditions in the actual world or the poet's newly developed awareness of that world causes the disintegration of his ideal Faeryland is to over-simplify the issue. What the poet confronts directly here is not merely that the world is fallen and disparate from the ideal, but that Faeryland cannot be kept detached from that world, and is itself disparate from the ideal. Here he presents all the disturbing elements that were left in the background in Book II: his poetic world is not autonomous, and he, like Marinell, has no authority to fashion in it a vision of peace and harmony; like Proteus, he can make no final claims to the authority he formerly professed. The act of creation that could produce the ideal Faeryland of Book II also insists that Faeryland ultimately is part of the actual world where those ideals cannot be permanently possessed, a world from which those ideals recede as soon as they draw near. The poet does not

see conflict between Faeryland and actuality, he sees congruence; he does not so much acknowledge that "real life" contra-
dicts his art, but that it defines and structures it. He does not
lose confidence in his ability to "deal with the facts of social
existence"; he loses confidence in his ability to create a golden
world independent of those facts—in fact, here he illustrates his
inability *not* to deal with those facts. The poem does not
suddenly change because it must admit a disturbing reality; it
demonstrates the implications of its own nature, whose reliance
on and participation in that disturbing reality have already been
adumbrated.[14] The successive books of *The Faerie Queene* do
not "grow increasingly tenuous and inconclusive";[15] rather the
poet realizes and acknowledges that they have been, all along,
tenuous and inconclusive. The poet does not simply come to
terms with the state of the world—something he has always
been aware of—but comes to terms with the status of his own
fiction, which subscribes to the actual, betrays his lack of
autonomy, and reveals his inability to fashion and authorize
ideal resolutions.

Rutgers University

NOTES

This paper was presented at the session sponsored by the Spenser Society at
the 1982 MLA Convention. In my notes I have tried to take account of critical
works that were not available when I first wrote the paper.

1. In the following discussion I make some points similar to A. Leigh
DeNeef's in *Spenser and the Motives of Metaphor* (Durham, N. C.: Duke
University Press, 1982). However, we diverge on a basic issue, and our
arguments seem finally to move in opposite directions. DeNeef claims in
general that Spenser ultimately tries to defend his "metaphoric faerieland"
against the "literal-minded" perception and portrayal of absolute disparities
between, *e.g.*, ideality and reality, fiction and fact, and (while acknowledging
that Spenser occasionally succumbs to such disparities to ward off abuses), he
focuses primarily on Spenser's attempt to "void their dichotomies" (p. 106). I
have focused instead on the alternative perspective: the ways in which such
dichotomies—however impossible to maintain—are crucial to his conception
of his art, and on how their dissolution or "accommodation" is seen as a
threat or challenge to rather than a justification of it.

2. See Carol Kaske, "Spenser's Pluralistic Universe: The View from the
Mount of Contemplation" in *Contemporary Thoughts on Edmund Spenser*,

Richard C. Frushell and B. J. Vondersmith, eds. (Carbondale: Southern Illinois University Press, 1975), pp. 127–130, although her ultimate point is that, while the worlds are contradictory and irreconcilable, "Spenser refuses to take sides as to which is the truer picture of man"; and Harry Berger, Jr., *The Allegorical Temper: Vision and Reality in Book II of Spenser's "Faerie Queene"* (New Haven, Conn.: Yale University Press, 1957), p. 104.

3. *The Faerie Queene*, II.x.5–9. All quotations are from the Variorum Edition, ed. Edwin Greenlaw, *et al.* (Baltimore: Johns Hopkins University Press, 1932–57).

4. Denis Donoghue, *Thieves of Fire* (New York: Oxford University Press, 1974), p. 17. For other discussions of the Promethean origins of the Faery race, *cf.* Thomas P. Roche, Jr., *The Kindly Flame: A Study of the Third and Fourth Books of Spenser's "Faerie Queene"* (Princeton, N.J.: Princeton University Press, 1964), pp. 34–37; Berger, pp. 107–111; and Kaske, pp. 127–128. Michael O'Connell, *Mirror and Veil: The Historical Dimension of Spenser's "Faerie Queene"* (Chapel Hill: University of North Carolina Press, 1977) also sees the Promethean story's significance in its emphasis on the fact that the ideal of Faeryland is created and fictional (p. 81), but he does not see the negative implications that imbue this story of creation.

5. *Cf.* Roche, who maintains that "Faeryland is the ideal world of the highest, most virtuous *human* achievements" (p. 45); and O'Connell, who contends that since the ideal "risks becoming remote," Faeryland "must be placed in the context of a world in which earthly, infected will is still very active" (p. 81).

6. Inconclusiveness, incompleteness, and loose ends are the hallmark of *The Faerie Queene*. The narrator's self-consciousness and uneasiness about this unfinished quality, and his Ariostan transitions that call attention to it, are newly developed, beginning in Book III, firmly established by Book IV. See Allan H. Gilbert, "Spenser's Imitations from Ariosto," *PMLA*, 34 (1919), 225–232.

7. The only narrative problems the narrator announces in this section are ones of compression; *i.e.*, he invokes the conventional difficulty of the self-proclaimed transcriber, without incurring any of the risks of the maker. In my characterization of the narrator's role here (or, rather, my acceptance of his characterization of it) I am taking a perspective different from those critics who see the account of the river marriage as a triumph of the poet and poetry, an explicit image of the power of art and the imagination at work. (See, *e.g.*, A. Bartlett Giamatti, *Play of Double Senses: Spenser's "Faerie Queene"* [Englewood Cliffs, N. J.: Prentice–Hall, 1975], pp. 130–133).

8. Paul Alpers also notes this point in *The Poetry of "The Faerie Queene"* (Princeton, N.J.: Princeton University Press, 1967), p. 121.

9. By "Faeryland" I am referring here to the fictional world of the poem itself in which its major characters move and act and in which their stories unfold.

10. O'Connell also discusses the Book II chronicles together with the river marriage, but he sees in Book IV a withdrawal into "a more private poetic world," and he claims that in this section, "Spenser is broadening his claim for the importance of his own poetic world" (p. 89). Once we take into account the details of the Florimell and Marinell story and their relation to the Thames

and the Medway, however, this sort of position becomes, I think, difficult to maintain. DeNeef, on the other hand, does make the comparison between the two stories, noting that the river marriage "excludes man from its celebration. . . . The world of man, it seems, . . . [is] controlled by destructive and deforming forces." However, since DeNeef follows critics like Giamatti in seeing the river marriage as the *poet's* victory, he concludes with an interpretation opposite to mine: "Freely ranging in his own golden world, the poet seems to have turned away from the brazen one . . ." (p. 124). In my reading, the final cantos of Book IV attest to the poet's *inability* to range freely within his own golden world, and to the identification (rather than the detachment) of the poet's created world and the brazen world. The general shape of my discussion of the Book IV "marriages" is in several respects closer to Jonathan Goldberg's (in *Endlesse Worke: Spenser and the Structures of Discourse* [Baltimore: Johns Hopkins University Press, 1981]), who analyzes the ways in which the "Authority of an Other" shapes the text as the "world and word meet" variously in these episodes (pp. 122–165). In his view, however, if I understand him correctly, this "other" that shapes the text is to be associated with the reality of political, social, and courtly *fictions* that manifest royal power and authority, whereas I argue that it is the reality of actual existence— limited, disorderly, disruptive—that shapes the poet's art, which is differentiated from the orderly union represented by the natural river marriage.

11. Harry Berger's comments on Spenser's "dynamic" conception of the *disconcordia concors* and the lack of absolute resolutions or triumphs in *The Faerie Queene* (in "The Spenserian Dynamics," *Studies in English Literature, 1500–1900,* 8 [1968], 1–18) inform my discussion here, though again I cannot accept the rigid distinctions he erects between human and faery.

12. Roger Sale, *Reading Spenser: An Introduction to "The Faerie Queene"* (New York: Random House, 1968), pp. 171–181. (Sale locates this change beginning in Book V.)

13. Harry Berger, Jr., "The Prospect of Imagination: Spenser and the Limits of Poetry," *Studies in English Literature, 1500–1900,* 1 (1961), 98, 97, 104. See also Richard Neuse, "Book VI as Conclusion to *The Faerie Queene,*" *ELH,* 35 (1968), 329–353.

14. Other critics have recently suggested that Spenser is confronting the implications of his own poetry more than the exigencies of the actual world, but they have focused on different characterizations of his poetry. See, *e.g.,* Madelon Gohlke, "Embattled Allegory: Book II of *The Faerie Queene,*" *English Literary Renaissance,* 8 (1978), 123–140, who argues that Spenser is "coming to terms with the limitations of his genre," a genre that is based on a "*separation*" between moral ideals and fallen human reality. While I agree that such a separation exists on one level, my point is that Spenser confronts the limitations imposed by an inability or failure to *maintain* that separation in his delineation of the relation between Faeryland and the actual world, and hence his inability to create his own image of those ideals. *Cf.* also DeNeef, who claims that in Book V, Spenser concedes that his bleak vision is caused not by the condition of reality, but by his own poetic strategy, which has emphasized a *disparity* between reality and fiction, and which he thus must refashion to accommodate the fiction, the ideal, to the actual (pp. 124–133). More similar to my position is Goldberg's claim that the increased sense of problems in

narration in Book IV are caused not by external pressures but by "the nature of narration itself " that denies closure (p. 29), and his focus on how "the social situation of the text is figured in the text" (p. 128). However, Goldberg's commitment to the Bartheian notion of a "writerly text" as an explanatory principle leads him in a different direction: *e.g.*, when he discusses the dissolution of boundaries between what is "inside" and "outside" the text, stating that the poem cannot be said to replicate " 'uninvented reality' " if reality is itself a "textual invention" (p. 29). When he does address the issue of the "external as the nontextual" (p. 123) later in his book, in the chapter entitled "The Authority of the Other," his primary concern there is, as I mentioned in Note 10, with the social and courtly *fictions* of royal power that surround Queen Elizabeth, and he still speaks of the "*fiction* that the text has a referent" outside of itself (p. 126). Yet while I do not share Goldberg's specifically political definition of the Authority and hence of the producer of the text, or his view of what constitutes the "reality" that is external to and brought into the text, I do very much share his perception that (in the terms of his discourse) "When the word enters society, or society enters the word, the word is destroyed" (p. 169).

15. Berger, "Prospect of Imagination," 97. Berger seems to waver between saying that the poet withdraws from the actual into Faerie, and that the actual invades Faerie. In his later version of this article, "A Secret Discipline: *The Faerie Queene*, Book VI," in *Form and Convention in the Poetry of Edmund Spenser*, ed. William Nelson, English Institute Essays (New York: Columbia University Press, 1961), pp. 35–75, he emphasizes the conflict between these two ideas and concludes that "the vision must be bounded and shaped by the sense that it is not reality; and it must yield to reality at last" (p. 75).

DAVID W. BURCHMORE

Triamond, Agape, and the Fates: Neoplatonic Cosmology in Spenser's Legend of Friendship

I

*T*HE STORY of Agape and her three sons, Priamond, Diamond, and Triamond, is an allegory concerning the role of Love in the creation and preservation of the "three worlds" according to Neoplatonic cosmology.[1] As developed by Ficino and Pico at the end of the fifteenth century in Florence, the doctrine of the three worlds was of fundamental importance in the work of such influential writers as Leone Ebreo, Francesco Giorgio, Reuchlin, and Agrippa; and it was passed on by a host of lesser followers throughout Europe in the sixteenth century.[2] Francis I studied Pico's system in a pair of unpublished treatises written by his chaplain, Jean Thenaud, in 1519 and 1536.[3] By the 1570s a spate of publications had popularized this cosmology in France, among the most significant being Guy and Nicholas Le Fevre de la Boderie's translations of Pico's *Heptaplus* and Giorgio's *Harmonia mundi* (Plate 1).[4] In England, John Colet engaged in correspondence with Ficino, quoted Pico on the subject of the three worlds, and played host to Agrippa during the latter's visit to London in 1510.[5] During the Elizabethan era, there is evidence for interest in the more esoteric aspects of Neoplatonic syncretism in "private circles such as Sir Philip Sidney's group of courtiers studying number in the three worlds with John Dee;"[6] and we find significant descriptions of the three worlds in Barnabe Googe's translation of Palingenius, Michael Drayton's *Endimion and Phoebe*, and Spenser's *Fowre Hymnes*.[7] To this roster we may add the philosopher Everard Digby, whose little known *Theoria Analytica* is a systematic exploration of the three paths to knowledge in the three worlds according to Reuchlin (Plate 2). A fellow student when Spenser arrived at Cambridge in 1569, Digby was giving public lectures there by 1573.[8] His

book was published in 1579 by Henry Bynneman, the same
man who published *A Theatre for Worldlings* in 1569 and the
Spenser-Harvey correspondence in 1580.

The concept of the three worlds, and the philosophy that lay
behind it, was thus a significant part of Spenser's cultural
heritage. Of course the story of Agape and her offspring is not
meant to be a precise representation of any philosophical system; but in order to establish a potential range of meaning for
Spenser's allegory, we have to know something about the
doctrine of the three worlds and the elaborate pattern of analogies and correspondences associated with it. The Triamond
brothers have been said to represent not only the harmony of
the three worlds united by Love, but also the unity of man's
tripartite soul[9] and the "three kinds of love" enumerated
elsewhere in Book IV (*cf.* Plate 3).[10] As we shall see, all of these
meanings are in fact compatible, and their combination in a
single figure is sanctioned by the habit of analogical thought so
characteristic of Renaissance Neoplatonic syncretism.

Though later compounded with additions from the Chris-
tianized Cabala by Pico and others, the triadic division of the
universe was fundamentally Platonic—or, more properly, Platonistic—in origin. The crucial text, cited by Ficino and Pico
alike, was the *Timaeus*, which states that when he framed the
universe the Demiurge "fashioned mind within soul and soul
within body, to the end that the work he accomplished might
be by nature as excellent and perfect as possible."[11] According to
Ficino's *Commentary on the Symposium*, therefore, the three
worlds are the Angelic Mind, the World Soul, and the Body of
the World,[12] as diagrammed here by the eclectic philosopher and
physician Cornelius Gemma (Plate 4). This hierarchy is metaphysical rather than spatial; it places the element of Soul, as a
substance which is composite and mixed, between the sensible
world of material things and the intelligible realm of ideas (Plate
5). As early as the time of Plato's successor Xenocrates, however, this ontological hierarchy had been associated with the
division of the universe into those regions beneath the heavens,
in the heavens, and outside the heavens,[13] so that Pico explains
in his *Oration on the Dignity of Man* that God "had adorned the
super-celestial region with minds. He had animated the celestial
globes with eternal souls; and he had filled with a diverse
throng of animals the cast off and residual parts of the lower

world" before proceeding to the creation of man (Plate 6).[14] Pico's scheme is illustrated here by Charles de Bouelles, one of the earliest writers to introduce the doctrines of the Florentine academy in France.[15] By virtue of his rational soul, man is placed "in the center of the universe"; he shares sense with the brute beasts and intellect with the angels, while his reason can turn in either direction.

These three cognitive powers of the rational soul—sense, reason, and intellect—establish one sense in which man is a microcosm of the three worlds. Since each of these powers is accompanied by an appetite, they also give rise to the three kinds of love so commonly distinguished by the Neoplatonists: sensual, rational, and intellectual—or, as they are sometimes called, bestial, human, and divine.[16] Spenser describes these three kinds of love in Book III when he speaks of that "sacred fire"

> . . . ykindled first aboue,
> Emongst th'eternall spheres and lamping sky
> And thence pourd into men, which men call Loue;
> Not that same, which doth base affections moue
> In brutish minds, and filthy lust inflame,
> But that sweet fit, that doth true beautie loue,
> And choseth vertue for his dearest Dame.
>
> (III.iii.1)

Another important sense in which man is a microcosm of the three worlds is illustrated in a manuscript of Thenaud's *Introduction in the Cabala* (Plate 7), a digest of the philosophy of Pico and Reuchlin prepared for Francis I in 1536. In the *Timaeus*, Plato had placed the appetitive, spirited, and logical parts of the soul in three different parts of the body: the lower belly, the chest, and the head.[17] This placement gave rise to endless variations throughout the Middle Ages and Renaissance. In Chalcidius and others, the three parts of the soul assigned to those regions of the body are called concupiscible, irascible, and rational;[18] in Bartholomaeus Anglicus and many of the scholastic theologians, they are the "natural" power of generation, nutrition and growth, the "vital" power of life and heat, and the "animal" power of sense and movement.[19] According to Pico, who is followed by Agrippa in Plate 8, they are the powers of generation, life, and knowledge residing in the genitals, the heart, and the brain.[20] Pico's scheme is also reproduced by Pietro Bongo, in Plate 9.

What matters, of course, is not the precise identification of the different parts of the soul, but the triadic arrangement by which they constitute a microcosm of the three worlds and an image of the Trinity. Thus in an elaborate table of triadic correspondences in his *De Arte Cyclognomica*, Cornelius Gemma brings together all of the various divisions we have listed.[21] Gemma's 33 categories are surpassed by the 42 entries in Charles de Bouelle's *Book of Wisdom*, which along with the intellectual, celestial, and sensible worlds includes the old Augustinian trinity of memory, intellect, and will and the familiar scholastic tripartition of the soul into the vegetative, sensitive, and rational powers (Plate 10).

This last category is of special interest to us, since, as Professor Nohrnberg has shown, the scholastic doctrine of the generation of the human soul bears a striking resemblance to the progression of lives in Agape's three sons.[22] According to Aquinas, the vegetative soul exists from the beginning, the sensitive soul is produced at the moment of generation, and finally the rational soul is created by God. But the lower souls are not simply added to the higher; they are corrupted and replaced by a higher soul which contains the perfection of the lower forms. Thus in the end man has not three souls, but one "perfect" soul which is simultaneously vegetative, sensitive, and rational, the less perfect souls having passed away in the process of generation.[23]

Aquinas also explains that to each power of the soul pertains a different form of appetite, and each appetite gives rise to a different kind of love. He thus distinguishes another three kinds of love, which he calls "natural," "sensitive," and "rational" or "intellectual."[24] It is these "three kinds of loue" that Spenser lists in canto 9 of Book IV, arguing that "the band of vertuous mind" is better than "The deare affection vnto kindred sweet, / Or raging fire of loue to woman kind:"

> For naturall affection soone doth cesse,
>   And quenched is with *Cupids* greater flame;
>   But faithful friendship doth them both suppresse,
>   And them with maystring discipline doth tame.
>   (IV.ix.2)

The gradual progression or growth through these three loves is illustrated in the story of Triamond, who moves upward from natural affection for his brothers to love for Canacee to eventual friendship with Cambell. In maturing to this final point, however, Triamond has not outgrown the earlier kinds. Like each of the other members of the perfect tetrad of friends formed at the end of the episode, Triamond is held by a triple bond: natural affection for his sister Cambina, sensitive love for his wife Canacee, and rational friendship for his former enemy Cambell.[25]

In short, it is not only possible that the Triamond brothers could simultaneously represent three worlds, three parts of the soul, and three kinds of love; given the analogical basis of the cosmology that Spenser is allegorizing, it is inevitable. The great advantage of Spenser's allegorical shorthand is that he can create a diversely suggestive figure like Triamond without having to work out in any precise or detailed fashion the elaborate system of correspondences for which he stands. When Spenser says of the brothers that

> These three did loue each other dearely well,
> And with so firme affection were allyde,
> As if but one soule in them all did dwell,
> Which did her powre into three parts diuyde,
>   (IV.ii.43)

his meaning is not restricted to the vegetative, sensitive, and rational powers; it can include any three powers of the soul which are regarded as forming an analogous triad. The essential point, in Pico's words, is that "the law of God's wisdom decreed among them a pact of peace and friendship in conformity with the kinship and mutual harmony of their natures." And it is this same power of Love, or Empedoclean "friendship," that binds the three worlds of the cosmos into one harmonious universe.[26]

II

In the story of Agape's visit to the Fates in Demogorgon's Hall, Spenser illustrates the unifying effect of love in opposition to the powers of chaos and discord. The purpose of the episode, Roche suggests, is to "foster an awed respect" for the dark

forces of universal creation "without the puppet strings of one-
for-one equivalents."[27] Yet in designing his allegory, Spenser
drew upon a well-established network of associations that is
essential to the meaning of the tale. Demogorgon, identified by
the mythographers with the unnamed and unknowable "high
lord of the triple world" in Statius' *Thebaid*,[28] was recognized by
Giraldus and Abraham Fraunce as the Platonic Demiurge,
creator of the tripartite universe.[29] As his servants and compan-
ions, the three Fates were naturally believed to assist in the
process of creation. According to Xenocrates (as quoted by
Gianfrancesco Pico), the three Fates correspond to the three
worlds, Atropos being assigned to the supercelestial or intellectual, Lachesis to the celestial or composite, and Clotho to the
sublunary or sensible realm.[30] With some variation in order,
Plutarch expresses similar views in several of the *Moralia*,
explaining that the middle of the three Fates "holds together
and intertwines, so far as is feasible, things mortal and divine,
terrestrial and heavenly."[31] In the *De Facie* he maintains that the
central Fate "mingles and binds together" the three elements of
mind, soul, and body in the creation of the individual.[32] In the
De Fato he associates the three Fates with the three parts of the
World Soul as it spreads throughout the three regions of the
universe: Lachesis is the sublunary or earthly region, Atropos
the wandering planets, and Clotho the region of the fixed
stars.[33] Again with differences in order, this last view was
transmitted to the Middle Ages by Chalcidius and Bernardus
Silvestris;[34] and it is cited in the Renaissance by Ficino, Pico, Le
Roy, Giraldus, and others.[35]

The ultimate source for ascribing a cosmogonic role to the
Fates was the "Myth of Er" in Book X of the *Republic*, where
Plato describes them as "seated round about" the great adamantine spindle of Necessity forming the axis of the universe. Plato
was notoriously inconsistent in his description of the scene,
referring to the axis as both a spindle and a distaff: at one point
he says that the "spindle" turned on the knees of Necessity,
while at another he says that all the spheres turned "around the
distaff, which was driven home through the middle of the
eighth."[36] Consequently there is some uncertainty among Renaissance sources about the manner in which the myth should
be represented. In Blaise de Vigenère's commentary on Philostratus (following the authority of Valeriano's *Hieroglyphica*),

Lachesis is robed with stars, Atropos is in black, while Clotho wears a crown adorned with the seven planets and holds "a distaff incredibly tall, which seems to reach from the earth to heaven."[37] Cartari, on the other hand, calls the object a "spindle," and it is so represented by his illustrators (Plate 11).[38]

In any case Plato's myth was well known in the Renaissance, and the scene was even acted out in the famous *Intermezzi* staged in Florence to celebrate the wedding of Grand Duke Ferdinand de' Medici in 1589 (Plate 12). According to the account of the production published in the same year,[39] the stage was filled with three banks of clouds representing the three regions of the universe. On the lowest were the Sirens, who had descended from the heavens to sing the praises of the bride. On the highest, in the realm of Ideas, were twelve figures representing virtues possessed by the married couple. In the middle, (accompanied by the seven planets and Astraea) Necessity and the three Fates were seated around the cosmic spindle itself (Plate 13).

Spenser recalls this Platonic image in his own description of the Fates, for when Agape sought them out in Demogorgon's Hall

> There she them found, all sitting round about
> The direfull distaffe standing in the mid.
> (IV.ii.48)

Like the illuminator of Thenaud's *Introduction in the Cabala* (Plate 14), Spenser combines the Platonic tableau with the more familiar image of the Fates as spinners. Milton performs a similar conflation of imagery in the *Arcades* when he describes the Fates as "those that hold the vital sheares / And turn the Adamantine spindle round, / On which the fate of Gods and men is wound."[40]

In Spenser's account, the figure of Necessity has disappeared, to be replaced by Agape herself: "She them saluting, there by them sate still, / Beholding how the thrids of life they span." In making the Fates accede, however grudgingly, to Agape's wishes, Spenser is following the often cited authority of the Orphic *Hymn to Venus,* which (as Ficino puts it) "placed Love before Necessity, saying that Love governs the three Fates and engenders all."[41] By joining the life-threads of Agape's children, the Fates are effectively uniting the three worlds and the three parts of the soul, thus fulfilling the role assigned to them by the Neoplatonists.

III

Spenser has also placed the stanza describing "the direfull distaffe standing in the mid" at the exact numerological midpoint of the first four cantos and proem of Book IV. Thanks to the work of Hieatt and others, we know that Spenser used the key-phrase "in the midst" to signal the presence of a deliberate centerpiece in each of the first three books;[42] and in fact there is another such midpoint in Book V, describing Britomart's identification with Isis "in the midst of her felicity." What we seem to have in Book IV is a group of complementary midpoints, for just one stanza from the center of the last four cantos we find the circle of maidens surrounding Amoret in the Temple of Venus described in language which seems calculated to recall the earlier scene:

> Thus sate they all a round in seemely rate
> And in the midst of them a goodly mayd.
> (IV.x.52)

Even more impressive than this deliberate verbal echo, however, is the emphatic centrality of the image described: Amoret is placed "euen in the lap of *Womanhood*," encircled by a ring of maidens at the foot of Venus' statue, "right in the midst" of the hundred altars set "round about" the "inmost" temple "within the compasse of that Islands space" (IV.x.21–52).

There is no key-phrase "in the midst" to mark the center of the middle four cantos, but what we find there is significant. The central episode describes Amoret's captivity in the Cave of Lust, and the precise midpoint falls between two stanzas just after Amoret has been thrown into his den:

> Then when she lookt about, and nothing found
> But darknesse and dread horrour, where she dwelt,
> She almost fell againe into a swound,
> Ne wist whether aboue she were, or vnder ground.
> (IV.vii.9)

In one sense this is a non-center, a negation of the other two. Its location is nowhere, although it is described with the same words Spenser elsewhere applies to the fallen angels in hell, "Where they in darknesse and dread horror dwell" (*HHL*, 90). In another sense the episode may be regarded as a kind of demonic parody of Agape in Demogorgon's Hall: that was a cosmogonic myth; this is a vision of sterility and destruction. There we saw Agape begetting and sustaining her three sons; here we witness Lust preparing to devour his three victims ("And of vs three to morrow he will sure eate one," laments Aemylia). There Agape persuaded the three Fates to lengthen her sons lives; here Aemylia reports that "fates peruerse / With guilefull loue did secretly agree" to work her destruction.

Taken as a group, these three centers (Hall of Demogorgon, Temple of Venus, and Cave of Lust) might be viewed as corresponding to the three worlds, and the three central figures (Agape, Amoret, and Lust) equated with the three kinds of love which the Neoplatonists called Divine, Human, and Bestial. It is not difficult to explain why Spenser might adopt such a scheme in Book IV. Friendship, as he conceived it, is both a personal virtue governing social relationships and a cosmic force which secures the harmony of the universe and its component parts. It is appropriate that his Legend of Friendship should imitate that concord. There was ample precedent in the many Neoplatonic treatises on love which are divided into three books, such as Pico's Commentary on Benivieni or Leone Ebreo's *Dialoghi d'amore*. In the preface to the last book of his Commentary on the *Symposium*, Louis Le Roy states that having confined his discussion in the first two books to "bodily and human love," he will proceed to expound "divine love" in the third.[43]

Other philosophical treatises follow the same pattern. In the opening paragraph of the *De Occulta Philosophia Libri Tres*, Agrippa states his intention to embody the triple world in his work; so that, in the words of an encomium prefixed to the English translation, "his *Three Books* with the *Three Worlds* shall stand."[44] Perhaps the most famous example of such a structure is the *De Harmonia Mundi Totius Cantica Tria* of Francesco Giorgio, who according to Guy Le Fevre de la Boderie took the "unique and triple world" as his pattern, and "in order to imitate as closely as possible the order of the world, just as its

Maker and Architect had done, first made and divided this 'harmony of the world' into three canticles and each canticle into eight tones or books."[45] Less famous, but more intriguing from our point of view, is the example of Everard Digby's *Theoria Analytica*. Its three books are devoted to the three "paths" or "keys" to knowledge in the three worlds, with the highest in the middle; its three central chapters are set aside for the definitions of those three worlds (again with the highest in the middle); and a pyramidal diagram of all three worlds is placed in the middle of the center chapter (Plate 15).

With this kind of symbolic structure fashionable even in Spenser's England, it is not surprising that he should make use of it in his own allegorical treatment of the function of love in the three worlds. And the tripartite structure Spenser imposes on Book IV, however artificial it may be, has the additional effect of creating three "groups" of four cantos each. Given the symbolic importance of the "four groups" or "tetrads" of perfect friends that has been so thoroughly established by Fowler and others,[46] this is probably not coincidental. We have already noted that the most perfect tetrad of friends, which includes the eponymous heroes Cambell and Triamond, is united by a triple bond of threefold love; and it might be said that the canto-tetrads, with the three kinds of love represented at their centers, are meant to reproduce that symbolism in the structure of the book.

Charlottesville, Virginia

NOTES

A draft of this essay was presented at the special sessions on "Spenser: The Cultural Heritage," at the Sixteenth International Congress on Medieval Studies in Kalamazoo, Michigan, 7–10 May, 1984. Quotations of Spenser are from the *Poetical Works*, ed. J. C. Smith and E. DeSelincourt (London: Oxford University Press, 1912).

1. First recognized by Thomas P. Roche, Jr., in *The Kindly Flame: A Study of the Third and Fourth Books of Spenser's "Faerie Queene"* (Princeton, N.J.: Princeton University Press, 1964), pp. 15–31. See also Maurice Evans, *Spenser's Anatomy of Heroism: A Commentary on "The Faerie Queene"* (Cambridge: Cambridge University Press, 1970), p. 184; Ronald Arthur Horton, *The Unity of "The Faerie Queene"* (Athens: University of Georgia Press,

1979), p. 105; and Jonathan Goldberg, *Endlesse Worke: Spenser and the Structures of Discourse* (Baltimore: Johns Hopkins University Press, 1981), p. 27.

2. See generally Nesca A. Robb, *Neoplatonism of the Italian Renaissance* (London: Unwin, 1935) pp. 64–66 (Pico) and p. 75 (Ficino); Charles Trinkaus, *In Our Image and Likeness: Humanity and Divinity in Italian Humanist Thought* (Chicago: University of Chicago Press, 1970), II, 476–478 (Ficino) and 506–508 (Pico); Christopher Butler, *Number Symbolism* (New York: Barnes & Noble, 1970), pp. 54–71; and S. K. Heninger, Jr., *Touches of Sweet Harmony: Pythagorean Cosmology and Renaissance Poetics* (San Marino, Calif.: Huntington Library, 1974), pp. 341 and 360.

3. On Thenaud, see Lynn Thorndike, *A History of Magic and Experimental Science*, 8 vols. (New York: Columbia University Press, 1941), VI, 453; Joseph Leon Blau, *The Christian Interpretation of The Cabala in the Renaissance* (New York: Columbia University Press, 1944), pp. 89–98; F. Secret, "Jean Thénaud, voyager et kabbaliste de la renaissance," *Bibliothèque d'humanisme et de renaissance*, 16 (1953), 139–144; and F. Secret, *Les Kabbalistes chrétiens de la renaissance* (Paris: Dunod, 1964), pp. 153–177. I have consulted the treatise of 1536 in a microfilm of MS fr. 167 of the Bibliothèque publique et universitaire, Geneva (illustrated here in Plates 6 and 14). On this MS, see *L'Enlumineur de Charlemagne à François Ier: Manuscrits de la Bibliothèque publique et universitaire*, ed. Bernard Gaguebin (Geneva: Braillard, 1976), pp. 149–152.

4. See François Secret, *L'Esoterisme de Guy Le Fevre de la Boderie* (Geneva: Droz, 1969). For commentary on the diagram reproduced in Plate 1, see S. K. Heninger, Jr., *The Cosmographical Glass: Renaissance Diagrams of the Universe* (San Marino, Calif.: Huntington Library, 1977), pp. 92–95; and also Maren-Sofie Røstvig, *The Hidden Sense and Other Essays*, Norwegian Studies in English, No. 9 (Oslo: Universitetsforlaget, and New York: Humanities Press, 1963), p. 46; and Frances A. Yates, *The Occult Philosophy in the Elizabethan Age* (London: Routledge, 1979), pp. 33–34. For other French sources, see note 20, below.

5. Leland Miles, *John Colet and the Platonic Tradition* (La Salle: Open Court, 1961); *John Colet and Marsilio Ficino*, ed. Sears R. Jayne (London: Oxford University Press, 1963). Pico's system of the Three Worlds is reflected in Ch. xii of Colet's "Ennaratio in Epistolam primum S. Pauli ad Corinthios," in *An Exposition of St. Paul's First Epistle to the Corinthians*, ed. and trans. J. H. Lupton (London, 1874), pp. 126–133 and 250–254; and in "Epistola II" of the *Letters to Radulphus on the Mosaic Account of the Creation*, ed. and trans. J. H. Lupton (London, 1876), pp. 10 and 170–171.

6. Frances A. Yates, *Giordano Bruno and the Hermetic Tradition* (Chicago: University of Chicago Press, 1964), p. 187. John Dee paraphrases Agrippa on the Three Worlds in his preface to Billingsly's translation of Euclid (1570): see Yates, *The Occult Philosophy*, pp. 44–45.

7. The hierarchy of worlds is described by Spenser in the *Hymn of Heavenly Beautie*, lines 36–77. For commentary thereon, see Josephine Waters Bennett, "Spenser's Venus and the Goddess Nature of the *Cantos of Mutabilitie*," *Studies in Philology*, 30 (1933), 160–161; Heninger, *Cosmographical Glass*, pp. 86–87; and Yates, *Occult Philosophy*, pp. 96–97. For other poetic treatments, compare Michael Drayton's *Endimion and Phoebe*, lines 663–680 (sublunary), 681–734 (celestial), and 879–904 (angelic world); and Barnabe Googe's translation

of Palingenius' *The Zodiake of Life*, ed. R. Tuve (1576; facs. rpt. New York, 1947), p. 229 ("Pisces," lines 169–194).

8. On Digby, see J. Freudenthal, "Beitrage zur Geschichte der englischen Philosophie," *Archiv für Geschichte der Philosophie*, Band IV, Heft 3–4 (1891), 450–477 and 578–603; W. R. Sorley, *A History of English Philosophy* (Cambridge, Cambridge University Press, 1920), pp. 9–10; and Meyrick H. Carré, *Phases of Thought in England* (Oxford: Clarendon Press, 1949), pp. 198–199. The Three Worlds in Digby's *Theoria Analytica* do not correspond to those in Ficino and Pico; rather they follow the scheme adopted by Reuchlin in *De Arte Cabalistica Libri Tres* (Hagenau, 1517). The same system was used by Pietro Galatino; see C. G. Nauert, Jr., *Agrippa and the Crisis of Renaissance Thought*, Illinois Studies in Social Science, No. 55 (Urbana: University of Illinois Press, 1965), p. 266, n. 13.

9. See the authorities cited in n. 1, above, and the extensive discussion in James Nohrnberg, *The Analogy of "The Faerie Queene"* (Princeton, N.J.: Princeton University Press, 1976), pp. 608–615. See also Alastair Fowler, *Spenser and the Numbers of Time* (New York: Barnes & Noble, 1964), p. 28, n. 1; and John E. Hankins, *Source and Meaning in Spenser's Allegory* (London: Oxford University Press, 1971), p. 144.

10. In a previous article I have suggested that the image of Agape and her "three louely babes" was derived from the common representation of Charity (*cf.* Plate 3) with three infants symbolizing the "threefold power" of love: "The Unfolding of Britomart: Mythic Iconography in *The Faerie Queene*," in *Renaissance Papers 1977*, ed. Dennis Donovan and A. Leigh DeNeef (Durham: Southeastern Renaissance Conference, 1977), p. 11 and Fig. 1. For other examples of this emblem in renaissance art, see Edgar Wind, "Charity: The Case History of A Pattern," *Journal of the Warburg and Courtauld Institutes*, 1 (1937), 322–330. That the "three kinds of loue" enumerated by Spenser at IV.ix.1 are embodied in the Triamond episode was first suggested by Jefferson B. Fletcher, "'The Legend of Cambel and Triamond' in the *Faerie Queene*," *Studies in Philology*, 35 (1938), 195–201. See also Nohrnberg, pp. 615–619; and David R. Pichaske, "*The Faerie Queene* IV.ii and iii: Spenser on the Genesis of Friendship," *Studies in English Literature, 1500–1900*, 17 (Winter, 1977), 81–93 (Pichaske's discussion of the Aristotelian "sources," however, is misleading).

11. *Timaeus*, 30B. Rather than genuine Platonic doctrine, this may be viewed as Plato's summary of Pythagorean cosmology through the character of the philosopher Tiameus. The triadic division of the universe is best referred to as "Platonistic," since it was fully developed only by Plato's early followers Xenocrates and Posidonius (who emphasized the placement of soul as a mediating principle between the sensible and intelligible realms). See Philip Merlan, *From Platonism to Neoplatonism* (The Hague: Nijhoff, 1953), p. 185; *The Cambridge History of Late Classical and Early Medieval Philosophy*, ed. A. H. Armstrong (Cambridge: Cambridge University Press, 1970), pp. 15–19 and 62; and Walter Burkert, *Lore and Science in Ancient Pythagoreanism*, trans. E. L. Minar, Jr. (Cambridge, Mass.: Harvard University Press, 1972), p. 245. This tripartition was adopted by the classical Neoplatonists (including Plotinus, Porphyry, Iamblichus, and Proclus) and thence passed on to the Neoplatonists of the Renaissance. See the "Triadic Division of the Universe,

and Pletho's Use of Proclus," in Milton V. Anastos, "Pletho's Calendar and Liturgy," *Dumbarton Oaks Papers*, 4 (1948), 289–299.

12. *In Convivium Platonis De Amore Commentarium*, I, iii, in *Opera Omnia* (Basle, 1561), II, 1321.

13. As reported by Sextus Empiricus, "Xenocrates says that there are three forms of existence, the sensible, the intelligible, and the composite or opinable; and of these the sensible is that which exists within the Heaven, and the intelligible that which belongs to all things outside the Heaven, and the opinable and composite that of the Heaven itself." *Against the Logicians*, I, 147, in *Works*, trans. R. G. Bury, Loeb Classical Library, II (London and Cambridge, Mass.: William Heinemann and Harvard University Press, 1935), p. 81. This passage was quoted verbatim by Gianfrancesco Pico in *Examen van. doct. Gent.*, II, xiii, in *Opera Omnia*, II (Basle, 1573), p. 841. A similar view, described as "what the Delphians say," is reported by Plutarch: "the whole universe is divided into three regions: the first is that of the fixed stars, the second that of the planets, and the last the sublunary region; they are all knit and ordered together in harmonious formulae." *Quaestiones Conviviales*, IX, 14, 4 (745B), in *Moralia*, IX, ed. E. L. Minar, Jr., F. H. Sandbach and W. C. Helmbold, Loeb Classical Library (London and Cambridge, Mass.: William Heinemann and Harvard University Press, 1961), pp. 276–277. For the spatial tripartition of the universe in various other forms, see the commentary on "Tripartition de la Nature" in *Apulée: Opuscules philosophiques et fragments*, ed. Jean Beaujeu (Paris: Budé, 1973), pp. 203–206. For an early use of the phrase "three worlds" in this context, *cf.* the Emperor Julian's "Hymn to Helios," *Oratio* IV, 148A.

14. "Supercaelestem regionem mentibus decoraret; aetherios globos aeternis animis vegetarat; excrementarias ac feculentas inferioris mundi partes omnigena animalium turba complerat." *De Hominis Dignitate, Heptaplus, De Ente et Uno, e scritti vari*, ed. E. Garin (Florence: Vallecchi, 1942), p. 104. Pico generally refers to the Three Worlds as the "supercelestial," "celestial" and "sublunary," but his system varies from Ficino's only in terminology. See Trinkaus, II, 507–508. Thus in the *Heptaplus* he explains that "antiquity imagined three worlds. Highest is the ultramundane, which theologians call angelic and philosophers intelligible; next to that is the celestial world, and last of all this sublunary world which we inhabit" ("tres mundos figurat antiquitas. Supremum omnium ultramundanum, quem theologi angelicum, philosophi autem intellectualem vocant . . . Proximum huic caelestem; postremum omnium sublunarem hinc, quem nos incolimus"). *Heptaplus*, Proem 2; ed. Garin, p. 184.

15. Bouelles actually speaks of four worlds, including the "divine"; but (as Ficino points out) the realm of God should not properly be counted as a world: "summum illum Deum, non mundum dicimus." *De Amore*, I, iii, in *Opera Omnia*, II, 1321. On Bouelles see Ernst Cassirer, *Individuum und Kosmos in der Philosophie der Renaissance*, Studien der Bibliothek Warburg, No. 10 (Leipzig: Teubner, 1927), pp. 299–412; and Joseph M. Victor, *Charles de Bouelles, 1479–1553: An Intellectual Biography*, Travaux d' humanisme et de renaissance, No. 161 (Geneva: Droz, 1978). According to Thorndike, VI, 439–443, Erasmus regarded the works of Bouelles as "unreadable."

On man as the center of the universe, see Pico, *Heptaplus*, III, vii; IV, ii; and

V, vi. See also Erwin Panofsky, *Studies in Iconology: Humanistic Themes in the Art of the Renaissance* (1939; rpt. New York: Harper & Row, 1972), pp. 135– 137; Trinkaus, II, 476–478; and compare Ficino's disciple Francesco Cattani da Diacetto, *De Amore*, II, iii: "Anima media est inter mundum intelligibilem & corpus, veluti Mundi nodus atque vinculum." *Opera Omnia* (Basle, 1563), p. 109.

16. "As desire generally follows knowledge, so severall knowing are annexed to several desiring Powers. We distinguish the knowing into three degrees; Sence, Reason, Intellect . . . Thus in our Soul . . . there may be three Loves; one in the Intellect, Angelical; the second Humane; the third Sensual." Thomas Stanley, trans., *A Platonick Discourse Upon Love*, Bk. II, Sects. iv and xxii, in *Poems and Translations of Thomas Stanley*, ed. G. M. Crump (London: Oxford University Press, 1962), pp. 206 and 217 (translating Pico's Commentary on Benivieni, II, v and xxvi in *Opera Omnia* (Basle, 1557); II, vii and III, iv in Garin ed.). Compare Leone Ebreo, *Dialoghi d'amore*, ed. S. Caramella (Bari: Laterza, 1929), p. 367; Mario Equicola, *Di natura d'amore* (Venice, 1563), fols. 70–71; Giordano Bruno, *De gli eroici furore*, I, ii; and Baldassare Castiglione, *Il Cortegiano*, IV, li. John Charles Nelson, *Renaissance Theory of Love* (New York: Columbia University Press, 1958), pp. 77–78, traces such discussions to Ficino's *De Amore*, VI, viii. The correspondence between the Three Worlds, three parts of the soul and three kinds of love is suggested in the lower diagram from Cornelius Gemma in Plate 3, which is a garbled schematization of Ficino's *De Amore*, VI, viii and VII, xiii–xiv. Behind all of these theories lies Plato's *Republic*, IX, 580D–581E: "the three parts [of the soul] have also, it seems to me, three kinds of pleasure, one peculiar to each, and similarly three appetites and controls." Thus, according to Apuleius, "Plato tres amores hoc genere dinumerat, quod sit unus diuinus cum incorrupta mente et uirtutis ratione conueniens, non paenitendus; alter degeneris animi et corruptissimae uoluptatis; tertius ex utroque permixtus, mediocris ingenii et cupidinis modicae." *De Dogmate Platonis*, XIV, in *Opuscules philosophiques*, p. 91.

17. *Timaeus*, 44D and 69D–72E.

18. *Timaeus a Calcidio Translatus Commentarioque Instructus*, ed. J. H. Waszink, 2nd ed., Corpus Platonicum Medii Aevi: Plato Latinus, No. 4 (London: Warburg Institute, and Leiden: Brill, 1975), pp. 245–246 (Chs. ccxxxi– ccxxxii). Compare Macrobius, *Commentarii in Somnium Scipionis*, I, xiv, 5– 13; and Bernardus Silvestris, *Cosmographia*, II, 13–14. According to Chalcidius, the world soul is triplex, and is divided among the three regions of the universe (the fixed sphere, the planets, and the sublunary region): "Erit ergo animae aplanes ratio, planetes ut iracundia et cupiditas ceterique huius modi motus quorum concentu fit totius mundi vita modificata," p. 148 (Ch. xcv). Compare Thomas Rychard's sixteenth-century commentary on III m. 9 of Boethius' *De Consolatione Philosophiae*, appended to the 1525 edition of John Walton's fourteenth-century translation: "He calleth the soule of the vvorlde . . . Of treble kynde. For fyrst he is partener of the kende of angeles viche ben of vniforme kynde / that ys to say of simple nature / pure / and vnmedled: viche Plato calleth the same and euer-abidynge mater / that ys to seyn of perdurable kende. The seconde part of hys kende / may be called the alliance to the erthly thinges vvyche ben varyable and corruptible and diuers in ther

beynge. The thyrd part of his kende / is medlede of thes both / that ys his allyance to the spheres of sterres and of planetes viche ben in parte meueable and in parte vnmeueable. . . . When he hath sotelly treted of the soule of the vvorlde / than goethe he to the soule of man and sayth that in maner leke as god hath made the soule of the vvorlde of iii naturs / so hathe he made the soule of man." Ed. Mark Science, Early English Text Society, OS No. 170 (London, 1927), pp. 370–371.

19. These are three powers of the soul as it functions in the body: "on hatte *naturalis* and is in the livere. þe oþir hatte *vitalis* and also *spiritualis* and ha **haþ** place in þe herte, þe **þridde** ridde hatte *animalis* and **haaþ** place in þe brayn." *On the Properties of Things: John Trevisa's Translation of Bartholomeus Anglicus' De Proprietatibus Rerum*, III, 14, ed. M. C. Seymour, *et al.*, I (London: Oxford University Press, 1975), p. 103. These are sometimes said to be parts of the sensitive soul; *cf.* the popular *Compendii Theologiae Veritatis* formerly attributed to Albertus Magnus, in his *Opera Omnia*, ed. A. Borgnet (Paris: Vives, 1890–94), Vol. 34, p. 68; and compare Thomas Aquinas, *Summa Theologica*, I, q. 78, art. 1 ad 4.

20. *Heptaplus*, Conclusion: "tres mundos, intellectualem, coelestem & corruptibilem, per tres homines partes aptissime figurat." *Opera Omnia* (Basle, 1555), p. 61. Pico's system was immensely influential throughout the Renaissance, and his description of the human microcosm reappears in a host of later authorities. *Cf.* Agrippa's *Dialogus de Homine*, ed. Paolo Zambelli, *Rivista critica di storia della filosofia*, anno XIII, fasc. iii (Florence, 1958), pp. 60–61; John Colet, "Ennaratio in Epist. Primum ad Cor.," pp. 133 and 253; and Leone Ebreo, *Dialoghi d' amore*, II: "Tutti questi tre mondi e' quali hai esplicati, generabile, celeste e intellettuale, si contengono ne l'uomo come in microcosmos; e si truovono in lui non solamente diversi in virtú e operazione, ma ancor divisi per membri, parte e luoghi del corpo humano" (ed. Caramella, pp. 90–91). Guy Le Fevre de la Boderie, in his preface to the French translation of Francesco Giorgio, writes that "chacun homme est la sommaire & l'abregé du grand monde distingué en 3. mipartimens, ainsi que l'homme contient trois estages ou sieges principaux de la vie naturelle ou vegetable, vitale ou sensitive, & animale ou motive, à sçavoir le foye, le coeur, & le cerveau." (Paris, 1570), sig. A5ᵛ. Guy explores this idea further in *La Galliade ou de la révolution des arts* (Paris, 1578), and in *L'Encyclie des secrets de l'éternité* (Anvers, 1571). See also Guy's disciple Blaise de Vigenere, *Traicte des chiffres* (Paris, 1586), fol. 26; and *Les Images de Philostrate* (Paris, 1614), pp. 6–8 and 88–89. Louis Le Roy summarizes Pico in the commentary accompanying his translation of Plato's *Symposium*, placing reason in the head, concupiscence in the liver, and ire in the heart. "Ainsi en l'integrité de la substance humaine, furent assemblées les substances de toutes les natures du monde. Ce qui ne se peut dire d'autre creature quelconque, Angelique, celeste, & sensible." *Le Sympose de Platon* (Paris, 1559), fols. 137ᵛ–138ᵛ. For late examples of Pico's influence in England, see Helkiah Crooke, *Microcosmographia: A Description of the Body of Man* (London, 1615), where "the Collation of man with the world" equates the head with the "Supreame and Angelicall part of the worlde," the venter with "the middle and celestiall part," and the lower belly with "the sublunary part" (pp. 6–7). The illustration from Thenaud in Plate 7 may be compared with the famous diagram in Robert Fludd, *Utriusque cosmi* . . .

historia (Oppenheim, 1617–19), III, 83, reproduced in Heninger, *Harmony*, Fig. 42; and in *Cosmographical Glass*, Fig. 84.

21. The full table is reproduced in Heninger, *Harmony*, pp. 80–81. Under the heading "In Microcosmo Homine" it includes:

Anima.	Spiritus.	Corpus.
Anima rationalis.	Anima irascibilis.	Anima cōcupiscibilis &
Intellectus.	Ratio.	vegetatrix.
Spiritus animalis.	Spiritus vitalis.	Imaginatrix virtus.
Cerebrum et nerui.	Cor & arteriae.	Naturalis Spiritus.
		Hepar & venae.

"In Mundo Maiore" includes "Caelum. Aether. Sublunaris regio." For background on Cornelius Gemma, see Thorndike, VI, 406–409.

22. Nohrnberg, *Analogy*, pp. 612–613.

23. *Cf.* Aquinas, *Summa Theologica*, I, q. 118, art. 2 ad 2, and I, q. 77, art. 8 resp. (the sensitive and nutritive powers do not remain "actually," but they remain "virtually" in the soul, as in their principle or root). Hence Triamond has not a "triple" soul, but a "perfect" one, and is properly named Telamond (from the Greek, τελιος, or "perfect").

24. Not to be confused with the three kinds of love discussed by the Neoplatonists, these arise respectively in the vegetative, sensitive, and rational parts of the soul. See Aquinas, *Summa Theologica*, Ia IIae, q. 26, art. 1 resp.; Ia IIae, q. 17, art. 8; I, q. 80, art. 1; and I, q. 60, art. 1. Compare Leone Ebreo, *Dialoghi d'amore*, II: "Il conoscimento e l'appetito e, per consequente, l'amor è di tre modi: naturale, sensitivo e rational volontario" (p. 67). According to Giovanni Caldiera, "viventia perfectissima sicut homines post cognitionem, post electionem obiecta sequuntur; per hos igitur tres appetitus tria amorum genera distinguimus quia primus amor est naturalis, secundus sensitivus, et tertius intellectivus." *De Concordia Poetarum, Philosophorum et Theologorum* (Venice, 1557), quoted in Trinkaus, II, 871, n. 75. See also *Les Six Livres de Mario Equicola d'Alveto . . . De la nature d'amour*, trans. Gabriel Chappuys (Paris, 1584), fol. 124. Since the lower souls are contained in the higher, the lesser loves are found together with the greater, and "perfect" love is triplex in nature. "True friendship tieth (though with diuers respects) children to their parents, kinred to kinred, the husband to the wife, and the minds of men of valour & virtue fast together, as a thing agreeable to all the qualities which the soule containeth." Lodowick Bryskett, *A Discourse of Civill Life*, ed. Thomas E. Wright, San Fernando State College Renaissance Editions, No. 4 (Northridge, Calif., 1970), p. 162.

25. As suggested by Fletcher, " 'Legend of Cambell and Triamond,' " pp. 197–198. Compare the explanatory note and diagram in A. C. Hamilton's edition of *The Faerie Queene* (New York: Longman, 1977), p. 451.

26. *Heptaplus*, Expositio: "inter eas foedus pacis & amicitiae, ex naturam cognatione & mutuo consensu, per sapientiae Dei legem sanctitum est," *Opera Omnia*, p. 62 (p. 382 in Garin ed.). For the "friendship" of the three parts of the soul, see Plato's *Republic*, IV, 442D and 443C. On the harmony of the universe, and the mutual love which binds its parts together, see Ficino's *De Amore*, III, iii, in *Opera Omnia*, II, 1330.

27. *Kindly Flame*, pp. 19–20.

28. Demogorgon originated as a corruption of Lactantius Placidus' gloss to

the phrase "triplicis mundi summum" in Statius' *Thebaid*, IV, 516. See D. C. Allen, *Mysteriously Meant: The Rediscovery of Pagan Symbolism and Allegorical Interpretation in the Renaissance* (Baltimore: Johns Hopkins University Press, 1970), p. 216. Boccaccio quotes the same line from Statius in his discussion of Demogorgon in the *Genealogie Deorum Gentilium Libri*, ed. V. Romano, Scrittori d'Italia, Nos. 200–201 (Bari: Laterza, 1951), I, 14. By the "triple world" Statius meant the classical division of land, sea, and air; compare Ovid, *Metamorphoses*, XV, 859 and XII, 39–40. For other examples of this topos, see G. Carl Galinsky, *Aeneas, Sicily and Rome* (Princeton, N.J.: Princeton University Press, 1969), pp. 216–217. Of course, the "triple world" is ruled by love, or Venus; see Ovid, *Fasti*, IV, 91–95; and compare Boethius, *De Consolatione Philosophiae*, II m. 8, 14–15: "terras ac pelagus regens / et caelo imperitans amor."

29. Giraldus was the first to explain that "Demogorgon" in Lactantius' gloss was a corruption of the word δημίουργον used by Plato and others. Giraldus, too, quotes the phrase "triplicis mundi summum" from Statius. Lilio Gregorio Gyraldo, *De Deis Gentium* (Basle, 1548), "Epistola Nuncupatoria," sig. 3ᵛ. Compare Abraham Fraunce, *The Third Part of the Countesse of Pembrokes Yuychurche* (London, 1592), fol. 6ᵛ: "By Demogorgon, or peraduenture, *Demiurgon*, is here understood that one & only creator of all."

30. Gianfrancesco Pico supplies this information in the same passage cited above, n. 13, again drawing his knowledge of Xenocrates from Sextus Empiricus, *Against the Logicians*, I, 149.

31. *Quaestiones Convivales*, IX, 14, 4 (745B–C), in *Moralia*, IX, pp. 276–277. See the quotation in n. 13, above; each of the three regions there described has a Fate as its guardian. The order Atropos/Clotho/Lachesis derives from Plato's *Laws*, XII, 960C.

32. *De Facie*, 945C–D, in Plutarch, *Moralia*, XII, ed. H. Cherniss and W. C. Helmbold, Loeb Classical Library (London and Cambridge, Mass.: William Heinemann and Harvard University Press, 1957), pp. 220–221. "Atropos enthroned in the sun initiates generation, Clotho in motion on the moon mingles and binds together, and finally on earth Lachesis too puts her hand to the task." Clotho is uniting the mind (νοῦς) with the soul (ψυχή); and Lachesis joins them to the inanimate (ἄψυχον) body. Earlier it is said that the earth provides man's body, the moon his soul, and the sun his intellect (943A). Compare *De Genio Socratis*, 591B–E, where Atropos is in the invisible, Clotho in the sun, Lachesis in the moon, and they preside over the conjunction (σύνδεσμων) of mind, soul, and body. *Moralia*, VII, ed. P. H. De Lacy, and B. Einarson (Cambridge, Mass.: Harvard University Press, 1959), pp. 468–471. Both of these dialogues were available in the French translation by Jaques Amyot, *Les Oeuvres morales & meslées de Plutarque* (Paris, 1572).

33. *De Fato*, 2 (568E–F), in *Moralia*, VII, 312–315. "Fate as a substance appears to be the entire soul of the universe in all three of its subdivisions, the fixed portion, the portion supposed to wander, and third, the portion below the heavens in the region of the earth; of these the highest is Clotho, the next Atropos, and the lowest Lachesis." Lachesis is also said to "twine or plait together" (συμπλέκουσα) these parts.

34. Chalcidius, Ch. cxliv (on Timaeus 41D–E): "uero substantia positum fatum mundi anima est, tripertita in aplanem sphaerem inque eam quae

putatur erratica et in sublunarem tertiam; quarum elatum quidem ad superna dici Atropon, mediam Clotho, imam Lachesin" (ed. Waszink, pp. 182–183). Compare Bernardus Silvestris, *Cosmographia*, II, ll: "Atropos governs the sphere of the firmament, Clotho the planets' wanderings, Lachesis the affairs of the earth." *The Cosmographia of Bernardus Silvestris*, trans. Winthrop Wetherbee, Records of Civilization: Sources and Studies, No. 89 (New York: Columbia University Press, 1973), p. 115.

35. Each of the passages from Plutarch's *Moralia* discussed above, nn. 31–33, is quoted and explained by Blaise de Vigenère in his commentary of Philostratus, first published in 1578. *Les Images de Philostrate*, "Pelops," (Paris, 1614), pp. 141–142. Louis LeRoy quotes at length from the *De Fato* in his commentary on Plato's *Timaeus*. The soul of the world "est divisee en trois parties, la premiere celle qui n'erre point, la seconde celle que l'on estime errer, & la troisiesme celle qui est au dessoubs du ciel, a l'entour de la terre, desquelles trois parties de l'vniuers, la plus haute s'appelle Clotho, la seconde se nomme Atropos, & la plus basse Lachesis, laquelle reçoit les influences & efficaces de ses deux soeurs celestes, & les transmet & attache aux choses terretres, qui sont dessoubs son gouvernment." Le Roy then directs his readers to the Myth of Er in Plato's Republic for further illumination: "mais quãt aux particularitez de tout cela, il y a vne autre fable ẽs liures de la republique qui les donne couertmẽt a entendre." *Le Timee de Platon* (Paris, 1582), fol. 48. Giraldus reports that "sunt uero qui Parcas ita interpretenter. per Clothon septem planetas, per Lachesin res subl[un]ares: per Atropon autem Aplanen, id est inerrantem sphaeram." Syntagma VI, in *De Deis Gentium* (Basle, 1548), p. 284. Pico expresses the same view in his Commentary on Benivieni, ed. Garin, II, xxiv, p. 517; and compare Ficino, *Theologica Platonica*, XVII, 3, in *Opera Omnia*, I, 392; and Epitome to *Republic* X, *Opera Omnia*, II, 1454. Ficino offers the slightly different view that Lachesis is the firmament, Clotho the seven planets, and Atropos is Saturn, in Epitome to *Laws*, XII, *Opera Omnia*, II, 1524. This is repeated by Louis Le Roy in *Le Phedon* (Paris, 1581), fol. 120ᵛ; by Blaise de Vigenere, *Les Images*, p. 142, and by Giovanni Pierio Valeriano Bolzani, *Hieroglyphica*, XLVIII (Basle, 1556), pp. 356–357.

36. *Republic*, X, 616C–617D. For the "spindle" (ἄτρακτος) see 616C and 617A; for the "distaff" (ἠλᾱκάτη) see 616C and E. Renaissance translators were uncertain how to reconcile the two terms. Ficino translates both as *fusum* (spindle). *Omni Divini Platonis Opera tra[ns]latione Marsilii Ficini* (Lyon, 1548), p. 455. He is followed by Le Roy, who translates the section of the *Republic* concerning "le fuseau de necessite" in *Le Phedon*, fol. 116. The Italian translation by Pamphilo Fiorimbene, *La Republica di Platone tradotta dalla lingua greca nella thoscana* (Venice, 1544), p. 444, also renders both as *fusaiolo*. On the other hand, the Latin translation by Jean de Serres (Serranus), published in Stephanus' edition of Plato, renders both words as *colus* (distaff). *Platonis Augustiss, Philosophi, Omnium quae Extant Operum Tomus Secundus* (Paris, 1578), p. 616. This edition was dedicated to Queen Elizabeth, and was more popular in England than Ficino's. See Robert Ellrodt, *Neoplatonism in the Poetry of Spenser* (Geneva: Droz, 1960), p. 96, n. 6.

For other Renaissance treatments of Plato's Myth of Er, see Giraldus, Syntagma VI, *De Deis Gentium*, pp. 285–286; and Sabinus' commentary on

Ovid, *Metamorphoses*, II, 654, in *Fabularum Ovidii Interpretatio Tradita in Academia Regiomontana a Georgio Sabino* (Frankfurt, 1589), pp. 73–74. The same commentary is printed among the works of Melancthon, in *Opera*, ed. K. G. Bretschneider and H. E. Bindseil (Brunswick: Schwetschke, 1834–60), XIX, col. 527.

37. *Les Images*, p. 143 ("vne quenouille longue a merueilles, qui semble atteindre de la terre iusqu'au ciel"). *Cf.* Valeriano, *Hieroglyphica*, XLVIII, p. 356 ("colum . . . ingentem admodum").

38. Cartari calls it a "gran fuso di diamante." *Delle Imagini de gli Dei de gli antichi* (Venice, 1647), p. 161. The cut from the French version by Antoine du Verdier (Lyon, 1581) is reproduced in DeWitt T. Starnes and E. W. Talbert, *Classical Myth and Legend in Renaissance Dictionaries* (Chapel Hill: University of North Carolina Press, 1955), p. 370.

39. Bastiano de' Rossi, *Descrizione dell'Apparato e degli Intermedi Fatti per la Commedia rappresentata in Firenze. Nelle nozze de' Serenissimi Don Ferdinando Medici, e Madama Cristina di Loreno Gran Duchi di Toscana* (Florence, 1589), pp. 18–32. In the midst of the Fates was placed "il fuso, il qual parea di Diamante, e sì grande, che con la cocca entrava ne' Cieli, come un fuso ordinario in un fusaiuolo" (p. 25). For discussion of the entire festival, see Aby Warburg, "I costumi teatrali per gli intermezzi del 1559: I disegni di Bernardo Buontalenti e il *Libro di conti* di Emilio de' Cavalieri," in *Gesammelte Schriften*, I (Leipzig: Teubner, 1932); and Roy Strong, *Splendor at Court: Renaissance Spectacle and the Theater of Power* (Boston: Houghton Mifflin, 1973), pp. 180–185.

40. *Arcades*, 65–67. For a full discussion of the "classical" image of the Fates as spinners, along with the Platonic conception and others, see Starnes and Talbert, Appendix I, pp. 340–386. They assume that Spenser's description of the Fates in IV.ii.48 is merely the "common" one found in the Latin tag (quoted in E. K.'s gloss to November, 148 of *The Shepheardes Calendar*): "Clotho colum baiulat, Lachesis trahit, Atropos occat." But it was quite common to conflate the poetic and philosophical images; in the descriptions of the Fates by Valeriano and De Vigenère mentioned above, n. 37, Lachesis spins a multitude of threads while Atropos cuts them with scissors and tosses the partly filled spools to the ground. This tableau is probably the source for Ariosto's treatment of the Fates in *Orlando Furioso*, XXXIV–XXXV.

41. Ficino, *De Amore*, V, xi; *Opera Omnia*, II, 1340. See the Orphic Hymn No. 55, "To Aphrodite," lines 5–7; in *Orphei Hymni*, ed. G. Quandt (Berlin: Weidman, 1962), p. 39. In Ficino's paraphrase, "tribus fatis imperas, & generas omnia, quae in coelo sunt & quae in terra, & quae in mari." The lines were frequently quoted; *cf.* Pico's *Commentary on Benivieni*, ed. Garin, II, xxiv (p. 517); and Mario Equicola, *De la nature d'amour*, fol. 114 (to Venus): "O Celeste Deesse . . . Tu as subiugué le monde, & tu commandes aux trois soeurs fatales;" and fol. 142ᵛ (to Love): "O Amour, tu es la cause & la principe de la vie, la reparation de nature, le soutien de la race humaine, conseruateur d'icelle, & toute puissante liaison de l'vniuers . . . Orphee te prefere à la nécessité, te faisant commander aux trois Parques."

42. See Michael Bayback, Paul Delany and A. Kent Hieatt, "Placement 'In the Middest' in *The Faerie Queene*," *Papers on Language and Literature*, 5 (1969), 227–234; rpt. in *Silent Poetry: Essays in Numerological Analysis*, ed. Alastair Fowler (London: Routledge, 1970), pp. 141–152. For the midpoint in *Colin*

Clout, see David W. Burchmore, "The Image of the Centre in *Colin Clouts Come Home Againe*," *The Review of English Studies*, N.S. 28 (1977), 393–406. A. K. Hieatt, in *Chaucer, Spenser, and Milton: Mythopoeic Continuities and Transformations* (Montreal: McGill-Queen's University Press, 1975), pp. 85–88, suggests that Spenser abandoned his scheme of midpoints in the second edition of *The Faerie Queene*. Professor Hieatt now agrees, however, that Book V contains an equally significant midpoint.

43. "Il y a trois choses en nous, le corps, l'ame & l'intellect, qui ont leurs propres beautez, & Amours separez . . . Or auons nous iusques icy presque tousiours parlé de l'Amour corporel & humain . . . Reste maintenant à parler de la perfaicte beauté, qui est l'intellectuele & de l'Amour diuin." *Le Sympose de Platon, ou de l'Amour et de beauté . . . avec trois liures de Commentaires* (Paris, 1559), fols. 136ᵛ–137. Le Roy quotes extensively from Pico on the "trois mondes" at fol. 164ᵛ. See further Werner L. Gundersheimer, *The Life and Works of Louis Le Roy*, Travaux d'humanisme et de renaissance, No. 82 (Geneva: Droz, 1966), pp. 37–40.

44. "An Encomium on the three Books of Cornelius Agrippa Knight, by Eugenius Philalethes," in *Three Books of Occult Philosophy*, trans. J[ohn] F[rench] (London, 1651), sig. A2. Agrippa's work opens as follows: "Cum triplex sit mundus, elementalis, coelestis & intellectualis . . . Horum omnium ordinem & processum, tribus his libris nūc tradere conabor: quorum primus cōtineat Magiam naturalem, alter coelestem, tertius ceremonialem." *De Occulta Philosophia Libri III* (n.p., 1533), p. I. Rǿstvig suggests that Pico's Commentary on Benivieni is similarly organized, "the overall pattern of the three books being that of the Platonic triad defined in the first sentence." *Hidden Sense*, p. 26.

45. "Donc nostre autheur imitant au plus pres qu'il a peu l'ordre du monde, ancois l'Ouurier & Architect d'iceluy, a premierement diuisé & comparty ceste harmonie du monde en trois Cantiques, chasque Cantique en 8: Tons ou Liures." *L'Harmonie du monde diuisée en trois cantiques. par François Georges . . . plus L'Heptaple de Iean Picus Comte de la Mirande* (Paris, 1579), sig. A iii. See further Rǿstvig, p. 28; and Butler, p. 56. According to the preface by Jacques Davy Du Perron (Bishop of Evreux), Pontus de Tyard sought in *L'Univers* to describe the world "à l'imitation de Platon & de son devancier Timée." Furthermore, although the work is not divided into three books, "pour estre vniuersellement Vniuers, embrasse les trois mondes, Intelligible, Celeste, & Visible, où demeurent les Idees, les raisons, & les formes, en l'entendement, en l'ame, & en la matiere . . . &, cōme le miroir de tout ce qui est, rapporte aux yeux de l'esprit les cognoissances, Metaphysique, Mathematique, & Physique, de ce qui est ou separé de la matiere, ou consideré sans matiere, ou meslé dans la matiere. . . . Ainsi l'Autheur retient les parties du Theologien, Mathemeticien & Physicien, au Timee adioustant le Parmenide, quand il parle de la diuinité sur le milieu du second Curieux, & du Ciel au commencement du premier, & des Elemens sur la seconde partie du mesme." *Deux discours de la nature du Monde et de ces parties* (Paris, 1578), "Avant-Discours." See further Yates, *Giordano Bruno*, p. 174.

46. See Fowler, *Spenser and the Numbers of Time*, Ch. IV, "The Tetrad," pp. 24–33; Nohrnberg, *Analogy*, pp. 621–623; and Hieatt, *Chaucer, Spenser and Milton*, Ch. 6, "Four Groups," pp. 75–94.

R. J. MANNING

Deuicefull Sights: Spenser's Emblematic Practice in *The Faerie Queene,* V. 1–3

T HE LAST line of the third canto of Book Five dispatches the Knight of Justice on "his first aduenture" (V,iii,40,9), and at the outset of the fourth Artegall proposes

> To follow his aduentures first intent,
> Which long agoe he taken had in hond.
>   (V.iv.3.6–7)[1]

This brings into question the whole nature and function of what precedes: if Artegall is only at this point beginning his quest, what relation do the deeds of the first three cantos have to the rest of the book, and how are we to judge them? One response has been to dismiss this section as largely irrelevant to the fable of justice,[2] a "false start" before the real concerns of the book begin at canto four.[3] A more hostile interpretation views Artegall's initial dispensing of Justice as "ironic," "a parody" in comparison to the equity later represented by Britomart. Accordingly the justice of the early cantos is seen as essentially flawed: "simplistic, furious, even vengeful," "perfunctory, robotistic,"[4] an "inhuman principle."[5] The beauty of this "ironic" reading is that it seems to rescue Spenser from the apparently barbarous implications of his fable. The violence of Book Five, which even so perceptive a critic as Lewis condemned as the product of a corrupt imagination,[6] has tended to alienate it from modern affections; the recourse to irony implies that Spenser, too, rejected, at least in part, the more distasteful aspects of sixteenth-century "justice." "Irony," however, comes rather too easily and conveniently to the aid of this argument. Throughout, Artegall's achievements are overtly lauded in honorific terms: in canto one he is "best skild in righteous lore" (4.9), "adore[d]," and highly regarded "for his great iustice"

(30.1–2); in canto two "honorable" and famed for his exceeding "noblesse" (1.1 and 8); in canto three his prowess is adjudged worthy "the honour of the prize" (13.9); the only dissenters from his justice are discredited murderers, extortionists, and cheats.

There is an obvious gap between Spenser's plain, unashamed praise of his virtuous exemplar and modern unease, disapproval, incomprehension, or interpretative slickness which misses the point in spite of its finesse. The problem need not even involve a failure of historical sympathy, simply overcome by recognizing the fact that sixteenth-century notions of justice differ from our own.[7] Although Spenser's habit of building into "the imagery of the *Faerie Queene*, at strategic points, the traditional emblems of the virtue he was writing"[8] has been well established, this basic poetic strategy has been overlooked by interpreters of these cantos. In the first three cantos of Book Five, Spenser inserts numerous traditional emblematic representations of Justice. Strangely, the one book devoted to the iconography of Book Five omits any reference to the emblems discussed in this article,[9] and most have hitherto gone unnoticed. Once the allusions are recognized, it may be seen that these early cantos portray Artegall's judicial virtues. What critics probably respond to when they describe the early cantos as a "false start" is a different narrative mode: one where traditional symbols are close to the surface of the poem. The beginning may be more emblematically schematic, but certainly not false. The narrative materials of these early cantos not only conceal emblematic allusions, but also unfold the significance of the traditional images of the titular virtue. Once this principle is accepted, I hope to demonstrate that the early cantos develop according to a significant moral scheme which establishes the preeminence of the virtue of Justice.

Canto I: The Headless Lady and the Knight with the Broken Sword.

As soon as Artegall embarks on his "new inquest" he encounters three characters: a lamenting "Squire in squallid weed" (13.7), "an headlesse Ladie" (14.3), and a knight bearing as his device "a broken sword within a bloodie field" (19.8). Each is, in fact, a hieroglyph of justice, although it is a tribute to

Spenser's powers of encompassing abstractions that they also function as credible agents in his narrative. It is usual to remark that Artegall resolves his first judicial problem according to the precedent set by Solomon in I Kings 3: Solomon is confronted by two women, each swearing she is the mother of the one child; Artegall is confronted by the knight and the squire who claim to love the same lady. Artegall, like Solomon, threatens to resolve the argument by cutting the disputed property in half, apportioning equal shares to the claimants. The squire, like the true mother, chooses to give up the claim rather than assent to the death of the beloved. Dissent reveals true love, and on that basis the righteous judge confidently awards the whole lady (or, in Solomon's case, child) to the right party. The episode is often seen as a justification of Artegall's legal credentials, placing him within a tradition of legal cunning which extends back to Solomon, the exemplary king and judge of the Old Testament.[10] The parallel is clearly beyond doubt, but little comment has been made on Spenser's changes to the circumstances of the biblical narrative, the substitution of the Knight and the squire for the two harlots, and the headless and living ladies for the child.

The headless lady is an ancient hieroglyph of justice. Diodorus Siculus reports that in Egypt near the Gates of Truth is placed a statue of a headless woman which represents justice (see Plate 16).[11] Gyraldi, Cartari, and Alexander of Naples in their compendia of gods and goddesses note that the Egyptians represented justice without a head, but advance no reason for this.[12] Curio, in his additions to Valeriano's *Hieroglyphica,* follows verbatim Gyraldi's description of headless justice, but adds this explanation: the statue symbolizes the necessary impartiality of justice, for in making his decision, the judge should be influenced by nobody.[13] Curio further explains, "in Athens in the Areopagus, the accused were ordered to give their defence with their heads veiled, lest they should move the emotions of the judges: therefore her [*i.e.* justice's] head is placed among the stars, contemplating God alone, and because of this cannot be seen by us. Furthermore the judge's verdict should be concealed up till the very last moment, according to the maxim, it is hidden, so fraud cannot contaminate it."[14]

Other features of Spenser's story derive from a different emblem in Valeriano's *Hieroglyphica*: justice drags behind her two captive women, one carries a broken sword, the other rests upon a staff. The two women personify extreme attitudes to the legal process which justice must avoid: the one with the broken sword symbolizes excessive rigor or severity, typified by a lack of restraint; the other represents dilatoriness, her conscience unaroused by any crime, however atrocious. Justice must avoid on the one hand over-rigorous severity, on the other indifference and sloth. From these two extremes Justice should construct a virtuous compromise.[15] Spenser identifies his knight with one captive by emblazoning her broken sword on his shield; although the squire does not lean upon a staff, Spenser plainly indicates the diffidence which relates him to the other extreme of dilatory justice. Clothing the squire in "squallid weed" (13.7), Spenser portrays the neglect and sloth which Valeriano signified by the woman's leaning posture: the OED, citing this passage, defines "squalid" as "foul through neglect."[16] As his clothes testify to one kind of neglect, so his subsequent actions show his judicial negligence.

The first emblematic image—that of the headless lady—comments upon the brutal, sinful world in which Artegall must prosecute his quest. The preliminaries of the canto tell how, when wickedness began to abound, Astræa, the teacher of justice,

> Return'd to heauen, whence she deriu'd her race;
> Where she hath now an euerlasting place,
> Mongst those twelue signes, which nightly we doe see
> The heauens bright-shining baudricke to enchace;
> And is the *Virgin*, sixt in her degree.
>
> (11.4–8)

The constelled Virgo-Astræa was depicted as a headless woman (see Plate 16).[17] That Spenser defers the description of the decapitated lady till after Artegall embarks on his quest serves to confirm the brutality of the world Astræa quit; but it also affirms that Justice, even in this benighted world, can be found, if sought. His first case is termed an "inquest" (13.1)—that is, a judicial inquiry designed to find the truth. It is therefore iconographically appropriate that it should concern a headless lady, the ancient hieroglyph that stood by the Gates of Truth. The insertion of this emblem into the narrative poses the problem—"How does one discover truth?"—while the allusion to the second, that of Justice and her two captives, implies the answer—by judicial impartiality coupled with understanding. He must avoid any easy solution based on either over-zealous, hasty vindictiveness, or slothful indifference.

Artegall favors neither the knight nor the squire, but appears to sympathize first with one, then with the other. His response to the sight of the decapitated corpse is similar to the squire's: one "rews" the loss of his lady, the other is "moved at that ruefull sight." But whereas the squire collapses into inaction under the weight of his grief, Artegall acquires an inner "zeal of vengeance." Artegall, like the squire, wishes the cause to be decided painlessly; but, unlike the squire, he is not prepared to accept a false confession of guilt to resolve the case the more easily. The inquiry must not only produce a result, but the result must be just. Artegall's proposal for resolving the dispute bears at first sight an uncanny resemblance to Sir Sanglier's treatment of his lady: the Knight offers at first to exchange ladies with the Squire, as Artegall proposes an exchange, albeit of a more grisly kind, when he suggests the equal division of both dead and living ladies. His initial request refused, Sir Sanglier took the Squire's lady by force and abandoned his own. When his own lady objected, begging the Knight not to abandon but to kill her instead, Sir Sanglier immediately strikes off her head. Artegall suggests a similar act of mutilation upon the surviving lady as a way of resolving the present dispute. It appears that Artegall is prepared to adopt a similarly ruthless distributive "justice," to that practised by Sir Sanglier. This is impartial, or "headless," but it takes no account of the rights of either party, and so fails to give to the deserving what is right, an essential part of distributive justice. [18]

The squire's dissent upsets this plan. In fact, Artegall relies upon the squire's reluctance in order to counter Sir Sanglier's impulsive acceptance of the quick solution. The squire's earlier diffidence proceeded from despair of ever reaching a just decision and from a desire to reach a decision with as little effort as possible; his present confession, while still unjust and quietistic, recognizes degrees of injustice. It is better to keep the lady alive, even in the wrong hands, than to kill her. By paying attention to emotions, to his own love for the lady, the squire alters the basis upon which the judicial decision is reached: he changes the emphasis from legalism to love.

But while we may respect the impulses behind the Squire's

decision, it still leads to injustice. The lady is still in the wrong hands. Artegall endorses the Squire's position but tries to reach a just decision. His distribution of the property is designed to give the deserving what is right:

> thine I deeme
> The liuing Lady, which from thee he reaued:
> For worthy thou of her doest rightly seeme.
> And you, Sir Knight, that loue so light esteeme,
> As that ye would for little leaue the same,
> Take here your owne, that doth you best beseeme,
> And with it beare the burden of defame;
> Your owne dead Ladies head, to tell abrode your shame.
>
> (28.2−9)

Sir Sanglier is assigned the grisly token of the dead lady's head, an explicit condemnation of his crime,[19] while the Squire is assigned the whole lady. Out of the two extremes represented by the squire and the knight, Artegall constructs an equitable decision. The solution is not founded upon callous legalism, but upon love. It was for this reason that Renaissance mythographers related the wings of Nemesis to the wings of Cupid (see Plate 17).[20]

Canto II: The Lady without Hands and the Giant with the Scales.

The three events in Canto Two are related in so far as each deals with financial abuse of Justice. The story of Pollente and the Toll Bridge is an obvious allegory of illegal extortion, but Spenser employs a more elusive iconography when treating the Lady Munera and the Giant.

Munera, as her name suggests, represents Justice corrupted by bribery. She is described in stanza 10 as a beautiful woman with golden hands and silver feet. When Talus, Artegall's page apprehends her, he ruthlessly lops off these limbs:

> But he her suppliant hands, those hands of gold,
> And eke her feete, those feete of siluer trye,
> Which sought vnrighteousnesse, and iustice sold,
> Chopt off, and nayld on high, that all might them behold.
>
> (26.6−9)

These hands of gold, which "iustice sold," and the feet of silver, which "sought vnrighteousnesse," are apt, if original, identifying attributes for a figure meant to represent bribery. Nevertheless, the punishment that Talus inflicts on her appears, and has been condemned as, unnecessarily severe in its ruthlessness.[21] But his action is only repellent if we regard Munera as a real person and forget the emblematic character of the abstraction which she is: as a general rule it is the fate of many, if not most, iconographical personifications to be beaten, bound, or have some other form of violence practiced upon them.

There is, in fact, considerable iconological wit employed in the punishment of Munera, for in cutting off her hands Talus reforms her into a traditional image of Justice. In Alciati's emblem, IN SENATUM BONI PRINCIPIS, the just ministers are all depicted without hands (see Plate 18).[22] Since they have no hands, they are unable to take bribes, and in that way the integrity of justice is preserved: "they neither desire gifts, nor allow themselves to be moved by promises or bribes."[23] The image is an ancient one, deriving from Plutarch's *De Iside et Osiride*,[24] and enjoyed considerable currency:[25] Faxardo, for example, bases his emblem, CUSTODIUNT NON CARPIUNT, on the same idea: "The Thebans represented the Integrity of Ministers, especially those of Justice, by a Statue without hands: if all Ministers were like these Statues, the Exchequer would be more secure, and Nations better governed."[26] Although the judges in Alciati's emblem are not shown without feet, they are depicted sitting down. Minos, in his commentary on Alciati, notes the importance of stability in making decisions, and that this steadiness is indicated by the judges' sitting posture.[27] Spenser's humor here is rather grim: by depriving Munera of feet, Talus may be said to force her to sit down. With neither hands nor feet Munera assumes, albeit unwillingly, the form of the traditional image of Justice.

Behind this episode, then, lies the traditional emblem of handless Justice. Spenser added the golden hands to symbolize Munera's corruption, and to remind us that she departs from the right image of true Justice. The silver feet are added as analogues of the golden hands.[28] When the iron groom, Talus, prunes these excrescences, he restores the traditional image of Justice to its proper state. Later Spenser enunciates the principle, that it is "better to reforme, then to cut off the ill" (V.x.2,9); but in this case "to cut off" is "to reforme."

The allusion to the emblem of handless Justice spells out the common theme of the three events in this canto: the correction of economic abuses of Justice. The episode of the Giant with the scales that concludes the canto represents the distortion of justice by avaricious self-interest. The scales are, of course, a traditional attribute of Justice;[29] Astræa herself trains the infant Artegall in their use (V.i.7). It is, therefore, at first difficult to see why Spenser should assign "an huge great paire of ballance" (30.3) to his arrogant Giant. The relevant allegorical context is Spenser's iconography of Avarice, who, in the pageant of the seven deadly sins, "right and wrong ylike in equall ballaunce waide" (I.iv.27.9). Similarly the Giant attempts to "weigh the wrong or right" (45.3).

Further, the Giant's unequal attempts to balance his scales recall Guillaume de la Perrière's emblem of Roman justice corrupted by financial interest:

> The Proverbe saith a man must never passe
> Nor peize his ballance with unequall weights,
> As once in Rome a happie custome was,
> Where equitie maintained without sleights,
> And Justice was the Monarks looking glasse,
> Till Avarice possessed their conceits:
> Then civill discord set their hearts at warre
> And caused each man his owne good to marre.[30]

The scales, normally an attribute of Justice, become in the Giant's hands the instruments by which he and his followers hope to readjust the social, economic, and cosmic order to their own advantage.[31] The hope of financial gain encourages the giant in his vain ambition to re-order the universe, and tempts the rabble to overthrow civil order. In some ways the mob is more pathetic than Munera and Pollente, as their gain lies only in expectation. Their greedy appetite for riches is satirically portrayed when they congregate around the demagogue, like "flies about an hony crocke" (33.3). Their mercenary motives plainly emerge after the Giant's demise:

> For well they hoped to haue got great good,
> And wondrous riches by his innouation.
>   (51.6–7)

The threat posed by economic abuses increases as the canto progresses: Pollente's local tyranny over his toll-bridge gives way to Munera's large dominion over "all the countrey lying ny" (9.7), and finally erupts into the attempted rebellion of the common people, the followers of the Giant, who pose a threat to the whole God-ordained order. The progression from land-owners' extortion to popular uprising shows that no class, no matter how wretched or hopeless their lot, is immune from this vice.

Canto III: The Sun and the Bridle, Attributes of Nemesis.

Book Five Canto Three concerns the threat posed by emotional excesses to the administration of Justice. The two emotions specifically dealt with are pride and anger. The events of the canto revolve around two attributes of the goddess Nemesis: the sun and the bridle. The power of the Goddess Nemesis was traditionally associated with the Sun. In most Plantin editions of Alciati, the illustration to Emblem 27, NEC VERBO, NEC FACTO QUENQUAM LAEDENDUM (Plate 19), probably executed by Assuerus Van Londerzeel,[32] shows the sun shining over the Goddess's left shoulder. Cartari connects this planetary association with the goddess's opposition to pride: "for the sun has this property, that wherever it appears, it obscures the brilliance of all other lights, and often causes that which appeared dark before to become apparent and to shine."[33] Nemesis oppresses the excessively proud and exalts the humble; she reveals hidden truth, by blotting out the false and distracting splendor of the boastful.[34] In this canto Braggadochio resumes his role as the cowardly, arrogant boaster, and the False Florimell reappears to distract the "vulgar" with her splendid, if fraudulent, beauty.[35] Although both have escaped exposure up till now, it is entirely appropriate that retribution should come at this point in the Legend of Justice, as the faults of both render them prey to the attentions of the goddess Nemesis.

To conceal his identity in the tournament, Artegall borrows Braggadochio's shield; later, by displaying this shield Braggadochio attempts to claim the prize for valour, properly won by Artegall. The trick, it has been noticed, is based on a similar incident in *Orlando Furioso*: Martano steals the armour, in which Grifone fought with distinction at King Noradino's tournament, and tries to pass himself off as the valorous knight.[36] The resemblance is fairly broad: in both incidents a boastful coward tries to claim credit for being a better knight than he is. Ariosto's narrative is rather generalized; Spenser, however, makes the double imposture revolve around a precise and significant image: the identifying attribute on the shield, the device, depicts "the Sunne brode blazed in a golden field" (14.9). As we have seen, the image is associated with Nemesis, and is one of the means by which Spenser converts Ariosto's story into a fable relevant to the Legend of Justice. The other, of course, is that Ariosto lets Martano succeed, and Grifone is imprisoned and beaten; Spenser does not allow Braggadochio to get away with his deception. Artegall's true, brilliant worth reveals Braggadochio for the counterfeit he is. When the just knight's true achievement is put against the false splendor of the boaster, then the fraud is apparent. Braggadochio is undone according to the archetype of Nemesis: truth is revealed, by putting the false against the true; in such a comparison the distracting splendor of the boastful is immediately exposed. Braggadochio can offer only the vain image, whereas Artegall shows the "wounds," the "sword," and the "arme" that won the day (22.1–4). In just such a way, the emblematist Aneau assures us, counterfeit shadows vanish before the noon-day sun of true virtue.[37] The fate of Braggadochio's boastful *impresa* is that it is "blotted out" (37.7).[38]

The disgrace of the False Florimell is accomplished in analogous terms: when the "snowy lady" faces the true Florimell it is as though "two sunnes appeare in the azure skye" (19.1). But, as before, when "the true saint" is set beside "the image," then the imposter is shown for the worthless thing she is: "Th'enchaunted Damzell vanisht into nought" (24.6). Spenser's mythographic allusions in the illustrative epic simile direct us to the meaning of this confrontation:

> As when the daughter of *Thaumantes* faire,
> Hath in a watry cloud displayed wide
> Her goodly bow, which paints the liquid ayre;
> That all men wonder at her colours pride;
> All suddenly, ere one can looke aside,
> The glorious picture vanisheth away.
>
> (25.1–6)

The delusive beauty of the False Florimell is imaged as a rainbow. Spenser's *"Thaumantes"* is almost certainly, though incorrectly, derived from Virgil's "Thaumantias" in *Aeneid*, IX,5. Commentators on this Virgilian passage interpreted Iris, the daughter of Thaumantis, as Eris, the goddess of Discord, sent to provoke disorder and confusion.[39] This the False Florimell certainly does, both here and earlier in Satyrane's tournament, where she is the occasion of "troublous stirre" (IV.v.25). The simile emphasizes her "pride," but her offence against Nemesis is signalled even more allusively: in the *Aeneid* Virgil twice describes the rainbow as producing its effects through its opposition to the sun. So famous was the tag that in the Renaissance the rainbow device was accompanied by the allusive motto, ADVERSO SOLE.[40] The moral implications would not be lost on Spenser, though probably not intended by Virgil.[41] When the false, distracting rival vanishes, Artegall immediately awards the "honor," the "golden belt" of chastity, to Florimell (27–28). Florimell's excellence, which had been called into question by the appearance of the dastardly Braggadochio and his "Franion," is now fully vindicated, and appears even greater through this trial. Artegall, acting as Nemesis, has caused her virtue to shine, when it appeared dark or doubtful before.[42]

Both incidents, then, can be seen to revolve around one attribute of Nemesis, the sun. However, as soon as Florimell is vindicated, Guyon makes his way through the crowd, to lay his hand on the "golden bit" of his horse, stolen by Braggadochio Book II, Canto 3. This dramatically introduces the image of the bridle, which forms the basis of the rest of the canto. Just as the Van Londerzeel illustration balances the sun on the left, against the bridle on the right, so the canto itself is divided between these two attributes. As the Knight of Temperance, Guyon may properly lay claim to the bridle, as it is an attribute of his virtue.[43] However, the bridle in this canto is appropriate to Nemesis. Geffrey Whitney associates her "biting bitte" with her power to restrain the wicked:

> With biting bitte, where with the lewde shee staies:
> And pulles them backe, when harme they doe intende.[44]

Both he and Cartari claim that Nemesis's bridle shows that men ought to restrain their tongues and to do all things with moderation: she checks men,

> when they take in wicked speeche delite,
> And biddes them still beware for to offende,
> And square theire deedes, in all things vnto righte. [45]

Nemesis, then, punishes those who indulge in wicked speech, and encourages moderation and restraint. These are the deeds which in fact characterize the last section of this canto.

His theft proved against him, Braggadochio resorts to verbal abuse: he "reuil'd, and rated, and disdayned" (35.8), to such a point that he incenses Artegall with his "lewd word" (36.1). Artegall's response is obviously extreme, for he considers killing the offender. Guyon counsels restraint, in accordance with the best traditions of Nemesis, who "pulles back" when "harme" is intended. [46] Not that Braggadochio escapes retribution, but his punishment is more in line with the goddess's powers. Just as she is accustomed to "pulle them backe, when harme they do intende," so the iron groom, Talus, "by the backe the boaster hent" and draws him from the hall (37.2–3). The recreant is convicted of "shame," "dishonour," "base villanie," and "defame" (38.6–9). His crime is finally categorized as "lewdnes" (38.9), and as such it comes under the special jurisdiction of Nemesis. He duly receives the goddess's usual punishment:

> But wicked Impes, that lewdlie runne their race,
> Shee hales them backe, at lengthe to their deface. [47]

Braggadochio's lewd race has now been run, and its end is "defame" (38.8).

"This Faire Furrowes End": Justice, Queen of Virtues.

Where normally we would expect the topos of conclusion to come at the end of the poem, or at least at the end of a book, Spenser unexpectedly invokes his at the end of Canto Three:

> And turne we here to this faire furrowes end
> Our wearie yokes, to gather fresher sprights.
> (40.6–7) [48]

He implies two things: from a wider narrative perspective, he has brought the careers of several characters, suspended across many books, to a just conclusion; from a more local perspective, he implies that these first three cantos form a distinct structural unit, a "faire furrow," in the Legend of Justice as a whole.[49]

James E. Phillips, in a stimulating and perceptive article, argues that "Spenser's seemingly miscellaneous narrative materials . . . have been consistently selected and arranged to develop analytically the idea of justice as he and his age understood it."[50] Unfortunately, the analytic scheme he employs, though interesting, is rather too vague to offer any precise analogy to Spenser's narrative. The principle he puts forward is, however, sound, and I hope to show in this section that Spenser's rhetorical disposition of these three early cantos corresponds in detail to two schemes: Cicero's theory of the moral virtues and a Platonic discussion of the soul.

Platonists related each moral virtue to a corresponding part of the soul: Prudence was assigned to the rational faculty, Fortitude to the irascible, and Temperance to the concupiscent. Justice, the fourth virtue, they believed, was shared equally between these three parts, and it was celebrated as the universal virtue ("nunc uniuersae uirtutis nuncupatione conplectitur").[51] Apuleius set forth this principle, and Salmasius could still refer to it some fifty years after *The Faerie Queene* was first published.[52] True to this principle, Spenser associates Justice with each of the moral virtues in turn: with Prudence in Canto One, Fortitude in Two, and Temperance in Three.

The most obvious and overt connection is established in Canto Three, where the Patron of Temperance himself plays an important role. As we have seen, the bridle, that figures prominently in the iconography of the canto, serves as an identifying attribute of both Temperance and Justice, and signals the cooperation of the two virtues. In the *De Inventione*, Cicero defined temperance as the "firm control exercised over lust and other improper impulses" ("Temperantia est . . . in libidinem atque in alios non rectos impetus . . . firma et moderata dominatio") and characterized its parts as "continence, clemency, and modesty" ("Eius partes continentia, clementia, modestia").[53] In Canto Three, Spenser anatomizes Temperance and its parts according to Cicero's scheme: "Firm control . . . over lust" is symbolized by Florimell's "golden belt" (27.1), the cestus, which Spenser allegorizes elsewhere as a sign of the binding of "lasciuious desire," and restraint of "loose affections" (IV.v.4.7–8). In this canto it represents specifically "continence," the first division of Cicero's *Temperantia*:

> Such power it had, that to no womans wast
> By any skill or labour it would sit,
> Vnlesse that she were continent and chast.
>
> (28.6–8)

The other parts of Temperance are to be found elsewhere in the canto: "Clementia," forbearance, is exhibited when Guyon restrains Artegall from venting his wrath on Braggadochio:

> Saying, Sir knight, it would dishonour bee
> To you, that are our iudge of equity,
> To wreake your wrath on such a carle as hee.
>
> (36.6–8)

This exactly fits the Ciceronian definition: "Clemency is a kindly and gentle restraint of spirits that have been provoked to dislike of a person of inferior rank" ("Clementia, per quam animi temere in odium alicuius inferioris concitati comitate retinentur").[54] "Modesty," the third and last part of Temperance, is approved in Florimell's "bashfull shamefastnesse" (23.3). Temperance, then, no less than Justice, characterizes the action of Canto Three.

In Canto Two Artegall "to perils great for iustice sake proceedes" (1.9), and thereby shows his Fortitude, which Cicero defines as "the quality by which one undertakes dangerous tasks" ("Fortitudo est considerata periculorum susceptio").[55] Each event in the canto displays an aspect of *Fortitudo*, and each opponent Artegall defeats represents some defect which the courageous man ought to overcome. Pollente, as his name implies, is "puissant and strong" (7.2),[56] but he uses his might for unjust ends. The moral philosopher was careful to distinguish between mere physical courage and the virtue of Fortitude, which should in all things be consistent with Justice: "even the courage that is prompt to face danger, if it is inspired not by public spirit, but by its own selfish purposes, should have the name of effrontery rather than of courage" ("verum

etiam animus paratus ad periculum, si sua cupiditate, non
utilitate communi impellitur, audaciae potius nomen habeat
quam fortitudinis").[57] In spite of the fact that Pollente is "a man
of great defence" (5.3), "expert in battell" (5.4), "puissant and
strong" (7.2), his strength leads him not to virtue, but to
extortion: he fights for "spoile" (9.1), "sua cupiditate," to fill
the "coffers" of Munera's "wicked threasury" (9.4). He exhibits
the impudent boldness of the wrongdoer, "emboldned" by
Munera's "wicked charmes" (5.5). Pollente, then, represents
mere "effrontery" ("audacia"), Artegall true courage.

The Saracen's might causes "all men for feare" his "passage
for to shonne" (4.9); but when Artegall "thitherward forthright
his ready way did make" (10.9), he displays the first aspect of
Fortitude, which "consisteth in not fearing anything."[58] Although it was admitted that "strength . . . is needfull to
prowesse,"[59] battles that involved brute strength were considered the least worthy manifestation of courage: "to mix rashly
in the fray and to fight hand to hand with the enemy is but a
barbarous and brutish kind of business" ("temere autem in acie
versari et manu cum hoste confligere immane quiddam et
beluarum simile est") only to be resorted to "when the stress of
circumstances demands it" ("cum tempus necessitasque postulat").[60] Artegall's battle with Pollente is a furious affair, and
perhaps exhibits the least admirable aspects of his courage.
Certainly, Spenser's epic simile in stanza fifteen does not minimize the brutishness of the encounter:

> As when a Dolphin and a Sele are met,
> In the wide champian of the Ocean plaine:
> With cruell chaufe their courages they whet,
> The maysterdome of each by force to gaine,
> And dreadfull battaile twixt them do darraine:
> They snuf, they snort, they bounce, they rage, they rore,
> That all the sea disturbed with their traine,
> Doth frie with fome aboue the surges hore.
> Such was betwixt these two the troublesome vprore.

This contest to gain "maysterdome . . . by force" is described in
beastly terms, as befits the kind of Fortitude here displayed:
"beluarum simile est" in Cicero's phrase. But while Dunseath
chooses to emphasize the "degrading effect"[61] of this simile,

there can be no doubt that it does portray "courages" (1.3) and "force" (1.4). Artegall does not shirk the fight, when circumstances demand it ("cum tempus necessitasque postulat"). Ultimately the outcome of the battle approves the knight's "puissance" (17.8), and Pollente becomes a warning to all those who abuse "power" (19.6–9).

In his next encounters, Artegall displays more worthy aspects of Fortitude. When Artegall overcomes the blandishments of the Lady Munera, he displays the second mark of Fortitude: the disdain of temporal goods. "Beware of ambition for wealth," advised Cicero, "for there is nothing so characteristic of narrowness and littleness of soul as the love of riches; and there is nothing more honourable and noble than to be indifferent to money" ("pecuniae fugienda cupiditas; nihil enim est tam angusti animi tamque parvi quam amare divitias, nihil honestius magnificentiusque quam pecuniam contemnere").[62] Finally, Artegall employs the force of argument to defeat the Giant, and this marks a more noble degree of fortitude, than that evidenced in his defeat of Pollente: "cedant arma togae."[63] But to characterize the victory in terms of mere eloquence[64] is to underestimate the meaning and nature of his triumph. Alpers comes closest to the significance of the incident when he sees the purpose of Artegall's argument as directed towards the acceptance of one's lot.[65] Alpers does not develop this line, but to Cicero man's ability to withstand the vicissitudes of life was the supreme test of his fortitude: "That achievement is most glorious in the eyes of the world," Cicero claimed, "which is won with a spirit great, exalted, and superior to the vicissitudes of earthly life" ("splendidissimum videri, quod animo magno elatoque humanasque res despiciente factum sit").[66] In his reply to the Giant, Artegall accepts the "vicissitudes of earthly life":

> They liue, they die, like as he doth ordaine,
>   Ne euer any asketh reason why.
> The hils doe not the lowly dales disdaine;
> The dales doe not the lofty hils enuy.
> He maketh Kings to sit in souerainty;
> He maketh subiects to their powre obay;
> He pulleth downe, he setteth vp on hy;
> He giues to this, from that he takes away.
> For all we haue is his: what he list doe, he may.
>   (ii.41)

This Christian fortitude can look upon even death with calm assurance: "a strong and lofty spirit is entirely free from anxiety and sorrow. It makes light of death, for the dead are only as they were before they were born" ("sic robustus animus et excelsus omni est liber cura et angore, cum et mortem contemnit, qua qui affecti sunt in eadem causa sunt qua antequam nati").[67]

> Likewise the earth is not augmented more,
>   By all that dying into it doe fade.
> For of the earth they formed were of yore,
> How euer gay their blossome or their blade
> Doe flourish now, they into dust shall vade.
> What wrong then is it, if that when they die,
>   They turne to that, whereof they first were made?
> All in the powre of their great Maker lie:
> All creatures must obey the voice of the most hie.
>
>   (ii.40)

The three contests in Canto Two then exhibit Artegall's fortitude.

The iconography of Artegall's first case and its allusion to the Judgment of Solomon establish the presence of the virtue of Prudence in Canto One. *Prudentia*, according to Cicero, consisted in "the search after truth and its discovery" ("indagatio atque inventio veri").[68] As I have argued earlier, Spenser's allusion to the ancient hieroglyph of the headless lady indicates that the case is concerned with the discovery of truth, "inventio veri"; the seeking of truth here relates Justice to the moral preoccupations of Prudence. Artegall's judgment of the knight and the squire firmly establishes his expertise in this virtue, which Cicero elsewhere defines as "rerum bonarum et malarum . . . scientia."[69] Artegall's adherence to Solomon's example shows him proficient not only in "judicial cunning,"[70] but in the virtue of wisdom. His "judgment," the Spenserian pun insists, consists not only in judicial decision-making, but in knowledge of men. Solomon's petition to the Lord was that he should have "wisedom and knowledge" to judge the people.[71] In I Kings 3, immediately before his judgment of the two harlots, Solomon prayed, "Giue therefore vnto thy seruant an vnderstanding heart, to iudge thy people: that I may discerne betweene good and bad."[72] The following narrative shows that he has been

granted that "vnderstanding heart." In analogous fashion Artegall's judgment of the knight and the squire shows that he has
the wisdom of Solomon.

In the first three cantos of Book Five, then, Spenser illustrates
the cooperation of the three other cardinal virtues with Justice,
and that Justice exercises control over the three faculties of the
soul: over Reason in Canto One, the Irascible in Canto Two,
and the Concupiscent in Three. These conclusions are capable
of the following tabular summary:

CANTO 1	PRUDENCE	REASON
CANTO 2	FORTITUDE	ANGER
CANTO 3	TEMPERANCE	CONCUPISCENCE

However, since it was believed that the virtues were interfused
one with another ("haec coniunctio confusioque virtutum")[73]
the scheme is capable of a more complex application: one critic,
for example, has related Munera's punishment to Temperance;[74]
memory and foresight, aspects of *Prudentia*, are to be found in
Canto Two;[75] Artegall exhibits anger in Canto Three.[76] These
complications may be explained in terms of the interdepen-
dence of the virtues, and may be regarded as little more than
finesses on the scheme outlined above. Finally the view that
emerges from these cantos is that Justice is supreme among the
virtues and in some measure includes all the rest.

Indeed, Spenser in these cantos is concerned to show that
without Justice Prudence and Fortitude are no virtues at all.
Artegall's prudential "sleight" by which he discovers truth
(i.24.9), is to be compared with the "sleight" (ii.7.5) by which
Pollente entraps the unwary, and with the trickery ("slight") by
which Braggadochio purloined Guyon's horse (iii.30.9).
"Sleight," then, unless put to the service of Justice, is an aid to
criminal fraud or extortion. I have already examined that mere
bodily strength, in the case of Pollente, is no virtue of itself, and
can be used equally in the cause of right and unrighteousness.
Events in Marinell's tournament also show that strength alone
is no guarantee of the success of the brave. As Spenser laments:

> But what on earth can alwayes happie stand?
> The greater prowesse greater perils find.
>
> (iii.9.1–2)

Justice, the moral philosophers agreed, was the only virtue which was always good, and therefore considered the most perfect and the most important: Justice without Temperance could still be useful (consider, perhaps, Artegall's violent defeat of Pollente); in the absence of Justice Prudence can be turned to criminal cunning; Justice without Fortitude is still Justice, but Fortitude without Justice is not a virtue, but a vice.[77]

The implications for a reading of Spenser are clear: narrative materials unfold and develop consistently and logically in terms of a moral scheme, to which Spenser's iconography is adjusted with tact and relevance. Although the material in these cantos is derived from moral and emblematic commonplaces, there is nothing stale about his treatment of it: he combines these familiar symbols and notions with a range, freshness, and occasional deviousness of invention, which is consistently logical, yet manages always to surprise. Those that invoke "irony" and "parody" simply fail to take Spenser seriously enough, underrating and misunderstanding his "deuicefull art" (x.1.1). But, as Spenser himself laments, "So feeble skill of perfect things the vulgar has" (iii.17.9). And above all else what these critics ignore is that to the moral philosopher justice was perhaps the most perfect of things. As Cicero states

> But in the whole moral sphere of which we are speaking there is nothing more glorious nor of wider range than the solidarity of mankind, that species of alliance and partnership of interests and that actual affection which exists between man and man, which, coming into existence immediately upon our birth, owing to the fact that children are loved by their parents and the family as a whole is bound together by ties of marriage and parenthood, gradually spreads its influence beyond the home, first by blood relationships, then by connections through marriage, later by friendships, afterwards by the bonds of neighbourhood then to fellow-citizens and political allies and friends, and lastly by embracing the whole of the human race. This sentiment, assigning each his own and maintaining with generosity and equity that human solidarity and alliance of which I speak, is termed Justice.[78]

It is with some measure of philosophic exactness that Spenser follows his Legend of Friendship with his Legend of Justice.

Book Four is largely concerned with matters of alliance, with the family, parents and children, the ties of marriage, the connections through marriage, and friendships. Many narrative strands are brought to their conclusion under the eye of the Knight of Justice, who oversees the end of the "fair furrow," just as the moral content of Book Four is completed in these first cantos of Five. But the function of these first cantos is not only to despatch unfinished business. These opening cantos establish the preeminence of Justice.

When Spenser introduces the tournament at the Spousals of Florimell and Marinell, he employs a rhetorical *occupatio*, implying some degree of poetic modesty:

> To tell the glorie of the feast that day,
>   The goodly seruice, the deuicefull sights,
>   The bridegromes state, the brides most rich aray,
>   The pride of Ladies, and the worth of knights,
>   The royall banquets, and the rare delights
>   Were worke fit for an Herauld, not for me:
>   But for so much as to my lot here lights,
>   That with this present treatise doth agree,
> True vertue to aduance, shall here recounted bee.
>
> (V.iii.3)

In addition to telling us what he will not, Spenser also tells us what he does describe. If there are "deuicefull sights" in these cantos, they "agree" with "this present treatise," and their function is "True vertue to aduance." As we have seen, in these first three cantos Spenser is true to his word, for he consistently depends upon "deuices" relevant to his titular virtue. Furthermore, they "agree" with the tenor and tone of the rest of his "treatise": in drawing on predominantly "Egyptian," hieroglyphic material (Diodorus's headless lady in Egypt: the Theban handless judges from Plutarch's *De Iside et Osiride*), he prepares us for the symbolism of his core canto in Isis Church, and for Artegall's identification with Osiris.

The Queen's University of Belfast

Notes

1. *The Works of Edmund Spenser: A Variorum Edition*, vol. v, ed. Edwin Greenlaw, Charles Grosvenor Osgood, Frederick Morgan Padelford, and Ray Heffner (Baltimore: Johns Hopkins University Press, 1936). All quotations are from this edition, hereinafter cited as *Variorum*.
I would like to thank Professor Alastair Fowler, who has discussed the ideas in this chapter with me. I take full responsibility, however, for my conclusions.

2. Judith H. Anderson, " 'Nor Man It Is': The Knight of Justice in Book V of Spenser's *Faerie Queene*," rpt. in *Essential Articles for the Study of Edmund Spenser*, ed. A. C. Hamilton (Hamden, Conn.: Archon Books, 1972), p. 458.

3. T. K. Dunseath, *Spenser's Allegory of Justice in Book Five of "The Faerie Queene"* (Princeton, N.J.: Princeton University Press, 1968), pp. 86ff.

4. Anderson, pp. 447, 452, 453.

5. Anderson, p. 456. Paul J. Alpers characterizes it as "detestable" in *The Poetry of "The Faerie Queene"* (Princeton, N.J.: Princeton University Press, 1967), p. 299; Graham Hough refers to the "brutal and summary methods" of Justice, in *A Preface to "The Faerie Queene"* (London: Gerald Duckworth & Co., 1962), p. 195.

6. C. S. Lewis, *The Allegory of Love, A Study in Medieval Tradition* (Oxford: Clarendon Press, 1936), p. 349.

7. An approach taken most notably by James E. Phillips, "Renaissance Concepts of Justice and the Structure of *The Faerie Queene*, Book V," rpt. Hamilton, pp. 471–487, and by Frank Kermode, "*The Faerie Queene*, I and V," in *Shakespeare, Spenser, Donne* (London: Routledge & Kegan Paul, 1971), 33–59.

8. Alastair Fowler, "Emblems of Temperance in *The Faerie Queene*, II," *Review of English Studies*, n.s. ii (1960), 143.

9. Jane Aptekar, *Icons of Justice: Iconography and Thematic Imagery in Book V of the "Faerie Queene"* (New York: Columbia University Press, 1969).

10. Aptekar, pp. 23 and 122; William Nelson, *The Poetry of Edmund Spenser* (New York: Columbia University Press, 1963), p. 265; and Kathleen Williams, *Spenser's "Faerie Queene": The World of Glass* (London: Routledge & Kegan Paul, 1966), p. 160.

11. Diodorus Siculus, *Bibliotheca Historica*, 1, 96, 9, tr. C. H. Oldfather, Loeb Classical Library, Vol. 1, London and New York: William Heinemann and G. P. Putnam's Sons, 1938.

12. L. G. Gyraldi, *De Deis Gentium* (Lyons, 1565), p. 30; Vincenzo Cartari, *Imagini dei Dei de gli antichi* (Lyons, 1581), p. 391; Alexander ab Alexandro, *Genialium dierum libri sex* (Paris, 1561), p. 213.

13. C. A. Curio's two books of additions to Valeriano first appeared in the Basle 1567 ed. of Valeriano's *Hieroglyphica*: "Caput vero ei non tam ademisse mihi videntur, quam inter sidera occultasse, vt indicarent a iudice neminem videri debere," *Eruditissimi viri hieroglyphicorum commentariorum liber prior*, in Valeriano, *Hieroglyphica* (Lyons, 1602), p. 635.

14. "vnde Athenis in Areopago, rei velato capite caussam dicere iubebantur, ne iudicum affectus mouere possent: condit ergo caput inter sidera, solum

Deum intuens, et ideo a nobis cerni non potest: debet enim iudicis mens ad extremum vsque, donec sententia sit lata, occulta esse, ne qua fraus strui possit," Valeriano, p. 635. In the more modern iconography of Justice, similar ideas are indicated by the blindfolding of Justice. Iaques Hurault, *Politike, Moral and Martial Discourses*, tr. Arthur Golding (London, 1595), p. 193, states: "The Thebans, to show what iustice is, did paint in their courts . . . the images of princes without eyes: to shew that in Iudgment kings ought not to be surprised with any affection."

15. "Sedenim species haec duas secum mulieres captiuas trahit, vnam quae fractum ensem manu praetendit, alteram quae conto innititur, duo ex hoc figmento vitia domita indicantes, vt ex vtriusque medio virtutem ipsam adstruerent, per fractum scilicet ensem seueritatem nimiam retusam cohibitamve intelligentes: per contum, lentitudinem ad ferulam reuocatam, qua iudicia plus aequo producebantur. Inde enim contatio, quae retardationem significat. Lenti vero sunt, qui nullo atroci quantumlibet scelere concitantur, neque publicis neque priuatis iniuriis commouentur." Valeriano, lib. 42, p. 453 (all contractions have been silently expanded).

16. *OED*, *s.v.* "Squalid" 2a.

17. The illustration that accompanies Curio's description of headless justice is titled "Astraea." It shows the astrological sign Virgo, between the Lion and the Scales.

18. "Iustitia est habitus animi communi utilitate conservata suam cuique tribuens dignitatem" (Cicero, *De Inventione*, II, liii, 160, tr. H. M. Hubbell, Loeb Classical Library, London and Cambridge, Mass.: William Heinemann and Harvard University Press, 1949). Distributive justice according to the traditional iconography of the scales of Justice, should not strive for equal treatment of the parties in the case, but should aim to award rewards and punishment according to the deserts of both parties: "Sedenim apud veteres aliter traditum inueni, qui iustitiam cum libratis omnino lancibus in laeua figurabant, sed in dextera . . . fasces cum adalligata securi statuabant, merita aequaque ex huiusmodi hieroglyphico praemia merentibus impendi, atque distribui, hinc scelerum conuictis castigationem impendere significantes" Valeriano, lib. 42, p. 453.

19. Cesare Ripa, *Iconologia* (Rome, 1603), *s.v.* Homicidio, images the murderer as holding "una testa humana tronca dal busto." Ottavo Scarlattini, *L'Huomo e sue Parte* (Bologna, 1684), p. 28, relates the woman's head to an image explicitly designed to terrify those who disregard the law: "*Terrore*: un Capo di Donna così deforme, e sparruto, che lo spavento ad esprimere, e far intendere il suo sembiante non havrebbe potuto scegluere figura più mostruosa di questa. Pausanio Intelligente . . . promulgò una Legge, che dovesse ciò esser insteso questo per la figura, Imagine del Terrore . . . Questo dovrebbero havere avanti a gli occhi quelli, che malamente oprando si gettano dietro alle spalle la divina Giustitia. . . ."

20. Pausanias reports that the people of Smyrna were the first to depict Nemesis with wings to resemble Cupid. See Cartari, p. 390, referring to Pausanias, *Description of Greece* 1. 33. 7, Loeb Classical Library, tr. W. H. S. Jones *et al.*, 5 vols. (London and Cambridge, Mass.: William Heinemann and Harvard University Press, 1918–35). "Neither this nor any other statue of Nemesis has wings, for not even the holiest wooden images of the Smyr-

naeans have them, but later artists, convinced that the goddess manifests herself as a consequence of love, give wings to Nemesis as they do to Love."

21. See, for example, Aptekar, p. 231 n.9.

22. *Emblematum liber*, Augsburg, 1531, sig. D1^v; in eds. after 1574 the standard numbering is Emblem 144.

23. "Cur sine sunt manibus? capiant ne xænia, nec se/Pollicitis flecti muneribusve sinant.

24. *De Iside et Osiride, Moralia*, Vol. v, tr. F. Cole Babbitt (London, 1957), describes the Theban statues of judges without hands, "to indicate that justice is not influenced by gifts or by intercession" (*Moralia*, 355).

25. See also Cartari, *The Fountain of Ancient Fiction* (London, 1599), sigs. k3^v–k4; N. Caussin, *Polyhistor Symbolicus* (Paris, 1618), p. 252; Valeriano, p. 363; Hurault, p. 193.

26. Diego Saavedro Faxardo, *The Royal Politician*, tr. J. Astry (London, 1700), Emblem 53, vol. 2, pp. 18–19.

27. Minos's note in Alciati, *Emblemata* (Lyons, 1614), pp. 515ff.

28. Valeriano, lib. 35, p. 365 mentions feet as a hieroglyph of *VACILLA-TIO*. The "silver feet" may suggest that she wavered according to the silver she was given.

29. See, for example, Tervarent, *s.v. Balance* I. Attribut de la Justice.

30. Guillaume de la Perrière, *The Theater of Fine Devices*, tr. Thomas Combe (London, 1614), sig. B3^r. The same emblem appears in C. Paradin and D. Simeoni, *Symbola Heroica* (Antwerp, 1563), p. 172. The proverb is drawn from Diogenes Laertius, *De clarorum philosophorum vitis*, VIII. 17.

31. The giant's standing "vpon a rocke" (30,1–2) links him with *Fortuna*, who stands on a stone ("Saxoque instare in globoso praedicant volubili," Gyraldi, p. 388); Justice sits ("Staua vna Vergine nuda a sedere sopra vn sasso quadro," Cartari, p. 391).

32. Henry Green, *Andrea Alciati and his Books of Emblems* (London: Trübner & Co., 1872), p. 207 interprets the monogram A thus, although he admits, p. 211, that there have been other contenders. The first ed. to use this cut is Antwerp 1577 and numerous others followed. This plate was known in England, being used for Geoffrey Whitney, *A Choice of Emblemes* (Leyden, 1586), p. 19.

33. Cartari, p. 388: "Percio che'l Sole è di questa natura, che douunque appare, oscura lo splendore di ogni altro lume, a fa spesso apparire, e risplendere quello, che prima staua occulto, e pareua oscuro." The idea derives from Macrobius, *Saturnalia*, 1.22.1. See also Gyraldi, p. 393: "Macrobius vero, Nemesin contra superbiam coli, esseque Solis potestatem arbitratus est. cuius haec natura sit, ut fulgentia obscuret et quae sunt in obscuro illuminet."

34. See Cartari, p. 388: "Nemesi . . . opprime i troppo superbi, e solleua gli humili, e à ben viuere gli aiuta. Et in summa era creduta questa Dea punire tutti quelli, li quali troppo si insuperbiuano del bene, che haueuano." Gyraldi, p. 393 expresses the same idea: "Nemesis, nunc erectas mentium humanarum cervices opprimere, et enervare videtur: nunc bonos ab imo suscitans, ad bene vivendum extollit." Minos in his note on Alciati's Emblem 27 traces the idea back to Seneca, *Hercules Furens*, 384f.: "Dominare tumidus, spirtus altos gere; /Sequitur superbos ultor a tergo Deus" (pp. 129f). For Nemesis's opposition

to pride, see Pausanias, *Description of Greece*, ATTICA, xxxiii. 2–3. Erasmus, *Adagia*, *s.v.* Adrastia, ed. (Geneva, 1606), col. 1855, claims that the ancients regarded Nemesis as the punisher of insolence and arrogance, whose duty was to punish immoderate desires.

35. Braggadochio appears first in II, iii and False Florimell in III, viii.

36. See Alfred B. Gough, ed., *The Faerie Queene, Book V* (Oxford: Clarendon Press, 1918), p. 197.

37. Aneau, *Imagination poétique* (Lyons 1552), p. 54: SOUVERAINE VERTU EFFACE LA FAULSE APPARENCE DE VERTU.

38. Upton first noted the heraldic spoof: see *Variorum*, p. 187.

39. "Iris, quasi *eris* dicta est: nunquam enim ad conciliationem mittitur . . . sed ad disturbationem," *Vergilii Maronis Bucolica, Georgica, et Aeneis, nunc cum veris commentariis Tib. Donati et Servii* (Basle, 1551), Aeneid, 1X, 2n.

40. See Filippo Picinelli, *Mundus symbolicus* (Cologne, 1695), p. 96, referring to Vergil, *Aeneid*, v, 89.

41. Virgil was praised for his scientific accuracy, see *Aeneid*, iv, 701 n. ed. cit.

42. Cartari, p. 388: "fa spesso apparire, e risplendere quello, che prima staua occulto."

43. The bridle as attribute of Temperance, see Crouch's emblem 11, SERVA MODUM, from *Delights for the Ingenious* (London, 1681), p. 42.

44. Whitney, p. 19. See also Alciati, Emblem 27; Tervarent, *s.v.* Mors avec les rênes. II. Attribut de Némésis.

45. According to Cartari, p. 388, Nemesis's bridle shows that men ought to restrict their tongues and do all things in moderation ("debbono gli huomini porre freno alla lingua, e fare tutto con misura").

46. Whitney, p. 19.

47. Whitney, p. 19.

48. Spenser uses this topos at the conclusion of the *Faerie Queene*, 1590 ed. For the topos of conclusion see E. Curtius, *European Literature in the Latin Middle Ages*, tr. Willard R. Trask (Princeton, N.J.: Princeton University Press, 1963), pp. 69–71.

49. Upton interpreted this in the latter sense, *Variorum*, p. 193.

50. Phillips, p. 472.

51. Apuleius, *De Platone et Eius Dogmate*, 228–229, in *Opuscules Philosophiques* (Paris, 1973), pp. 84f. J. Stobaeus, *Pythagoreorum Quorundam Fragmenta Ethica* (Basle, 1582), p. 720, sets out the same scheme.

52. C. Salmasius, *Notae et Animadversiones in Epictetum et Simplicium* (Leyden, 1640), p. 162.

53. II, liv, 164.

54. II, liv, 164.

55. II, liv, 163.

56. Thomas Cooper, *Thesaurus* (London, 1573), *s.v. Pollens*: "he that can doe much and is of great power"; *s.v. Pollentia*; "might, puissance, power." Peter Bayley, *Edmund Spenser: Prince of Poets* (London: Hutchinson, 1971), p. 138, sees Pollente as "ruthless power."

57. Cicero, *De Officiis*, tr. Walter Miller (Loeb Classical Library, London and Cambridge, Mass.: William Heinemann and Harvard University Press, 1975), I, xix, 63.

58. Hurault, p. 276.

59. Hurault, p. 278; "exercendum tamen corpus," Cicero, *De Officiis*, I, xxiii, 79.

60. *De Officiis*, I, xxiii, 81.

61. P. 89.

62. *De Officiis*, I, xx, 68; "*Fortitude* . . . iudgeth honors, riches, and worldlie goods, an vnworthie recompence for his valiant acts" (Pierre de la Primaudaye, *The French Academie*, tr. T. B. [London, 1586], p. 270).

63. *De Officiis*, I, xxii, 77.

64. Aptekar, p. 35, for example.

65. P. 300.

66. *De Officiis*, I, xviii, 61.

67. Cicero, *De Finibus Bonorum et Malorum*, tr. H. Rackham (London and Cambridge, Mass.: William Heinemann and Harvard University Press, 1914; rpt. 1971), I, xv, 49.

68. *De Officiis*, I, v, 15; see also, I, vi, 18.

69. *De Inventione*, II, liii, 160.

70. Aptekar, pp. 122ff; Nelson, p. 265.

71. 1 Kings 3:12 (Geneva version).

72. I Kings 3:9. I. Weemse, *The Portraiture of the Image of God in Man*, third ed. (London, 1636), sig. Aa3, notes that Solomon, of the Old Testament judges, was "most remarkable . . . for his wisedome."

73. *De Finibus*, V, xxiii, 67; "quae quattuor . . . inter se colligata atque implicata sunt," *De Officiis*, I, v, 15.

74. James Nohrnberg, *The Analogy of "The Faerie Queene"* (Princeton, N.J.: Princeton University Press, 1976), pp. 392ff. The allusion to Alciati's Emblem 31, ABSTINENTIA, confirms my earlier iconographic reading. As Aneau notes, the meaning of the emblem is that "Le iuste Iuge ne doibt recevoir dons" (*Emblemes d'Alciat* [Lyons, 1549], p. 54).

75. 2.7; 12.9.

76. 36. 1, 8.

77. "La Giustitia . . . è stata sempre tenuta da sauii per Reina, e signora delle Virtù morali. . . . Tra i Filosofi ancora si tenne, che la Prudenza per se stessa senza la Giustitia nulla rileuasse, ma che per il contrario la Giustitia sia di sua natura utilissima a ciascuno senza la Temperanza, e senza la Prudenza, affermando, che si come la Fortezza senza la Giustitia non solamente non è buona, ma vitio, che per il contrario la Giustitia senza la Fortezza è sempre virtu" (I. Ruscelli, *Le Imprese Illustri* (Venetia, 1583), lib. IV. 4–5).

78. "In omni autem honesto de quo loquimur nihil est tam illustre nec quod latius pateat quam coniunctio inter homines hominum et quasi quaedam societas et communicatio utilitatum et ipsa caritas generis humani, quae nata a primo satu, quod a procreatoribus nati diliguntur et tota domus coniugio et stirpe coniungitur, serpit sensim foras, cognationibus primum, tum affinitatibus, deinde amicitiis, post vicinitatibus, tum civibus et iis qui publice socii atque amici sunt, deinde totius complexu gentis humanae; quae animi affectio suum cuique tribuens atque hanc quam dico societatem coniunctionis humanae munifice et aeque tuens iustitia dicitur," (*De Finibus*, V, xxiii, 65).

SETH WEINER

Minims and Grace Notes: Spenser's Acidalian Vision and Sixteenth-Century Music

OUR UNDERSTANDING of Spenser's Acidalian vision in the sixth book of *The Faerie Queene*, like our understanding of so many set pieces in Medieval and Renaissance literature, reflects the collaboration of the literary critic and the art historian. From a purely literary point of view, Spenser's main event—the dance of the three classical Graces about a nameless country lass—will probably always remain as fundamentally elusive as it originally was to Sir Calidore, whose intrusion, we recall, made it disappear. But thanks to the efforts of distinguished scholars of the sister arts, we can at least say something germane about the iconography of that dance.[1] My purpose in this essay is not to gainsay what these scholars have said, nor even to suggest that some key iconographic detail is wanting in their accounts. Rather, I wish to validate and corroborate what is now commonly accepted about the scene in terms of the other sister art— music—which, I feel, has not received adequate attention.

Music can be a rather slippery term, and I shall consider it in a number of its guises—most obviously, of course, as a common trope for *poetry*; but then, more specifically, as a set of practical rules for performance and composition; and, finally, as a speculative science concerning ideas of cosmic harmony and their reflections in the sublunary world. Spenser compresses all of these senses of *music* into a single witty word when he looks back at the whole Acidalian episode and calls it a *minim* inspired by a mere country girl:

> Sunne of the world, great glory of the sky,
> That all the earth doest lighten with thy rayes,
> Great *Gloriana*, greatest Maiesty,

> Pardon thy shepheard, mongst so many layes,
> As he hath sung of thee in all his dayes,
> To make one minime of thy poore handmayd.
>
> (6.10.28)[2]

In view of the fact that Spenser's *minim* has been so celebrated as an instance of musical wordplay, it is surprising that the word's musical sense remains generally misunderstood by literary scholars. My point of departure, then, will be to provide a full and detailed gloss for this complex word. A proper musical understanding of minims can tell us much about the whole Acidalian episode, especially about certain numerological relationships governing the Graces' dance. These numerological matters, in turn, support and enhance the insights offered by critical analysis as well as by art historical study. In the end, I shall return to the precincts of the art historian in order to reassess the vexed question of how Spenser positioned his three Graces. I shall suggest a new choreography based not only on iconographic, but also on musical, numerological, and literary considerations. My point, in part, is to show that one kind of analysis informs another. Surely such an enterprise lives up to the spirit of Spenser's book of courtesy which, by rights, must concern itself deeply with integrating the civilized arts in terms both of theory and utility.

*   *   *

A *minim* is what we in America call a half-note. In England, the term *minim* is still used. To understand the special importance of minims for Spenser, we must know something about the system used in late sixteenth-century England for measuring musical rhythms. At first glance, measuring rhythms might seem remote from the Graces' dance which, as the art historians have shown, reflects the notion of giving and receiving benefits in a harmonious, disciplined, and well-integrated social order. But the dance moves to the rhythm of Colin Clout's piping, which is also his poem. Put another way, the minim, or little song inspired by a lowly country lass, sets the measure for nothing less than the stately dance of courteous, civilized living.[3] One might point in this connection to St. Augustine's well-known definition of music, in its broadest philosophical sense, as *recte modulandi scientia*—the skill of moving (or measuring) well. Renaissance musicians repeated this formulation often, among them Thomas Morley in his *Plain and Easy Introduction to Practical Music*, which appeared in England in 1597, one year after Spenser's passage.[4]

Moving well—in music as in life—requires an orderly segmenting of time. In Spenser's passage, no one conducts for Colin Clout, so we must assume he has a strong internal sense of his musical beat—what Renaissance musicians would have called the *tactus* or *stroke*. Though the process of beating time in music is common knowledge, rehearsing the basic concepts as expressed by Renaissance practitioners is particularly useful for understanding Spenser's passage. As the names *tactus* and *stroke* imply, the beat was usually thought of in terms of moving the hands, though, as in Colin's case, these motions need not have been literally carried out. Morley's brief description—"a successive motion of the hand directing the quantity of every note and rest in the song with equal measure"—is clear and typical.[5] The important word is *equal*: the *tactus* reduced all motion, no matter how fractured, to equality: all notes and rests had to fit into the equal swaths of time marked out by successive beats. But the *tactus* fulfilled more than the practical function of holding a composition together. It had philosophical implications as well. In his *De Musica* (*ca.* 387), passages of which pervade the musical treatises of the Renaissance, St. Augustine saw the beat (he called it *percussio*) as a principle of unity amidst multeity or, put another way, as a reflection of the eternity and stillness that transcend and contain the flux of time.[6]

The terminology for describing how various musical notes (including the minim) relate to the *tactus* provides further illustration of the odd interfusion of technical details (*practical music*) with abstract ideas (*speculative music*). In modern music, the quarter note (or crotchet) commonly serves as basis for the beat: one crotchet equals one stroke. In Spenser's time, this office was usually performed by the semibreve (our whole note). Modern notation prescribes a fixed proportional relationship between notes: twentieth-century minims, for example, always last half as long as twentieth-century semibreves. During the Renaissance, two proportional relationships were possible: one, like ours, was based on two, the other on three. The first was called *imperfect* and the second, *perfect*. These names suggest something of the kind of quasi-mystical thinking that

originally undergirded the system of mensural notation.[7] By
Spenser's time, the terms were used simply as a matter of
course: we do not find writers like Morley telling us about
fickleness and constancy, or femininity and masculinity, or
Platonic Lamdas and the Trinity, or any other aspects of the
symbolism clustered about the numbers two and three. Yet, in
an age as numerologically aware as the Renaissance, it is hard to
imagine a composer deciding on a suitable rhythm for his
composition without some of this lore wafting through his
mind. In any event, given that the semibreve defined the *tactus*,
the note that had to be fitted to the semibreve—the note, that is,
which determined whether the rhythm would be perfect or
imperfect—was none other than the minim. And, as the musical treatises of the period suggest, the word *minim* itself was
commonly associated with *perfect*, rather than with *imperfect*
time. Thomas Ravenscroft sums up late sixteenth- and early
seventeenth-century usage on this point quite clearly:

> *Tact*, *Touch* or *Time*, is, a certaine *Motion* of the hand
> (whereby the quantity of *Notes* and *Rests* are directed) by an
> equall *Measure* . . . The Auncients [by whom Ravenscroft
> means musicians of the fifteenth century] obserued three
> . . . But these our dayes obserue but two . . .
>   The first is the *Perfect Diuision* of the *Semi-breue* which is
> by 3. the which we call *Minime Time*. . . .
>   The second is the *Imperfect Diuision* of the *Semi-breue*
> which is by 2. the which we terme *the Semi-breue Time*.[8]

Ravenscroft published his treatise in 1614 but lifted this passage
from earlier writers whom he cites in marginal glosses.[9] And in
any event, a use of the term *minim time* just as suggestive for
Spenser's passage as Ravenscroft's appears in a short tract
published about the same time as the second installment of *The
Faerie Queene*: William Bathe's *Briefe Introduction to the Skill of
Song* (*ca.* 1596), issued originally in 1584 as *A Briefe Introduction
to the True Art of Musicke*.[10] It is not a premier musical treatise,
especially in comparison with Morley's impressive work. Bathe
is interesting, though, because his work is likely to reflect the
most common rather than the most learned usage of musical
terms—the usage, that is, which someone like Spenser would
have known. Like most educated men, Spenser was probably

trained as a boy in the rudiments of singing and playing: at least we know that his schoolmaster, Richard Mulcaster, recommended that boys be taught these skills. Bathe, like Mulcaster, was also interested in teaching boys. He felt his book to be quite practical and accessible and even boasts, in the preface, of eight-year-olds who in one month mastered the rigors of sight-singing through the Bathe method.[11]

Bathe's description of *tactus* is much like Ravenscroft's, except that he calls *minim time, three minim time*. To beat three minim time properly, one moves the hand down for the duration of two minims and up for the duration of one. These two partial strokes constitute one full stroke which is equal in time to the semibreve. But in actual practice, Bathe explains, people often beat one full stroke per minim, especially in three minim time, though they may do so in semibreve time as well. Bathe calls this practical beat *minim time*. Here the minim and not the semibreve becomes the basic unit of time that keeps music moving well.[12]

In ordinary performance practice, then, the minim virtually held musical compositions together, while the actual term *minim* was habitually associated with perfect rather than with imperfect time. These are the musical commonplaces that inform Spenser's literary wit in the gallant apology offered to Gloriana at the end of the Acidalian episode. On the one hand, Spenser (as the pastoral poet, Colin Clout) commits a truancy: his duty (as the author of England's official dynastic epic) is to praise Gloriana, not her handmaid. His exaltation of that maid must therefore be seen as minimal—as a mere trifle or a small indulgence easily enough atoned for by a witty disclaimer. But, on the other hand, this trifle happens to contain a vision of ideal social order central to the whole conception of *The Faerie Queene*. And that country maid happens to be Colin Clout's poetic inspiration, without which there would be neither pastoral poem nor epic poem. Here the musical senses of *minim* become important. The lass and the song and dance depending on her constitute the basic *mora* to which the whole poem can be reduced and from which it proceeds. Calling that *mora* a *minim* invites us to compare *The Faerie Queene* to a vast musical composition moving in perfect, or minim, time. So Spenser chose the term deftly, for it strides the blast between all the irreconcilable oppositions that the wit of the Acidalian episode requires us to hold in balance—personal and public, pastoral and epic, trivial and vital, temporal and timeless, concrete and ineffable.[13]

In concentrating so much wit into a single word of a single stanza, Spenser surely intended not only to celebrate what he simultaneously apologizes for, but also to make his courtly readers rethink what comes before the envoy. In this connection, the musical senses of *minim* can be made to apply retrospectively to the dance of the Graces in a number of illuminating ways. If minim time, or three minim time (to use Bathe's term), means the perfect division of the *tactus* by three, the spectacle of the *three* Graces moving well about *one* maiden (as Augustine might have put it) suggests a dance in perfect time. In the musical notation of Spenser's era, the sign denoting minim time was a circle or a semi-circle enclosing a dot: ⊙ or ☉ [14] This looks almost like a diagram of the ring of Graces surrounding Colin Clout's lass. Musical theorists saw the dot as conferring perfection on the semibreve—that is, as insuring that three minims elapsed in the time of one pulse.[15] In a sense, the "iolly Shepheards lasse" functions as such a dot: Colin Clout pipes to her alone, so the perfect music that comprehends his whole vision moves to her measure or, put another way, she confers perfection (in the musical sense) on the poem describing the vision. Appropriately enough (and again recalling the sign of perfection) she is said to grace the entire cosmic dance—the three Graces and the hundred naked maidens encircling them—like a precious gem set in the midst of a ring:

> And in the middest of those same three, was placed
> Another Damzell, as a precious gemme,
> Amidst a ring most richly well enchaced,
> That with her goodly presence all the rest much graced.
>   (6.10.12)[16]

If the dance, seen physically, is almost an emblem for minim time, one should be able to describe its movement and configuration in terms of the number three and the ideas clustered about that number. This involves a decisive move away from musical practice to music considered as a speculative science—a science that rubs shoulders with geometry and arithmetic and with the arcane mysteries of number. The importance of triads in classical and Christian thought need not be labored: an epithet like "perfect" in "perfect time" is almost its own sermon. Trinitarian thinking has a long tradition. When Pico della Mirandola writes that vestiges of the holy Trinity leave their impress on all creation, he not only echoes Ficino, but also St. Augustine, who developed the idea systematically in Books IX–XV of *De Trinitate*. Ficino echoes this same treatise when he writes in *De amore* that

> The Trinity was regarded by the Pythagorean philosophers as the measure of all things; the reason being, I surmise, that God governs things by threes, and that the things themselves also are determined by threes.[17]

The "governing" and "determining" of which Ficino speaks are accomplished by a series of unfoldings: *ones* unfold into *threes* and each three gives rise to successive groups of three. But since Renaissance intellectuals often think backwards from particulars to their source, *infolding* (the opposite of *unfolding*) also becomes important: the triune relationships inhering in any fully developed set of phenomena, that is, always lead the mind back to the unity from which these phenomena originally proceeded.[18] The whole process might be thought of organically in terms of the way a seed unfolds through time into the roots, trunk, branches, and leaves of a tree. Conversely, the tree is inchoate in the seed, which therefore infolds the whole process of growth and change that will show forth in the tree's unfolding.

The movement of Spenser's dance is just such an organic process of unfolding and infolding. These reciprocal motions inhere in the poetry describing the dance, so in a metaphoric sense, at least, they inform Spenser's (or Colin's) music. But this music—or, more properly, the dance that moves to it—can also be described precisely as a dynamic of triadic unfoldings and infoldings. I shall therefore proceed from a literary to a numerological description, the one being nothing more than a mathematical analogue for the other.

To begin with, then, the reciprocity of unfolding and infolding finds nice expression in the shifting conceptions of the dance's central figure. To just the extent that she confers perfection on Colin's song, she is herself perfected by the other dancers. From lowly status, she is "aduaunst to be another Grace" (6.10.16) even though she already surpasses all the Graces in beauty ("But she that in the midst of them did stand, / Seem'd all the rest in beauty to excell" [6.10.14]), and even though she contains within herself all the qualities of the Graces:

> Another Grace she well deserues to be,
> In whom so many Graces gathered are.
>   (6.10.27)

The poet himself realizes that his vision almost fragments her:

> But that fourth Mayd, which there amidst them traced,
> Who can aread, what creature mote she bee,
> Whether a creature, or a goddesse graced
> With heauenly gifts from heuen first enraced?
> But what so sure she was, she worthy was,
> To be the fourth with those three other placed:
> Yet was she certes but a countrey lasse,
> Yet she all other countrey lasses farre did passe.
>   (6.10.25)

Paradoxically, of course, the same vision that fragments the poet's perception of his mistress also makes a harmony of the contrasts. It is a harmony of reciprocity—a circle like the dance itself. The country lass inspires the poet's vision which, incarnated as his poem, returns to grace her. Insofar as the Graces' dance symbolizes the giving and receiving of civilized benefits within an orderly, integrated society, the fact that they grace and are graced by Colin's mistress mirrors perfectly the relationship between the poem (a civilized benefit) and the ultimate source from which it unfolds.

The dancers' actual motion embodies the pressure of this unfolding and its concomitant infolding almost physically:

> All they without [the hundred naked maidens] were
>   raunged in a ring,
> And daunced round; but in the midst of them
> Three other Ladies did both daunce and sing,
> The whilest the rest them round about did hemme,
> And like a girlond did in compasse stemme:

And in the middest of those same three, was placed
Another Damzell, as a precious gemme,
Amidst a ring most richly well enchaced,
That with her goodly presence all the rest much graced.

(6.10.12)

Several commentators[19] have noted the way Spenser moves us inward from the hundred naked maidens through the Graces, and finally to Colin's mistress: the process of infolding seems obvious enough. Unfolding is no less self-evident in the way the country lass graces the dance, which is another way of saying that the whole gracious affair emanates from her. But more impressive and certainly just as noteworthy is the way the verse itself holds the unfolding and the infolding in dynamic tension. The hundred maidens *hemme* the Graces about—which, in one sense, means they are like the border at the outer edge of an elegant garment. But *hemme* also means to confine, to limit and to constrain: the hundred maidens receive their impetus from the Graces but also exert a reciprocal pressure. The word *stemme* has the same force as *hemme*: it means to encircle, but also to stop or to check.

A push and tug—unfolding and infolding leaning against each other—defines the discipline of the dance. But what, specifically and mathematically, is *perfect* about this situation? The answer, obviously, must lie in the numbers—the one hundred maidens and the four figures whom they *hemme* and *stemme*. To understand the way these numbers function, I must invoke the Pythagorean commonplace of creation out of the monad. The monad is the number one, or unity—unlimited and eternal, a number, yet above all number, and the source of all number. In physical terms, the monad is a point, dimensionless and without any perceptible existence, yet defining a fixed and real position: so it is, that reasoning combined with a little leap of faith bridges the infinite gap between the One, immortal and unchanged, and the created universe. *Two* points determine a line, which does have dimension; *three* points define a plane, and *four* a solid. Thus, as S. K. Heninger expresses it,

a time-space continuum springs from the abyss. The number 4, the final possibility of extension in our three-dimensional world, serves as an ideogram for the creation *in toto*.

> The tetrad . . . furnishes an elementary scheme for the
> extended universe, the skeletal diagram for cosmos.[20]

The sum of the first four numerals is ten $(1+2+3+4=10)$, the
decad, representing, in Heninger's phrase (p. 84), "the limit of
the universe," since the tetrad cannot exceed it.

In Spenser's dance, the inner cluster mirrors the concept of
the tetrad closely: the mysterious figure in the center (a sort of
monad) is extended in time and space by the three moving
Graces. The problem seems to come with the one hundred
maidens. One hundred relates proportionally to the decad, but
that is not good enough to warrant a numerological argument.
Yet, on inspection, one hundred poses no problem at all: in fact,
it is a *perfect* unfolding of the tetrad—an unfolding, that is, in
terms of threes, for one hundred is the sum of the *cubes* of the
tetrad:[21]

$$1^3 + 2^3 + 3^3 + 4^3 = 100.$$

The fact that there are one hundred maidens, then, exerts an
infolding force by insuring that the relationship between the
inner and outer figures is perfect. And the inner figures unfold
cubically (that is perfectly) into the outer ring. In a sense, the
perfection of minim time can be said to unfold into a series of
more general triadic relationships that need own no strictly
musical connection but which are all musical in Spenser's
context because they bridle the motion of the Graces' dance,
making that dance conform to St. Augustine's idea of what
music is: the skill of moving well. Furthermore, the triadic
Pythagorean harmony that defines Spenser's dance complements the symbolism usually associated with the Graces and the
maidens—that is, the unfolding of inward courtesy, private and
deep in the soul's inner sanctum, into the civilities and shared
decencies that make society an ongoing concern. Spenser is
telling us that the music of the universe resonates with the
music of civilized institutions.

In the *Solitaire Premier* of Pontus de Tyard, a French poet and
philosopher with whose work the so-called Sidney Circle, and
Spenser among them, may have been familiar, I find another
piece of musical lore centering on the Graces—another triune
unfolding of universal harmony—that complements and ex-

tends what has thus far been pointed out.[22] Pontus recounts a legend of St. Augustine's explaining how the nine muses unfolded from the three Graces.[23] These three originals were, in turn, often associated with three pitches on the ancient Greek scale—the Hypate, or lowest pitch, the Mese, a pitch of middle range, and the Nete, or highest pitch before the octave (the first, fourth, and seventh tones, to be precise). He explains further that the other four tones of the scale (the octave does not count because it merely repeats the first tone) were defined, or named, by their positions in relation to the basic three (e.g., the paranete, or sixth tone, is adjacent to the Nete).[24] In a sense, then, the seven-toned Greek scale, each tone commonly linked with a planet in accounts of celestial harmony,[25] can be seen as an extension of three Grace-notes—not in the modern sense of that term, established in the first part of the seventeenth century, but three quite literal Grace-notes notwithstanding.

In applying what Pontus de Tyard says of Grace-notes to Spenser's Graces, I am no longer dealing with rhythmic motion but with pitch. Technically, therefore, I cannot say the Hypate, Mese, and Nete are an unfolding of minim time. But insofar as they are a triadic shorthand for universal harmony, I consider them quite relevant. Indeed, a glance at the title page (see Plate 20) to Francinus Gafurius's important and influential *Practica Musicae* (1496) shows a nice conflation of rhythm and pitch. The "singing" of the planets is propelled, as it were, by the triadic rhythm of the Graces' dance directed by Apollo and pictured at the top of the page.[26] Besides, both rhythm and pitch are required for music to be anything more than an abstraction, and whether we are thinking in terms of minims or of Greek scales, the Graces (who sing as well as dance in Spenser's account) function centrally as "unfolders:" they symbolize the very process by which the abstract is extended into the concrete.

This last observation leads me to my final remarks, which will take up the positioning of the Graces in Spenser's poem. Their positions, I think, should have something to do with the iconography of unfolding, and I wish to propose that they are arranged in a circle facing outward. But before justifying my surmise, I must say something about the general drift of scholarship on this issue. That there is an issue at all comes from the fact that two classical sources relate the Graces to Spenser's

virtue of courtesy, and each demands a slightly different configuration. The first is Seneca's *De beneficiis*.[27] Seneca pictures the
Graces moving in a circle that symbolizes the cycle of liberality—giving, receiving, and returning benefits. The second explanation comes in Servius' commentary on *The Aeneid* and
implies a choreography somewhat more vague than Seneca's.
For Servius, two Graces continually come towards us and one
always faces away, signifying that we receive two benefits for
every one we bestow. Thematically, the two interpretations are
perfectly compatible. Thus, E. K., following the precedent of
Renaissance dictionaries like Thomas Cooper's *Thesaurus linguae Romanae & Britannicae* (1565) or Charles Stephanus' *Dic-
tionarium Historicum ac Poeticum* (1553), can run them easily
together in his notes to the Graces' dance in *The Shepheardes
Calender*.[28] Physically, though, Servius' dance implies a two-
fold and Seneca's a three-fold motion. Spenser's rather detailed
description in *The Faerie Queene* therefore seems to demand that
we make a choice:

> And eeke them selues so in their daunce they bore,
> That two of them still forward seem'd to bee,
> But one still towards shew'd her selfe afore;
> That good should from vs goe, then come in greater store.
>
> (6.10.24)

On the face of it, this description favors Servius. The last
line, especially, seems to offer a nicely condensed statement of
his view. The problem is that, at first glance, the description
makes little physical sense: all the Graces seem to be facing us
like a line of chorus girls, to borrow a phrase from Humphrey
Tonkin. To obviate this problem, most commentators accept
the editorial emendation of *forward* (the reading in the first two
imprints of 1596 and 1609) to *froward* (the 1611 reading) meaning *fromward*, or *away from us*. The editors find their chief
support in E. K. who uses *fromwarde* in his note on the Graces
cited above. With this change comes physical sense—*two* Graces
facing away from us and *one* coming towards us—but a new
problem: can we find a Renaissance precedent for Spenser's
departure from Servius? The most likely candidate is Pico della
Mirandola in his commentary on Benivieni:[29]

One of the Graces is painted with her face towards us, as coming forward and not returning. The other two, because they belong to the intellect and the will, the operations of which are reflexive, are therefore painted with their faces away from us, as if returning; thus things come to us from the Gods and from us to the Gods they return.

Here, as Tonkin points out (p. 254), "Pico is describing not a Servian exchange of gifts but the operations of Beauty, an altogether less mundane way of reading the Graces." Since Beauty, like Light, is a Divine effluence, Pico's remarks open the way for linking the classical Graces to God's grace. Tonkin (p. 254) cites Alexander Ross's *Mystogogus Poeticus* (1648), which, though rather late, is a summation of traditional lore and identifies the classical Graces with the three theological virtues (the Divine Graces) quite explicitly. The tell-tale puns, so appealing to Renaissance intellectuals, on *grace* and on *charites*, the Greek name for the Graces, are too obvious for comment. And Spenser himself suggests the link structurally in *The Faerie Queene*. As has been many times pointed out, the Acidalian scene in Book VI corresponds closely to the House of Holiness in Book I. Each episode occurs in its book's tenth canto and presents a sort of infolding of the chief virtue. More to our point, each episode centers on three ladies, the Graces in Book VI having their analogue in the figures of Faith, Hope, and Charity (Fidelia, Speranza, and Charissa) in Book I. Faith and Hope are virgins because they look away from the things of this world toward the beatitude of the next. Charity is married and fecund because she manifests the workings of God's love *in* this world.[30] The analogy here to Spenser's modification of Servius is nice: two Graces (like Faith and Hope) face away from us; one (like Charity) comes towards us.

But if these explanations be true, the last line of Spenser's stanza now looks problematic: how can it be a simple statement of Servian lore? As Tonkin is quick to note, it is not. Given the vagaries of sixteenth-century spelling, the word *then* could just as well be *than*, in which case the line would read:

That good should from vs goe, *than* come in greater store.

If both readings (*then* and *than*) are possible and therefore simultaneously valid, the line means that we owe more than we receive *and* that we receive more than we give. Such ambiguity is perfectly consonant with the mystery of Divine grace—or, as Tonkin so eloquently puts it, the ambiguity "precisely exemplifies the mystery of God's relationship to man as Paul expresses it: it is supreme benefit and supreme obligation."[31]

In proposing another formation for the Graces, I do not wish to gainsay any of the scholarship I have just summarized; I wish merely to complement it. I do not, however, think it necessary to accept the reading *froward* in order to make the points that someone like Tonkin, for instance, makes. Thomas P. Roche, who retains the original reading in his edition of *The Faerie Queene*, suggests in his note on the passage that *forward* could mean simply that two Graces are "nearer the viewer without specifying that they are dorsally or frontally displayed" (p. 1228). That way, Spenser's description is sufficiently vague to accommodate all permutations and combinations: it embraces Servius and Seneca as well as St. Paul. But I would find the purposes of inclusiveness and accommodation, as well as mere physical coherency, served better if the Graces were all facing outward. *Forward*, as well as *toward*, could simply mean facing forward—that is *outward*—*without specifying any set relationship to a fixed viewer*. After all, Calidore is no longer *seeing* the dance at this point. It has vanished and Colin Clout is recreating it poetically. But if my suggestion is valid, why is the position of one Grace *contrasted* with that of the other two—

> That two of them still forward seem'd to bee,
> *But* one still towards shew'd her selfe afore?

The answer is that all three are moving in a circle: the contrast insures that we do *not* imagine a chorus line. Sometimes two Graces are facing us, while one is facing away (but she is still facing *toward* some other viewer because she is directed outward). Sometimes one Grace is *toward* us and two are facing away (but still *forward* in relation to someone viewing the circle from another point).

What, then, are the advantages this configuration has for understanding Spenser's passage? For one thing, Seneca is accommodated more neatly to Servius and St. Paul (at least physically) than he is in any other scheme. More importantly, the new choreography points to some interesting artistic analogues that strengthen the case for linking the Graces with the three theological virtues. The most telling is an urn designed to carry the heart of the French King, Henry II.[32] The urn, executed between 1560 and 1563, sits atop a ring of Graces, all three facing outward, carved from a single block of marble by the sculptor Germain Pilon. The sculptor and his mentors were doubtless inspired by the elegant ring of outward-facing Graces supporting an incense burner that Raphael had designed for Henry II's father, Francis I. But they must also have had other models that were not so light and airy. As Victoria Goldberg puts it: "How could the Graces presume to carry one king's heart when they had scarcely finished dispensing his father's perfume?"[33] Her answer hinges on the relation cited above between the Graces and the theological virtues, and she finds admirable examples of Faith, Hope, and Charity portrayed back to back in a ring, much as Pilon depicts the Graces. Nicola Pisano's Holy Water Basin in Pistoia, for example, exhibits the Virtues this way, as does Giovanni Pisano in the group he carved around the column supporting his pulpit in Pisa.[34] Such correspondences between outward-facing Virtues and Graces deepen our understanding of Spenser's linking of his Graces in Book VI with the Virtues in Book I. The relationship, as we can see now, is enforced not only by the structure of the poem, but by the disposition of the Graces as well.[35]

Finally, three outward-facing Graces (with all their classical and Christian associations) provide the best possible emblem for triadic unfolding and infolding. Turning away from the ineffable and looking out on the tangible world of motion and change, they represent, almost diagrammatically, the unfolding of Eternity into time. Eternity is incarnated in minim time — that is, in terms of the number three. The rhythm of time is therefore triadic and sets the pace for the triune harmony of the cosmic scale. Resonating with the rhythm of time and the music of the cosmos is the dance of our life as it unfolds in our civilized institutions. As the Graces circle endlessly about, their perfect (that is, three-fold) music permeates the Senecan cycle of liberality. As they face now towards us, now away from us in different permutations and combinations, we move kaleidoscopically between the Servian exchange of benefits and the spiritual give and take that characterizes the workings of Faith, Hope, and Charity. With this passage from the order of civil life to the order of Grace, the great unfolding of minim time begins to infold and return to the Perfection whence it came. Even as we live the life prescribed by Servius or Seneca, we glimpse the life beyond time when everything—every leaf-fall and the numbering of every hair—is wrapt up suddenly into Eternity and held still.

University of California, Los Angeles

NOTES

1. The Acidalian vision occupies the first twenty-eight stanzas of *FQ*, VI, x. Some of the commentaries to which I refer are: Edgar Wind, *Pagan Mysteries in the Renaissance* (Harmondsworth: Penguin Books, rev. and enlarged, 1967 [1958]), pp. 26–53 and 113–128; E. H. Gombrich, "Botticelli's Mythologies," in *Symbolic Images: Studies in the Art of the Renaissance* (Oxford: Phaidon Press, 1978), pp. 31–82; De Witt T. Starnes and Ernest William Talbert, *Classical Myth and Legend in Renaissance Dictionaries* (Chapel Hill: University of North Carolina Press, 1955), pp. 44–111; Lila Geller, "The Acidalian Vision: Spenser's Graces in Book VI of *The Faerie Queene*," *Review of English Studies*, n.s. 23 (1972), 267–277; Humphrey Tonkin, *Spenser's Courteous Pastoral* (Oxford: Clarendon Press, 1972), pp. 248–264. See also the excellent note in Thomas P. Roche's edition of *The Faerie Queene* (New Haven, Conn.: Yale University Press, 1981 [1978]), pp. 1227–1228.

2. This and all following quotations from *FQ* are from Roche's ed. cited in note 1.

3. The syntax of Colin Clout's apology is, of course, ambiguous, and the *minim* may refer to the "poore handmayd" herself as well as to the whole Acidalian episode. That is, we may read the line as "To make one minime [about] thy poore handmayd" or, alternatively, to make out of "thy poore handmayd" a tiny part ("one minime") of the huge poem that, as a whole, blazons forth your (Gloriana's) praise. Spenser probably intends both senses: the *minim* is at once the song that moves the Graces' dance and also the inspiration that moves the song.

4. Thomas Morley, *A Plain and Easy Introduction to Practical Music*, ed. R. Alec Harman; foreword by Thurston Dart (New York: W. W. Norton, 1973 [1963]). Augustine (*De Musica*) is quoted on p. 101.

5. Morley, ed. Harman, p. 19. Andreas Ornithoparcus, *Musicae activae micrologus libris quator digestus* (Leipzig, 1517) defines *tactus* first generally (without reference to hand motion), and only subsequently in terms of such motion:

Tact is a successiue motion in singing, directing the equalitie of the measure: Or it is a certaine motion, made by the hand, etc. (tr. in 1609 by John Dowland as *Andreas Ornithoparcus his Micrologus, or Introduction Containing the Art of Singing*. Passage on p. 46.)

Ornithoparcus's treatise and Dowland's translation are conveniently available in facsimile as *A Compendium of Musical Practice*, ed. Gustave Reese and Steven Ledbetter (New York: Dover Publications, 1973).

6. A full treatment of the substance of St. Augustine's *De Musica* and its use by Renaissance theorists of music can be found in my "Renaissance Prosodic Thought as a Branch of *Musica Speculativa*" (Ph.D. dissertation, Princeton University, 1981), pp.128–180.

7. Earlier theorists actually made numerological points about perfect time. For examples, see Manfred Bukofzer, "Speculative Thinking in Medieval Music," *Speculum*, 17 (1942), 177–180.

8. Thomas Ravenscroft, *A Briefe Discovrse of the true (but neglected) vse of Charactring the Degrees, by their Perfection, Imperfection, and Diminution in Measurable Musicke*, etc. (London, 1614), pp. 20–21.

9. One is Morley, whose definition of *tactus* the attentive reader will have already recognized. The second is Nicolaus Listenius, whose *Musica* appeared in 1537 and was re-issued eight times between 1541 and 1557. I do not know which edition Ravenscroft saw. I have seen 1548. Ravenscroft refers to cap. 10, Part II, which deals with *tactus* and lists three kinds—major, in which a breve receives a beat; minor, in which the semibreve or two minims receive a beat; and *specialis*, in which a note other than a semibreve and augmented in some way receives the beat (Fol. Fii). The third treatise Ravenscroft lists is Sebald Heyden, *De arte canendi* (1540). Ravenscroft cites Book II, cap. 5 on Proportions. These are discussed in relation to *tactus*. Of interest is the so-called proportion of inequality "when the number of notes and the number of *tactus* differ, as when we sing two, three, four, or more semibreves to one *tactus*, or when we give two, three, four, or more *tactus* to each semibreve" (*De arte canendi*, tr. Clement A. Miller [American Institute of Musicology, 1972], p. 83). Into the last category here, we can easily fit what Ravenscroft calls *minim time*.

Ravenscroft may have cited Heyden incorrectly, however. He may have intended Book I, cap. 5, rather than Book II. Book I, cap. 5 deals with *tactus*, and begins with a passage that sounds just like Morley (with a finger substituted for a hand):

Tactus est digiti motus, aut nutus, ad temporis tractum, in uices aequales diuisum, omnium Notularum, ac Pausarum quantitates coaptans. (p. 40 of 1540 ed.)

10. It is unclear to me whether the 1596 ed. is an overhaul or a mere reprinting of 1584. No copy of 1584 seems to be available for inspection either here or in England. Sir John Hawkins, the eighteenth-century musical historian who rivalled Dr. Burney, claims to have compared both issues (he even quotes the title page of 1584). He says 1596 is an overhaul. But the

following entries in *The Stationers Register* (ed. Arber, III, 71 and 95), suggest a mere reprinting:

> *III, 71*: Thomas Easte/Entred for his Copie under bothe the wardens handes. *A brief introduction to the skill of songe concerning the practice* sett forth by William Bath gent 22 Sept, 1596.
> *III, 95*: Ultimo Octobris, 1597
> Thomas Easte Entred for his copie under th[e] [h]ands of the Wardens, A briefe Introduction to the true arte of musicke, sett forth by William Bathe Student at Oxford. y^t was a former copie printed by Abell Jeffes *anno* 1584 And is by him sett over to master *East* as appeareth by his letter written to the wardens to have it nowe entred for Master Eastes copye.

In any event, if Bathe's exact words as quoted did not precede Spenser's passage, they were at least exactly contemporary with it.

11. Bathe's educational concerns and methods—Ramistic in outlook—are most in evidence in his *Janua Linguarum*, a sort of proto-Berlitz Latin course published in 1611. The book was reissued throughout the seventeenth century and throughout Europe in numerous recensions by many authors. See T. Corcoran, *Studies in the History of Classical Teaching* (London: Longman's, Green and Co., 1911), Part I.

12. Bathe does not actually mention partial and whole strokes, but his passage makes no sense without these concepts. Partial and whole strokes were commonplaces: Ornithoparcus, *e.g.*, distinguishes between "the whole or totall *Tact*" and the "lesser *Tact*" or "Semitact." This last, he says, is "allowed of onely by the vnlearned," an attitude that supports my contention about Bathe's emphasis on common practice rather than learned correctness. (See Dowland's tr. of Ornithoparcus, p. 46).

Following are Bathe's actual words:

> There be 2. kindes of time, Semibreefe time, & three minim time. Semibreefe time is the striking vp & downe of the hand equally in length continuing. Three minim time is the striking downe & then vp of the hand equally in length, making each latter stroke, iust halfe the former. . . .
>
> In tuning Songs of Semibreefe time, you must put of the notes, as much as maketh a minim lēgth to euery mouing of the hand, likewise in the minim time, saue that to euery stroke there goeth but a minim length.
>
> Heere note that these two kindes of time, may by deuided into minim time, by keeping all strokes equall in length, putting a minim length to euery whole stroke. (fol. B1)

*   *   *   *   *

> Some keepe Semibreefe time, as sufficient easie of it selfe, and doe not diuide it into minim time.
>
> Three minim time is more difficult, and therefore some doe diuide it into minim time. (fol. B7)

13. Oppositions—such as that of pastoral to epic or of truancy to the carrying out of duty—have, in some form, determined much of the commentary on the pastoral oasis in Book VI. An early article in this vein is J. C. Maxwell, "The Truancy of Calidore," *ELH*, 19 (1952), 143–149, arguing that Spenser can only fully display courtesy in the "truant" scenes and that this somewhat vitiates his usual allegorical mode based on the quest motif: he never manages a comfortable literary reconciling of truancy and quest. Arnold Williams, *Flower on a Lowly Stalk: The Sixth Book of the Faerie Queene* (East Lansing: Michigan State University Press, 1967), organizes a whole chapter (pp. 75–84) around "Premise and Anti-Premise," attempting to set up a sort of Hegelian thesis/antithesis/synthesis scheme. William V. Nestrick, "The Virtuous and Gentle Discipline of Gentlemen and Poets," *ELH*, 29 (1962), 357–371, organizes his essay around the opposition of freedom to discipline. Harold Toliver, *Pastoral Forms and Attitudes* (Berkeley: University of California Press, 1971), 63–82, especially stresses dereliction of duty in his assessment of pastoral experience. Laurence Lerner, *The Uses of Nostalgia: Studies in Pastoral Poetry* (London: Chatto & Windus, 1972), 151–162, stresses simplicity vs. learning and sophistication. Paradoxically, the Acidalian scene always "takes us further from the court, and less far" (p. 156)—*e.g.*, we move inward from the elegant, courtly 100 maidens to the three Graces with all the learned iconography known only to educated courtiers, to the climax of the whole thing—a simple country lass. This same progression is viewed in a completely different (and I think less deft) way—as Spenser's effacing his ideal vision by having its source turn out to be only a country maid—by A. Leigh De Neef, " 'Who now does follow the foule Blatant Beast': Spenser's Self-Effacing Fictions," *Renaissance Papers* (1978), 11–21. Edward Tayler, *Nature and Art in Renaissance Literature* (New York: Columbia University Press, 1964), 102–121, organizes his discussion, as his title makes clear, around the classic opposition between nature and art.

I find Paul Alpers, *The Poetry of "The Faerie Queene"* (Princeton, N. J.: Princeton University Press, 1967), quite helpful on this whole issue of oppositions. What he says of the stanzas opening Canto X can by easy application be said of the whole Acidalian scene:

> The two points of view [pastoral and courtly] are unequivocally stated, and there is no attempt or desire to qualify one by the other. . . . Spenser is content to treat the elements of a complex moral case as distinct and self-contained moral perspectives, and feels no need to combine them into a single structure of judgment.   (p. 285)

On the related issue of the place of the Acidalian episode in the poem as a whole and what this placement tells us about poets and poetry, see Donald Cheney, *Spenser's Image of Nature: Wild Man and Shepherd in "The Faerie Queene"* (New Haven, Conn.: Yale University Press, 1966), pp. 229–230; the Nestrick article noted above; Richard Mallette, "Poet and Hero in Book VI of 'The Faerie Queene,' " *Modern Language Review*, 72 (1977), 257–267; Susanne Woods, "Closure in *The Faerie Queene*," *Journal of English and Germanic Philology*, 76 (1977), 195–216; and Tonkin, *op.cit.*, p. 138 and p. 304.

14. See Morley, ed. Harman, p. 24; Ornithoparcus, tr. Dowland, p. 43. A circle with a dot in its center is also the planetary sign for the sun, a fact that may make Spenser's conventional address to Gloriana—"Sunne of the world"—more witty on reflection than it is at first glance.

15. Ornithoparcus, p. 43, equates absence of a dot with imperfecting of the time. Morley, pp. 119ff., discusses the function of dots in perfecting time, though he is as concerned with dots placed after notes as with those placed within mensural signs.

16. Of course, the gem set in the midst of a ring is physically ambiguous, as Tonkin points out, p. 139. The lass is in the center of a circle as in the perfect mensural sign, but she is also on the circumference of a circle, as a gem is on the circumference of a ring—perhaps to mirror the fact that she is at once one of the Graces *and* the source of their grace. Geller (p. 269) makes the rather nice point that the image of the gem wafts the notion of art and the arts of civilized living across this natural scene. The dance becomes a perfect balance of art and nature, a mutual disciplining of one by the other. Tayler, pp. 115–118, is also illuminating on this balance of art and nature.

17. See Wind, pp. 41 and 42, from whom I take these passages. Ficino: *Divinam trinitatem in rebus cunctis agnosces.* Pico: *Est trinitatis divinae in creatura multiplex vestigium.* Augustine: *Tria in Charitate, velut vestigium Trinitatis.* The longer passage from Ficino is from his *De amore* and is translated by Wind. Wind writes more of pagan, Augustinian, Medieval, and Renaissance triads on pp. 241–255.

18. I shall make much use of the concepts of unfolding and infolding and am much indebted to two articles by Gerald Snare, who applies these ideas profitably to Spenser's Acidalian vision. See "The Poetics of Vision: Patterns of Grace and Courtesy in *The Faerie Queene*, VI," *Renaissance Papers* (1974), pp. 1–8, and "Spenser's Fourth Grace," *Journal of the Warburg and Courtauld Institutes*, 34 (1971), pp. 350–355. For purposes of illustration, a rather simple example of triadic unfolding and infolding can be found in the work of the French Neoplatonic poet and philosopher Pontus de Tyard, the chief theorist for Baïf's *Academie de Poesie et de Musique* founded at Paris in 1570. For Tyard, knowledge (in its perfect form, eternal and indivisible) unfolds itself in our fallen world according to three basic disciplines—Philosophy, Rhetoric, and Mathematics. Each discipline in turn produces three sub-disciplines. Philosophy gives rise to theology, moral philosophy, and natural philosophy. Rhetoric has three branches: demonstrative, deliberative, and judicial. And Mathematics unfolds as arithmetic, music, and geometry. Of course, one studies these nine subjects in order to return to the perfect, unfallen knowledge from which they flow, so the process of infolding follows that of unfolding. See Pontus de Tyard, *Oeuvres: Le Solitaire Premier* (1552 and subsequent eds.), ed. Silvio F. Baridon (Lille: Librairie Giard; Geneva: Librairie Droz, 1950), pp. 36–38. See also Frances Yates, *The French Academies of the Sixteenth Century* (London: The Warburg Institute, University of London, 1947), p. 83. Pp. 77–94 provide an excellent summary of Tyard's whole philosophical *oeuvre*, with most space devoted to *Le Solitaire Premier*. See also Kathleen M. Hall, *Pontus de Tyard and his Discours Philosophiques* (Oxford: Clarendon Press, 1963). I find Hall's treatment of Tyard's sources particularly useful. I refer to Tyard

advisedly in this note, for I shall advert to him in a subsequent section of my essay.

19. *E.g.*, Tonkin, pp. 136–137; Lerner, cited above in note 13; and Snare, *Renaissance Papers,* (1974), pp. 3–4.

20. S. K. Heninger Jr., *Touches of Sweet Harmony* (San Marino, Calif.: Huntington Library Press, 1974), p. 79.

21. This equation is not infrequently cited in the Renaissance and is a Pythagorean commonplace. See Alastair Fowler, *Spenser and the Numbers of Time* (New York: Barnes & Noble, Inc., 1964), p. 276. Another interesting suggestion on the 100 maidens is given by R. F. Hill, "Colin Clout's Courtesy," *Modern Language Review,* 57 (1962), 492–503. Hill suggests (p. 493) a link with the 100 altars (each with its own maiden) surrounding Venus in the Temple of Venus in *FQ*, IV. Of course, this still leaves the number 100 unexplained.

22. On possible links between Spenser and Pontus de Tyard, see Snare, *Renaissance Papers,* p. 5 n. 3. See also Nan Cooke Carpenter, "Spenser and Timotheus: A Musical Gloss on E. K.'s Gloss," *PMLA,* 71 (1956). Carpenter seems a bit too confident about Spenser's (or at least E. K.'s) having read Pontus in order to learn about the modal affects. On general links between the Leicester, or Sidney, Circle (the so-called Areopagus) and the French academicians see Jan van Dorsten, *Poets, Patrons, and Professors: Sir Philip Sidney, Daniel Rogers and the Leiden Humanists* (Leiden: University Press; London: Oxford University Press, 1962) and *The Radical Arts* (Leiden: University Press; London: Oxford University Press, 1970). See also James E. Phillips, "Daniel Rogers: A Neo-Latin Link Between the Pléiade and Sidney's 'Areopagus,' " in J. E. Phillips and D. C. Allen, *Neo-Latin Poetry in the Sixteenth and Seventeenth Centuries* (Los Angeles: Clark Memorial Library Seminar Papers, 1965).

23. *Solitaire Premier,* ed. Baridon, p. 35. Pontus speaks directly of Muses here, but makes them interchangeable with Graces. On links between the Muses and the Graces in general, see James Nohrnberg, *The Analogy of "The Faerie Queene"* (Princeton, N.J.: Princeton University Press, 1976), p. 674 and p. 679. See also Lila Geller, "The Three Graces in Spenser's *Faerie Queene*: Image and Structure in Books III and VI" (Ph.D. dissertation, University of California, Los Angeles, 1969) for extensive treatment of the linkage.

24. *Solitaire Premier,* pp. 29–30.

25. See, *e.g.*, the figure in the text showing the title page to Francinus Gafurius' *Practica Musicae* (1496). Tyard's seven notes are somewhat unusual: eight is a more common number. Morley (p. 110) reproduces a chart linking eight Muses, eight Greek notes, eight modes, and seven planets plus the fixed stars. His source is a short treatise in a ms. (Lansdown 763; formerly Waltham Holy Cross) owned by Thomas Tallis and presumably passed on to William Byrd, Morley's teacher and Tallis's pupil.

26. The iconography of the serpent in the figure is also intriguing and germane to this essay, since it involves a triadic unfolding. The three heads (one leonine surrounded by two dog-like) link this serpent with Apollo, in whose service such a beast is often found in mythographic treatises. So Apollo, who controls the triadic Graces' dance also controls the serpent whose

three Cerberus-like heads show that the three-fold rhythm of universal time extends right down to the underworld. Further, the looped tail of the serpent is an image of eternity. "Gafurius thus makes it diagrammatically clear [says Wind] that Time issues from Eternity, that the linear progression of the serpent depends on its attachment to the topmost sphere where its tail coils in a circle" (p. 266).

27. For Senecan Graces, see especially Wind, pp. 26–35.

28. Starnes and Talbert, *Classical Myth and Legend*, pp. 50–53.

29. Quoted by Tonkin, p. 254; Geller, p. 273; and Kathleen Williams, *Spenser's Faerie Queene: The World of Glass* (Berkeley and Los Angeles: University of California Press, 1966), p. 213. Williams quotes Thomas Stanley's seventeenth-century translation and recension of Pico, *A Platonick Discourse upon Love* (1651). I have quoted Tonkin's translation.

A quite interesting suggestion on a Renaissance precedent for Spenser's departure from Servius is made by Mason Tung, "Spenser's Graces and Costalius' *Pegma*," *English Miscellany*, 23 (1972), 9–14. Costalius's emblem of the Graces matches Spenser's description—two Graces forward (but recessed) and one toward—and the explanation for the emblem has some suggestive verbal parallels with Spenser's passage. Tung's theory, of course, has the virtue of requiring no textual emendation of *forward* to *froward*.

30. I follow Roche's note here, p. 1228.

31. Tonkin, p. 257.

32. Henry's urn is discussed thoroughly and its iconography traced by Victoria Goldberg, "Graces, Muses, and Arts: The Urns of Henry II and Francis I," *Journal of the Warburg and Courtauld Institutes*, 29 (1966), 206–218.

33. *Ibid.*, p. 206.

34. *Ibid.*, p. 208.

35. There is yet more about Henry's urn that is tantalizing in terms of the men and matter in this essay. The intellectual *milieu* in which Pilon's Graces were conceived and born was that of the *Pléiade*, soon to become the inspiration for Baïf's *Academie de Poesie et de Musique*. Pontus de Tyard, the theorist for these groups, had already written his *Solitaire Premier* in which he discusses the Muses and Graces. It is quite possible, in fact, that he, or perhaps the great Ronsard, mentor of the *Pléiade*, was involved in designing the iconographic programme that Pilon followed. Both Tyard and Ronsard are known to have done such work on other occasions, and Ronsard was to collaborate with Pilon a few years later in designing the entry of Charles IX. Goldberg speculates learnedly on who might have been responsible for Pilon's programme on p. 212.

HAROLD L. WEATHERBY

The Old Theology: Spenser's Dame Nature and the Transfiguration

S PENSER'S MUTABILITIE asks that God, "the highest him," the "Father of Gods and men" (vi, 35), judge her quarrel with Jove. When Nature comes instead, the Titaness, though irascible and sensitive to slights, offers no objection. Her acquiescence suggests that Nature *is* God, and Spenser underscores that suggestion by comparing Nature's radiance with the transfigured Christ's:

> Her garment was so bright and wondrous sheene,
> That my fraile wit cannot deuize to what
> It to compare, nor finde like stuffe to that,
> As those three sacred *Saints*, though else most wise,
> Yet on mount *Thabor* quite their wits forgat,
> When they their glorious Lord in strange disguise
> Transfigur'd sawe; his garments so did daze their eyes.
>
> (vii, 7)

The simile stops short of complete identification, but if Spenser in Dame Nature's presence is like the apostles in Christ's, Nature's Christlikeness seems to follow.

All this is rather stranger than critics have allowed. They have turned (with Spenser's encouragement) to Chaucer and the school of Chartres and (without his encouragement) to Boethius, the Florentine Neo-Platonists, Nicholas of Cusa, and half a dozen others to explain how Nature can double for God.[1] The Transfiguration simile has proven less tractable and has been largely ignored, though Josephine Waters Bennett argued fifty years ago (in an article enshrined in the *Variorum* and still widely cited) for Nature as the *anima mundi* and hence as "another personification of the Logos."[2] Spenserian scholarship seems satisfied with these citations, but they are inadequate in

two ways. First they do not go far enough in respect of
Nature's deification. Alane's and Dan Geffrey's Nature may
legitimately be characterized as God's vicar whereas Spenser's,
in C. S. Lewis's phrase, "is really an image of God himself."[3]
Between vicarious representation and identification there is a
great difference, and Spenser seems to insist on the latter. Lewis
quotes, "For, euen the gods to thee, as men to gods do seeme"
(vii, 15), suggesting that Nature is precisely the "Father of Gods
and men," for whom Mutabilitie has asked. In order to describe
her adequately Spenser requires "fresh sparks of that immortall
fire, / Which learned minds inflameth with desire / Of *heauenly
things*" (vii, 2, italics added). Moreover the events on Arlo, over
which Nature presides, are "things doen in heauen."

The second difficulty with the conventional citations is that
they are insufficiently Christian in tone and emphasis to account
for Spenser's representation. Bernardus's *Noys* and Alane's
Natura are, to be sure, manifestations of the Logos, but the
conception and the language are more nearly philosophical than
theological, Platonist than Christian. Spenser's Dame is much
more homely, less a personification of a concept from the
schools than of Christ from the Bible. Florentine Neo-Platonist
citations present the same difficulty; to say that Nature is
"another personification of the Logos" is to imply that Christ is
also just *another*—an implication at odds with Spenser's language. Rather Christ is the "glorious Lord . . . Transfigur'd,"
beheld in awe by "three sacred *Saints*"; the formulation is
insistently Christian—as much so as Mutabilitie's personal
characterization of God, as Father and as "the highest him."
The god of whom Nature is a vicar and the Logos of whom she
may be another personification are the gods of the philosophers;
the God with whom Spenser identifies Dame Nature seems to
be the God of our fathers, and His Son, the glorified Savior,
Jesus as His disciples beheld Him.

Did Spenser have a precedent for such a conception, or did he
make it up himself? The latter seems unlikely both for theological and literary reasons. The orthodoxy of his day, whether
Protestant or Catholic, would have regarded Nature's deification, much less her Christification, as heretical. Reformers
differed with the Schoolmen as to the degree of damage done to
Nature by the Fall; but as to the fundamental distinction
between Nature and Grace, there was no serious disagreement.[4]

Nature was wholly other than and radically subordinate to
God, and to present her otherwise would have been to identify
oneself with a heresy such as Bruno's pantheism. There is no
evidence from the poem that Spenser intends any such identification; the narrator's tone and posture is consistently orthodox.
Mutabilitie is the heretic; Spenser and the deified Dame Nature
defend the traditional religion.[5] We suspect therefore a Christian
precedent for deification. On the strictly literary side of the
argument, such traditional symbols as Nature and God are not
subject to reconstruction at a poet's whim. As James Hutton
remarks in reference to another Spenserian eccentricity, "traditional *topoi* tend to carry their metaphors with them and to
resist others."[6] Such conservatism militates against originality
and suggests that what appears in any given instance to be the
violation of convention may in fact be an alternative tradition.
Is there any such alternative in this instance? Can we discover a
theology which is at the same time orthodoxly Christian and
yet susceptible to the concept of Nature's deification?

I

We can, but not where we are accustomed to look for
Spenserian sources and analogues. Christian deification comes,
rather, from the East, from the writings of the Greek Church
Fathers—Irenaeus, Athanasius, John Chrysostom, Basil the
Great, Gregory of Nyssa, Maximus the Confessor, and John of
Damascus, to mention only the best known. Had it been
historically possible for those theologians of the first eight
centuries to read the Mutabilitie Cantos, they would not, I
believe, have been startled by Spenser's making Nature God—
the God of the Bible and of the Church. For they all do exactly
that in their discussions of the Incarnation and its effects. This is
the doctrine of *theosis*, which from earliest times has been a
distinguishing characteristic of Greek Christianity: that man
was made God by virtue of God's becoming man and that
through man's body, deified by Christ's body, the rest of the
physical creation participates in the life of the Holy Trinity.[7]
Therefore Nature becomes God in the very way Spenser's
allegory indicates—in Christ.

That is not to say that the Greek Fathers talk a great deal
about Nature as such; they do not. Moreover, I know no

Eastern instance of Nature's allegorical personification, much
less of her being granted the status of a deity in her own right.
All those details of Spenser's representation are characteristically Western and almost certainly derive from the sources
conventionally cited. But if *Physis*, unlike *Natura*, never became
a goddess, she did become divine. Instead of representing
Nature as a make-believe divinity, the Eastern fathers conceive
her—or more precisely what the Western *her* signifies—as a
divinized reality. The West personified Nature and made her a
goddess because it considered the creation a semi-autonomous
order of existence to which Grace was superadded; without
Grace, Nature was still Nature and could be represented as
such. The Eastern Fathers thought of Grace as ontological or
organic; without it—which is to say, without deification—
Nature as an order of being, subject to conception and definition (and thus of personification), does not exist. The West
taught that Adam's sin deprived Nature of the superaddition of
Grace which Christ's sacrifice restored; the East understood
Adam's defacement of the image of God in the creature as
having altogether undone the creature. In a sense there was
nothing left for Christ to restore; redemption, which is theosis,
literally effects a new creation.[8] On that showing Nature can
only be accurately represented as Spenser represents her—as
deified in Christ. Except in His flesh the cosmos is not a cosmos
at all but a chaos. Creation presupposes deification; to be
"natural" is to be divine.

From an Eastern point of view, therefore, the familiar Western personification would have to be assimilated to Christ in
order to achieve metaphysical status. Such, I suggest, is the
point of view which Spenser takes in the Mutabilitie Cantos—
that his intention is to adapt conventional Western allegory to
Eastern theology, retaining the familiar figure of *natura* while
subjecting it to a theological reinterpretation and expansion; to
retain the form but bestow a new and explicitly Christian
meaning upon it. If I am correct, we must read the Cantos on
two levels, taking account of the Western literary conventions
which govern the allegory and at the same time reinterpreting
those conventions in view of a Christian theology of deification.

That such was Spenser's conscious and deliberate intention is
strongly suggested by his reference to the Transfiguration. "The

light on Thabor"—the phrase in Greek Patrology has the character of an epithet—is as much an Eastern signature as theosis itself, and the two are integral to one another (as they are in Spenser's representation). The Eastern Fathers did not conceive Christ's Transfiguration simply as a revelation of His divinity (the almost exclusive Western emphasis) but also as the theosis of His humanity and, through that humanity, of all creatures. Thus the illumination of His face and clothing becomes an epiphany of the illumination of the cosmos, and the transfigured Christ a kind of metonymy (as Spenser's simile suggests) for a deified Nature. This cosmic interpretation of the light on Thabor is so pervasive in Eastern theology as to defy exact documentation. According to Vladimir Lossky it appears for the first time in the writings of St. Irenaeus (d. 202); thereafter it becomes the cornerstone of the doctrine of universal deification, and Spenser could have encountered it almost anywhere in Greek Patristic work.[9]

But could Spenser have read that work? If we are predisposed to think not—to jump to the conclusion that Greek Patrology was wholly remote from Renaissance interests—that is probably because we know less than we should about early Patristic editions.[10] All the Fathers whom I have named and all the classic texts on theosis and the Transfiguration are to be found in sixteenth-century Western European editions, some in the original Greek, some in Latin translation, some in both. Most of these are major scholarly publications from distinguished houses—Froben in Basil, Estienne in Geneva, Chaudiere in Paris, Aldine in Venice.[11] No less a figure than Erasmus was responsible for a number of the Latin translations. Editing and translating the Greek Fathers was a part of the humanist enterprise, and anyone with Spenser's tastes and education is likely to have been aware of it.

Admittedly none of the major Patristic *opera* comes from England, but there is evidence of their English circulation.[12] We know, for instance, that Erasmus's Chrysostom (Froben, 1530) was acquired by the Pembroke library before Spenser matriculated there.[13] Though the absence of ancient accession records makes dating of acquisitions uncertain, we may reasonably suppose that other sixteenth-century Patristic editions now in Cambridge libraries were acquired near the time of their publication (many can be shown to have been there since at least the

seventeenth century). There is also evidence that scholars pur-
chased these books for their private libraries; contemporary
inventories of Cambridge men who died in residence (and not a
few did) reveal numerous Greek Patristic *opera*.[14] In all, seventy-
two scholars owned two hundred fifty-three copies of the ten
principal Greek Fathers. Most of these editions are not identifi-
able, and there is no way to prove that Spenser saw them. Their
very presence however, and in considerable numbers, indicates
that his Cambridge contemporaries were reading Eastern Patrology. (Lancelot Andrewes, one of the best Patristic scholars
of the period, was among those contemporaries, both at Merchant Taylors' and at Pembroke.)

There were religious as well as humanist motives for this
activity. In the ecclesiastical controversy of the day, the Reformers appealed frequently to Byzantine against Latin Christianity. Archbishop Jewel, for instance, quotes from Chrysostom interchangeably with Calvin; and Cranmer, in his preface
to the Great Bible, appeals to the authority of Chrysostom and
Basil.[15] The entire Book of Common Prayer contains only one
ascription of authorship, and that is Eastern—"a prayer of St.
Chrysostom." A little later, Hooker's familiarity with the principal Greek Fathers is manifest in the *Laws of Ecclesiastical Polity*.
Anyone who was as familiar with the Protestant-Catholic
controversy as Book One of *The Faerie Queene* shows Spenser
to have been would almost certainly have been familiar as well
with these Greek Patristic citations, and he makes an allusion to
Greek Christendom in his characterization of Una as daughter
of the Eastern Emperor.[16]

Are deification of Nature and her transfiguration also allusions? Did Spenser expect his readers to recognize, for instance,
the theology of St. Athanasius? In 1556 Froben published Petrus
Nannius's Latin translation of *De Incarnatione*, the work in
which Athanasius presents his fullest discussion of theosis.[17]
There he makes the (to Western ears) remarkable statement that
God "was made man that we might be made gods."[18] In the *we*
Athanasius intends all creation, all that Dame Nature personifies. In the beginning the Father created through the Son. It is
therefore appropriate that the "renewal of nature [has been]
effected by the Word who was its initial author and maker."[19]
The Incarnation is to be understood as reconstituting the cosmos; Christ made a new creation, one which is united directly

to the Creator in a way the old was not. God was "not far from [the world] before [the Incarnation] since nothing in creation is left empty of Him," but now He entered it in a new way.[20] That newness pertains specifically to Christ's victory over death, for it is mortality which radically separated the old creation from God, excluding Nature from participation in the divine life. By triumphing over death in the flesh through His own death and resurrection, Christ, according to Athanasius, "consumed death in men as stubble in fire."[21] Delivered from mortality man becomes a god (for the gods are *athanatoi*); and because the victory over death is in the flesh, all material things partake of deification. The divine energies now, therefore, flood the cosmos; Christ in the most literal, even physical, sense fills all things. He took flesh "that He might work in man and show Himself everywhere, leaving nothing empty and destitute of His divinity and knowledge."[22]

Spenser could also be alluding to St. Irenaeus, whom we have already mentioned as an early exponent of the link between theosis and Transfiguration. Irenaeus develops that motif in considerable detail in the fourth book of his principal treatise, the *Contra haereses*, which was published in twelve Latin editions between 1526 and 1596.[23] (The frequency of publication is surprising to us, who regard him as an obscure early Father; sixteenth-century perceptions were evidently different.) Irenaeus's emphasis is upon the deifying power of the light which shone from Christ on Thabor (we are reminded of Dame Nature's sacred radiance). "The Word was made flesh . . . so that the light of the Father might enter the flesh of the Lord and from His glorious flesh might come to us." The fruit of that encounter is theosis—man's, Nature's, becoming divine: "and thus man might attain to incorruption, being compassed with the light of the Father."[24] Irenaeus repeats the theme, with some variation, half a dozen times in as many paragraphs: "just as those who see the light are within the light and receive its splendor, so those who see God are within God, perceiving His splendor. And the brightness quickens them." God "having been seen gives life to those who see Him. . . . Men therefore will see God [Irenaeus is still referring to the Transfiguration] and live by the vision, made immortal."[25] Dame Nature's brightness also quickens; "having been seen" she "gives life," for when "all creatures" behold her on Arlo, Mutabilitie, the

source of death, is vanquished and creation made immortal—
"none no more change shall see" (vii, 57, 59).

Spenser could also have found deification in the most popular
of the Greek Fathers, St. John Chrysostom, in his homilies on
St. Matthew—ready to hand in the Froben edition at Pembroke.[26] Chrysostom's very first sermon introduces theosis in
reference to the distinction between Law and Grace, Old Testament and New. "In the Old Testament, when Moses had gone
up into the mountain, God came down; in the New, *when our
nature . . . had been raised up into Heaven*, the Holy Spirit came
down from Heaven."[27] "Could anything equal such good tid-
ings as these? God on earth, man in Heaven, all mingled
together—Angels were joining [their] choirs with men, and
men were being added to angelic choirs and to the other
celestial and supernal powers."[28] With probable reference to the
Transfiguration Chrysostom says that "not only in cities and
places of assembly but in the very tops of mountains. . . . there
especially you may see evangelical wisdom flower and choirs of
angels shine forth in a human body and heavenly discourse
shine completely on earth."[29] Chrysostom is even more explicit
in his second homily, with reference to Christ's nativity: "He
deigned to be the son of David, *that He might make you the son of
God.* . . . For it is far more difficult according to human reason
for God to become man than for a man to be deified as the son
of God. When therefore you have heard that the son of God is
the son both of David and of Adam, cease to doubt, since you,
the son of Adam, are the son of God. . . . Thus He was born
after the flesh, that you might be born after the Spirit; He was
born of woman, *that you might cease to be the son of woman.*"[30]
Chrysostom is also explicit about the cosmic dimension of
theosis; in reference to Isaiah's prophecy that "all flesh shall see
the salvation of God," he adds, "But truly all lands and sea, and
the whole race of man."[31]

Eastern liturgy resounds with these same themes, and all the
Byzantine liturgical books were printed several times over in
the sixteenth century.[32] In Christ's Epiphany (the Baptism),
"The creation finds itself set free, / And those in darkness are
now made sons of light." "Let the whole earthly creation clothe
itself in white / For this day it is raised up from its fall from
heaven."[33] In the blessing of water (also at Epiphany) the
Eastern Church sings, "Today the whole creation shines with

light from on high. . . . Today things above keep feast with
things below, and things below commune with things above."[34]
At Christmas, "Heaven and earth are united . . . for Christ is
born. Today has God come upon earth, and man gone up to
heaven."[35] The Transfiguration liturgy, as we should expect, is
particularly rich in such references: the light on Thabor has
"sanctified . . . all the inhabited earth." Christ on the mountain
"made the nature that had grown dark in Adam to shine again
as lightning, transforming it into the glory and splendour of
[His] own divinity."[36]

II

The way Nature had grown dark in Adam, by becoming
mutable, is another theme common to Spenser and the Greek
Fathers: Mutability is the disease which theosis (the Transfiguration) is to cure. Maximus the Confessor offers a precise
formulation of the Eastern doctrine—"The wrong choice made
by Adam brought in passion, corruption, and mortality."[37]
When Adam sinned, he subjected himself to the desires of the
flesh; to live under the power of those desires is to be subject to
change and decay; to change and decay is ultimately to die. The
difference between this doctrine of the Fall and the Western
must be understood in order to see how Eastern Spenser's
allegory is. The Latin Church, at least after Augustine, taught
that Adam's principal legacy is sin; mutability, passion, and
death are sin's consequences. All men inherited Adam's sin and
guilt and are therefore subject to his punishment. The Eastern
doctrine stands that conception on its head—not that in Adam
we all sin but that in Adam we all die. Sin is the consequence
rather than the cause of mutability. Here the divergence between the two Christianities is most radical: the West teaches
that we die because we sin, the East that we sin because we die,
or are going to die.[38] A moribund Nature, subject to passion
and mutability, lacks the strength to resist sin. In that context
we understand the importance of theosis for the Greek Fathers:
because death is the cause of sin, deliverance from sin entails the
conquest of death. Christ could not take away the sins of the
world without making the world immortal, without setting it
free from change. Until the creation is deified, man will continue to change and die and therefore to sin. Whereas the

Western Church baptizes chiefly for the remission of sins, the principal emphasis in Eastern baptismal liturgy is upon union with Christ in his victory over death; without that victory, remission of sins would be to no effect.

Spenser's allegory of the Fall at the beginning of Mutabilitie Six corresponds in most respects with Eastern teaching. Oddly, no critics seem to have noticed how strange it is for a sixteenth-century English Christian to have proceeded as Spenser does in this matter—how unlike, say, Milton's his account of Paradise's loss. Spenser substitutes Mutabilitie for a personification of sin; he does not even use the word *sin*. *Bad* and *wrong* come into the world, but Mutabilitie is blamed for these, not they for her. She, not sin, perverted "all which Nature had establisht first / In good estate, and in meet order ranged" (vi, 5). She, not sin, is responsible for death: she "death for life exchanged foolishlie: / Since which, all liuing wights haue learn'd to die." And she is the source of evil, having broken the laws "of Iustice, and of Policie; / And wrong of right, and bad of good did make" (vi, 6). In other words, sin is the result of change and death rather than their reason, the "pittious worke of MVTABILITIE" rather than the cause of our becoming mutable.[39]

Spenser is also Eastern in making passion the principal agent of change. Mutabilitie's very disposition—her rebelliousness and irascibility—signifies her bondage to the flesh, as do several other facets of her characterization: she is descended from "great *Earth*, great *Chaos* child" (vi, 26); when Spenser says she gathered "spirit of her natures pride" (vi, 26) he hints broadly at sexual impulse; when she beholds Cynthia's palace, she burns with the passion of envy "in her ambitious spright" (vi, 10); and she is sister, we are reminded, to such passionate deities as Hecate and Bellona (vi, 3). Nor is she unique in her slavery to desire: Spenser depicts all changing beings as passionate. Faunus brings the curse of mutability and death upon Ireland by his inordinate sexual desire. When Diana and her maidens clothe him, for punishment, in "Deares skin" (vi, 50), Spenser may be remembering another Patristic commonplace—that the skins in which God clothes Adam and Eve signify the passions to which they had subjected themselves.[40] But Diana, though she punishes Faunus, is not herself exempt from passion, either as huntress or as planetary deity; Cynthia "that neuer still did stand" (vi, 8) repays concupiscence with irascibility (vi, 51).

None of the deities are exempt; all of them, as Mutabilitie rightly claims, are subject to change, and all, even Jove, are subject likewise to passion. He too was once a usurper, and at Mutabilitie's appeal to "the highest him" Jove "wexed wroth" (vi, 35). When Nature says to Mutabilitie, "thy *decay* thou seekst by thy *desire*" (vii, 59, italics added), she articulates the law of change and death in a fallen cosmos: *all* creatures desire, therefore change, decay, and die.

The cosmic extent of change is also a Patristic commonplace. Whereas Western theology and poetry in the Middle Ages conceived of change as sublunary and believed the superlunary heavens, on account of their perfect, circular motion and quint-essential constitution, to be impassible and incorruptible, Greek Christianity for the most part ignored such distinctions. St. Basil in the *Hexaemeron* makes open fun of astrologers, who seek signs in the heavens because they believe the heavens to be stable. Basil flatly denies that; astrology is ridiculous because the heavens are as mutable as the earth. "What could be more ridiculous? The Ram, from which you derive the nativity of man, it is [nothing more than] the twelfth part of the heaven, in which, when the sun enters, it touches upon signs of spring. . . . How then [do you find] there the principal causes which determine the life of men?" Everything changes—the seasons, the days, the planets, and even the "fixed" stars. "I would ask them [the astrologers] if the figures of the stars do not alter (ἀμείβεται) a thousand times a day?" If even those highest stars change, is it not foolish to trust in the stability of any part of the cosmos?[41]

Basil's argument closely resembles Mutabilitie's. Having violated the lunar boundary and proved thereby that change rules everywhere else, she too ascends finally to the *stellatum*: "Onely the starrie skie doth still remaine" (vii, 55). Her argument, of course, is that *still* is how it doth not remain; rather, as Basil says, "the figures of the stars . . . alter a thousand times a day": "the Starres and Signes therein still [always] moue" (vii, 55). Mutabilitie does not, of course, speak for Spenser, but Nature, who does, makes no attempt to refute this part of her adversary's argument. Rather she concedes the point: "all things stedfastnes doe hate" (vii, 58)—an admission which may have been shocking to Spenser's orthodox contemporaries but which is wholly consonant with Eastern Christian theology.

III

Parallels such as these suggest Greek Patristic influence on the Mutabilitie Cantos, but they obviously do not demonstrate Spenser's indebtedness to any particular work or works. Though I have quoted nothing he could not have read in a sixteenth-century edition, my aim has been to illustrate an accessible tradition rather than to prove that he was drawing this or that detail from one Church Father or another. There is, however, one Patristic treatise which resembles the Mutabilitie Cantos in enough detail to suggest that it may, in fact, have been a source.

In 1577 the Parisian, humanist monk Jacobus Billius edited and translated John of Damascus.[42] This is one of the major Renaissance Patristic editions and contains several treatises never before published in the West. Among them is the Damascene's famous homily on the Transfiguration[43]—still regarded as a standard source for the Eastern doctrine of the light on Thabor, primarily because of its comprehensiveness. Coming at the end of the Patristic period, John of Damascus, in all his writings, summarizes and gives precise form to themes developed less systematically by his predecessors. In the case of the Transfiguration (and the related doctrines of theosis and mutability) he offers a compendium of earlier Patristic teaching. What Spenser could have found scattered through the entire corpus of Greek Patrology, he could have found there as in a digest. Furthermore 1577 is exactly the time when we might expect Spenser to have been reading theology and drawing upon it for his future poetry—the year after his graduation from Cambridge, the year before his residence at Rochester, and about three years before he began work on *The Faerie Queene*.

John of Damascus begins his homily by rephrasing Irenaeus's and Athanasius's doctrine of theosis—that God was made man so man might be made God: "The Word was made flesh, and the flesh was made the Word, although neither departed from its own nature." The second clause provides the premise for all that follows: if human flesh has been transmuted into the Word of the Father *without departing from its own nature*, that nature without ceasing to be itself has been deified. Therefore on Thabor the "eyes of men" see "the unseen things, an earthly body shining forth with divine splendor, a mortal body welling forth the glory of the Godhead." The union is not apparent but real: "The glory did not accrue to the body from without but from within, from the [more-than-divine] Godhead of the Word of God united to it hypostatically in an ineffable manner." In what manner? "How can unmixed things be mixed and yet remain distinct? How do things not capable of combination combine into one nor depart from the essential dispositions of their own natures?" The answer lies in the mystery of the Incarnation: "through the infleshing of the immutable Word and through the incomprehensible, immutable theosis of mortal flesh."[44] "The glory of the Godhead becomes also the glory of the body."[45]

Here, as in earlier Patristic treatments of deification, the Incarnation is to be understood not simply in itself but as the principle of creation's theosis. John of Damascus leaves no doubt that when he speaks of "the glory of the body," he intends Christ's body only primarily, not exclusively; not only Christ's humanity but "human things" in general take on divinity—literally, "become of God" (θεοῦ . . . τὰ ἀνθρώπινα γίνεται). Correspondingly divine things become "of man" (ἀνθρώπου . . . τὰ θεῖα). [46] The perfect ἀντίδοσις (communimunicatio idiomatum) in Christ extends its effects to all men: "Man is deified by God's being made man" (θεοῦται . . . ἄνθρωπος ἐν τῷ θεὸν ἀνθρωπίζεσθαι). God "united the archetype [Christ, the Logos] to the image [man, for man was created in that image]," "in Himself making human nature divine" (ἐν ἑαυτῷ θεουργῶν τὸ ἀνθρωπινόν). [47] "Because of this things human mingle everywhere with things divine."[48]

Because of this too Nature other than human nature is deified, for man is a microcosm and what pertains to him pertains by extension to the rest of creation. God "wrought pancosmic salvation (παγκόσμιον σωτηρίαν)"—which is to say, pancosmic deification—"in His only begotten Son," for man, whom the Son became, is inherently or potentially pancosmic, "bearing in himself the knot of all substances both visible and invisible—for man is both these things." "The good will of the Father welded together (συνεκρότησεν) the union (συνάφειαν) of all things in the only-begotten Son," and the Son in turn unites that union to the Father. "Truly the Lord and Creator and Ruler of all things was pleased to become in His only-begotten and consubstantial Son the connection of Godhead and manhood and through this *of all created things*, so that God might be all in all."[49] (John makes the relation between human and cosmic deification even clearer in his homily on the Nativity, also in a two-text version in Billius's edition: "The Creator has transmuted *all nature* into a better state through the mediation of humanity. For if man, who holds a middle place between spirit and matter, is the bond of the whole creation visible and invisible, the creative word of God, by uniting Himself to human nature, *has united Himself thereby to the entire creation* [ἑνωθεὶς ὁ δημιουργὸς Λόγος τοῦ θεοῦ τῇ φύσει τῶν ἀνθρώπων, δι' αὐτῆς ἁπάσῃ τῇ κτίσει ἥνωται].)[50] Here we have a clear theological rationale for presenting *natura* as Spenser does.

The Transfiguration is central to this doctrine of cosmic theosis, for Christ on Thabor did more than merely reveal the ultimate deification of the universe. Rather, as Irenaeus also taught, He effected it. "All things belonging to the one in-fleshed divine Word were in common, both things of the flesh and of the uncircumscribed Godhead"; but the divine glory and the mortal passibility (δόξα and πάθη) have different sources. More therefore than union was required for deification; mortal passibility had to be suffused with divine glory, and that is what the Transfiguration accomplished. When Christ's face "shone as the sun," he imparted his light to the physical creation so that it too might shine: "the divinity conquered and gave its own radiance and glory to the body" and by macrocosmic extension to all bodies.[51] "This is the Light which wins the victory over all of Nature. This is the Life which has conquered the cosmos."[52]

That conquest means, as it does for Spenser, victory over change; John, like his predecessors, regards mutability as the antithesis of transfiguring light. In Christ, "Heaven was established and earth made firm and remains unshaken";[53] the reference is simultaneously to the original creation in its prelapsarian condition and to the result of theosis by which heaven and earth are reconstituted in firmness, free from change and decay. When men ascend Thabor by contemplation and are thereby conformed to Christ's glory, they enter the Kingdom of God and are "freed from the revolution of the external world."[54] *Revolution* translates περιφορᾶς, literally a "bearing round." Estienne's *Thesaurus* (1572) defines it as *circumlatio* and *circumfero—sol ut circumferatur.* John of Damascus's reference is, in effect, to the "ever-whirling wheele / Of *Change*, the which all mortall things doth sway" (vi, 1), which Mutabilitie personifies and over which a deified Nature triumphs.

The way John interprets that triumph is also Spenserian—not simply by abolishing change but by accepting and transcending it. He develops a paradox of mutable immutability (or immutable mutability) which is strikingly similar to Dame Nature's constitution; she is "Still moouing" (a paradox in itself) "yet vnmoued from her sted" (vii, 13). John says much the same of Christ: "The same one, being man, is without beginning in the Godhead and, being God, began in manhood." "O strange exchanges . . . showing man without beginning [which is to say changeless] and Him who is without beginning to take a created beginning [to become changeable] in bodily fashion."[55] God as man becomes mutable; man as God becomes immutable. Christ is at once both because His flesh, though deified, did not depart "from its own nature." Therefore the creation deified in Him also becomes, at once, "Still moouing"; the mutable is made immutable without (impossibly and paradoxically) ceasing to be mutable. In view of Spenser's Transfiguration simile such theology seems a more likely source for Dame Nature than the usual Chartrian and Neo-Platonic glosses. John of Damascus sheds light on another facet of the same paradox—that creatures "by their change their being doe dilate" and "worke their owne perfection so by fate," their fate being, presumably, their changeable condition (vii, 58). Deified flesh does precisely that—not only retains its own nature but "through its own nature" (διὰ τῆς οἰκείας) goes to God. By union with the Logos flesh, even as flesh, has sufficiency of divine power that "*through itself* it might be strengthened and instructed and become habituated to divine things."[56] That is virtually to say that through union with the Godhead in Christ creatures, though still in a creaturely way, effect their own deification—by changing become changeless, "worke their *owne* perfection" (italics added).

Dame Nature promises more, however, than perpetual paradox, and so does John of Damascus. Though Spenser beholds Nature's transfigured glory, he still looks forward to the time she has promised "when no more *Change* shall be" (viii, 2). Similarly the light on Thabor is a harbinger of a greater glory to come.

Eschatology is built into the scriptural accounts of the Transfiguration. In each version (Matthew 17:1–8; Mark 9:2–8; Luke
9:28–36) the ascent of Thabor ensues directly upon Christ's
saying to his disciples, "There be some of them that stand here,
which shall not taste of death, till they have seen the Sonne of
man come in his kingdome" (Matthew 16:28). Those referred
to are evidently Peter, James, and John, and the sight of the Son
coming in glory is clearly *both* the second advent and the
Transfiguration. Certainly that is the way the Greek Fathers
interpret Christ's statement. Chrysostom's commentary is representative of the tradition—when Christ comes again, in His
Kingdom, we shall not only behold Him in "far greater brightness" (than on Thabor), but we shall participate in His glory.
Then "shall the righteous shine forth as the sun, indeed much
more than the sun" just as, in anticipation of the ultimate
epiphany of deification, Christ "did shine as the sunne."[57]
Spenser could have found the same interpretation in Irenaeus—
in the discussion of theosis to which we have already alluded.
When Irenaeus says, "The Word was made flesh" so that "man
might come to incorruption, being compassed with the light of
the Father," his reference is simultaneously to the deification
effected on Thabor and the fruit of that deification—its perfect
fulfillment in the age to come. As Vladimir Loosky interprets
the passage "The prophetic vision [on Thabor] was already a
participation in the final state . . . in the 'Kingdom of God
coming in power.' "[58] Pseudo-Dionysius, whose Western reputation requires no documentation, makes the same connections
between deification, Transfiguration, and the last day, and his
brief exposition became a *locus classicus* in subsequent Patristic
exegesis, including John of Damascus's homily. The Transfiguration both reveals and anticipates the glory to come when we
shall become "incorruptible and immortal and . . . fulfilled with
[Christ's] visible Theophany in holy contemplations, the which
shall shine about us with radiant beams of glory (even as once
of old it shone around the Disciples at the Divine Transfiguration)."[59] That such an interpretation is an established reading in
Patristic exegesis is indicated by St. Basil's allusion in a homily
on the forty-fifth Psalm: "Peter and the Sons of Thunder saw
[Christ's] beauty in the mount, surpassing the sun in His
splendor, and they were deemed worthy to perceive with their
eyes [lit., to receive into their eyes— ὀφθαλμοῖς λαβεῖν] *the
beginning of His coming in glory.*"[60]

John of Damascus, recapitulating and digesting as usual, says
that in this present life our souls are like those of the three
disciples on Thabor (to whom Spenser, we recall, compares
himself), "burdened with this earthly tabernacle of the body";
but at the last day, "when the just shall shine as the sun . . .
being delivered from the necessities of the body, they will be as
the angels, incorruptible, with the Lord, in [His] great and
manifest revelation from heaven."[61] The use of *tabernacle*
(σκηνή) alludes to Peter's misguided desire to stop short of
the final glory by building three tabernacles on Thabor and
remaining there rather than descending the mountain and perse-
vering in the world until the Second Coming—not unlike Red
Crosse's temptation on the Mount of Contemplation. To have
done so would have been to interpret the Transfiguration only
as an epiphany and not also as a prophecy, and John insists on
both. Christ on Thabor manifested what He also predicted and
predicted what He manifested; hence the Transfiguration demands both enjoyment and anticipation, which are precisely
Spenser's responses to Dame Nature's radiance. The cosmos
becomes at the Judgment Day what in Christ it already is and
on Thabor has been shown to be—still another paradox and one
which may explain why Nature is "Vnseene of any, yet of all
beheld" (vii, 13). It could also account for the sudden shift from
the cosmic jubilation of Canto Seven to the discontent and
eschatological aspiration in the two stanzas of Eight. Like Peter
and the Sons of Thunder Spenser must forego a tabernacle on
the mountain of vision and wait in a world where, in spite of
Nature's transfiguration, Mutabilitie "beares the greatest
sway." What some commentators have taken to be a change of
attitude on Spenser's part may be a mystery inherent in the
exegetical tradition.

But patience seems to be rewarded; there are hints of eschatological consummation at the end of Canto Seven where Spenser
presents a version of the Judgment Day—judgment upon,
victory over, change and death. So subtly as almost to disguise
what he is doing, he unveils Nature, suggesting by doing so the
final apocalypse. In the fifth and sixth stanzas we are told "Her
head and face was hid" because it was either too terrible or
(Spenser's opinion) too "beautious" to look upon: the divine
cannot be beheld directly but only "like an image in a glass."
But of course Spenser knew that at the last day we will behold
Him "face to face"—which is precisely how all creatures behold

the hitherto veiled Nature when, the revels being ended, she sits for judgment.

The first hint of her disclosure is that she is staring at the ground. How can we know? We were told she was veiled. Apparently no longer: "all creatures," we learn, are "looking in her face." While we are adjusting ourselves to that discovery, "At length, she looking vp with chearefull view, / The silence brake." The unveiling is inseparable from judgment—"The silence brake, and *gaue her doome* in speeches few" (vii, 57). Spenser's coyness is probably designed to surprise us with what we ought to be expecting—as much as to say, if you had comprehended the allegory and what a deified and transfigured Nature signifies, you would have recognized the implicit eschatology and have anticipated what you are now seeing. I interpret the understated character of Nature's departure to be owing to the same motive: "Then was that whole assembly quite dismist, / And *Natur's* selfe did vanish, whither no man wist" (vii, 59). With an adverse judgment against Mutabilitie, the work of deification is complete; things *have* turned to themselves again and worked their own perfection. Death has been conquered, change overcome by change itself. Nature, therefore, has come to an end, and the life of the age to come is beginning. What was both revealed and prophesied on Thabor (or Arlo) at the beginning of the Canto is brought to fruition at the end. The time *has* come "that all shall changed bee, / And from [hence] forth, none no more change shall see." "This," says John of Damascus (quoting Psalm Seventy-Six), " 'is the change of the right hand [which is Christ] of the most High,' These are the things which the eye has not seen and the ear has not heard" (except the eyes and ears of the select apostles on Thabor and of the Poet on Arlo) but which "all creatures" will see and hear "in the age to come" (and do see and hear at the end of Canto Seven).[62]

Another element in John of Damascus's eschatology may be reflected in Spenser's numbering of the cantos and stanzas. In the hexaemeral tradition six signifies the day or age of this present life, for God made the world in six days; seven is the day of God's rest and creation's completion or fullness—the Sabbath. Eight signifies the day beyond the world and beyond time (or change)—the day of the Resurrection and of the coming of the Kingdom, of the new and deified creation. Saint

Augustine's formulation is representative of this numerology as it develops both among the Greek and Latin Fathers: "After this period God shall rest as on the seventh day, when He shall give us . . . rest in Himself. . . . the Seventh shall be our Sabbath, which shall be brought to a close, not by an evening, but by the Lord's day as an eighth and eternal day . . . prefiguring the eternal repose not only of the spirit, but also of the body."[63] Several critics, most notably Alastair Fowler, have suggested that the Mutabilitie Cantos presuppose this numerology—the seventh containing "the assembly of the orders of creation" and the eighth looking "forward to the last things. . . . that eighth day when the seven-fold cosmos will be made new and eternal."[64] Fowler relies altogether on Western sources—Augustine, Hugh of St. Victor, and Du Bartas—and does not notice (and no one else has noticed) that the Eastern Fathers tie this conception directly to the Transfiguration and the related theme of deification. By placing the Transfiguration simile in the seventh stanza of the seventh canto of the seventh book, Spenser may be alluding to the Patristic doctrine that the theophany on Thabor completes the creation by revealing the glory of the eighth day in the seventh, thereby translating the created into the uncreated, the temporal into the eternal.

The basis for this conception is a discrepancy in the Gospel accounts. Matthew and Mark say the ascent of Thabor occurred six days after the prophecy of the Second Coming while Luke says after "eight dayes." John of Damascus follows Chrysostom and others in taking this discrepancy as occasion for numerological interpretation. Matthew and Mark, says John, speak of six days because in six "God by a word effected the constitution of all visible things"; Luke says eight days because eight "bears the figure of the age to come; for the present life is concluded in seven ages, but in the eighth the life of the age to come is named." Christ on Thabor manifested both the conclusion and the prediction, anticipating the eighth day when "the things of the eighth [are] revealed in perfection." Then Christ "will be seen by His perfect servants" whereas now He is seen by imperfect servants, "by His apostles on Mount Thabor."[65] John does not specify whether the Transfiguration occurs in the sixth or seventh day; indeed the distinction between sixth or seventh tends to blur when either or both is set in contrast to the eighth. (Similarly the Sabbath and the eighth day tend to coalesce in contrast to the sixth, as we see in Augustine's formulation.) If then Spenser intends this numerology, his representation is fully within the boundaries of the exegetical tradition. By comparing himself with Christ's "imperfect servants" on Thabor (and indeed emphasizing his and their imperfection), he identifies himself as one of those who before the eighth day looks forward to the "things of the eighth." In the seventh he beholds a type of the Transfiguration which both reveals and whets his longing for the theosis of creation, the "Sabaoths sight." (If Spenser is indeed conceiving that sight in the context of the Transfiguration and of the eighth day, the 1611 spelling, *Sabaoth*, rather than Upton's *Sabbath*, is almost certainly correct; for the eighth day transcends the Sabbath, and the Son's Second Coming in His Kingdom, which the Transfiguration anticipates, would presuppose the presence of God's hosts.)

Besides these broad theological parallels there are two passages in John of Damascus which read like glosses on Spenserian peculiarities. In introducing the Transfiguration simile Spenser says Dame Nature's face was brighter than the sun—"It the Sunne a thousand times did pass" (vii, 6). In the Gospel accounts of the Transfiguration, however, Christ's face shone only "*as* the sunne." The amplification may be owing to John's discontent with St. Matthew's comparison: "What are you saying, O Evangelist? Why do you compare things essentially incomparable? Why have you placed side by side and put together things which cannot by their nature be put together?" How did the "light unbearable and unapproachable" shine only "as the sun which is beheld by all?" Such rhetoric, by calling attention to the thinness of Matthew's figure, invites such hyperbole as Spenser's magnifying the simile a thousand times. Moreover, Matthew's imagined response to John's challenge suggests a relation to the transfigured Christ similar to that in which Spenser stands to Nature. Spenser cannot behold Nature's face for its brightness, and his wit is too frail to describe the radiance of her clothing; Matthew says he writes for "those bound by the flesh," who cannot endure the intensity of the light on Thabor. For their sakes he takes the sun for his simile, as the "most beautiful and radiant among bodies—not as wholly of the same essence, for it is altogether impossible to represent the uncreated being in the created." Christ's face shone *as* the sun, "not that He was not more brilliant than the sun, but only so much could the beholders see."[66] Because Nature's transfigured face is a thousand times more brilliant than the sun, Spenser the beholder can*not* see.

In the same stanza and context we learn that Nature's face, again because of its brilliance, cannot be seen "but like an image in a glass" (vii, 6); the phrase serves as a bridge into the Transfiguration simile in the succeeding stanza. Spenser's source is the third chapter of Second Corinthians: "But we all beholde as in a mirrour the glory of the Lord with open face" (II Cor. 3:18). The allusion has long been recognized by editors, but none of them has commented on the appropriateness of the Pauline verse to the Transfiguration. Moreover I have found no scriptural glosses, Protestant or Catholic, which make that connection, and Eastern Patristic discussions of the Transfiguration—save one—are silent on the subject. That one is John of Damascus. The motif of the veil is traditional: Christ on Thabor removed the veil which covered Moses's face on Sinai, for on the second mountain grace superseded law. The usual Patristic citation is the tenth and eleventh chapters of Hebrews which develop the veil symbolism (though without reference to Thabor). John follows that tradition and quotes from Hebrews, but he also introduces the simile from Second Corinthians, implying that Paul is himself referring to Thabor (as well he may have been). John in any event takes the reference for granted, fitting the Pauline phrase so seamlessly into his own syntax that a reader unfamiliar with Scripture would not recognize a quotation: "The law had a shadow of things to come, not the truth itself, as one may hear from the writer Paul. And at that time Israel was not able to look intently at the glory of Moses's face, a glory which was being abolished; *but we with face unveiled behold as in a mirror the glory of the Lord*, being *transfigured* from glory into greater glory, as by the Spirit of the Lord."[67] *Transfigured* in this context is arresting: it translates (μεταμορφούμενοι) which is the same Greek verb used to describe the illumination of Christ's face on the mountain—"He was transfigured (μετεμορφώθη) before them" (Matthew 17:2). (In Greek theology and liturgy the *Transfiguration* is the *Metamorphosis*.) None of the English Bibles translates Paul's verb as *transfigured*, and thus all obscure the probable allusion to Thabor which John of Damascus discerns.[68] Spenser is much more likely therefore to have caught the reference by reading John's homily than by reading the Bible, and since John's use of Second Corinthians is untraditional, his homily seems a particularly likely source. Nor, reading Billius's edition, could Spenser have been in doubt about the quotation: "2. Cor. 3" appears in the margin.

IV

Common then to Spenser and John of Damascus is a Nature deified—quite literally made God—in Christ, an epiphany of that deification in the Transfiguration, an anticipation (also in the Transfiguration) of the age to come when the epiphany on Thabor (or Arlo) will be fulfilled, a heavy emphasis upon mutability as the principal consequence of the Fall, a corresponding emphasis on the universality of mutability and on the paradox of change's being conquered by change, an employment (if the numbering of Spenser's stanzas is deliberate) of the sixth, seventh, and eighth days of the hexaemeral tradition as eschatological symbols, a deliberate departure from the language of Scripture to emphasize the intensity of Christ's and Nature's radiance, and an untraditional citation of Second Corinthians as a gloss on the Transfiguration. Not only do all these elements appear in John of Damascus's homily; they are so linked there as to constitute an order of ideas very nearly identical with Spenser's. Though such resemblances fall short of demonstrative proof of Patristic (or, more immediately, Damascene) influence on *The Faerie Queene*, they point to the probability of such. Certainly none of the literary or philosophical texts with which the Mutabilitie Cantos are customarily glossed (nor all of them taken together) affords so exact a set of correspondences, and none accounts so well for Spenser's theology of Nature. As I suggested in reference to the personification of Nature, we should not discount those other sources altogether; Spenser was nothing if not eclectic, and his debt to Chaucer and Alane is a matter of record. I suggest, however, that he subsumed the familiar Western material within the more comprehensive Eastern pattern—that the Chartrian and Neo-Platonic elements so frequently cited are better understood as embellishments than as substantial philosophical components of these cantos; that the habit of thought is Eastern. Perhaps that is to claim too much, but the ease with which Spenser's allusion to the Transfiguration fits itself into the larger pattern of deification and eschatological anticipation resembles the ease with which the same motifs combine in Patristic commentaries and bespeaks a way of thinking and perceiving rather than a mere borrowing of sources. Have we discovered, perhaps, a Greek Patristic Spenser to add to C. S. Lewis's list? More study will be required to answer the question, but the possibility is certainly there; we may have failed to see in *The Faerie Queene* what we did not expect to see.

One question remains: why should Spenser appeal from Western Christianity to Eastern? We have already hinted at an answer in what we have said about the East's conception of cosmic mutability. Mutabilitie is supposed to represent the discoveries of the "New Philosophy" and her strong showing against Jove to reflect Spenser's alarm at those discoveries—at finding change where, in Lewis Owen's words, "It was not thought to exist before."[69] We have seen, however, that in Greek Christendom there was nowhere where change was not thought to be. Since the only permanence anticipated was not above the moon but in the eighth day when the prophecy of the Transfiguration would be consummated, the discovery of universal mutability could not pose a threat to orthodoxy. How better then to respond to such a threat than by turning from traditional Western views, which could not accommodate the new facts, to Eastern views, which could? By doing so Spenser could admit eveything which the "New Philosophy" taught and in the very process of that admission defend a Christian interpretation of the world. In the belief that Christ conquered death *by death*, made flesh God by *becoming flesh*, and effected immutability by *becoming mutable*, he can admit without fear, as Dame Nature serenely does, that "all things stedfastnes doe hate / And changed be." The Mutabilitie Cantos may manifest less of the New Philosophy than of the oldest Christian theology.

Vanderbilt University

NOTES

1. A good summary of this scholarship is to be found in S. P. Zitner's Introduction to his edition of *The Mutabilitie Cantos* (London: Thomas Nelson, 1968), pp. 48–50. Zitner argues for Chartrian rather than Florentine influence, as does Robert Ellrodt in *Neoplatonism in the Poetry of Edmund Spenser* (Geneva: Librairie E. Droz, 1960), pp. 63 ff.

2. "Spenser's Venus and the Goddess Nature of the *Cantos of Mutabilitie*," *Studies in Philology*, 30 (1933), 160–192. This is summarized in the *Variorum* (vi, 410 ff.).

3. *Spenser's Images of Life*, ed. Alastair Fowler (Cambridge: Cambridge University Press, 1967), p. 15. One wonders how literally Lewis meant *image*; since Nature is assimilated to Christ, who is the "express image" of the Father, his phrasing is exact and provocative.

4. No clearer exposition of this is available than Professor A. S. P. Woodhouse's in his famous article ("Nature and Grace in *The Faerie Queene*," *ELH*, 16 [1949], 194–228). If he is correct about Spenser's attitudes toward Nature and Grace in earlier portions of *The Faerie Queene* and if my interpretation of the Mutabilitie Cantos is valid, Spenser seems to have changed his mind in the course of writing the poem.

5. I agree with Angelo M. Pellegrini ("Bruno, Sidney, and Spenser," *Studies in Philology*, 40 [1943], 128–144) that there is no indication of Bruno's influence on Spenser, and I disagree on the same matter with G. F. Waller ("Transition in Renaissance Ideas of Time and the Place of Giordano Bruno," *Neophilologus*, 55 [1977], 3–15).

6. "Spenser's 'Adamantine Chains': A Cosmological Metaphor," in Hutton's *Essays on Renaissance Poetry*, ed. Rita Guerlac (Ithaca: Cornell University Press, 1980), p. 171.

7. One of the best discussions of this matter and of the distinctions between East and West is M. Lot Borodine's *La deification de l'homme selon la doctrine des pères grecs* (Paris: Editions du Cerf, 1970).

8. "The Eastern tradition knows nothing of 'pure nature' to which grace is added as a supernatural gift. For it, there is no natural or 'normal' state, since grace is implied in the act of creation itself. . . . 'Pure nature,' for Eastern theology, would thus be a philosophical fiction corresponding neither to the original state of creation, nor to its present condition which is 'against nature,' nor to the state of deification which belongs to the age to come." Vladimir Lossky, *The Mystical Theology of the Eastern Church* (Crestwood, N. Y.: St. Vladimir's Seminary Press, 1976), p. 101.

9. The relation between deification and the Transfiguration is discussed in all its aspects by Lossky in *The Vision of God*, trans. Asheleigh Moorehouse (Leighton Buzzard, England: Faith Press, 1973).

10. How little is surprising; there has been no systematic effort to identify and catalogue these. Migne provides some help, for he relies in many instances on the texts of Renaissance editions. See also Deno John Geanakoplos, *Interaction of the "Sibling" Byzantine and Western Cultures in the Middle Ages and Italian Renaissance (330–1600)* (New Haven, Conn.: Yale University Press, 1976).

11. For partial listings see H. M. Adams, *Catalogue of Books Printed on the*

Continent of Europe, 1501–1600, in Cambridge Libraries, 2 vols. (Cambridge: Cambridge University Press, 1967), and Emile Legrand, *Bibliographie Hellénique des xv^c et xvi^c siècles,* 4 vols. (Paris: G.-P. Maisonneuve & Larose, 1962).

12. On English publication of the Greek Fathers see William P. Haaugaard, "Renaissance Patristic Scholarship and Theology in Sixteenth-Century England," *Sixteenth Century Journal,* 10 (1979), 37–60.

13. Bishop Matthew Wren's 1617 list of books in the Pembroke College library contains the following entry: "Chrysostomus lat. in 5 vol. (accessit A° 1536)." The edition is D. Ioannis Chrysostomi . . . opera, quae hactenus versa sunt omnia, ad Graecorum codicum collationem multis in locis per utriusque linguae peritos emendata. . . . Basileae, in officina Frobeniana, Mense Avgvsto, Anno M. D. XXX.

14. John Welles, BD, Pembroke, deceased, 1569 (the year of Spenser's matriculation there) had "in his studdye" *Opera Crisostomi,* 5 voluminibus (very likely the Froben edition), *Opera basilij magni* 1 volume, along with a *Testamentum novum grece & Latine* and a Lexicon *grecum.* Other sixteenth-century inventories reveal seventeen copies of Athanasius, seventeen of Cyril of Alexandria, seven of Dionysius the Areopagite, twenty-three of Gregory the Theologian, twelve of Irenaeus, twenty-five of John of Damascus, thirty-three of Basil the Great and one hundred nine of John Chrysostom.

15. See Jewel's *An Apology of the Church of England,* ed. J. E. Booty (Ithaca, N.Y.: Cornell University Press, 1963) and *The First Authorized English Bible and the Cranmer Preface,* ed. Harold R. Willoughby (Chicago: University of Chicago Press, 1942).

16. See Frank Kermode, "*The Faerie Queene,* I and V," *Bulletin of the John Rylands Library,* 47 (1965), 123–150 for a convincing interpretation of Una as a symbol of "the primitive Eastern Church." See also Thomas H. Cain, *Praise in "The Faerie Queene"* (Lincoln, Nebraska: University of Nebraska Press, 1978), pp. 76 ff.

17. *Athanasii Magni . . . opera in quatour Tomos distributa: quorum tres sunt à Petro Nannio . . . latinius redittis . . .* (Basil: Froben, 1556). There were no Greek editions of Athanasius until 1601, but Spenser would have had access to several Latin translations of *De Incarnatione.* The first of these appeared in Vicenza in 1482. Subsequent translations came from Paris (1519 and 1520), Strasbourg (1522), Cologne (1532), and Lyon (1533). The Froben edition was the standard text until the Benedictine edition of 1698. If Spenser read the *De Incarnatione,* he probably did so in Nannius's translation, from which I quote here. For a full account of editions see *Sources Chrétiennes,* 199 (Paris: Editions du Cerf, 1973), pp. 163–165.

18. *Is enim ideo homo factus est, ut nos dii efficeremur.* (54, 3), Nannius (1556), I, 71 (*PG,* 25: 191–192).

19. *ut ita naturae instaurationem, à verbo ipsius ab initio authore & conditore factam, digne ritéque contemplari possimus.* (1, 4), Nannius (1556), I, 36 (*PG,* 25: 97–98).

20. *non quidem antea inde longinquus (nihil quippe ab eo vacuum relinquitur in rebus creatis . . . .)* (8, 1), Nannius (1556), I, 40 (*PG,* 25: 109–110).

21. *mortem in illis quasi stipulam in igne consumens.* (8, 4), Nannius (1556), I, 40 (*PG,* 25: 109–110).

22. *ut . . . in homine operaretur, & seipsum undecunque ostenderet, nihil desertum*

destitutumque relinquens à sua divinitate & cognitione. (45.1), Nannius (1556), I, 66 (*PG*, 25: 175–176).

23. Nine of those are of Erasmus's translation, which appeared first in Basil (Froben) in 1526 and was reprinted in 1528, 1534, 1548, 1560, 1563, 1567, and 1571 by various publishers. There were also translations by Gallasius (Paris, 1570) and Feuardent (Paris, 1575 and Cologne, 1596). For a partial account of these see *Sources Chrétiennes*, 100 (Paris, 1965), pp. 34–38. I quote here from Erasmus's translation in the Paris edition of 1545 by Mathurin Dupuys.

24. *Quando verbum caro factum est . . . ut in carnem domini occurrat paterna lux, & à carne eius rutila veniat in nos, & sic homo deveniat in incorruptelam, circundatus paterno lumine.* (4, 20), Erasmus (1545), p. 359 (*PG*, 7:1033).

25. *Quemadmodum enim videntes lumen intra lumen sunt & claritatem eius recipiunt, sic & qui vident deum, intra deum sunt, percipientes eius claritatem. vivificat autem eos claritas. . . . visus vitam praestat iis, qui vident eum. . . . Homines igitur videbunt deum, & vivent per visionem, immortales facti.* (4, 20), Erasmus (1545), p. 361 (*PG*, 7: 1035–1036).

26. See note 13. I quote from this edition.

27. *Et in veteri quidem testamento cum Moses ascendisset in montem, descendit deus. In novo vero cum nostra in coelum . . . esset elevata natura, spiritus sanctus descendit de coelo.* (1, 1), Erasmus (1530), III, 5 (*PG*, 57: 15–16).

28. *Nunquid possit esse aequale his tam bonis nunciis? Deus in terris, homo in coelo: facta est omnium una permixtio, angelia cum hominibus iungebant choros, homines choris addebantur angelicis, atque coelestibus aliis, supernísque virtutibus.* (1, 2), Erasmus (1530), III, 6 (*PG*, 57: 15–16).

29. *Et non in urbibus solum atque plateis, sed in ipsis quoque verticibus montium. Etenim ibi maxime evangelicam videas florere philosophiam, & angelorum choros in humano corpore refulgere, conversationémque omnino coelestem in terris micare.* (1, 5), Erasmus (1530), III, 9 (*PG*, 57: 20).

30. *filius David esse dignatus est, modò ut te filium faceret dei. . . . Quantum enim ad cogitationes hominum pertinet, multo est difficilius deum hominem fieri, quàm hominem dei filium consecrari. Cum ergo audieris, quia [Gr. ὅτι] filius dei, filius sit & David & Adae, dubitare iam desine, cum tu qui filius es Adae, sis filius dei. . . . Natus est enim secundum carnem, ut tu nascerere spiritu: natus est ex muliere, ut tu desineres filius esse mulieris.* (2, 2), Erasmus (1530), III, 13 (*PG*, 57: 25–26).

31. *sed omnes terrae prorsus, ac maria, atque universum humanum genus.* (10, 3), Erasmus (1530), III, 66 (*PG*, 57: 187).

32. See Legrand for listings. I have quoted here from an English translation of *The Festal Menaion* by Mother Mary and Kallistos Ware (London: Faber and Faber, 1969).

33. Second canon for matins, eighth canticle, *FM*, p. 378.

34. *FM*, p. 355.

35. From Great Compline for the Nativity, *FM*, p. 263.

36. From Great Vespers for the Transfiguration, *FM*, pp. 474 and 477.

37. Quoted by John Meyendorff in *Byzantine Theology: Historical Trends and Doctrinal Themes* (New York: Fordham University Press, 1974), p. 145.

38. The Scripture at issue is Romans 5:12, the phrase, ἐφ'ᾧ πάντες ἥμαρτον. The Vulgate renders this *in quo omnes peccaverunt,* "in whom [Adam] all have sinned." The Greek pronoun, however, can be neuter as well as masculine so may be translated "because of which" with reference

to death (ὁ θάνατος). That is the way the Greek Fathers interpreted St. Paul's statement: "Therefore, as through one man sin came into the world and through sin death, and thus death passed to all men, *because of which* all have sinned." See Meyendorff, pp. 143–146.

39. Basil the Great in the *Hexaemeron* homilies says that mutability preceded the fall: "the cosmos was designed as a fitting place of sojourn for everything in the process of birth and death." Everything in the physical creation except human souls was made subject to "the passage of time . . . always driving on and flowing by and never stopping its course"—all that prior to Adam's trespass. The original sin subjected the human soul to this temporal bondage by making it subject to the passions of the body. *Hexaemeron*, I, 4–5 (*PG*, 29: 11–14). Spenser could have read this in either of two Erasmian editions: *En amice lector thesaurum damus inestimabilem D. Basilium . . .* (Basil ex officina Frobeniana, 1532); *Divi Basilii magni, Opera graeca quae ad nos extant omnia* (Basil: Froben, 1551). There were Latin translations as well. For a listing of sixteenth-century editions see *Sources Chrétiennes*, 160 (Paris: Editions du Cerf, 1970), pp. 135–143. I translate here from the 1551 Froben edition, pp. 2–3.

40. See, for instance, St. Gregory of Nyssa, *De Virginitate (PG, 46: 373–374)* and *De Anima et Resurrectione (PG, 46: 147–150)*.

41. I quote here from the Froben edition of 1551, pp. 26–27; see note 39. τούτων τὶ ἄν γένοιτο καταγελαστότερον; ὁ κριὸς ἀφ' οὗ τὴν γένεσιν τοῦ ἀνθρώπου λαμβάνεις, οὐρανοῦ μέρος ἐστὶ τὸ δωδέκατον, ἐν ᾧ γενόμενος ὁ ἥλιος, ἐαρινῶν σημείων ἐφάπτει . . . πῶς οὖν ἐκεῖθεν τὰς προηγουμένας αἰτίας λέγων ὑπάρχειν τοῖς τῶν ἀνθρώπων βίος . . . ; (6, 6) πρῶτον μὲν οὖν ἐκεῖνο αὐτοὺς ἐρωτήσωμεν, εἰ μὴ ἐφ' ἐκάστης ἡμέρας μυριάκις ἀμείβεται τῶν ἀστέρων τὰ σχήματα

42. Sancti Ioannis Damasceni *Opera . . .* per D. Iacobum Billium Prunaeum, S. Michaelis in eremo Coenobiarcham. Parisiis: Apud Guillelmum Chaudiere . . . 1577.

43. The Transfiguration homily is printed in both Greek and Latin in parallel columns. For the most part this edition is Billius's Latin translation; only two other works appear in a two-text version. Also the Transfiguration homily is one of several listed in the table of contents as *nunc primum in lucem exeunt*. Both of those distinctions might have served to call it to Spenser's attention. In the following passages I have translated from the Greek text (comparing it with Billius's translation), and I have included in parentheses a few Greek phrases which are of particular interest. (I have also added italics to my English version; there are no emphases in the Greek.) My assumption in working from the Greek rather than the Latin is that Spenser read both languages and would have been more interested in the original than in a contemporary translation. There is no compelling reason to doubt his knowing Greek; it made part of the curriculum both at Merchant Taylors' and at Cambridge, and Spenser is unlikely to have completed a Master's degree without the capacity at least to construe Greek, even if not to read it fluently. With the exception of a few difficult passages, John of Damascus's Greek is easily translated and should have been readily accessible, especially in view of the parallel Latin text.

Migne reproduces Billius's Greek text with a few alterations (and numerous errors). Since Billius's Latin is not available, I give the passages in question in the notes.

44. *Nam & verbum caro, & caro verbum facta est, etiamsi neutrum horum à sua natura desciuerit.*

Nunc visa sunt, quae hominum oculis cerni non poterant, nimirùm terrenum corpus divinum splendorem emittens, mortale corpus deitatis gloriam fontis instar fundens.

Non externè corpori gloria accessit, sed interne ex Dei Verbe deitate (ὑπερθέου θεότητος), *modo quodam omnem sermonem excedente ipsi personaliter unita.*

Quonam pacto, quae misceri nequeunt, inter se miscentur, & tamen ab omni confusione libera manent! Quonam modo ea, quae inter se coire non possunt, in unum coëunt, nec tamen propriam naturae suae rationem excedunt!

tum per immutabilem Verbi incarnationem, tum per mortalis carnis immutabilem atque omnem mentis captum superantem deificationem. (2), Billius, 357ᵛ – 358ʳ (*PG*, 96: 547 – 548).

45. *divinitatísque gloria corpori quoque gloriam conciliavit.* Here the Latin is free; the Greek reads, καὶ ἡ θεότητους δόξα, καὶ δόξα τοῦ σόματος γίνεται (12), Billius, 362ᵛ (*PG*, 96: 563 – 564).

46. *tum Deus humana, tum homo divina sibi asciscit.* (2), Billius, 358ʳ (*PG*, 96: 549 – 550).

47. *divinitatem homo consequitur, dum Deus humanitatem suscipit.*

genus humanum in seipso innovans: atque imagini exemplar miscetur. (3 & 4), Billius, 358ᵛ – 359ʳ (*PG*, 96: 551 – 552).

Here Billius's translation is inexact and weakens the force of the original, by rendering θεουργῶν as *innovans*—*renewing* rather than *deifying* human nature. One suspects as motive for this free reading in a largely literal translation a Western Catholic distaste for (or perhaps simply incomprehension of) the Patristic doctrine of man's theosis. A reader comparing the parallel texts (as we can imagine Spenser's doing) would certainly notice the discrepancy and have the Greek emphasis on deification brought forcibly to his attention.

48. *Ob eam causam divinis humana nunquamnon miscet.* (10), Billius, 362ʳ (*PG*, 96: 561 – 562).

49. *in unigenito suo Filio universi orbis salutatem operata est.*

Nam cum parvus mendus homo sit, ut qui essentiae omnis, tum in aspectum cadentis, tum oculorum aciem fugientis, nodum ac vinculum in seipso ferat.

Benigna Patris voluntas in unigenito Filio rerum omnium connexionem effecit.

revera benigna omnium rerum domini & creatoris ac gubernatoris voluntas hoc tulit, ut in unigenito & consubstantiali Filio suo divinitatis & humanitatis, ac per eam conditarum omnium rerum, connexio fieret, ut sit Deus omnia in omnibus. (18), Billius, 365ᵛ (*PG*, 96: 573 – 574).

50. Par. 1; I have translated from Billius's Greek text as it is reproduced, with slight alterations, in *Sources Chrétiennes*, 80 (Paris: Editions du Cerf, 1961), pp. 47– 48; italics added.

51. *vincit divinitas, atque claritatem suam & gloriam ita corpori impertit.* (13), Billius, 363ᵛ (*PG*, 96: 565 – 566).

52. *Hoc lumen adversus omnem naturam palmam obtinet. Haec vita est quae de mundo triumphavit.* (16), Billius, 364ᵛ (*PG*, 96: 569 – 570).

53. *coeli firmati sunt, terráque constabilita est, atque inconcussa manet.* (6), Billius, 360ʳ (*PG*, 96: 555 – 556).

54. *ab externa huiusce mundi iactatione velut in libertatem vindicati.* (10), Billius, 362ʳ (*PG*, 96: 561–562). *iactatione* is inadequate to translate περιφωρᾶς. My interpretation assumes Spenser's knowing the Greek and understanding its implications.

55. *idem ipse cum homo sit, deitatis ratione principio caret, & cum Deus sit, humanitatis respectu initium capit.*

O novam & admirandam commutationem . . . quam miro modo hominem principii expertem ostendit, & eum, qui principio caret, corporeo modo creatum initium capere! (3), Billius, 358ᵛ (*PG*, 96: 551–552).

56. *carnemque per naturam suam grassari permitteret, ut per seipsam & robur concipiat, & erudiatur atque ad praestantiorum disciplinam & habitum perveniat.* (10), Billius, 362ʳ (*PG*, 96: 561–562).

57. *Tunc quasi sol iusti, immo vero multo magis, quàm sol resplendebunt.* (56, 4), Erasmus (1530), III, 324–325 (*PG*, 58: 555–556).

58. Lossky, *The Vision of God*, p. 35.

59. *The Divine Names* (1, 4) (*PG*, 3: 591–592). I quote from the translation by C. E. Rolt (London: Macmillan, 1940), p. 58. (See note 65.)

60. *Viderunt etiam ipsius pulchritudinem Petrus et filii tonitruii in monte, fulgore suo splendorem solis superantem, atque habiti sunt digni, qui gloriosi ejus adventus exordia oculis perciperent.* (*PG*, 29: 399–400).

61. *terreno hoc corporis tabernaculo premuntur, post . . . quando fulgebunt iusti sicut sol, atque corporeis necessitatibus liberati, tanquam angeli cum Domino immortales erunt, in magna & illustri è coelis revelatione. . . .* (20), Billius, 366ᵛ (*PG*, 96: 575–576).

62. *Haec mutatio dexterae excelsi. Haec sunt quae oculos non vidit, nec auris audivit. . . . Ita in futuro seculo semper cum Domino erimus, Christum cernentes divinitatis luce refulgentem.* (15), Billius, 364ᵛ (*PG*, 96: 569–570).

63. *The City of God*, xxii. For a full explication of the Eastern conception of the eighth day see Jean Danielou, *The Bible and the Liturgy* (Ann Arbor: Servant Books, 1979), pp. 262–275.

64. *Spenser and the Numbers of Time* (London: Routledge & Kegan Paul, 1964), p. 58.

65. *Quinetiam sex dierum spatio rerum omnium quae in oculorum sensum cadunt, congeriem Deus sermone suo effecit. . . . Octonarius autem idcircò adhibetur, quia futuri aevi figuram gerit. Etenim septem seculis praesens vita concluditur. Octava verò futura vita praedicatur. . . . ut in octava, ea quae ad octavem pertinebant, perfectis revelarentur. . . . Sic Dominus à perfectis famulis suis conspicietur, quemadmodum in monte Thabor ab Apostolis conspectus est.* (8), Billius, 361ʳ–361ᵛ (*PG*, 96: 559–560). Here John of Damascus cites the passage from Pseudo-Dionysius to which we have alluded (see note 59).

66. *Quid ais Euangelista? Quid ea, quae verè incomparabilia sunt, comparas? Quid ea confers ac componis, quae nullum collationem admittunt? . . . Luménne illud, quod ferri, propriusque adiri non potest, instar huius quod ab omnibus conspicitur, effulsit? . . . verùm quia mihi cum iis, qui carnis catenis vincti sunt, oratio est, id quod inter corpora praestantissimum ac praeclarissimum est, exempli causa arripio: non quòd quàm similimum ipsi sit (neque enim fieri potest, ut quod increatum est, in rebus creatis ita exprimatur, ut nullum omnino discrimen insit).* (13), Billius, 363ʳ (*PG*, 96: 565–566).

67. *Umbram enim, ut ex Paulo audire licet, futurorum lex habebat, non ipsam*

veritatem. Ac tum Israëliticus populus in Mosis faciem, quae abolenda erat, intendere non potuit. Nos autem revelata facie Domini gloriam intuemur, a gloria in maiorem gloriam transformati, tanquam à Domino Spiritu. (17), Billius, 363ʳ (*PG*, 96: 571–572).

68. Wyclif and Rheims read *transformed*; the rest, simply *changed*.

69. "Mutable in Eternity: Spenser's Despair and the Multiple Forms of Mutabilitie," *Journal of Medieval and Renaissance Studies*, 2 (1972), 61.

CAROL A. STILLMAN

Politics, Precedence, and the Order of the Dedicatory Sonnets in *The Faerie Queene*

THE DEDICATORY sonnets are our only means for distinguishing the two issues of the 1590 *Faerie Queene*; they also present one of its few textual problems, that of determining the sonnets' proper order and the circumstances of their printing. Most older editions position them pretty much at random. The *Variorum* reproduces (correctly) the arrangement of the second issue, without, however, providing a rationale for that order beyond the fact that it represents the printer's final intentions. Editors assume the order is the printer's whim, not the author's plan. They also believe that the second issue was needed because of last-minute additions made by Spenser under political pressures. I will argue here that there are stronger grounds for accepting the second issue's order, and that the theory explaining the two issues is unnecessary.

The contents of the issues need first to be detailed. From the states of the surviving copies of the 1590 edition, it is apparent that the printer initially included only ten of the seventeen poems—those to Hatton, Essex, Oxford, Northumberland, Ormond, Howard, Grey, Raleigh, Lady Carew, and "All the Ladies." Then, before the type had been distributed, he attempted to add the seven remaining sonnets by making a cancel which contained all but the last two addressed to Lady Carew and "the Ladies" (which were on a separate leaf), to produce the arrangement that follows: Hatton, Burghley, Oxford, Northumberland, Cumberland, Essex, Ormond, Howard, Hunsdon, Grey, Buckhurst, Walsingham, Norris, Raleigh, the Countess of Pembroke, Lady Carew, and "the Ladies." In binding, some copies were mistakenly made up of only the first issue's ten sonnets, or those ten plus the fifteen of the cancel intended to supercede them.[1]

In spite of the muddled state of the text, we can be certain that the order of the second issue has Spenser's authority, for the simple reason that neither he nor the printer had any choice in the matter. Poems addressed to noblemen had to be presented according to the heraldic rules for precedence. The chief officials of the crown come first, then the peers, then the gentlemen, followed by the ladies, all ranked by the dignity of their families, offices, and titles. In his *Honor, Military and Civill*, Sir William Segar, Garter King-at-Arms, provides the details for this complicated etiquette that allow us to justify the ordering of the sonnets.[2]

As Segar illustrates in his examples of two of Elizabeth's proceedings, the Lord High Chancellor (Hatton) always precedes the Lord High Treasurer (Burghley), and so Spenser preserves their ranking in his dedications.[3] Oxford is entitled to first place among the earls because he is the Lord High Chamberlain (see below) and because he has the most ancient title. Within each rank of the aristocracy, the peers take their places by the time span the family has possessed the title, ("the ancientie of his Ancestors creation," Segar says).[4] However, English lords go before Irish lords of the same degree.[5] Thus, the sonnets present in succession the seventeenth Earl of Oxford (created 1142), the ninth Earl of Northumberland (created 1416), the third Earl of Cumberland (created 1525), the second Earl of Essex (created 1572), and the Irish Earl of Ormond and Ossory.[6]

In Segar's proceedings, as in the dedications, Howard and Hunsdon come first among the barons for their offices as Lord High Admiral and Lord Chamberlain of the Household.[7] As a general rule, holders of important offices take their places before all others of their rank. A few of the highest officials take precedence regardless of their aristocratic titles. Segar cites an act of Henry VIII's reign that established the system for seating the great officers of the Crown in Parliament. The Lord High Chamberlain (Oxford), the Lord High Constable, the Earl Marshal, the Lord Admiral (Howard), the Lord Steward, the Lord Chamberlain (Hunsdon), Segar says, "are placed in all assemblies of Councell, after Lord privie Seale [who follows the Lord Chancellor, the Lord Treasurer, and the Lord President of the Privy Council], according to their degrees, and estates, So that if he be a Baron, to sit above all Barons: and if he be an Earle, above all Earles."[8] Oxford's earldom therefore places him well before his fellow officers, Howard and Hunsdon, who are only barons. Howard's 1597 elevation to Earl of Nottingham gave him precedence over an indignant Essex, until the Queen pacified her favorite by making him Earl Marshal, an office ranked just above Lord Admiral.[9]

In Spenser's dedications, the fourteenth Lord Grey of Wilton (created 1290) and the first Lord Buckhurst (created 1567) properly follow the two office-holding barons, again placed by the time of the family's tenure of the title. As Principal Secretary, Walsingham comes first among the knights but after the lords, "being no baron," and so Segar shows his place in the two proceedings he records.[10] Norris takes precedence over Raleigh for his office as Lord President of Munster and for his birth as the second son of a baron, Henry Norris of Rycote. Segar again provides the rule: "all Barons yonger sonnes shal precede all Batcheler Knights."[11] A knight bachelor is one who is not enrolled in a special order of knighthood, such as the Garter or the Bath.

Spenser's dedications conclude with poems to ladies, one first to Mary Sidney, the Countess of Pembroke, followed by one to Elizabeth Spencer, Lady Carew. The principles are fundamentally the same as those used to rank the gentlemen. In proceeding, the women follow the men and are placed among themselves according to the nobility of their husbands, or, if unmarried, of their fathers.[12] Here the countess precedes the baronet's wife. One final sonnet, addressed "To all the Ladies," closes this politely and properly ordered series of dedications.

Spenser's editors and bibliographers have been more interested in speculating why seven sonnets had to be added than in understanding the arrangement of the cancel. The standard explanation for the occurrence of these late additions—proposed by Gollancz, seconded by Johnson, and quoted with approval in the *Variorum*—is as follows.[13] Spenser originally wrote only the first issue's ten sonnets; while the volume was being printed, his friends convinced him it would be impolitic to omit Burghley. Spenser therefore hastily composed a sonnet to Burghley and took advantage of the occasion to add new dedications to six other gentlemen.

The theory is not plausible. There is little sense in arguing that Spenser threw in the extra six sonnets for good measure if his purpose in making the alteration was solely to add one addressed to the Lord Treasurer. The dedications may not be deeply moving, but they are finely crafted poems. Johnson recognizes that the change must have been made "almost immediately" after the first issue was completed, since the type had not yet been distributed when the second issue was prepared.[14] Not even Edmund Spenser can toss off seven sonnets at a sitting.

The evidence for Spenser's animosity towards Burghley is also weak. Spenser would naturally dislike the lord's cautious foreign policy, but otherwise his supposed hatred for Burghley is based upon a strained reading of "Mother Hubberds Tale," on an apocryphal tale that Burghley later delayed paying his pension, and on the identification of "the rugged forhead" mentioned in Book Four's proem with Burghley.[15] Even if one accepts this last point as valid, there is still no evidence for Spenser's ill will towards Burghley in 1590. I suggest instead that the omission of the seven sonnets from the first issue was due to some minor oversight of the printer, the poet, or an intermediary. The mistake was soon discovered and rectified by inserting the missing dedications in strict accordance with the heraldic rules for precedence.

University of Notre Dame

NOTES

1. My description of the textual problems of the sonnets is drawn from Francis R. Johnson, *A Critical Bibliography of the Works of Edmund Spenser* (Baltimore: Johns Hopkins University Press, 1933), pp. 11–18.

2. (London, 1602). Segar provides by far the best contemporary account of precedence. Also useful are: John Selden, *Titles of Honor*, 2nd ed. (London, 1631) and Thomas Milles, *The Catalogue of Honor* (London, 1610). The Early English Text Society prints the undated manuscript of a "Cornellis van dalw"; it appears to be notes made out of Segar, since it follows his wording closely. "A Book of Precedence," *EETS*, ex. ser., VIII, ed. F. J. Furnivall (London: Kegan Paul, 1869), pp. 13–28. One can also infer many of Segar's rules from the proceedings recorded in John Nichols, *The Progresses and Public Processions of Queen Elizabeth*, 3 vols. (London: John Nichols, 1823; rpt. New York:

AMS Press, 1969). Some additional confirmation can be derived from two nineteenth-century authorities, Charles R. Dodd, *A Manual of Dignities, Privilege, and Precedence* (London: Whittaker & Co., 1844) and William J. Thoms, *The Book of the Court*, 2nd ed. (London: Henry G. Bohn, 1844).

3. Segar, pp. 241–247. Also Thoms, p. 477, and Dodd, p. 32.

4. Segar, p. 240.

5. Segar does not discuss the placement of Irish peers, probably because the Anglo-Irish lords were rarely present at court and could not sit in the House of Lords. When Buckingham began selling Irish titles, the issue of precedence was hotly debated. "Certainly no Irish or Scottish peer could sit in the English house of lords, nor did such a peer outrank an English peer of the same grade in England. But an English peer was outranked by any Irish or Scottish peer of a higher grade, a fact that rankled in the breast of many an English baron who found himself displaced on a commission or in any place of authority by an Irish or Scottish viscount." Charles R. Mayes, "The Early Stuarts and the Irish Peerage," *English Historical Review*, 73 (1958), 227–251.

6. My source for these numbers and dates is George E. Cokayne, *The Complete Peerage*, 13 vols. (London: St. Catherine Press, 1910).

7. Segar, pp. 242, 246.

8. Segar, p. 243. Selden quotes the act in full, II, 902–905, and so does Milles, pp. 62–63.

9. J. E. Neale, *Queen Elizabeth I* (London: Jonathan Cape, 1934; rpt. New York: Doubleday [Anchor], 1957), p. 360.

10. Segar, pp. 242, 246.

11. Segar, p. 241.

12. Segar, p. 240. If, however, a noble lady marries a mere knight or esquire, she takes place by her father's status, not her husband's.

13. The relevant passages in Gollancz and Johnson are cited in full in the *Variorum*, V, 428–429. Or see Johnson, pp. 15–16.

14. Johnson, p. 15. McKerrow says that Elizabethan printers normally distributed the type after printing each gathering, sometimes after every few leaves. (Ronald B. McKerrow, *An Introduction to Bibliography* [Oxford: Clarendon Press, 1927], pp. 60, 175).

15. Thomas Fuller is apparently the first to tell the story of the pension, and it is frequently repeated and embroidered throughout the seventeenth and eighteenth centuries. The venerable tradition of Spenser's hatred for Burghley seems to have developed around this tale. See R. M. Cummings, *Spenser: The Critical Heritage* (London: Routledge & Kegan Paul, 1971), pp. 320–321 and 327–329. Also Jewel Wurtsbaugh discusses the anecdote in *Two Centuries of Spenserian Scholarship* (Baltimore: Johns Hopkins University Press, 1936), pp. 22–26.

A passage in Nashe's *Pierce Penniless* is also adduced as evidence for Spenser's grudging inclusion of the detestable Burghley. Pierce praises *The Faerie Queene* but chides Spenser for failing to provide a dedication to "thrice noble *Amyntas*." He proceeds to compose his own sonnet to that "renoumed Lord." McKerrow suggests the unnamed peer might be the Earl of Derby; the *Variorum* editors apparently believe that Nashe must have read a copy which lacked the cancel: therefore he must mean Burghley. I think the context shows that Nashe is enjoying a little joke: the mystery lord does not exist. Pierce complains at length of the ingratitude of patrons before lavishing compliments on his "magnificent rewarder of vertue," Amyntas. A dedication to an unnamed lord is obviously pointless—but so are all dedications, since all lords are stingy. Nashe might be directing a gibe at Spenser as well, for seeking favor with so many. He might as well, Nashe hints, add another dedication to "the unknown lord," just in case he overlooked anyone important (Thomas Nashe, *Works*, ed. Ronald B. McKerrow, corrected by F. P. Wilson, 5 vols. [Oxford: Basil Blackwell, 1958], I, 241–244).

DOUGLAS ANDERSON

"Vnto My Selfe Alone": Spenser's Plenary Epithalamion

I

*A*FTER OBSERVING with characteristic candor that, in his judgment, the *Amoretti* "are not among our greatest sonnets," C. S. Lewis continues a sweeping essay on Spenser by affirming that the *Epithalamion* "belongs to a different world."[1] It is a "buoyant poem" covering not only the whole of a marriage day but also harmonizing "all the diverse associations of marriage," which Lewis cheerfully enumerates: "summer, landscape, neighbours, pageantry, religion, riotous eating and drinking, sensuality, moonlight." "Those who have attempted to write poetry," he concludes, "will know how very much easier it is to express sorrow than joy. That is what makes the *Epithalamion* matchless. Music has often reached that jocundity; poetry seldom." Lewis is controversial in many of his opinions, but this view of *Epithalamion* is not one of them. The comprehensive joy he finds in the poem is shared by most sympathetic readers and confirmed by virtually every scholar who has written on it, though not always with Lewis's eloquence.[2] This prevailing sense of marital "jocundity," however, has tended to overshadow elements of *Epithalamion* which may, upon examination, prove to be less markedly joyful.

Qualities of Spenser's marriage ode which seem to me nearly, if not quite equally, as decisive as its buoyancy and harmony are silence and isolation. The poet frankly, and conventionally, courts these conditions in his final stanzas, bidding the marriage dancers "ceasse" and be gone, welcoming night, conjuring away night's troubling noises:

> Bvt let stil Silence trew night watches keepe,
> That sacred peace may in assurance rayne,
> And tymely sleep, when it is tyme to sleepe,
> May poure his limbs forth on your pleasant playne.
> (353–356)[3]

At this rather advanced hour in his wedding day, of course, the poet is less interested in silence for its own sake than he is in concealment, "prety stealthes," and "snatches of delight." Epithalamia traditionally close with a blessing upon the lovers' union and a tactful allusion to the wedding night's romantic promise. A more perplexing variety of silence and isolation influences the tone of the opening stanza, where Spenser goes out of his way to establish a solitude that is not simply conventional or romantically suggestive but is a part of the entire poem's dramatic climate. In the song which follows, the poet tells us, only his own voice will be heard, singing to himself:

> Ne let the same of any be enuide:
> So Orpheus did for his owne bride,
> So I vnto my selfe alone will sing,
> The woods shall to me answer and my Eccho ring.
>   (15–18)

The familiar Alexandrine, which in one form or another acts as a refrain to each subsequent stanza, here has the effect of emphasizing the loneliness to which Spenser has just called our attention. At happier moments in the poem, as countless readers have observed, the line affirms nature's participation in the wedding joy. But in this initial appearance, the echoing woods suggest not natural reciprocity but the absence of human company. The echo is singularly and hauntingly empty.

The opening invocation, moreover, is both traditional and oddly mournful. Spenser reminds the Muses of the "sadder tenor" by which they have often taught nature to condole with their own sorrows and (as we have seen) compares himself to Orpheus, a troubling allusion in a poem ostensibly commemorating fulfilled love. Enid Welsford has pointed out that the classical songs of Orpheus which Spenser is clearly thinking of here are not joyful epithalamia but laments over the loss of Eurydice.[4] The "wished day," the wedding day around which *Epithalamion* revolves, Spenser assures us shall compensate for "al the paynes and sorrowes past"; and in a reprise of his invocation, his diction is plaintive rather than festive and confident:

> O fayrest Phoebus, father of the Muse,
> If euer I did honour thee aright,

Or sing the thing, that mote thy mind delight,
Doe not thy seruants simple boone refuse,
But let this day let this one day be myne,
Let all the rest be thine.

(121–126)

The celebration seems neither a fulfillment nor a commencement but only a momentary hiatus, "this one day," for which
the poet repeatedly pleads. The lines carry with them a nearly
inaudible background of resignation and loss.

This solemn undertone—so at odds with the apparently
joyous spirit of the poem, as readers have come to see it—lends
special interest as well to the mysteriously deep sleep of the
bride in the early stanzas. After dispatching several extraterres-
trial emissaries and marking the morning's progress, the poet
himself grows impatient: "Ah my deere love why do ye sleepe
thus long, / When meeter were that ye should now awake"
(85). To be sure, shortly after this direct appeal, she appears
"out of her dreame," but never throughout the scenes that
follow does she seem anything less than entranced. Although
Spenser praises her "fayre eyes like stars that dimmed were /
With darksome cloud," the clouds break only momentarily in
the sixth stanza before closing once more. She never gazes upon
her lover again—indeed, she "suffers not one looke to glaunce
awry" in any direction save downward—and all the kinetic
description of the wedding day thereafter serves in some
measure to intensify our sense of this motionless, abstracted,
passive figure in the midst of the dance, with "sad eyes stil
fastened on the ground" (234).

I do not mean to rebuke Spenser because his bride is not
companionable or because he permits thoughts of sadness to
disturb the matrimonial atmosphere. But I am convinced that
the poem's allusive richness and complex tone require us at least
to consider the possibility that Spenser found expressive opportunities in his poetical marriage gift which may have outgrown
the personal occasion (or occasions) for which he began writing.[5] One line of development apparently led him to explore the
possibility of blurring the distinction between an individual,
earthly marriage sacrament and the visionary, unearthly "marriage" prophesied for the end of time.[6] A second, but no less
decisive, set of interests may have encouraged Spenser to

explore throughout the poem a range of ambiguities in the theme of marriage. These ambiguities pervade not only *Epithalamion* itself but extend as well to the conclusion of the sonnet sequence to which it is joined. A further look at Spenser's diction and at the closing lines of the *Amoretti* may make this observation clearer.

II

It is worth noting at the outset that Spenser systematically deepens our sense of the bride's miraculous quietude and passivity. At times, indeed, she seems removed from her surroundings in being and in time as well as in virtue. When finally she emerges from her "bowre" in full view of Spenser's richly imagined "public," he tells us she comes:

> Lyke Phoebe from her chamber of the East,
> Arysing forth to run her mighty race,
> Clad all in white, that seemes a virgin best.
> So well it her beseemes that ye would weene
> Some angell she had beene.
>   (148–153)

And a few lines later, he assures us that her physical beauty bears no comparison to her spiritual gifts: "Had ye once seene these her celestial threasures, / And unrevealed pleasures, / Then would ye wonder and her prayses sing. / That al the woods should answer and your echo ring" (200–203). Such lines establish the bride as a fit emblem of "Unspotted fayth and comely womanhood" with all the hyperbolic zeal a neoplatonic lover could wish, but they do so by quietly insisting on the inaccessibility of such perfection. At the climax of the marriage ceremony, the poet himself is momentarily baffled by his bride's perplexing reticence: "Why blush ye love to give to me your hand / The pledge of all our band?" (238–239). Not even in the wedding chamber itself does Spenser permit our sense of her dramatic detachment to lapse. In some measure it is traditional in epithalamia that the bride be ceremonially ushered to her bed. But here again Spenser's emphasis falls less on the dignity of ceremony than on the relationship between the action taking place around the bride and the conspicuous stillness of the bride herself:

Spenser does allow us easy + only the threshold

Now bring the Bryde into the brydall boures.
Now night is come, now soone her disaray,
And in her bed her lay;
Lay her in lillies and in violets,
And silken courteins ouer her display,
And odourd sheetes, and Arras couerlets.
Behold how goodly my faire loue does ly
In proud humility;

(299–306)

The attention of the passage is equally divided between the
sensory appeal of the "boure" itself and the careful arranging
required to prepare this spectacle for viewing: now bring, now
"disaray," lay, lay, display, behold. No classical marriage song
before Spenser, not even the comparatively graphic Carmina 61
of Catullus, devotes such detail to the placing of the bride in her
bed.[7] Indeed, in virtually all of Spenser's chief predecessors, the
bridal chamber (when it is alluded to at all) may be lavishly and
joyfully decorated by attendant maids, but once the bride and
groom themselves arrive there, poet and celebrants discretely
retire. In one sense the exceptional treatment Spenser accords
this scene is wholly appropriate; this is the matrimonial climax
toward which the entire poem has directed its energies. But
Spenser's bride is not conducted to her chamber so much as she
is enshrined there. The lines have, in some measure, the solem-
nity of burial. The care which Spenser devoted to the description suggests that he may for the time being intend the tone to
reflect precisely this disturbing mixture of associations: solem-
nity and joy, earthly passion and unearthly stillness. The result
is a considerable enrichment of a conventional moment, for the
entire passage incorporates the tantalizing quality of its closing
oxymoron.

I hasten to add that matrimonial joy is certainly Spenser's
chief interest, though not necessarily his only one. Nor is his
treatment of the bride the only means he employs to enhance
the poem's suggestive power. Spenser exploits the biblical
tradition of the marriage metaphor in ways which quickly
transcend personal themes. Most students agree that *Epithalamion* celebrates the poet's wedding with Elizabeth Boyle on St.
Barnabas Day (June 11) 1594 in Cork. A. Kent Hieatt has based
his ingenious calendrical reading of the poem on these facts.[8]
Spenser alludes to the day and the place. He borrows freely

from the Song of Solomon as he describes his bride's appearance: Spenser's lines "Her paps lyke lillies budded, / Her snowie necke lyke to a marble towre," suggest the verses in Song IV: 4–5: "Thy necke is as the towre of David buylt for defense: a thousand shields hang therein, and all the targets of the strong men. Thy two breastes are as two yong roes that are twinnes, feding among the lilies."[9] I have already quoted the mild, sexual innuendo with which the poet greets the "stil Silence" of the nuptial night (353). Certainly these are the marks of an enraptured groom.

On one occasion, however, Spenser refers to his "groome" in the third person and alludes to the wedding day in language which may suggest more than simply buoyant spirits:

> Now is my loue all ready forth to come,
> Let all the virgins therefore well awayt,
> And ye fresh boyes that tend upon her groome
> Prepare your selues; for he is comming strayt.
> Set all your things in seemely good aray
> Fit for so ioyfull day,
> The ioyfulst day that euer sunne did see.
>
> (110–116)

The reference to the groom is particularly curious, for the phrasing is quite close to the prophesy of Isaiah and the exhortation of John the Baptist, crying in the wilderness, "Prepare the way of the Lord: make his pathes straight."[10] The "bridegroom" is, of course, a familiar metaphor for Jesus which the editors and translators of the Geneva Bible applied to the erotic ecstasy of the Song of Solomon, glossing it as an allegory for the "singular love of the bridegrome toward the bride. . . . Also the earnest affection of the Church which is inflamed with the love of Christ desiring to be more and more joyned to him in love, and not to be forsaken for anie spot or blemish that is in her."[11] Spenser seems to be thinking of this same gloss earlier in the poem when he urges the "Nymphes" of Mulla to tidy up before approaching his sleeping bride: "That when you come whereas my love doth lie, / No blemish she may spie" (65–66). These echoes of familiar, biblical themes and passages invariably complicate Spenser's description of his wedding day as the "joyfulst . . . that ever sunne did see." Two sorts of joy briefly mingle here: Spenser's distinctly secular and individual joy in his marriage, and the collective exultation with which Christians might be expected to greet the return of their "bridegroom." This passage, then, like the description of the bride's arrival in her marriage chamber, functions most fully when the reader's imagination is pulled in seemingly contradictory directions at once. The appeal, for us and for Spenser, is not so much in its clarity of meaning as in its flexibility.

The potentially apocalyptic overtones of biblical "epithalamia" appear to have influenced Spenser at other points in the poem as well. As the book of Revelation draws to a close, the Evangelist witnesses the beginnings of the climactic marriage between Christ and his church: "And I heard like a voyce of a great multitude, and as the voyce of manie waters, and as the voyce of strong thonderings, saying Hallelujah: for our Lord God almightie hathe reigned. Let us be glad and rejoice, and give glory to him; for the marriage of the Lamb is come, and his wife hathe made her selfe ready."[12] The joyous Choristers, shouts of "Io Hymen" which fill the firmament, and supernaturally "roring Organs" of Spenser's poem may owe something to John's explosive, heavenly music. To be sure, the festival of Revelations—if it may be viewed as "festive"—celebrates universal resurrection, the end of history, the summoning of the dead and sifting of souls. Events there encompass humanity. But on a less sweeping scale, Spenser has prepared us for this thematic richness—apocalypse, death, anticipated resurrection, reunion—in the charming, untitled song which precedes *Epithalamion* in William Ponsonby's first edition of 1594 and which is referred to in the variorum edition of Spenser's poems by the somewhat formidable term *Anacreontics.*

These eighty-or-so lines are a curious mixture of narrative threads. Spenser's chief concern appears to be with a vignette involving Cupid, Venus, and "A gentle Bee with his loud trumpet murm'ring," whose buzzing disturbs Cupid's nap:

> Whats this (quoth he) that giues so great a voyce,
>   that wakens men withall?
> In angry wize he flyes about,
>   and threatens all with corage stout.
>
> (6–9)

Venus observes that Cupid and the Bee are alike in their diminutive size and in the disproportionate pain they inflict on men. "Then eyther change thy cruelty," she charges her son, "or give lyke leave unto the fly" (20). Cupid is not inclined to be tolerant, however, and he pursues the Bee until he is stung

> The fly that I so much did scorne,
> hath hurt me with his little horne.
>   (29–30)

and runs for comfort to his mother. Nor does tearful experience teach "the wanton boy" to be merciful to men, for "since that time," the poet reports, "he wounded hath my selfe / with his sharpe dart of love" (55–56). The song closes with the poet languishing from these fresh wounds. *Epithalamion* immediately follows.

The tale is slight enough, though the Bee's loud "trumpet murm'ring" which "wakens men withall" may hint at the apocalyptic themes we have already detected in *Epithalamion*. Cupid and the Bee take up exactly sixty lines, which conclude with the poet suffering the "pining anguish" of unrequited love. Spenser has, however, introduced these sixty with twenty-two, unrelated lines in a different stanza form which allude to what appears to have been an earlier infatuation. This short preamble treats two, brief episodes. In the second and less interesting of the two, Cupid confuses the poet's "Dame" with his goddess mother, until the poet's own laughter alerts him to his error and he blushes for shame. Spenser's compliment to his lover's beauty is graceful and gallant but not much more. The two opening stanzas of the Anacreontic song, though, are less straightforward:

> In youth before I waxed old,
>   The blynd boy Venus baby,
> For want of cunning made me bold,
>   In bitter hyue to grope for honny.
>   But when he saw me stung and cry,
>   He tooke his wings and away did fly.
>
> As Diane hunted on a day,
>   She chaunst to come where Cupid lay,
>   his quiver by his head:
> One of his shafts she stole away,

And one of hers did close conuay,
  into the others stead:
  With that loue wounded my loues hart
  but Diane beasts with Cupids dart.
                                    (1–14)

This is, at most, a poetic sketch, perhaps a study for the more
elaborately treated bee sting which Cupid himself suffers a few
lines later. But the atmosphere of a comic fable, or of a gallant
compliment, is conspicuously absent. Instead, an "aged" poet
recalls a painful experience of thwarted love and then seems to
imply that the heart of his beloved was, in turn, wounded—not
by the mythical arrows which enamour but by those which kill.
Love itself is degraded by its chance lodgement in the hearts of
"beasts" and the fierce economy of the poet's vision of love's
"bitter hive" matches the paradoxical resonance of the bride's
"proud humility" in her nuptial bed. This cryptic song is so
strategically placed that Spenser appears to be teasing us with its
suggestive possibility. The story of Cupid and the Bee, indeed
Epithalamion itself, is set against a half-lit background of embit-
tered sorrow that is evoked but not quite fully expressed, as if
Spenser had sought simply to sound a note and then allow it to
fade into the texture of verse that follows. He has seen fit to
incorporate a poetic transition between his sonnets and his
marriage song which is, at best, ambiguous and which may, in
addition, announce his intention to intermingle with his more
joyful subjects some of the qualities of an elegy. Although the
narratives which Spenser presents in the *Anacreontics* are too
fragmented to provide a decisive orientation to *Epithalamion* as a
whole, they nevertheless alert the reader to the variety of
possibilities in Spenser's tone which we have been exploring in
earlier passages.
  The language with which he announces the end of the
wedding ceremony itself captures nicely the tonal complexity I
am trying to describe:

  Now al is done; bring home the bride againe,
  Bring home the triumph of our victory,
  Bring home with you the glory of her gaine,
  With ioyance bring her and with iollity.
  Neuer had man more ioyfull day then this,

> Whom heauen would heape with blis.
> Make feast therefore now all this liue long day,
> This day for euer to me holy is.
>
> (242–249)

Most commentators observe that "triumph" suggests the triumphal honors accorded to conquering generals in ancient Rome, and the abundance of classical allusion in the poem gives this reading great weight. But Spenser may have been equally concerned that readers detect his biblical sources in 1 Corinthians XV: 52–55:

> In a moment, in the twinkling of an eye at the last trumpet: for the trumpet shal blowe, and the dead shal be raised up incorruptible, and we shal be changed. For this corruptible must put on incorruption: and this mortal must put on immortality. So when this corruptible hathe put on incorruption, and this mortal hathe put on immortalitie, then shal be broght to passe the saying that is written, Death is swallowed up into victorie! O death, where is thy sting! O grave where is thy victorie!

This passage takes up a number of the metaphoric threads which we have considered here: the "trumpet murm'ring" of the troublesome little Bee, and the comical "sting" treated in the untitled song, as well as Spenser's use of "victory" in a context where a reader might conceivably be puzzled by the usage if it were not a deliberate attempt to enrich and extend a complex pattern of multiple meanings.

Moreover, Spenser's opening clause, "Now al is done," has not only a resonant finality to it which suggests doom as much as joyous fulfillment, but here too Spenser seems sensitive to biblical language. Two of the four Evangelists (Mark and Matthew) record that Jesus's last words on the cross were: "My God, My God, why hast thou forsaken me?" Luke attributes to him the less dramatic but more resigned: "Father, into thine hands I commend my spirit." With characteristic idiosyncrasy and evocative power, however, John reports that after he had "received of the vinegre" offered him by an onlooker, Jesus said simply, "It is finished." Unlike the forms of direct and public address to the Father recorded in the first three gospels, this short statement has a hushed, private quality, as if the dying man had been unwittingly overheard talking to himself.

The ever-helpful Geneva editors tell us that the words signify the beginning of the time of grace, that "all the ceremonies of the Law are ended" much as the "ceremony" described in *Epithalamion* too has just ended.[13] John overheard nearly the same sentence again in the vision reported in Chapter XVI of Revelation. After the seventh angel has poured out the seventh vial of the wrath of God, a loud voice speaking "out of the temple" says "It is done." The pattern of biblical allusion elsewhere in the poem makes it seem likely that this fateful announcement too has contributed to the diction of Spenser's marriage song. Nor does it seem at all improbable that Spenser intended his readers to respond to this admittedly broad range of sources and allusions in order that the poetry itself might touch, however lightly, upon the widest possible scope of thought and emotion. For a moment at the beginning of this climactic stanza, Spenser has evoked the image of the crucifixion with its complex sequence of imaginative corollaries: isolation, death, despair, resurrection, joy. Matrimonial joy is surely the dominant theme for Spenser's purposes, but all the others are present to some degree, even a curious sense of the singularity of the poet's experience: "Never had man more joyfull day then this. . . . This day forever *to me* holy is" (245–249 italics mine). The thematic seriousness and intensity of these first eight lines insulate them from the pagan celebration which follows to the point where the very abandon with which Spenser describes it suggests remoteness rather than involvement:

> Poure out the wine without restraint or stay,
> Poure not by cups, but by the belly full,
> Poure out to all that wull,
> And sprinkle all the postes and wals with wine,
> That they may sweat, and drunken be withall.
> Crowne ye God Bacchus with a coronall,
> And Hymen also crowne with wreathes of vine,
> And let the Graces daunce unto the rest;
> For they can doo it best:
>
> (250–258)

It seems clear that Spenser intends this picture of walls, posts, and in all likelihood dancers, covered in a "sweat" of wine to be anything but appealing.

In the following stanza, the poet exhorts the "yong men of the towne" to join the marriage celebration:

> Ring ye the bels, ye yong men of the towne,
> And leave your wonted labors for this day:
> This day is holy; doe ye write it downe,
> That ye for euer it remember may.
> This day the sunne is in his chiefest hight,
> With Barnaby the bright,
> From whence declining daily by degrees,
> He somewhat loseth of his heat and light,
> When once the Crab behind his back he sees.
> But for this time it ill ordained was,
> To chose the longest day in all the yeare,
> And shortest night, when longest fitter weare:
> Yet neuer day so long, but late would passe.
>
> (261–273)

The poet's solicitude that the day be forever remembered is an enthusiastic excess of the kind one might expect from a groom, but it carries with it as well an echo of the anxiety displayed in his earnest plea to Phoebus which we noted earlier: "Let this day let this one day be mine / Let all the rest be thine." The reflections on the summer solstice which follow are the natural and delightfully comic thoughts of a newly-wedded lover, eager for night to fall. But Spenser captures in them a sense of regret and fatality too, for from the height of the solstice the sun is ever "declining daily by degrees," losing heat and light. The final line in the passage, "Yet neuer day so long, but late would passe," serves equally well as the consolation of an impatient husband and as a sober reminder that days, youth, beauty, life, happiness—all, like the waning year, share the mortal property of "passing." Spenser's language in these two decisive stanzas is capable of uniting the narrative of his marriage day, a meditation on "sad Time," and a vision of heavenly triumph in a single, complex, and satisfying poetic performance.

III

The final lines of the poem call upon Juno, Hebe, Hymen, and Cinthia, asking that the new marriage be fruitful. Until "the chaste wombe" be filled "with tymely seed," the poet's songs and woodland echoes will cease. Certainly Spenser's recent marriage to Elizabeth Boyle has reasserted its claim here as his chief theme. But the richness of allusion which we have found operating elsewhere in the poem has by no means abated. The wedding night, which Spenser welcomes at long last, holds uniquely redemptive as well as romantic promise. Not only does night's "sable mantle" conceal the eager lovers (if one can imagine Spenser's bride "eager"), but it "defrays" the day's labor:

> Now welcome night, thou night so long expected,
> That long daies labour doest at last defray,
> And all my cares, which cruell love collected,
> Hast sumd in one, and cancelled for aye:
> Spread thy broad wing ouer my loue and me,
> That no man may vs see,
> And in thy sable mantle vs enwrap,
> From fear of perill and foule horror free.
>
> (315–322)

In light of the use made of religious themes elsewhere, one can hardly avoid the conclusion here—and perhaps again a few lines later when the poet prays that "the chaste wombe" may breed "our comfort"—that Spenser intends the lines to associate the groom's sense of peaceful release with the sense of collective "release" promised by the cancellation of human sin, "sumd in one" man and redeemed by sacrifice. The "perills" and "foule horrors" to which the poet refers seem, after all, a far more serious menace to sinners rather than to newlyweds. The passage invokes a species of peace which reaches far beyond the boundaries of a marriage song. The final, complete stanza gives these hints explicit, powerful treatment:

> And ye high heauens, the temple of the gods,
> In which a thousand torches flaming bright

Doe burne, that to vs wretched earthly clods
In dreadful darknesse lend desired light;
And all ye powers which in the same remayne,
More than we men can fayne,
Poure out your blessing on us plentiously,
And happy influence vpon us raine,
That we may raise a large posterity,
Which from the earth, which they may long possesse,
With lasting happinesse,
Vp to your haughty pallaces may mount,
And for the guerdon of theyr glorious merit
May heauenly tabernacles there inherit,
Of blessed Saints for to increase the count.
So let vs rest, sweet love, in hope of this,
And cease till then our tymely joyes to sing,
The woods no more vs answer, nor our eccho ring.

                                        (409–426)

The poet becomes, in effect, a second Adam, raising up a new
generation of men to take their proper places, not among
earthly creatures, but among saints and angels. The lines are a
sweeping expansion of the marriage theme on a scale compara-
ble with Genesis. Spenser seems, indeed, to refer to Genesis
some lines earlier when he recalls a moment when Jove lay with
Night itself "And begot Majesty" (331). The reference has
puzzled readers seeking a source in classical mythology.[14] But
by making the poetically commonplace substitution of Jove for
Jehovah, Spenser may well be alluding to the first moments of
the creation when "darkenes was upon the deep" and God said,
"Let there be light." Here surely are Spenser's transcendent
partners: God and darkness, Jove and Night. The fusion of the
marriage narrative with the most fundamental of religious texts
is in many ways a logical outgrowth of the treatment Spenser
has given throughout the poem to critical passages from Revelation and the crucifixion story. The confidence he places in his
redemptive vision explains the nearly magical sense of progres-
sive quiet he is able to obtain from a long list of night distur-
bances:

Let no lamenting cryes, nor dolefull teares,
Be heard all night within nor yet without:

Ne let false whispers, breeding hidden feares,
Breake gentle sleepe with misconceived dout.
Let no deluding dreames, nor dreadful sights
Make sudden sad affrights;
Ne let housefyres, nor lightnings helpelesse harmes,
Ne let the Pouke, nor other evill sprights,
Ne let mischivous witches with theyr charmes,
Ne let hob Goblins, names whose sence we see not,
Fray us with things that be not.

(334–344)

The more nuisances and superstitious terrors he mentions, the less insistent, less menacing and less audible, they become. Their very jumble is comically reassuring: false whispers, lamenting "cryes," and "housefyres" are lumped in with hobgoblins, "shriech oules," "croking" frogs, and the Pouke. Spenser has a melodic power over these singers of "drery accents." Out of their names he makes a kind of lullaby, the reiterated admonition "ne let" having something like the effect of a simple phrase or tune soothingly repeated over and over to calm a child.

I have, perhaps, belabored Spenser's jocund poem with undue scriptural zeal. But this discussion seems to me to be necessary for a fuller appreciation of the range of the verse. *Epithalamion* is by no means an allegory of the Christian pilgrimage. But Spenser is capable of enriching its language by incorporating precisely the sort of textual depth out of which allegory might be made. In this respect, the well-known ambiguities of the envoy are completely in harmony with the spirit of the poem as a whole:

Song made in lieu of many ornaments,
With which my loue should duly have bene dect,
Which cutting off through hasty accidents,
Ye would not stay your dew time to expect,
But promist both to recompens,
Be vnto her a goodly ornament,
And for short time an endlesse moniment.

(427–433)

The verse is undeniably difficult, partly because in it Spenser's syntax is unusually dense and partly because in these lines he re-establishes the ambiguous undertones which the restful, and finally prophetic, stanzas immediately preceding them have momentarily eclipsed. The word "moniment" alone is enough to trouble a scrupulous reader much as the allusion to Orpheus does at the poem's outset. But the envoy's complexity involves more than a single, problematic word. Spenser begins by addressing his "goodly" song but describing the "ornaments" for which the song itself (so he claims) is at best an inadequate substitution. The pronoun "which" in both cases seems to refer to these unrendered gifts, though its antecedent is by no means clear. The ornaments themselves, of course, are inanimate objects of the poet's will; they cannot of their own accord cut off "through hasty accidents." Nor is it reasonable to believe that Spenser means that his song itself is incomplete—that the music of *Epithalamion* "would not stay" its "dew time." I think it is plain enough that the poem explores its multiple subjects fully and closes only after having realized its greatest promise, foretold a glorious future, and come to rest.

It seems to me likely, then, that in the wistful, fourth line, "Ye would not stay your dew time to expect," Spenser is addressing neither his poem nor the ornaments for which it is a replacement, but a nameless listener who proved mysteriously unable to follow the song to its conclusion. The sense of human absence is pervasive here, just as in the first stanza of *Epithalamion* the woodland echoes gave fresh intensity to the poet's solitude and to the role of his song as "recompens." The phrasing of this compensatory thought itself is the poem's closing ambiguity, for the envoy's final line can convey futility as well as fulfillment. Under the restrictive influence of "short," the promise implicit in "endlesse" loses much of its consolatory power. Once again the imagination of the reader is confronted with subtly competing claims: a sense of limitation and the expectation of triumph, sadness and a profound contentment. Spenser appears to strive for a mixture of associations that, like an unusually complex musical chord, satisfies most deeply because of its fullness.

Milton's memorable Sonnet XXIII touches many of the same themes in language strikingly similar to that of *Epithalamion*:

Methought I saw my late espoused Saint
  Brought to me like Alcestis from the grave,
  Whom Jove's great Son to her glad Husband gave,
  Rescu'd from death by force though pale and faint.
Mine as whom washt from spot of childbed taint,
  Purification in the old Law did save,
  And such, as yet once more I trust to have
  Full sight of her in Heaven without restraint,
Came vested all in white, pure as her mind:
  Her face was veil'd, yet to my fancied sight,
  Love, sweetness, goodness, in her person shin'd
So clear, as in no face with more delight.
  But O, as to embrace me she inclin'd,
  I wak'd, she fled, and day brought back my night.[15]

Milton's sonnet is indisputably elegiac—a "marriage poem" of sorts, interwoven with a lament on human mortality and a vision of otherworldly recompense. Spenser's poem incorporates such qualities only as part of its background, part of the network of diverse associations to which C. S. Lewis calls our attention. But in the sonnet's compressed space, Milton has dramatized the identical spiritual predicament which pervades *Epithalamion*: a fragile balance between the powerful appeal of life and an experience of the ephemeral nature of human beauty.

Vassar College

NOTES

1. C. S. Lewis, *Studies in Medieval and Renaissance Literature* (Cambridge: Cambridge University Press, 1966), p. 130.

2. For a review of the critical opinion on *Epithalamion* see *The Works of Edmund Spenser: A Variorum Edition, Minor Poems*, 2 vols. Greenlaw *et al.*, eds. (Baltimore: Johns Hopkins University Press, 1954), II, 645ff. Since the publication of the *Variorum* edition, the most noteworthy work on *Epithalamion* in particular has been that of A. Kent Hieatt, *Short Time's Endless Monument* (New York: Columbia University Press, 1960), and the work of Enid Welsford cited below, Note 4. Robert S. Miola has commented recently on the *Anacreontics* in "Spenser's *Anacreontics*—A Mythological Metaphor," *Studies in Philology*, 77 (1980), pp. 50–66. Hereafter the *Variorum* edition will be cited as *Poems*.

3. I have used the text of *Epithalamion* and the *Anacreontics* in *Spenser, Poetical Works*, J. C. Smith and E. de Selincourt, eds. (London: Oxford University Press, 1912), pp. 580–584. All line numbers in parentheses refer to this edition.

4. Enid Welsford, *Spenser, Fowre Hymnes, Epithalamion: A Study of Edmund Spenser's Doctrine of Love* (Oxford: Basil Blackwell, 1967), p. 173. Welsford finds the allusion to Orpheus in the Georgics, IV, 464–466: "But [Orpheus], solacing love's anguish with his holow shell, sang of thee, sweet wife, of thee to himself . . . of thee as day declined." Perhaps a more probable source for Spenser's allusion is in Boethius's *The Consolation of Philosophy*. At the conclusion of Book III, Lady Philosophy retells the story of the loss of Eurydice: "Long ago the Thracian poet, Orpheus, mourned for his dead wife. With his sorrowful music he made the woodland dance and rivers stand still." The line from Boethius may have suggested to Spenser his echoing woods. See *The Consolation of Philosophy*, trans. Richard Green (Indianapolis: Bobbs-Merrill, 1962), pp. 73–74.

5. Some years ago Douglas Hamer inferred, largely on the basis of the Latin letters of Gabriel Harvey to Spenser, that Spenser himself had married sometime early in 1580, and may have begun composing *Epithalamion* to honor this first marriage, more than fourteen years earlier than the date to which the poem is customarily assigned. The evidence, though interesting, is very slight. See Douglas Hamer, "Spenser's Marriage" in *Review of English Studies*, 7 (1931), 271–290.

6. The editors of *Poems* have noted the indebtedness to Revelation in one or two lines, but no commentator to my knowledge has examined the poem's biblical sources as a systematic theme.

7. See *Catullus, Tibullus and Pervigilium Veneris* in the Loeb Classical Library Edition, trans. F. W. Cornish (Cambridge, Mass.: Harvard University Press, 1914), pp. 69–85.

8. A. Kent Hieatt, *Short Time's Endless Monument* (New York: Columbia University Press, 1960).

9. *The Geneva Bible: A Facsimile of the 1560 Edition*, Lloyd E. Berry, ed. (Madison: University of Wisconsin Press, 1969). All biblical citations are to the Geneva edition. I have silently modernized the sixteenth-century usage by adding consonants where the Geneva edition only employs diacritical marks.

10. See Isaiah 40:3 and Mark 1:3.

11. See the prefixed "Argument" to the Song of Solomon in the Geneva edition cited above.

12. Revelation 19:6–7.

13. See the marginal gloss in the Geneva edition, John 19:30.

14. Enid Welsford, *Spenser, Fowre Hymnes, Epithalamion: A Study of Edmund Spenser's Doctrine of Love* (Oxford: Basil Blackwell, 1967), p. 183.

15. John Milton, *Complete Poems and Major Prose*, ed. Merritt Y. Hughes (New York: Odyssey Press, 1957), p. 170.

II

SETH LERER

The Rhetoric of Fame:
Stephen Hawes's Aureate Diction

ONE TENDS to think of aureate diction as an embarrassing experiment in the history of English literature. Ever since Lewis labelled it a feature of the "Drab Age," critics have seen aureation as the product of fifteenth-century misreadings of Chaucer and as evidence of the warped aesthetics of John Lydgate and his followers.[1] In this spirit Alice Miskimin, in her recent book on the Renaissance Chaucer, considers Stephen Hawes's *Pastime of Pleasure* (1509), "one of the most crippled and myopic of early sixteenth century allegorical poems."[2] Readers have found in Hawes little else but slavish imitation of the already derivative Lydgate, and have seen in his defense of aureation a meager excuse for verbosity.[3] I would argue, however, that Hawes differs significantly from his fifteenth century predecessor in his theory of poetry and his practice of aureation. For Lydgate, words such as "enlumyn," "aureate," and "goldyn" signify the poet's power to reform and beautify his world. The "sugrid aureat licour" which falls from the Muses— or from God—inspires the poet to write. *Endyting* for Lydgate presupposed a two-fold process of illumination: while the poet received divine enlightenment in order to write, his task was to *enlumyn* his readership.[4]

While Lydgate's aureate terms were designed primarily to communicate a sense of inspiration, Hawes's aureation had a much different purpose. Lydgate was interested in the processes of poetry writing—in the relationship between God and the Muses and the poet. Hawes was interested in the effects of poetry—in the relationship of the poet and his reader. If Lydgate was fascinated with problems of inspiration, Hawes was possessed by problems of preservation. He developed an aureate diction which stressed the preserving power of poetry, its ability to make a poem's subject memorable and its author immortal.

Two historical events separated Lydgate and Hawes and were responsible for this shift. One was the discovery of complete texts of Cicero's philosophical works, and the ensuing humanist preoccupation with public service and literary fame.[5] The second, complementary development was the invention of printing.[6] What Hawes did was to incorporate Cicero's psychological and artistic metaphors for creation and perception into the technical language of book making. He developed a language of "impression," a language which linked remembering, writing, and printing as physical processes which could preserve a poet's work and ensure his fame. It is this term "impression" which Hawes would have also found in Chaucer, and which would have given him an insight into Chaucerian poetic and psychological theory denied to Lydgate.

The language of impression developed well before the advent of movable type. To Cicero, patterns of understanding were impressed on the mind as notions or concepts.[7] To John of Salisbury (*ca.* 1115–1180), the images of things were, in effect, impressed on the soul; in this way, sensation produced imagination.[8] This imagery was also to be found in Boethius' *Consolation of Philosophy*, and it no doubt entered the English language through Chaucer's *Boece*. In Book V, metrum 4 of the *Consolation* Boethius restates Stoic perception theory. The Stoics held that the mind was passive, merely receiving impressions from outside as a wax tablet receives printed words. In Chaucer's translation, the Stoics,

> wenden that ymages and sensibilities . . . weren enprientid into soules from bodyes withoute-forth . . . ; ryght as we ben wont somtyme by a swift poyntel to fycchen lettres enprientid in the smothness or pleyness of the table of wex. . . .   (Robinson, pp. 379–380)[9]

In the *Merchant's Tale*, this psychology explains January's thoughts on his impending marriage: "Heigh fantasye and curious bisynesse / Fro day to day gan in the soule impresse" (1577–1578). It explains how Criseyde's image remains fixed in Troilus' mind: "That in his hertes botme gan to stiken / Of hir his fixe and depe impressioun" (*Troilus and Criseyde*, I, 297–

298). The imagery appears repeatedly in that poem to offer a
coherent psychological vocabulary for experience and sensation.[10]

Hawes develops these metaphors to explain everything from
the workings of memory to the aesthetics of poetic diction. It is
with human and artistic memory that Hawes is fascinated
throughout the *Pastime of Pleasure*. In his extended treatment of
the five parts of classical oratory, the first such treatment in
English, he devotes great length to *memoria*.[11] But Hawes is
apparently not interested in ordinary remembrance—what classical theory called "natural memory"—but rather in mnemono-
technics, the art of memory celebrated by Cicero and Quintil-
ian and explained for modern readers by Frances Yates.[12] Here,
physical *loci* are used to retain parts of a speech or order an
argument. Hawes integrates the technical mnemonic language
into his larger metaphorical structures. He sees the memory as a
grounde on which *ymages* are placed, and these words translated
the *loci* and *imagines* of the *ad Herennium*.[13] His concern is not
with forensic oratory but with poetic narrative. Each image is a
sygnyfycacyon (1255) of both narrative and its moral import.
Implicit in this theory is the view of literature as a storehouse of
moral exempla; recollection is thus imbued with deep ethical
significance.[14]

In his explanation, Hawes preserves the imagery of writing
and impressions:

> So is enprynted / in his propre mynde
> Euery tale / with hole resemblaunce
> By this ymage / he dooth his mater fynde
> Eche after other / withouten varyaunce
> (1261–1264).[15]

The mind becomes a piece of paper or an engraver's plate on
which images, like words, are inscribed. When the poem's
hero, Grande Amoure, beholds the vision of his lady, he notes:

> But with my heed / I made her a token
> Whan she was gone / inwardly than wrought
> Vpon her beaute / my mynde retentyfe
> Her goodly fygure / I graued in my thought
> (1505–1508)

Her image remains "registered well in my remembraunce" (1753), like an entry in a log. He repeatedly notes how her "goodly countenaunce and fayre fygure" remain "engraued" in his mind (3881–3882). Later in the poem, Grande Amoure describes the Tower of Chivalry,

> That all of Iasper full wonderly was wrought
> As ony man can prynte in his thought
> And foure ymages aboue the toure there were
>   (3000–3002)

This passage states a central tenet of Hawes's aesthetic theory and his justification of aureation. Poetry and memory function as engravings or paintings, for they all store visual images. He notices golden images of lions on shields, whose pictures, like the explanatory "scrypture" beneath them, are "grauen" (4287–4290). As "symylytudes" (939, 985), poems and pictures represent figures, stories, or ideas. The figure of Atlas, in one case, "exemplifies" certain moral virtues. But more importantly, it is the story of Atlas, preserved in poetry, which provides that example. Hawes's defense of exemplary fable shares with Cicero a common critical vocabulary in which the terms of artistic representation describe literary processes.

Cicero employed the terms of art and art criticism to characterize a variety of literary and rhetorical concepts, from the principles of poetic imitation and pedagogic instruction to a defense of literature itself.[16] In *De Oratore* he has Antonius express the growth and development of the novice orator in words taken from the techniques of the plastic arts. The teacher molds the pupil as a sculptor works clay or casts bronze, and his words, *limare* and *adfingere*, refer to the processes of filing away irregularities in metal or of shaping a sculpture by adding clay.[17] But, from the student's viewpoint, Antonius shows how he must portray the model through practice, and the words *exprimere* and *effingere*—die casting or hand-shaping in wax— bring out the implicit associations of rhetor and artist Cicero had maintained throughout his writings.[18] Familiar to a Renaissance readership, and cited by Skelton, is the famous association of the sculptor Zeuxis with which the young Cicero opened Book II of *De Inventione*.[19] Elsewhere, poetry is defended in the terms of artistic imitation. Literature offers models of virtue, and readers may emulate literary ideals to formulate their own notions of character.[20] "How many pictures of high endeavor," he argues in *Pro Archia*, "the great authors of Greece and Rome have drawn for our use, and bequeathed to us not only for our contemplation, but for our emulation." [21] Literature, he concludes, surpasses the plastic arts, for a statue offers only a likeness (*imagine*) of the body, not of the soul. A great man should prefer to be remembered through writings, rather than portraits, for, "How much more anxious should we be to bequeathe an effigy of our minds and characters, wrought by supreme talent." [22] In the recently reconstructed *De Officiis*, fifteenth-century readers would have found Cicero's defense of exemplary fable also couched in these terms. Hypothetical narratives, he asserts, present *exempla* of moral conduct.[23] Human laws, too, appear in this language: "We possess no substantial, lifelike image of true law and genuine justice." All we are capable of is a mere outline sketch which imitates models presented by nature and truth.[24] Philosophical fables and human laws thus share an essentially imitative purpose and can be characterized in the language of artistic replication.

Hawes was clearly alive to the resonances of this artistic vocabulary when pressed into the service of literary criticism. The very title of his *Example of Vertu* (1503–04, printed 1509) plays off the old, Ciceronian sense of an *exemplum* as a literary representation, and the opening lines of Hawes's prologue reinforce the associations of moral literature, imitation, and book-making.[25] When, in the *Pastime of Pleasure*, he considers the purpose of poetry as "moralyzing the symylytude," he also focuses on artistic replication and interpretation. Poems are like pictures for both make resemblances. To take one brief case, Hell is presented "in terryble fygure" (1010). Cerberus survives in literature as the "deflouered pycture" (1013). Myths and texts are "fatall pyctures" (1028), and poets "depaynt" (1045) character and narrative. In an extended passage, Hawes links poetry and painting with history, using a classical example received, no doubt, through Chaucer.

> By the aduertence / of theyr storyes olde
> The fruyte werof / we maye full well beholde
> Depaynted on aras / how in antyquyte
> Dystroyed was / the grete cyte of Troye.
> (1077–1080)[26]

These theoretical concerns explain one repeated narrative feature of the *Pastime*. Everywhere he goes, Grande Amoure encounters painted towers, walls, or objects. Again and again, gold towers "enameled aboute / With noble storyes / . . . do appere without" (272–273). He sees a "famous story / well pyctured . . . / In the fayre hall / vpon the aras" (475–476); or "lytell turrets / with ymages of golde" (365). The Tower of Chivalry is

> Gargylde with beestes in sundry symylytude
> And many turrettes aboue the toures hye
> With ymages was sette full meruaylouslye.
>
> (2959–2961)

When he enters the tower, Grande Amoure sees, "of golde so pure / Of worthy Mars the meruaylous pycture / There was depaynted all aboute the wall" (3023–3025). What Hawes may have found in Chaucer's *Knight's Tale* (with its painted temples), in his *Book of the Duchesse* (with the room painted with scenes from the *Roman de la Rose*), or in the towers of the earlier English romances *Sir Orfeo* and *Floris and Blauncheflour*, he has transformed into a statement about narrative and poetry.[27] Grande Amoure has become a reader of images and signs. He is forced to interpret: "Whan I the scrypture ones or twyes hadde rede / And knewe therof all the hole effecte" (4298–4299). In addition to his didactic instruction at the hands of the Liberal Arts, and on top of his education in the field of battle, the protagonist is confronted with narrative images which he must decipher. The brilliant gold and enamel imagery of these pictures echoes the same vocabulary Hawes had used to describe poetic diction. His language is "Depaynted with golde / harde in construccyon" (912). Like Lydgate, Hawes has literalized the *colores* and *flores rhetorici* into literal colors and images. But unlike Lydgate, who had considered the poet's purpose "to adourne and make fair . . . peint and florishe,"[28] Hawes has gone a step further. Painting and poetry share a common aureate quality. In a deep sense, both arts have a single purpose. They are recepticals of history and fame. The destruction of Troy painted on the Tower of Chivalry depicts "noble actes to reygne memoryall" (3027). In the encapsulated biographies of great heroes at the poem's end, Hawes stresses how their deeds survived in written books and shared oral history: "I spred his dedes in tonges of memory," Fame says of Judas Machabee (5543).

For Hawes what makes aureate diction a suitable vehicle for poetry is both its luster and its physical hardness, and I want to explore one specific case of this theory in action. In the Godfrey Gobelive section of the poem, Hawes dramatizes the distinctions between the language of poetry and that of the common man. The grotesque dwarf Godfrey joins Grande Amoure after his excursion from the Tower of Chivalry. From his head to his toes, Godfrey is a figure of vice and corruption according to the standard iconographies (3494 ff.). When he addresses the knight, he spouts forth in the rude accents of his native Kent:

> Sotheych quod he whan I cham in kent
> At home I cham thogh I be hyther sent
> I cham a gentylman of moche noble kynne
> Thogh Iche be cladde in a knaues skynne.
>   (3510–3513)

This bit of philological naturalism, on a par with Chaucer's *Reeve's Tale*, reifies the theoretical statements about language Hawes makes through Lady Rhetoric.[29] Godfrey's rude provincialisms stand in sharp contrast both to the courtly discourse of Grande Amoure and the aureate diction of the poem's narrative. Godfrey's dialect becomes a skin of language far more revealing than the "knaues skynne" which he claims shields his gentlemanliness. As an allegorical figure of "false report," Godfrey represents an impediment to the knight's achievement of love and fame. But as a physical embodiment of a mundane language, the dwarf's appearance reveals the linguistic impediments to decorous communication in society.

Faced with such language in everyday speech, Hawes seeks through his poetry to refine and purify diction. His statement that aureate diction works by analogy, "As we do gold / from coper purify" (916), also returns us to the concrete nature of his imagery. In fact, Hawes seems possessed by the physicality of writing: by the feel of the pen, the touch of an engraving, or the weight of a book. Such an attitude informs his transformation of the tropes of rhetoric into palpable entities. Hawes turns the *loci* of invention into the places along Grande Amoure's pilgrimage; he turns the *sedes* of argument into the thrones on which Lady Rhetoric and Grammar sit. By making the world of words a world of things, Hawes suggests that allegorical poetry, like allegorical painting, is a process of making the imaginary real. He transforms the mental activity of education into the physical motion of the hero's journey, and in this respect the goals of his enterprise dovetail with the theories of "place logic" which developed towards the end of the fifteenth century. Ong has described in detail the ways in which this theory of argument spatialized thought. Mental activity became transformed into physical motion, as the act of finding an argument (*inventio*) became a physical search. In the same year that Hawes published the *Pastime of Pleasure* a Strassbourg printer brought out Murner's "Mnemonic Logic," a student handbook which presented on the page physical systems of reasoning and remembering. The student would move through various places of argument, progressing by steps to mastery of the topics. Ong has characterized Murner's text in words which, I think, pointedly apply to the movement of Hawes's poem.

> Murner's allegory itself is not pure allegory but a device for fixing his symbols in mnemonically servicable space. . . . The chief psychological implement is a sense of diagrammatic structure, strongly influenced by the mnemonic tradition which is evident from . . . his thinking of his whole book as a series of places moved through by steps.   (Ong, *Ramus,* p. 89)

The progress of the student mirrors the progress of Hawes's lover. The various places to which Grande Amoure arrives become, in this schema, imaginative seats of thought and argument. The literalizing of rhetorical method, the concretizing of aureate terms, and the attention given to mnemonic theory all point to Hawes's preoccupation with the spatial nature of thought. The experience of vision fixes everything literally on the page and figuratively in the book of memory.

By turning poetry into a seen thing, Hawes restates a fundamental link between literary activity and the pursuit of fame. With the advent of printing, his structures and metaphors are given new immediacy. The meaning of *impression* now moves from the psychological to the typographical. While the *OED* cites a 1508 quotation as the first use, in English, of "impress" meaning "to print," the Latin word *impressor* was early on used to characterize printers.[30] Fifteenth-century colophons record *impressit* as the word for "printed."[31] For Hawes, "impressions" become literal when, at the *Pastime*'s end, he echoes the envoi at the close of Chaucer's *Troilus*. Here, the poet fears not the misapprehensions of scribes, but, for the first time (*OED, s.v.* impression, 3), the typographical errors of printers:

> Go lytel boke I pray god the saue
> From mysse metrynge by wronge Impressyon.
> (5803–5804)

The implications of this rewriting signal an important shift in English literary attitudes. No longer are we in the manuscript culture of a Chaucer or a Petrarch, who could complain of scribal infidelity. Their texts, as Gerald Bruns acutely observes, remain "open" in that they are constantly subject to the vagaries of copyists. In print culture, though, texts end firmly and insistently "closed": once the author has approved their form, they may be reduplicated intact.[32] Elizabeth Eisenstein summarizes this new development from one very specific point of view: the idea of the errata sheet. She notes "a new capacity to locate textual errors with precision and to transmit this information simultaneously to scattered readers" (p. 80). Hawes thus calls attention to two key features of print culture and its impact on literary dissemination. First, books can be standardized and reproduced at will; corruption, when it does occur, results not from scribal diversity but from uniformly reprinting a single error.

Second, there is the preserving power of print. Hawes seeks to make "grete bokes to be in memory" (5815) like those of his master Lydgate. He attempts to preserve poetic fame not simply through writing but through publishing; and if he wishes to remain famous with Chaucer, it will be "in prynted bokes" (1337). His arguments counter the stance of his contemporary Johann Tritheimus, who in the last decades of the fifteenth century was busy praising scribes at the expense of the new print technology. Tritheimus claimed that manuscripts on vellum would last one thousand years, while paper books

would survive a mere two hundred.[33] But in lauding manuscript culture, Tritheimus misses the point, and he offers a
convenient foil for Hawes. The point, of course, is not the
survivability of a single book but the reduplicability of that
book. Hawes recognizes that in replication lies immortality,
and it is in this concept that the old Ciceronian model dovetails
with the new technology to speak directly to the Humanists'
renewed sense of the pursuit of personal distinction. The greatest guarantee of posthumous honor is literary achievement. The
imagery of concrete artifacts appears in Vergerius's *Ingenius
Moribus*, in a passage which addresses Hawes's own central
metaphors: "With a picture, an inscription, a coin, books share
a kind of immortality. In all these, memory is, as it were, made
permanent."[34]

The advent of printing could only reinforce this cultural
predisposition. Eisenstein has suggested that "the drive for
fame itself may have been affected by print-made immortality"
(p. 123). What she labels the "duplicative powers of print" (p.
113) are at the fore of Hawes's restatement of heroic fame at the
end of the *Pastime*. Hector lives "in full many bokes ryght
delycyous" (5527); Joseph's reputation is written down, "To
abyde in bokes without ony fayle" (5534); King Arthur's
worthy acts are "Perpetually for to be commendable / In ryall
bokes and Iestes Hystoriall" (5570). Finally, Lady Fame will
"cause for to be memoryall" the pilgrimage of Grande Amoure
(5586 ff.), and as she calls Dame Remembrance forth, it is clear
that this allegorical figure represents not merely memory, but
poetic writing.

> Commaundynge her ryght truely for to wryte
> Bothe of my actes and my gouernaunce
> Whiche than ryght sone began to endyte
> Of my feates of armes / in a shorte respyte
> Whose goodly storyes in tongues seuerall
> Aboute were sente for to be perpetuall.
>
> (5594–5599)

In the end, the goal of Grande Amoure's journey, and of
Hawes's energies, is the production of a text. We have witnessed the hero of the *Pastime* progress as a student and as a
reader, and with our reading, ideally, we too should grow. The

inescapable fact that Hawes writes to be printed and read, that he inscribes his imaginary reader in his own texts, leads me to conclude on a speculative note. Summarizing the developments of fifteenth-century humanism, Eisenstein implies that much of Renaissance activity was fundamentally concerned with the recovery of texts and the restructuring of educational systems around reading and writing.[35] The place of printing in such a self-consciously literate environment is thus vital to its success. In turn, any arguments about Cicero's place in this study may devolve not simply to the recovery of his texts in the early fifteenth century or the frequency of their publication at the century's close. They may also involve claims for a post-Petrarchan attempt to recapture something of the essence of "antiquity," a word which Hawes himself uses with great reverence when discussing the production and reproduction of literature.[36] There are, perhaps, two implications to this view. First, as books became staples of pedagogy, education became an instruction in the arts of reading.[37] Grande Amoure is thus a revealing transitional figure in the history of education: one of the last to sit at his masters' feet and learn by hearing; one of the first to read the signs and inscriptions which write the progress of his growth. Second, Hawes articulates for vernacular literature an attitude already established for the classics. We find at work in his contemporary Politian a new historical awareness: a growing sense of the need to preserve classical texts in classical forms and to edit the text into an edition of historical viability and authenticity.[38]

At the very least, however, we may find in Stephen Hawes a poet preeminently concerned with the concept of literary fame and with his own posthumous reputation. His central metaphors of printing and impression reinforce the idea of printed books as repositories of the memory of the poet's name. His long excurses on the triumvirate of English literature, Chaucer, Gower, and Lydgate, do more than comment on early Tudor reading tastes. Hawes attempts a fundamental statement about the canon of English literature and his own desire to be canonized. For aureate diction to become the rhetoric of fame, it was essential that Hawes find in the newly recovered works of Cicero and in the printing technology of his own day a vocabulary of replication and preservation. If his method and technique still firmly place him in the Drab Age, they also create the

environment in which a Sidney or a Spenser could look upon
this brazen world and turn it gold.[39]

Princeton University

NOTES

1. See C. S. Lewis, *English Literature in the Sixteenth Century Excluding
Drama*, Oxford History of English Literature, Volume III (Oxford: Claren-
don Press, 1954); Arthur Heiserman, *Skelton and Satire* (Chicago: University
of Chicago Press, 1961), pp. 199–200, 241–242; and the earlier study, Vere L.
Rubel, *Poetic Diction in the English Renaissance* (New York: Modern Language
Association of America, 1941), esp. pp. 31–46.
2. Alice S. Miskimin, *The Renaissance Chaucer* (New Haven, Conn.: Yale
University Press, 1975), p. 166.
3. See the frequent remarks and asides in Stanley E. Fish, *John Skelton's
Poetry* (New Haven, Conn.: Yale University Press, 1965), and the extended
discussion in Elizabeth J. Sweeting, *Early Tudor Criticism* (Oxford: Basil
Blackwell, 1940), pp. 1–22. For a more sympathetic view of Hawes, see the
Introduction to Florence W. Gluck and Alice B. Morgan, eds., *Stephen Hawes:
The Minor Poems*, EETS 271 (London: Oxford University Press, 1974), pp.
xxxi–xlvii.
4. For a comprehensive assessment of Lydgate's aureate diction, see Lois
Ebin, "Lydgate's Views on Poetry," *Annuale Mediaevale*, 18 (1977), 76–105.
Ebin notes how Lydgate uses the word "enlumyn" to refer specifically to
religious inspiration. He prays to God in the *Life of St. Edmund*, "Send doun of
grace thi licour aureate / Which enlumynyth these rhetoriciens," and Ebin
rightly calls attention to Lydgate's development of the definition of inspiration from Chaucer's *Parson's Tale*, "to illuminate or enlighten the heart or
mind" (Ebin, p. 79, n. 7).
I would add here that Hawes also develops a vocabulary for inspiration
based on another Chaucerian moment, the opening to the *General Prologue*,
especially the lines: "Of which vertu engendred is the flour; / Whan Zephirus
eek with his sweete breeth / Inspired hath in every holt and heeth" (A, 4–6).
(All quotations from Chaucer will be from F. N. Robinson, ed., *The Complete
Works of Geoffrey Chaucer* [Boston: Houghton, Mifflin, 1957]). Hawes transforms these lines on two occasions into a metaphor for poetic inspiration.
They provide him with a central paradigm (*i.e.*, breath as spirit) for expressing one aspect of his poetic theory and his allegorical descriptions. Thus,
Grande Amoure, in the *Pastime of Pleasure*, enters the archetypal love-garden,
which has become:

> Lyke a place of pleasure / most solacyous
> Encensynge out / the aromatyke odoure
> Of zepherus brethe / which that euery floure
> Through his fume / dothe always engendre.
> (64–70)

Similarly, the expression of knowledge granted by Lady Astronomy is described:

> She encensed out her aromatyke odoure
> The brethe of zepherus encreased the floure
> A myddes the medow fayre resplendysshaunt
> Was a pauylyon ryght hye and quadraunt.
>
> (2671–2674)

It is clear that Hawes replaces Chaucer's word "inspired" with his own unique use of the word "encense." According to the *OED*, this term meant both a literal breathing out of vapor or odor, and, more importantly, an enlightening movement, "to bring to sense, to inform or give knowledge" (*s. v.* insense, vb.). Both meanings were common in fifteenth century usage, and the *OED* cites Hawes surprisingly frequently to illustrate these meanings. A 1486 quote, however, reads, "Eternal sapience did insense me," suggesting that the word could, like Lydgate's *enlumyn*, carry a strong sense of divine or poetic inspiration and successfully translate Chaucer's *inspired*.

5. Among the many general studies on this subject, the ones which have contributed most to my argument include Roberto Weiss, *Humanism in England During the Fifteenth Century* (Oxford: Blackwell, 3rd. ed., 1963); Daniel Javitch, *Poetry and Courtliness in Renaissance England* (Princeton, N.J.: Princeton University Press, 1978). On the Ciceronian revival, see especially Hannah H. Gray, "Renaissance Humanism: The Pursuit of Eloquence," *Journal of the History of Ideas*, 24 (1963), 497–514; Hans Baron, "Cicero and the Roman Civic Spirit in the Middle Ages and Early Renaissance," *Bulletin of the John Rylands Library*, 22 (1938), 72–97. For a view countering Baron's thesis on Civic Humanism, and the role of Cicero in the process, see Jerrold E. Seigel, *Rhetoric and Philosophy in Renaissance Humanism* (Princeton, N.J.: Princeton University Press, 1968), esp. pp. 3–30. For one chronicle of the rediscovery of Ciceronian texts, see *Two Renaissance Book Hunters: The Letters of Poggius Bracciolini to Nicolaus de Nicoli*, trans. Phyllis G. Gordan (New York: Columbia University Press, 1974).

6. See Walter Ong, S.J., *Ramus, Method and the Decay of Dialogue* (Cambridge, Mass.: Harvard University Press, 1957), especially his remarks on the spatialization of thought and argument as a response to printing, pp. 83–119; Elizabeth Eisenstein, *The Printing Press as an Agent of Change* (Cambridge: Cambridge University Press, 1979), especially pp. 43–159; 163–225.

7. ". . . quarum rerum nullum subest corpus, est tamen quaedam conformatio insignita et impressa intellegentia, quam notionem voco," *Topica*, 27 (ed. and trans., H. M. Hubbel [Cambridge, Mass.: Harvard University Press, 1927]).

8. Echoing the Aristotelian theory behind Cicero's above statement, John of Salisbury writes, "Hanc autem asserit Aristotiles anime passionem, eo quod, dum exercetur, rerum imagines anime imprimantur; quod si una pro altera imprimatur, pro errore, quo fallitur in iudio, fallax uel falsa opinio nominatur" (From the *Metalogicon*, IV, 11, ed. C. C. I. Webb [Oxford: Clarendon Press, 1929], p. 177).

9. Boethius's Latin reads:

> Quondam porticus attulit
> Qui sensus et imagines
> Credant mentibus imprimi,
> Mos est aequore paginae,
> Obscuros nimium senes
> E corporibus extimis
> Ut quondam celeri stilo
> Quae nullas habeat notas
> Pressas figere litteras.

(ed. and trans., H. F. Stewart, E. K. Rand, revised S. J. Tester [Cambridge, Mass.: Harvard University Press, 1973]).

10. See the listing in J. S. P. Tatlock, ed., *A Concordance to the Complete Works of Geoffrey Chaucer*, (Washington, D.C.: The Carnegie Institution, 1927; rpt. Gloucester, Mass.: Peter Smith, 1963), *s. v.* Impressioun. Pandarus's advice at *Troilus*, II, 1371–1372, also uses the image. Of Love, he notes, "For in good herte it mot som routhe impresse, / To here and see the giltless in distresse."

11. This fact had been noted long ago by W. S. Howell, *Logic and Rhetoric in England, 1500–1700* (Princeton, N.J.: Princeton University Press, 1954), pp. 88 ff.

12. Frances Yates, *The Art of Memory* (Chicago: University of Chicago Press, 1966). Of the many studies capitalizing on her research, see, for example, Donald R. Howard, *The Idea of the Canterbury Tales* (Berkeley and Los Angeles: University of California Press, 1976), pp. 146–158; Grover A. Zinn, Jr., "Hugh of St. Victor and the Art of Memory," *Viator*, 5 (1974), who mentions Hawes's treatment on p. 220.

13. "Nam loci cerae aut chartae simillimi sunt, imagines litteris, dispositio et conlocatio imaginum scripturae, pronuntiatio lectioni" (*Rhetorica ad Herennium*, ed. and trans. Harry Caplan [Cambridge, Mass.: Harvard University Press, 1954], III, 30).

14. All quotations from Hawes are from W. E. Mead, ed., *The Pastime of Pleasure*, EETS O. S. 173 (London: Oxford University Press, 1928), and will be cited by line numbers in the text.

15. Earlier, Hawes had likened the selection of tales in a narrative to principles of mnemonic choice in a language reminiscent of Chaucer:

> Yf to the orature / many a sundry tale
> One after other / treatably be tolde
> Than sundry ymages / in his closed male
> Eche for a mater / he doth than well holde
> Lyke to the tale / he doth than so beholde.
> (1247–1251)

Hawes's use of the word "male" echoes Chaucer's catch phrase "unbuckle the male," used to describe the process of tale-telling (*CT*, A, 3115; X, 26). Zinn points to a passage in Hugh of St. Victor which describes a system of mnemonic *loci* by analogy to a moneychanger's purse. Hugh compares the ease with which the moneychanger reaches into his purse (*marsupium*) for his money, knowing precisely where each item is, with the alacrity and accuracy with which a man may reach into his thought to select the matter he needs to remember. The Chaucerian "male" is thus the mind as a purse. Other Middle English poets utilized Chaucer's phrase to describe tale telling (See the *MED*, *s. v.* male), notably Lydgate: "If ye shall tell youre owne tale . . . / Ye will unclose but a lytyll male, / Shewe of youre vices but a small parcele" (quoted from the *MED*).

16. Much of the following discussion develops from the material collected in Elaine Fantham, "Imitation and Evolution: The Discussion of Rhetorical Imitation in Cicero *De Oratore*, 2. 87–97 and Some Related Problems of Ciceronian Theory," *Classical Philology*, 73 (1978), 1–16. See also A. E. Douglas, "The Intellectual Background of Cicero's Rhetorica," in H. Temporini, ed., *Aufstieg und Niedergang der Römischen Welt*, I, no. 4 (Berlin: De Gruyter, 1973), especially pp. 108–115, "Art Criticism in Rhetorical Contexts." The classic statement of the theory of imitation in antiquity remains Richard McKeon, "Literary Criticism and the Concept of Imitation in Antiquity," reprinted in R. S. Crane, ed., *Critics and Criticism*, 2nd rev. edition (Chicago: University of Chicago Press, 1957), pp. 117–145.

17. Fantham, p. 14 and n. 13.

18. Fantham, p. 5 and n. 14.

19. *De Inventione*, ed. and trans., H. M. Hubbell (Cambridge, Mass.: Harvard University Press, 1927), II, i, 1–II, ii, 5. Skelton mentions the passage in the Latin gloss to one of the poems against Garnesche, A. Dyce, ed., *The Poetical Works of John Skelton* (London: Thomas Rodd, 1843), p. 126. The *De Inventione*, of course, was known throughout antiquity and the Middle Ages, and I do not mean to imply that it was one of the Humanists' recovered texts. I do wish to suggest that, only in the context of the complete Ciceronian corpus, could the imagery of the passage carry important literary and philosophical weight.

20. See Wesley Trimpi, "The Quality of Fiction," *Traditio*, 34 (1974), 31–40.

21. *Pro Archia*, 14, ed. and trans., N. H. Watts, *The Speeches of Cicero* (Cambridge, Mass.: Harvard University Press, 1965). The Latin reads: "Quam multas nobis imagines non solum ad intuendum, verum etiam ad imitandum fortissimorum virorum expressas scriptores et Graeci et Latini reliquerunt. . . ."

22. *Pro Archia*, 30. The Latin reads: "An statuas et imagines, non animorum simulacra, sed corporum, studiose multi summi homines reliquerunt, consiliorum relinquere ac virtutum nostrarum effigiem nonne multo malle debemus, summis ingeniis expressam et politam?"

23. *De Officiis*, III, ix, 39; see Trimpi, pp. 34–35.

24. *De Officiis*, III, xvii, 69, ed. and trans., Walter Miller (Cambridge, Mass.: Harvard University Press, 1913). The Latin reads: "Sed nos veri iuris germanaeque iustitiae solidam et expressam effigiem nullam tenemus, umbra et imaginibus utimur. Eas ipsas utinam sequeremur! feruntur enim ex optimis naturae et veritatis exemplis."

25. Ed. Gluck and Morgan, p. 4, 1–28.

26. Compare the opening images of the Dreamer's vision in the *House of Fame*. He sees "ymages / Of gold, stondynge in sondry stages" (121–122); "in portreyture," he sees the "figure" of Venus (131–132); finally, he beholds,

inscribed on a "table of bras" the opening lines of the *Aeneid*, and the story of the "destruction of Troye" follows (141ff.).

27. On the Medieval English traditions of wall painting and artistic visions in Romance, see John V. Fleming, "Chaucer and the Visual Arts," in D. M. Rose, ed., *New Perspectives in Chaucer Criticism* (Norman, Okla.: Pilgrim Press, 1982), pp. 121–136, and the bibliography cited therein.

28. Lydgate, *Troy Book*, II, 5029–5030 (quoted in Ebin, p. 80).

29. Comparison suggests itself with Caxton's well-known story of the Londoners trying to buy eggs in Kent, recounted in the preface to his *Eneydos* of 1490. Caxton's point is not simply philological either. He uses his observations to reflect on the diachronic and synchronic mutability of English: "And certaynly our langage now used varyeth ferre from that which was used and spoken when I was borne / For we englysshe men / ben borne under the domynacyon of the mone which is never stedfaste / but ever waverynge / wexynge one season / and waneth & decreaseth another season" (ed. W. J. B. Crotch, *The Prologues and Epilogues of William Caxton*, EETS O. S. 176 [London: Oxford University Press, 1928], p. 108). This sublunary characteristic is also echoed by Hawes, who sees Grande Amoure's courage as "lunatyke" (5270). Lady Rhetoric, too, dwells above the sublunary, mutable world of man (659–665). Thus, less than two decades apart, both Hawes and Caxton express the essential mutability of spoken English in the same local and metaphysical terms.

30. Eisenstein, p. 57, n. 52.

31. See Cora E. Lutz, "Manuscripts Copied from Printed Books," in *Essays on Manuscripts and Rare Books* (Hamden, Conn.: Archon, 1975), pp. 129–138, esp. p. 134.

32. Gerald Bruns, "The Originality of Texts in Manuscript Culture," *Comparative Literature*, 32 (1980), 113–129.

33. *In Praise of Scribes—De Laude Scriptorum*, ed. Klaus Arnold (Lawrence, Kansas: Coronado Press, 1974), p. 63. For discussions of this passage, see Eisenstein, pp. 14–15, and Howard, *Idea of the Canterbury Tales*, pp. 64–65.

34. Quoted in William H. Woodward, *Vittorino da Feltre and Other Humanist Educators* (Cambridge, Mass.: Harvard University Press, 1897), p. 105. Cicero, too, uses the language of art and physicality to distinguish true glory from popular fame. The one follows "no lofty image of virtue (*nullam eminentem effigiem virtutis*) but a shadowy phantom of glory (*sed adumbratam imaginem gloriae*)." True glory, however, "is a thing of real substance (*solida quaedam res*) and clearly wrought (*expressa*), not a phantom (*non adumbrata*)." From *Tusculan Disputations*, ed. and trans., J. E. King (Cambridge, Mass.: Harvard University Press, 1927), III, ii, 3.

35. See Eisenstein's remarks on p. 173.

36. Gluck and Morgan, p. 4, 1–7.

37. See Eisenstein, pp. 65–66.

38. For a comprehensive discussion of Politian's editorial and philological methods and his place in the history of classical scholarship, as well as for some of the larger implications of this particular study, see A. Grafton, "On the Scholarship of Politian and Its Context," *Journal of the Warburg and Courtauld Institutes*, 40 (1977), 150–188, esp. pp. 182–183.

39. An earlier version of this paper was read at the Sixteenth Congress on Medieval Studies, Kalamazoo, Michigan, 1981.

MASON TUNG

Spenser's "Emblematic" Imagery: A Study of Emblematics

*T*HAT SPENSER'S imagery appears "emblematic" is true because the poet sometimes creates his images in the same mode in which the emblem is made, but more frequently his imagery is only coincidentally emblematic because its comparisons are based on sources identical to those of the emblem—natural history, Aesop's fables, proverbial lore, and mythology.[1] Under the influence of medieval exegesis and Renaissance moralization of classical learning, these four sources tended to influence each other through their common pictorial motifs and moral teachings. In addition, the compendia of these sources were "emblematized" or assimilated into emblem books during the heyday of the emblem, the last quarter of the sixteenth century and the first quarter of the next.[2] Accordingly, it is not difficult to trace the sources of Spenser's images to emblem books, whereas they are in fact based on sources common to both poets and emblematists.[3] Moreover, Spenser's first practice—creating images in the "emblematic" mode—is the result more of making its tenor and its vehicle attain the same metaphorical relation that exists between the text (*i.e.*, the motto and the verse) and the picture of an emblem than of direct borrowing from emblem books. In other words, when Spenser controls his image with a moral the way the text of an emblem controls the details of its picture, he is creating an imagery that is generically "emblematic." It would be instructive, therefore, to examine those theoretical aspects of emblematics that are common to poetics. Some of these aspects are: the idea of *ut pictura poesis*, the mixing of *dulci* with *utile*, the revealing of the intelligible in the visible, and the ideal of expressing in images the similitude with vividness, *i.e.*, with both *enargeia* and *energeia* (the aim of the former is to achieve verisimilar representation, that of the latter, organic realism that

transforms an imitation into a witty invention).[4] In particular,
an exposition of the metaphorical function of an emblem's text
and picture in revealing the universal through the particular will
go a long way towards identifying the generic "emblematic"
mode of Spenser's imagery. But first it may be helpful to
illustrate from Spenser's works the coincidental nature of the
emblem-likeness of some of his images as a result of their
having been based on the four sources mentioned above.

I. Spenser's Imagery Based on the
Four Sources of the Emblem

Henri Estienne and Claude-François Menestrier, two contemporary critics, begin their respective surveys of theories and
rules of *devise* and emblem with an introductory discussion of
their sources.[5] Menestrier gives the following list: fables of the
ancients, metamorphoses, proverbs, the apologues of Aesop,
sentences, apothegms, axioms of sciences, examples of history,
and poetic fictions.[6] Both critics name the Egyptian hieroglyph-
ics as the ultimate source from which derived medals and coins,
cyphers and enigmas, heraldic arms and *devises* which were the
immediate predecessors of the emblem. Originated in France,
the *devise*, called *impresa* by the Italians, was imported into Italy
by the invading forces of Charles VIII and Lewis XII in 1499.[7]
The *devise*, which differed from the emblem in having only the
motto and the picture (whereas the emblem has in addition an
explicatory verse), was worn by the military leaders and troops
in their badges, coats of arms, insignias, and standards. Its first
theorist, Paolo Giovio, traced its origin to the Egyptian hiero-
glyphics in *Dialogo dell' Imprese Militari et Amoroso*.[8] The hiero-
glyphics—transmitted to the West by Horapollo and systema-
tized via the medieval herbals, Physiologus, and the bestiary by
Valeriano in his *Hieroglyphica* (1556)[9]—became in the Renaissance nothing more than moralized natural history.[10] This
natural history was readily available to renaissance men of
letters in the works of classical naturalists as well as—and along
with Aesop's fables, proverbial lore, and mythology—in numerous compendia, handbooks, manuals, dictionaries, and en-
cyclopediae. The following illustrations will introduce first the
images and their bases, then the parallels from emblem books,
followed by images that reflect the interconnections among the
sources.

1) Natural History[11]—Examples of Spenser's use of natural history may be found in his animal images. Spenser probably knew first hand the classical naturalists such as Aristotle and Pliny. But, for the purposes of this demonstration, a bestiary is chosen to provide pictures and texts that are representative of the classical and medieval traditions. The bestiary is based on that in the twelfth-century manuscript, now Cambridge University Library Ii.4.26, translated into English by T. H. White in 1954, to be cited as White, followed by page number. Parallels in an emblematized natural history are taken from Camerarius (see n.2 above, referred to hereafter by his name, followed by volume and emblem numbers, *e.g.*, 4.82 for volume 4, no. 82), who provides many references to textual and pictorial sources, which are recorded along with some of the texts and pictures of Camerarius in Henkel and Schöne's *Handbuch* (hereafter referred to as *HShb*, followed by column number).[12] Parallels to other emblem books may also be found in this *Handbuch*; those that are not in it will be mentioned here as the need arises.

Animal images without moral applications by Spenser are: "Snake casting off skin" (*FQ*, IV.iii.27.7–9) from White 187, Camerarius 4.82, *HShb* 634ff.; "viper's brood" (*Amoretti*, 2.6 & *FQ*, I. i. 25.9) from White 170, Camerarius 4.91, *HShb* 662; "Panther hiding his head," (*Amoretti*, 53. 1–4) from White, 14 & 17, Camerarius 2.37, *HShb* 405. Although Camerarius's fourth volume (1604) is too late for Spenser to use, there are other emblem books to which he could refer: Montenay's *Emblemes* of 1571, no. 41 on the snake, Beza's *Icones* of 1580, no. 32 on the viper, and Capaccio's *Imprese* of 1592, fol. 36ᵛ on the panther. But there is no hard evidence that he knew any of these emblem books; therefore, these animal images, though they could have been based on emblems, are only coincidentally "emblematic." Their real source via the bestiary is natural history.

In *Vanitie* Spenser illustrates the eleven visions with the moral that the great, mighty, and strong in nature are often overcome by the small, insignificant, and weak. Two illustrations in particular closely follow the bestiary; the ship held up by the small fish Remora (*Vanitie*, no. 9 from White 208) and the crocodile constrained by the little bird Tedula or Trochilus (*Vanitie*, no. 3 from White 169n). Alciati's *Emblemata* (1577), no. 82 and Camerarius 4.27 both deal with the holding power of remora; it is also in Giovio, p. 169, Corrozet's *Hecatom-*

graphie, Dviii^v, Sambucus's *Emblemata* (1564), p. 205, *Mikrokosmos* (1579), no. 66, and *HShb* 713. Camerarius refers to the relationship between the crocodile and trochilus in 2.98; it is also in Boria's *Empresas* (1581), p. 83 and Capaccio's *Imprese*, 2.59^v. The emblematists, following the naturalists, emphasize the marvels of ecology, the helpfulness of the little bird in cleaning the teeth of the voracious crocodile, whereas Spenser uses the little bird's forcing open the crocodile's jaws to show that "so small so mightie can constraine"—a case of changing the traditional moral to suit his own purposes and a typical way in which Spenser uses his sources. Despite the moral applications these images are far from being truly "emblematic," not only because Spenser based them on the bestiary but also because the *Vanitie* is modeled on *Petrarch* and *Bellay* which are but redactions of *Theatre*. Now *Theatre* can in no way be considered an emblem book in spite of its twenty woodcuts; it is properly an illustrated book of verse consisting of epigrams and sonnets.[13] Indeed, the connection between the moral and the description of the remora and the ship in *Vanitie* is not that between the motto and the picture of an emblem either. The moral, instead of controlling the details of the picture as in a bona fide emblem, is deduced from, or added onto, the story like that in an Aesop's fable (see below).

The tropological interpretation of animal behavior produces many proverbs that are used by poets and emblematists alike. In the following examples, references to Charles G. Smith's *Spenser's Proverb Lore* (1970) will be CGS, followed by numbers. "Turtle on bared branch" (*SC, November* 138 & *Amoretti*, 89.1) may be from White 145ff., Camerarius 3.64 "Idem cantus gemitusque," *HShb* 861, or the proverb "as true as a turtle to her mate" CGS 788; "eagle's eye beholding the sun" (*FQ*, I.x.47.6) from White 107, Camerarius 3.9 "Sustinuere diem," *HShb* 773f., or "only the eagle can gaze at the sun" CGS 199; "basilisk or cockatrice kills with looks" (*FQ*, IV.viii.39.7–9 & *Amoretti*, 49.10) from White 168ff., Camerarius 4.79 "Noxa nocenti," *HShb* 627, or "the basilisk's eye is fatal" CGS 40 and "the cockatrice kills with its look" CGS 109. Unlike the naturalists, the emblematists picture the basilisk facing a mirror and thus directing its lethal power ironically against itself (Plate 21). Spenser, on the other hand, seems to prefer the straightforward natural history to the ironic interpretation offered by the emblematists as further seen in Scève's *Délie* (1544), no. 21 "Mon regard par toy me tue," and Picinelli's *Mundus symbolicus* (1681), 7.22 "Ipsi peribit." Finally, "a cruel crafty crocodile" (*FQ*, I.v.18.4) may be from Giovio, p. 188 "Crocodili lacrimae" used later by Typotius's *Symbola* (1603), 3.107, Camerarius 4.66 "Devorat, et plorat" based on Camilli's *Imprese* (1586), 3.3 "Plorat, et devorat" or from the proverb "in the tears of a hypocrite is craft, not sorrow" CGS 758 and Erasmus, *Adagia*, 2.362. Proverbs intermingle not only with natural history but also with Aesop's fables.

2) Aesop's Fables[14]—References of fables will be to the uniform numbers developed by Ben Edwin Perry in *Aesopica* (1952) and in *Babrius and Phaedrus* (1965).[15] The stories of "the fox and the kid" in *May*[16] and "the wolf in sheep skin" in *September* of *SC* have no exact parallels in Aesop; Spenser seems to have conflated similar stories in Aesop 572, "The Kid and the Wolf" and 611 "The Fox and the Hens" for the first, and Aesop 705 "Dog, Wolf, and Ram" and 451 "The Wolf in Sheep's Clothing" for the second. Such a method of borrowing by conflating details from various fables to make new composites indicates the thoroughness of Spenser's familiarity with the Aesopic style and tradition.[17] Another example in which Spenser changes both the story and the moral is "the oak and the briar" in *February*: it has a parallel not only in Aesop 70 "Oak and Reed" but also in emblem books of Junius, *Emblemata* (1565), no. 43 and of Whitney, p. 220 "Vincit qui patitur." The moral in Aesop's fable, followed by the emblematists, points up the pride of the oak that, choosing to fight the wind, is broken by it, and the virtue of the reed that survives the storm with pliant patience, whereas Spenser's fable teaches a lesson of pride against the briar that wants the oak cut down and dies after the oak's protection has been destroyed.[18] Similarly, "the foolish fly or grasshopper" in *February* 38 and *October* 11 has a parallel in Aesop 373 which reappears in Faerno and in Whitney, p. 159 (see n.2. above). Faerno follows the fable tradition by giving a title, "FORMICA, ET CICADA," above the woodcut, below which is a verse, then comes the moral "Aetatis dum uer agitur, tum consule brumae." It is a familiar moral as it is in the Book of Proverbs, 6.6: "go to the ant, thou sluggard; consider her ways, and be wise." But Spenser has Cuddie in *October* complain about small reward due him after his feeding youth's

fancy (lines 7–18). Unlike the fable grasshopper who is unwilling to labor for food and wastes his time in singing for his own pleasure, Spenser's Cuddie spends his time entertaining his friends but receives no reward for his pains.

Fables are easily mingled with natural history and with proverbs as the following examples will show. The overly affectionate ape mother smothers her young to death (*SC, May* 95–102) with Spenser's pointed moral in a couplet, "So often times, when as good is meant, / Euil ensueth of wrong entent" may be paralleled in Aesop 218, "Ape's Twin Offspring," with this moral: "This is the nature of many men. Be thou ever an enemy to such, rather than a friend," also in White 34, the bestiary, with the twist that carrying the unwanted offspring on her back and the beloved one in her bosom, the mother ape discards the one she loves when pursued because it is hampering her escape. But some of the emblematists use a more subtle moral as seen both in Paradin's *Devises* (1551), p. 226 "Caecus amor prolis," and in Whitney, p. 188, whose moral is: "When foolishe loue forbiddes them to bee taughte." The fable about an eagle cracking shell fish on Aeschylus' head because it mistook the dramatist's bald head for a rock (*SC, July* 217–228) has partial parallels in Aesop 490 "Eagle and Crow" and 230 "Eagle and Tortoise." Pliny in *Natural History* (10.3) records the incident involving Aeschylus; such a legend is obviously in Spenser's view and has been used by the emblematists as well. To mention one among many, Covarrubias's *Emblemas* (1589), 1.44 "Vt lapsu graviore ruat," mentions Pliny in his prose commentary (for other emblematic examples, see *HShb* 613, 1165ff.). Finally, the fable about the dog who through greed loses the bone in his mouth upon seeing his reflection in the river (*SC, September* 59–61) has a close parallel in Aesop 133 "Dog with Meat & His Shadow," which appears in Faerno, no. 90 and in Whitney, p. 39 (Plate 22, Figure 1; CGS 700 and *HShb* 566ff.). It is also in White 66ff. with the moral: "Because it leaves the true food in the river out of greed for the shadow, it symbolizes those silly people who often leave that which is peculiarly of the law out of desire for some unknown thing," which is echoed in Spenser's "To leaue the good, that I had in honde / In hope of better, that was vncouth" (lines 59–60). Whether Spenser echoes the moral of Aesop or bestiary, or makes drastic changes of it, the fact remains that the moral is deduced from the fable; this is why the same fable can have a number of divergent morals. As long as the moral does not control the details of the image (or fable) in a metaphorical relation which exists between the text and the picture of an emblem, and as long as the emblematic sources are themselves borrowings from Aesop, Spenser's images based on fables are the most coincidentally "emblematic."

3) Proverbial Lore[19]—In the following examples based on proverbial lore, it will be seen that the one whose moral does not control the details of the story is but coincidentally "emblematic," but the other whose morals do control the details to a certain extent is more nearly generically "emblematic." In comparing Slander railing against Arthur and Amoret to a dog biting a stone (*FQ*, IV.viii.36.5–6; CGS 190), Spenser might have in view Alciati, no. 174 "Alius peccat, alius plectitur" (Plate 22, Figure 2; also in Whitney, p. 56, *cf. HShb* 562). The application of the moral is different, however; in Alciati the dog is condemned for forsaking its real enemy who threw the stone and for attacking the guiltless and innocent stone, whereas Spenser emphasizes the stupidity and blindness of Slander who continues to rail at Arthur and Amoret even though they have passed "the reach of eare." Of a more complicated instance is a group of proverbial sayings concerning the dichotomy of honey versus gall, of sweet versus bitter. By and large there are two main thoughts: one is that the sweet is not worth the gall; the other, the reward is worth the trouble and pain. Of the first are: *SC, March* 122–123 (CGS 477), *FQ*, I.iv.46.3–4 (CGS 745), *FQ*, IV.x.1.4–5 (CGS 477), and *FQ*, IV.x.3.8–9 and *SC, January* 54 (CGS 482). These are paralleled (and also as examples of the interpenetration of proverbs with mythology) in Alciati, no. 111 "Dulcia quandoque amara fieri," picturing Venus, Cupid, and beehive in a tree trunk, and no. 112 "Fere simile ex Theocrito," showing Venus, Cupid, and apiary; both are also borrowed in reversed order by Whitney, pp. 147 and 148 (see *HShb* 1758ff.). The story of Cupid's being stung by bees is probably based on the *Greek Anthology* (a major source of Alciati),[20] 9.548 as well as on Anacreon 40 and Theocritus 19. The second group that "A dram of sweet is worth a pound of sowre," *FQ*, I.iii.30.4 (CGS 743), *FQ*, VI.xi.1.8–9 (CGS 745), and *Amoretti*, 26.9–10 (CGS 745), has a parallel in La Perrière's *Le Théâtre* (1539), no. 30 and in Whitney, p. 165 "Post amara

dulcia" (see *HShb* 296 and 298). Spenser combines both groups
in the *Anacreontics* at the end of *Amoretti* where Cupid and Venus
act out these proverbs. Lines 37–38 apply to the first group:
"Full many thou hast pricked to the hart, / that pitty neuer
found," meaning gall is greater than sweet, while lines 49–50
reflect the second group: "Who would not oft be stung as this, /
to be so bath'd in Venus blis?"[21] By virtue of the presence of the
motto-like proverbs in these metaphorical comparisons, Spenser has "invented" a new emblem by appropriating and conflating several traditional proverbs and iconographical (mythological) traditions, resulting in a "witty invention" that theorists of
emblem as well as of poetry consider as having fulfilled the
highest ideal of the doctrine of imitation (see II below).

4) Mythology[22]—Through tropological interpretation of
classical myths, proverbs naturally intermingle with mythology as has already been shown above. Two examples without
the use of proverbs indicate the coincidental nature of some of
the "emblematic" images based on mythology. "*Niobes
vnhappy race*" (*FQ*, IV.vii.30.5–9), based on Ovid *Met* 6.146ff.
and Homer *Il* 24.602ff. and turned into emblem by Simeoni's
Ovidio, no. 77 (see n.2 above), is used by Spenser to demonstrate Belphoebe's speed in pursuing and killing the salvage
man in the manner of Diana's killing Niobe's children. In Ovid
as well as in emblems—Alciati, no. 67 "Superbia" and Whitney,
p. 13—the moral is on Niobe's pride and her just punishment.
Similarly, Phaeton's pride mixed with rashness causing his
demise, Ovid, *Met*, 2.85 and Simeoni, nos. 21 & 22, has been
treated by Alciati, no. 56 "In temerarios." Spenser, however,
dwells on Phaeton's horses being scared by the Scorpion in *FQ*,
V.viii.40.2 instead of on his pride or his boldness (although he
does deal with them in *FQ*, I.iv.9.1–4 and *FQ*, III.xi.38.3).

Myths intermingle with proverbs and other sources in the
following examples. Diggon's emblem "Inopem me copia fe-
cit" in *September* means "Plenty makes me poor" CGS 619 and
refers in *Amoretti* 35.8 and 83.7 to Narcissus (Ovid, *Met*, 3.466)
which is treated by Alciati no. 69 "Philautia" (Whitney, p. 149
"Amor sui"; see *HShb* 1627). This same proverb is applied to
plant life by Paradin, p. 244 "Mihi pondera, luxus" to show the
broken stalks of a bundle of heavy laden wheat (Whitney, p. 23)
and by Alciati no. 192 "In foecunditatem, sibi ipsi damnosam,"
to depict the moral of a wayside fruitful tree being bombarded

by children with stones and sticks for its fruits (Plate 23, Figure 1; Whitney, p. 174 and *HShb* 179). Alciati based his emblem on Aesop 250 "The Nut Tree," whose moral in Whitney's words is: "My proper fruicte my ruine doth procure: / If fruictlesse I, then had I growen in peace." Thus, proverbs have a way of applying a single wise saying to many different sources, creating a kind of eclecticism that is inherent in a borrower's source rather than the result of his borrowing.

Such is however not the case with Spenser's Occasion, the product of the poet's own eclecticism.[23] "To seize occasion by the forelock," CGS 777 and Erasmus, *Adagia*, 1.301.34, is treated by Spenser extensively and differently in *FQ*, II.iv.47–48 (though traditionally in *Amoretti*, 70.8) and has a parallel in Alciati no. 121 "In occasionem" (Plate 23, Figure 2) based on the *Greek Anthology* 16.275 (Whitney, p. 181, Plate 24; see *HShb* 1809–1811). Traditionally, *Occasio*, bald at the back of her head because of the forelock, holds a razor and stands on a globe or a wheel in the midst of the sea. The only traditional thing Spenser retained is the forelock, representing for Sir Guyon the opportunity to restrain wrath. Here again, Spenser has "invented" a new emblem according to the generic mode rather than following some emblematic models. Similarly, "Cupid's riding a lion" (*FQ*, III.xii.22) has been traced by Arthur Marotti to Lucian's *Dial. deor.* 12.2 (see n. 11 above), but most of the sources have Cupid driving a chariot drawn by two lions—the *Greek Anthology* 9.211, "Conti, Cartari," as well as Alciati no. 105 "Potentissimus affectus amor." In following Lucian, Spenser chooses to use only one lion instead of the more common two, but the moral remains the same, "Omnia vincit amor" CGS 481. However, in bringing concord to the warring parties, Cambina (*FQ*, IV.iii.39.1–3) is made by Spenser to replace Cupid on the traditional lion-drawn chariot, thereby suggesting that love is an ingredient in the constitution of concord, another example of his "witty invention."

From the above illustrations of the emblem-likeness of many of Spenser's images, it has been shown how easy it is to identify them as having been based on emblem books when in fact they are based on the four sources. This kind of misattribution is made all the more facile by the prolific assimilation of these sources into emblem books and by the interpenetrations among them. When no moral application is involved, the images based on these sources are simply coincidentally "emblematic." Those based on Aesop's fables are the most coincidentally "emblematic" because they resemble the fables in both appearance and moral inculcation. However, the fable's moral is deduced from its story, whereas the emblem's moral controls the details of its picture in a metaphorical relationship. To the extent Spenser controls his image with a moral as the emblematists do, he is "inventing" his imagery in the emblematic mode as has been shown above in varying degrees of perfection among such examples as "Cupid, Venus, and bees," "Occasion," "Concord in the lion-drawn chariot." To understand properly the metaphorical relationship between the emblem's text and its picture, an exposition of some aspects of emblematics will now be necessary.

II. Some Aspects of Emblematics

In addition to Spenser's controlling his images with morals in a metaphorical relation as do the emblematists, there are other aspects which also contribute to his achieving a generically "emblematic" invention. The delineation of these aspects will necessitate putting Spenser aside for the moment and dealing with some theoretical aspects of emblematics that are common to the arts of poetry and painting. In defining the relationship between the motto and the picture, theorists apply the Horatian "vtile dulci miscere" "the mixing of pleasure with teaching" to a relationship between body and soul. Just as the picture (equated with the body) pleases the eye (*dulce*), so the motto (equated with the soul) feeds the mind (*utile*).[24] And just as the body cannot exist without the soul, so a picture without its motto is unable to bring the true use of an emblem. (In poetry the vehicle and the tenor of an image may be considered its body and soul.)

From this definition Giovio developed his five rules; the first and the third deal with *utile* and *dulce*: "First, a just proportion or relation of the Soule to the Body" and third, "That above all things, it have a sweet appearance, which shall succeed, by inserting therein either Stars, Sun, Moon, Fire, Water, green Trees, mechanicall Instruments, diversified, and fantasticall Beasts and Birds" (E/B 21).[25] By "just proportion or relation" Giovio means that the body bears the correct proportion of

meaning to the soul, without which a *devise* or an emblem can
neither please nor teach. Girolamo Ruscelli, in *Le Imprese illustri*
(1566), explains that "the Figure and the Motto are its necessary
parts, the one to allure the eye, the other to invade the mind"
(E/B 23). Corollary to the mixing of *dulci* with *utile* is the issue
of obscurity versus clarity (the veiling of truth) which is dealt
with by Giovio's second and fifth rules. "That it be not so
obscure, as to need a Sybill to interprete it; nor yet so plain, as
the common people may comprehend it," and "that the Motto
. . . be in a strange language . . . to the end, that the intention of
it bee a little removed from common capacities" (E/B 21).
Scipione Ammirato, in *Il Rota* (1562), elaborates on these rules:
"it shall suffice that the more simple doe know the body of the
Devise, and that they clearly discerne it to be the figure of a Fish,
Bird, Horse, Tree, Temple, Bridge, or such like thing, either
naturall or artificiall . . . whilst the learned feast their understandings with the consideration of the propriety of the creatures represented, and of the usage of the things artificiall, untill
they have found out the true subject of the comparison, and
discovered the Authors designe, whose invention and subtility
they will doubtlesse commend" (E/B 32). Estienne himself
observes that since "the chief aim of the Embleme is to instruct
us, by subjecting the figure to our view, and the sense to our
understanding: therefore they must be something covert, sub-
tile, pleasant and significative. So that, if the pictures of it be too
common, it ought to have a mysticall sense; if they be something obscure, they must more clearly informe us by the
words, provided they be analogick and correspondent" (E/B
7ff.). Both Ammirato and Estienne mention "the subject of
comparison" and "words be analogick and correspondent" in
connection with the fact that the obscurity may be turned into
clarity through proper understanding of the author's intended
comparison or similitude. This brings up the centrality of the
metaphorical relationship between the picture and the text
which includes the motto and the verse.

The invisible conceit of the author's mind ("dark conceit") is
revealed to the viewer's mind when his eyes are struck pleas-
ingly by the natural quality (the visible) in the picture (the
body) through the similitude with the universal concept (the
intelligible) carried in the motto (the soul). To Ammirato "the
conjunction and copulation of the Body with the Soule is very

handsome, when it is made by comparison" (E/B 30). Estienne
provides the most cogent analysis of the metaphorical function
of the text and the picture: "Now as Metaphorick and trans-
ported termes alwaies appear to our understandings with two
significations, whereof the one is the proper and the other the
strange, externe and borrowed, by meanes of the Similitude,
which it hath in common with the first: Even so may we say,
that *Devises* present themselves to our understandings with two
significations; the one is, the naturall quality, or the usage of the
thing represented by the figure; and the other is, the meaning of
the Author. Now to come to the apprehension of the *Devise*, we
must abandon the first signification, and discover the second,
by means of the resemblance, which the quality or usage of the
thing figured hath with the conception of the Authors fancie"
(E/B 40 & 52). To a certain extent Estienne's definition of
metaphor is similar to that of Aristotle: "a metaphor is the
transfer of a name that belongs to something else either from
the genus to the species, or from the species to the genus, or
from one species to another, or according to analogy."[26] In
other words, it is the transferring of meaning from the vehicle
to the tenor, from the visible to the intelligible. John M.
Steadman reveals the reason why the metaphysical poets "combine familiar diction with an extensive resort to the metaphorical analogies"; they "may have been conditioned by Aristotle's
dual emphasis on clear diction and strange or 'foreign' metaphors" because Aristotle places metaphor "(along with antithesis and *energeia*) among the elegancies and 'approved beauties' of
style."[27] Buoyed by the Aristotelian high regard towards metaphor, the emblem theorists consider their genre as superior to
both poetry and painting. Antonio Possevino so claims in
Tractatio de poësi & pitura (1595): "The rationale of the emblem
lay in its uniting poetry and painting in a form that maintained
the values of each art, permitting one to be the interpreter of the
other."[28] In asserting the superiority of this union, French
theorists use *ut pictura poesis* or its corollary formula, "painting
is mute poetry; poetry is speaking picture"—attributed to
Simonides of Ceos by Plutarch—to argue their case. For instance, Pierre Le Moyne explains in *De l'art des devises* (1649):
"La merveille est, que cette Poësie sans Musique fait en un
moment avec cette figure et ce Mot, ce que l'autre Poësie ne
sçauroit faire qu'avec un long temps et de grands préparatifs

d'harmonies, de fictions et de machines."[29] Menestrier echoes
this sentiment: "Si la Peinture est une Poësie muette, & la Poësie
une Peinture parlante, l'Emblême qui a les beautez de l'un & de
l'autre, merite aussie ces deux noms. . . . Ce sont les images qui
sont la matière des Emblêmes, puisque les Emblêmes sont des
instructions qui doivent frapper les yeux, pour passer de-là
jusqu'à l'âme."[30] The emphasis on the supremacy of sight and
on the vividness of the imitation by painting brings up the issue
of *enargeia* versus *energeia* in relation to the doctrine of *ut pictura
poesis*[31] and the doctrine of imitation.

For that former doctrine, declares Hagstrum, "had originally
arisen in connection with the notion of *enargeia*, the vivid and
life-like reproduction in verbal art of natural detail."[32] According to Hagstrum, Aristotle has "recognized that a powerful
rhetorical effect is achieved by that orator who is able, as it
were, to set things before the eyes of his auditor by using words
that signify actuality. But to describe that effect, Aristotle uses
not the word *enargeia* but the homonymous word *energeia*
(*Rhetoric*, 3.11.1–2)." The difference between the two is as
follows: *enargeia*, explains Hagstrum, "implies the achievement
in verbal discourse of a natural quality or a pictorial quality that
is highly natural," whereas *energeia* "refers to the actualization
of potency, the realization of capacity or capability, the achievement in art and rhetoric of the dynamic and purposive life of
nature." Hagstrum goes on to elaborate what *energeia* means to
poetry and to the doctrine of imitation: "Poetry possesses
energeia when it has achieved its final form and produces its
proper pleasure, when it has achieved its own independent
being quite apart from its analogies with nature or another art,
and when it operates as an autonomous form with an effectual
working power of its own. . . . 'Imitation,' a term that had
bound the verbal and graphic arts together in antiquity but had
been replaced in official medieval philosophy by a new similitude between the work of art and unseen, unseeable reality,
became in the Renaissance a crucially important term of critical
meaning. . . . For Aristotle imitation meant doing in another
realm what nature does in hers: the achievement in matter other
than the original matter of a form that possesses unity of its
own and that, when fully realized, achieves its own end and
obeys its own laws."[33] In these passages the explanations of
Aristotelian *energeia* and Aristotelian imitation are essentially

the same. To Aristotle the ideal imitation enables an artist to "invent" a new reality that transcends its model and has its own organic life, that "when fully realized, achieves its own end and obeys its own laws"; *energeia*, a higher form of representation than *enargeia*, transcends the merely visible or verisimilar and reaches the intelligible which is what emblematists want their perfect emblem to achieve, "when it has achieved its final form and produces its proper pleasure," or in Estienne's words, when it has realized its "signification or Comparison understood, by meanes whereof we express more clearly, with more efficacy and livelinesse, a rare and particular conception of wit" (E/B 37).

Some of Spenser's images appear to be constructed along these generic lines of the emblem. They contain a picture, the visible body that imitates nature in a verisimilar or "painterly" manner and a motto, the intelligible soul that reveals the author's purposes and intention with the help of a verse explaining the subject and the meaning of the comparison (simile or metaphor). The Graces' dance in *FQ*, VI.x.22–24 is an outstanding example. The motto, "That good should from vs goe, then come in greater store," dictates the details of the picture, especially of how the three Graces should move: "That two of them still froward seem'd to bee, / But one still towards shew'd her selfe afore," meaning two of them going away from, one returning towards, the viewer. The way they dance, which is the central metaphor, is compared to the lesson they teach us "how to each degree and kynde / We should our selues demeane, to low, to hie; / To friends, to foes, which skill men call Ciuility." To be civil and gracious, in this context, means to bestow unmerited favor, to give more than to receive. As the allegorical core, the Graces' dance also controls the Legend of Courtesy by this motto in that both Calidore and Calepine are paragons of courtesy because they give more than they receive. In choosing this motto, Spenser is also transcending his traditional model in that most sources—with a rare exception or two, whether classical or Renaissance, whether textual or pictorial—show two Graces coming towards the viewer with the other going away from him and the opposite moral: to give in order to receive more in return.[34] To a certain extent Spenser has made an Aristotelian imitation and achieved the organic realism of *energeia*. His Graces' dance has its own end and obeys its own laws; it "has achieved its final form and produces its proper pleasure." Not just an isolated image or a set piece, "it operates as an autonomous form with an effectual working power of its own" and achieves "the dynamic and purposive life of nature." In short, it moves from the visible to the intelligible, from the particular to the universal, which is the goal of the emblem as well as of poetic imagery. The picture of the Graces' dance obviously pleases the eye (*dulce*) and its motto and verse instruct the mind (*utile*) through a metaphorical relation that brings about a non-traditional yet universal truth. In this example Spenser may be said to have "invented" an image in the generic "emblematic" mode.[35] It goes without saying that among Spenser's generically "emblematic" images only a few (such as Occasion or Malbecco) reach the perfection of the Graces' dance just as it is true that in any emblem book only a handful of emblems are made to perfection.

Thus, emblem as a genre, sharing a great many common concerns with poetry, is far from being homogeneous and univalent; it has many intermingling and interpenetrating sources which are often the direct sources of poetic imagery. What is true of Spenser's imagery is, to a greater or lesser extent, true of those of other Renaissance poets, including Shakespeare, Donne, Herbert, Crashaw, Milton. With the exception perhaps of Ben Jonson, who in his masques consciously drew upon emblem books and iconologies, the greater the "inventiveness" of Renaissance authors, the less inclined they were to rely on one particular source, least of all on emblem books. The truth is that the emblematists were latecomers to the Renaissance scene, drawing their materials from the same fund of classical and medieval heritage and resources which had for some time served all arts and letters.

University of Idaho

NOTES

1. The decision to deal only with these four in this study is an arbitrary one except for the fact that there are more images based on these than on others. For other sources, see P. M. Daly, *Literature in the Light of the Emblem* (Toronto: University of Toronto Press, 1979), pp. 9–36. Daly's survey of

"Recent Development in Emblem Theory" (pp. 36–53) is especially helpful to a better appreciation of emblematics; see my review of his book in *Milton Quarterly*, 14 (1980), 64–66. References in the text and in the notes to emblem books use the simplest forms; for full citations, see Mario Praz, *Studies in Seventeenth-Century Imagery*, Second Edition (Rome: Edizioni di Storia e Letteratura, 1964), "A Bibliography of Emblem-Books," pp. 241–576. Spenser's "Emblematic" images have been studied by Rosemary Freeman, *English Emblem Books* (London: Chatto & Windus, 1948; 2nd imp. 1967); John M. Steadman, "Una and the Clergy," *Journal of the Warburg and Courtauld Institutes*, 21 (1958), 134–137; A. D. S. Fowler, "Emblems of Temperance in *The Faerie Queene*, Book II," *Review of English Studies*, n.s. 11 (1960), 143–149; Rene Graziani, "Philip II's 'Impresa' and Spenser's Souldan," *Journal of the Warburg and Courtauld Institutes*, 27 (1964), 322–324; K. W. Scoular, *Natural Magic* (Oxford: Clarendon Press, 1965), pp. 154–161 (on emblematic hill and valley in *SC July*); Nicholas Brooke, *Shakespeare's Early Tragedies* (London: Methuen, 1968; on Spenser's emblematic technique); David M. Bergeron, "The Emblematic Nature of English Civic Pageantry," *Renaissance Drama*, 1 (1968), 167–198; Clarence Steinberg, "Atin, Pyrocles, and Cymocles: On Irish Emblems in *The Faerie Queene*," *PMLA*, 87 (1972), 192–200; Carolyn Prager, "Emblem and Motion in Spenser's *Prothalamion*," *Studies in Iconography*, 2 (1976), 114–120; James Nohrnberg, *The Analogy of "The Faerie Queene"* (Princeton, N.J.: Princeton University Press, 1976), pp. 95–99 and *passim*.

2. For instance, Joachim Camerarius, a natural historian who edited Pierandrea Matthioli's *De plantis* (1586) and an herbal *Hortus medicus et philosophibus* (1588), converted natural history into an emblem book. Between 1590 and 1604 he published in Nuremburg the *Symbolorum & Emblematum* in four volumes with one hundred emblems each. Volume 1 (1590) deals with "Herbaria," vol. 2 (1595) with "Animalibus Quadrupedibus," vol. 3 (1596) with "Volatilibus et Insectis," and vol. 4 (1604) with "Aquatilibus et Reptilibus." On the recto of each folio is the circular picture in the center with its motto above and its explicatory verse below (Plate 21). On each facing verso are references in Latin prose explaining the textual sources of this particular natural phenomenon in such classical naturalists as Aristotle, Aelian, Pliny, Plutarch, Oppian as well as in many church fathers and classical poets (Hesiod, Ovid, Propertius, *etc.*) and the pictorial sources in Alciati and other contemporary emblem and *devise* collections. Two collections of Aesop's fables were also emblematized: one by W. B. [William Barret] entitled *The Fables of Aesop . . . Translated into English Verse, and Morallized . . . Emblematically Illustrated with Picture* (1639) and the other by an anonymous author, *Aesops fables, with their moralls in verse . . . Illustrated with pictures and emblems* (1650). Emblematized proverbs are represented in Gilles Corrozet's *Hecatomgraphie C'est à dire les descriptions de cent figures & hystoires, contenantes plusieurs Appophtegmes Proverbes, Sentences & dictz des Anciens que des modernes* (1540). Otto van Veen devoted an entire emblem book to a single author's *sententiae* in *Emblemata Horatiana* (1607). Mythology was emblematized by Gabriele Simeoni's *La Vita et Metamorphoseo d'Ovidio, Figurato & abbruiato in forma d'Epigrammi* (1559), rendering the metamorphoses into 187 emblems.

Assimilation of these sources into emblem books may be seen in the works of their originator and popularizer, Andrea Alciati and his *Emblemata* (1st ed. 1531, last supervised ed. 1550); see Henry Green, *A. Alciati and His Books of Emblems* (1872) for a complete bibliography. This famous emblem collection draws its subjects from natural history, Aesop's fables, mythology, heraldry, profane and sacred histories, *devise* collections, proverbs and personifications (as typified later in Cesare Ripa's *Iconologia*, 1593, itself not an emblem book). Many of Alciati's imitators generally retain this formula of an eclectic gathering, most noticeably in Geoffrey Whitney's *A Choice of Emblemes* (1586).

The common pictorial motifs that facilitate the interpenetration of emblems with their sources may be attributable to the common producers of both kinds of books. For one famous instance among many, Christopher Plantin of Antwerp published, using the same artists and engravers for the cuts, all four types of sources as well as emblem books, including those of Alciati. Not infrequently woodblocks used in printing herbals and Aesop's fables are reused in printing emblem books. A case in point are the fourteen trees at the end of Alciati's *Emblemata* (Antwerp: C. Plantin, 1577) which are struck from the same blocks of Plantin's 1565 Rembert Dodoens's herbal, *Cruydt-Boech*. The best example of wholesale use of existing woodblocks to print an emblem collection is Whitney's *Choice* with which Spenser is said to have been familiar—Freeman, pp. 102–105 and Praz, p. 214. Out of a total of 247 woodcuts in *Choice*, 207 are identical to those used by Plantin in printing emblem books of Alciati, Sambucus, Junius, Paradin, and Gabriello Faerno's *Fabulae centum*, a regular collection of Aesop's fables. See Appendix II (pp. 79–85) of my essay, "Whitney's *A Choice of Emblemes* Revisited," *Studies in Bibliography*, 29 (1976), 32–101.

3. According to Daly, "the critic is greatly aided in his pursuit of sources by a knowledge of which books the writer in question actually possessed, and even more so by the marginal notes and other indications which some poets thoughtfully added concerning their sources" (p. 59). Spenser, to my knowledge, never identifies his "emblematic" sources nor reveals his knowledge or possession of any particular emblem books. Although it may be safe to assume that most Renaissance authors would be familiar with the emblem literature, it is safer to assume that they are more likely to be well versed in the sources of the emblem in that they have been tapping these sources for their images long before emblem books became popular.

4. See the fine study of the similarities among artis poeticae, picturae, and emblematicae by R. J. Clements in *Picta Poesis: Literary and Humanistic Theory in Renaissance Emblem Books* (Rome: Edizioni di Storia e Letteratura, 1960). Detailed studies of Spenser and the emblem have so far appeared only in unpublished theses and dissertations. Ellen G. Ward's "Spenser and the Emblem Writers," a Duke thesis (1936) is followed by Sister M. L. Beutner's "Spenser and the Emblem Writers," St. Louis University M. A. thesis (1941), Jack W. Jessee's "Spenser and the Emblem Books," Ph.D. dissertation, University of Kentucky (1955), D. M. Greene's "Medieval Background of the Elizabethan Emblem-Book," Ph.D. dissertation, University of California, Berkeley (1958), Jerry L. Mills's "Spenser's Emblem of Prudence: Four Studies in *The Faerie Queene*," Ph.D. dissertation, Harvard University (1968), and R. J. Manning's "Spenser's Use of Emblems in *The Faerie Queene*,"

Edinburgh University thesis (1978). Most of the attempts at identifying Spenser's images with emblem books succeed in confirming Spenser's eclecticism and great freedom in using his sources whatever kind they might be.

5. Henri Estienne, *L'Art de faire les devises* (Paris, 1645), tr. by Thomas Blount as *The Art of Making Devises* (London, 1646; rpt. 1650 ed. bound in the same volume as Abraham Fraunce's *Insignium Amorum*, 1588 and Adrian d'Amboise's *Traicte des devises*, 1620 as no. 7 of "The Philosophy of Images" ed. Stephen Orgel (New York: Garland Publishing Inc., 1979); hereafter referred to as Estienne/Blount. Claude-François Menestrier, *L'Art des Emblemes* (Lyons, 1662) and a later verson of the same title (Paris, 1684), rpt. respectively as nos. 15 and 18 of the same series "The Philosophy of Images."

6. P. 104; 1684 version of *L'Art*, p. 19.

7. Estienne/Blount, p. 20.

8. Rome, 1555; first illustrated ed., Lyons, 1559; rpt. 1574 which includes Gabriele Simeoni's *Imprese Heroiche et Morali* and Lodovico Domenichi's *Ragionamento*, bound with Samuel Daniel's tr. of Giovio as *The Worthy Tract of Jovius*, London, 1585, as no. 6 of "The Philosophy of Images," ed. Stephen Orgel (New York: Garland Publishing Inc., 1979).

9. For details see D. C. Allen, *Mysteriously Meant: The Rediscovery of Pagan Symbolism and Allegorical Interpretation in the Renaissance* (Baltimore: Johns Hopkins University Press, 1970), pp. 112–119, and Daly, pp. 11–21.

10. Called "the tropological approach to nature" by J. M. Steadman in *From Nature to Myth: Medieval and Renaissance Moral Symbols* (Pittsburgh: University of Pittsburgh Press, 1979), pp. 9 and 116; this is a collection of his articles published elsewhere earlier.

11. See Madeleine P. Cosman, "Spenser's Ark of Animals: Animal Imagery in *The Faerie Queene*," *Studies in English Literature, 1500–1900*, 3 (1963), 85–107; Arthur F. Marotti, "Animal Symbolism in *The Faerie Queene*; Tradition and the Poetic Context," *Studies in English Literature, 1500–1900*, 5 (1965), 69–86; Robert Wilcher, "Details from the Natural Histories in Marvell's Poetry," *Notes & Queries*, 15 (1968), 101–102, on Spenser's *Time*, ll. 216–217. There are not many studies on the relation between emblematics and natural history except perhaps the following: H. K. Hofmeier, *Die Emblemata und ihre Beziehungen zur Medizinsgeschichte*, "Düsseldorfer Arbeiten für Geschichte der Medizin," 1968, and Hans Kuhn, "Physiologus-traditionen i emblembøgerne," *Convivium: Årsskrift for Humaniora, Kunst og Forskning*, 1979, 108–125.

12. Arthur Henkel and Albrecht Schöne, *Emblemata, Handbuch zur Sinnbildkunst des XVI. und XVII. Jahrhunderts* (Stuttgart, 1967; rev. 1976). For an overview of the strengths and weaknesses of this invaluable handbook, see the review of the first edition by William S. Heckscher and Cameron F. Bunker in *Renaissance Quarterly*, 23 (1970), 59–80. As an example of the *Handbuch's* recording Camerarius's textual and pictorial sources with additions by the two editors, I quote the references to Camerarius 4.82, "Positis novus exuviis," of snake shedding its old skin in *HShb* 635: "Arist. Hist. an. 600b; Plin. nat. hist. VIII 98; Verg. georg. III 437, Aen. II 473; Nonn. Dionys. XLI 178ff.; Nicand. ther. 31ff.; Basil. comm. in Isiam, Proem. 1 (Migne, *PG*, 30, 120), de mor. serm. I 6 (Migne, *PG*, 32, 1128); Augustin. de doctr. Chr. XI 16; Herapoll. hierogl. I 2; physiol. c. 11; Epiph. ad Physiol. c. 13; Valerian. Hierogl. XIV 3; Bargagli, Impr. S. 454."

13. *Theatre* is regarded as the first emblem book printed in England—by C. H. Herford in *Literary Relations between England and Germany in the Sixteenth Century* (Cambridge: Cambridge University Press, 1886), p. 369, by Harold Stein, in *Studies in Spenser's Complaints* (New York: Oxford University Press, 1934), p. 11, and by Freeman n. 1, p. 51. Recent studies of *Theatre* are by Louis S. Friedland, "The Illustrations in *The Theatre for Worldlings*," *Huntington Library Quarterly*, 19 (1956), 107–120; Alfred W. Satterthwaite, "A Re-examination of Spenser's Translation of *Theatre*," *Philological Quarterly*, 38 (1959), 509–515; Leonard Forster, "The Translation of the 'Theatre for Worldlings,' " *English Studies*, 48 (1967), 27–34.

14. Since Louis S. Friedland's early study, "Spenser as a Fabulist," *South Atlantic Bulletin*, 12 (1937), 85–108, 133–154, 197–207, little is done on Spenser's relation to fable literature except perhaps John L. Lievsay's "Braggadocchio: Spenser's Legacy to the Character-Writers," *Modern Language Quarterly*, 2 (1941), 475–485 on boasters in Theophrastus, Aesop, Plautus, and Terence, and Nancy F. Dillard's 1973 University of Tennessee Ph.D. dissertation, "The English Fabular Tradition: Chaucer, Spenser, and Dryden." Recent studies on emblem and fable are more promising: Christian L. Küster, "Bemerkungen zum emblematischen Fabelbuch 'De Warachtighe Fabulen der dieren' von 1567," *Raggi Zeitschrift für Kunstgeschichte und Archäologie* [Basel], 9 (1969), 113–122; John Ewing Shell, "The Role of the Emblem and the Fable in the Didactic Literature of the 16th Century," Ph.D. dissertation, Rice University (1972); Barbara Tiemann, *Fabel und Emblem. Gilles Corrozet und die französische Renaissance-Fabel* (München, 1974); Monika Hueck, *Textstruktur und Gattungssystem. Studien zum Verhältnis von Emblem und Fabel im 16. und 17. Jahrhunderts* (Kronberg, 1975); Arnold C. Henderson, "Medieval Beasts and Modern Cages: The Making of Meaning in Fables and Bestiaries," *PMLA*, 97 (1982), 40–49.

15. Ben Edwin Perry, ed. and trans. *Babrius and Phaedrus*, Loeb Classical Library (Cambridge, Mass.: Harvard University Press, 1965) and the earlier *Aesopica . . . Vol. One Greek and Latin Texts* (Urbana, Ill.: University of Illinois Press, 1952) in which the uniform numbers were worked out and cross-referenced to those in Babrius, Phaedrus, Perotti's Appendix, Avianus as well as to modern eds. of Halm, Chambry, and Hausrath; see the "Tabula Comparativa," pp. 715–722.

16. See C. L. Wrenn, "On Re-reading Spenser's *Shepheardes Calender*," *Essays and Studies*, 29 (1943), 30–69.

17. In tracing the origin of fable collecting, Ben Perry has established the fact that the early collections were meant to provide orators with reference materials which they intended to rewrite to suit their particular purposes (*Babrius*, pp. xi–xvi). Referring to Perry's findings in a recent article, Arnold Henderson (n. 14 above) further notes that John Lydgate has urged writers to be true to Aesop's original intention by turning a fable to their own purposes (p. 41 and n. 2). It is highly probable, therefore, that Spenser is "inventing" his own fables in this proper tradition.

18. See Sidney Rosenzweig, "Ascham's *Schoolmaster* and Spenser's February Eclogue," *South Atlantic Bulletin*, 15 (1940), 103–109 answered by Louis S. Friedland, "Spenser's Fable of 'The Oak and the Briar,' " *South Atlantic Bulletin*, 16 (1941), 52–57; Warren E. Roberts, "Spenser's Fable of the Oak and the Briar," *Southern Folklore Quarterly*, 14 (1950), 150–154; Calvin

Huckabay and Everett H. Emerson, "The Fable of the Oak and the Briar," *Notes & Queries*, 1 (1954), 102–103; Louis S. Friedland, "A Source of Spenser's 'The Oak and the Briar,' " *Philological Quarterly*, 33 (1954), 222–224; Paul E. McLane, "Spenser's Oak and Briar," *Studies in Philology*, 52 (1955), 462–477.

19. In addition to Charles G. Smith's *Spenser's Proverb Lore* (Cambridge, Mass.: Harvard University Press, 1970), the following may be mentioned: Hoyt H. Hudson, *The Epigram in the English Renaissance* (Princeton, N.J.: Princeton University Press, 1947; rpt. New York: Octagon, 1966); Ronald M. Smith, "Three Obscure English Proverbs," *Modern Language Notes*, 65 (1950), 411–417; Irving P. Rothberg, "Covarrubias, Gracian and the *Greek Anthology*," *Studies in Philology*, 53 (1956), 540–552; James O. Crosby, "Quevedo, the *Greek Anthology*, and Horace," *Romance Philology*, 19 (1966), 435–449; Enid Howarth, "Venus Looking Glass: A Study of Books III and IV of *The Faerie Queene*," Ph.D. dissertation, University of New Mexico (1967); Charles C. Doyle, "Smoke and Fire: Spenser's Counter-Proverb," *Proverbium*, 18 (1972), 683–685.

20. Praz, pp. 25–31 and figs. 46–51; *cf.* Daly pp. 9–11.

21. See Janet Levarie, "Renaissance Anacreontics," *Comparative Literature*, 25 (1973), 211–239; and also L. C. John, *The Elizabethan Sonnet Sequence* (New York: Columbia University Press, 1938; rpt. New York: Russell & Russell, 1964), pp. 67–69; James Hutton, "Cupid and the Bee," *PMLA*, 56 (1941), 1036–1057; William C. Johnson, "Vow to Eternity: A Study of Spenser's *Amoretti*," Ph.D. dissertation, University of Iowa (1969); P. M. Cummings, "Spenser's *Amoretti* as an Allegory of Love," *Texas Studies in Literature and Language*, 12 (1970), 163–179.

22. Spenser's use of mythology is studied by Alice E. Sawtell, *The Sources of Spenser's Classical Mythology* (New York: Silver, Burdett & Co., 1896; rpt. Folcroft, Pa.: Folcroft Press, 1970); Henry G. Lotspeich, *Classical Mythology in the Poetry of Edmund Spenser* (Princeton, N.J.: Princeton University Press, 1932; rpt. New York: Gordian, 1965); and Wilhelm Lichtenegger, "Antike Mythologie in Spenser's *Faerie Queene*," Ph.D. dissertation, University of Graz (1941); John P. Cutts, "Sources of Britomartes," *Modern Language Notes*, 58 (1943), 607–610; John E. Hankins, "Spenser's Lucifera . . . ," *Modern Language Notes*, 59 (1944), 413–415; A. C. Hamilton, "Spenser's Treatment of Myth," *ELH*, 26 (1959), 335–354; Robert E. Hallowell, "Ronsard and the Gallic Hercules Myth," *Studies in the Renaissance*, 9 (1962), 242–255; Dewitt T. Starnes, "The Figure of Genius in the Renaissance," *Studies in the Renaissance*, 11 (1964), 234–244; T. K. Dunseath, *Spenser's Allegory of Justice in Book V of "The Faerie Queene"* (Princeton, N.J.: Princeton University Press, 1968); John P. Cutts, "Spenser's Mermaides," *ELH*, 5 (1968), 250–256; R. M. Cummings, "An Iconographical Puzzle: Spenser's Cupid at *FQ*, 2.8," *Journal of the Warburg and Courtauld Institutes*, 33 (1970), 317–321; John J. Mulryan, "Spenser as Mythologist in *Four Hymnes*," *Modern Language Studies*, 1 (1971), 13–16; Peter S. Hawkins, "From Mythography to Myth-making: Spenser and the Magna Mater Cybele," *The Sixteenth Century Journal*, 12 (1981), 51–64. More general studies are: Douglas Bush, *Mythology and the Renaissance Tradition in English Poetry* (Minneapolis: University of Minnesota Press, 1932; rev. New York: W. W. Norton, 1964); Jean Seznec, *The Survival of Pagan*

Gods (1940; 1st English ed. 1953, rpt. New York: Harper, 1961); Dewitt T. Starnes and Ernest W. Talbert, *Classical Myth and Legend in Renaissance Dictionaries* (Durham: Duke University Press, 1955); Edgar Wind, *Pagan Mysteries in the Renaissance* (New Haven, Conn.: Yale University Press, 1958; rev. ed. Harmondsworth, England: Penguin, 1967); Douglas Bush, *Pagan Myth and the Christian Tradition in English Poetry* (Philadelphia: American Philosophical Society, 1968); John J. Mulryan, "Natalis Comes' *Mythologiae*: Its Place in the Renaissance Mythological Tradition and Its Impact Upon English Renaissance Literature," Ph.D. dissertation, University of Minnesota (1969); Patricia Merivale, *Pan the Goat-God: His Myth in Modern Time* (Cambridge, Mass.: Harvard University Press, 1969); Barbara C. Garner, "Francis Bacon, Natalis Comes, and the Mythological Tradition," *Journal of the Warburg and Courtauld Institutes*, 33 (1970), 264–291; Harold Fisch, "*Antony and Cleopatra*: The Limits of Mythology," *Shakespeare Survey* 23, ed. Kenneth Muir (Cambridge: Cambridge University Press, 1970), pp. 59–67; Bodo Güthmüller, "Picta poesis Ovidiana," in *Renatae Litterae*, Klaus Heitmann and Eckhart Schroeder, eds. (Frankfurt am Main, 1973), pp. 171–192; Theodorus Nils a. Hoen, "Aspects of Classical Mythology in Renaissance Emblems, 1531–1640," Ph.D. dissertation, New York University, 1975.

23. See J. G. McManaway, " 'Occasion,' *FQ*, II. iv. 4–5," *Modern Language Notes*, 49 (1934), 391–393, cf. Praz, n. 1 p. 215; John Manning & Alastair Fowler, "The Iconography of Spenser's Occasion," *Journal of the Warburg and Courtauld Institutes*, 39 (1976), 263–266; David M. Burchmore, "The Medieval Sources [Boccaccio's *De casibus*] of Spenser's Occasion Episode," *Spenser Studies* 2, Patrick Cullen and Thomas P. Roche, Jr., eds. (Pittsburgh: University of Pittsburgh Press, 1981), pp. 93–120. On Spenser's eclecticism, *inter alia*, Graham Hough, "Spenser and Renaissance Iconography," *Essays in Criticism*, 11 (1961), 233–235, answering A. Fowler's view in *Essays in Criticism*, 10 (1960), 334–341 and making further exchanges with Fowler in 11 (1961), 236–238; Jean MacIntyre, "Spenser's *The Faerie Queene* III. xi. 47–48," *Explicator*, 24 (1966), item 69; James A. Heffernan, "William Wordsworth on Imagination: The Emblemizing Power," *PMLA*, 81 (1966), 389–399; C. S. Lewis, *Spenser's Image of Life*, ed. A. Fowler (Cambridge: Cambridge University Press, 1967); Wilhelm Füger, "Ungenutzte Perspektiven der Spenser-Deutung: Dargelegt an *TFQ* I viii 30–34," *DVLG*, 45 (1971), 252–301.

24. In the discussion of these chosen aspects, the theory of *devise* is considered as true of, and applicable to, the emblem because the emblem theorists agree in the main with the views of the *devise* theorists. They do differ in other aspects which are, however, not germane to the issues at hand. Spenser's view concerning the mixing of *dulci* with *utile* may be inferred from his emphasis on "doctrine by ensample" as seen in his "A Letter of the Authors": "But such, me seeme, should be satisfide with the vse of these dayes, seeing all things accounted by their showes, and nothing esteemed of, that is not delightfull and pleasing to commune sence. For this cause is Zenophon preferred before Plato, for that the one in the exquisite depth of his iudgement, formed a Commun welth such as it should be, but the other in the person of Cyrus and the Persians fashioned a gouernement such as might best be: So much more profitable and gratious is doctrine by ensample, then by

rule" ("Appendix I" in *Edmund Spenser: The Faerie Queene*, ed. A. C. Hamilton, [London: Longman, 1977], p. 737). See also J. W. Saunders, "The Façade of Morality," *ELH*, 19 (1952), 81–114; J. M. Steadman, "Felicity and End in Renaissance Epic and Ethics," *Journal of the History of Ideas*, 23 (1962), 117–132. On Spenser's poetics the following works may be consulted: Charles S. Baldwin, *Renaissance Literary Theory and Practice*, ed. D. L. Clark (New York: Columbia University Press, 1939); Rosemond Tuve, *Elizabethan and Metaphysical Imagery* (Chicago: University of Chicago Press, 1947); Maurice Evans, *English Poetry in the Sixteenth Century* (London: Hutchinson's University Library, 1955; rpt. New York: Norton, 1967); E. J. Clark, "Spenser's Theory of the English Poet," Ph.D. dissertation, Loyola University of Chicago (1956); Walter J. Ong, "From Allegory to Diagram in the Renaissance Mind," *Journal of Aesthetics and Art Criticism*, 17 (1959), 423–440; Carl R. Sonn, "Spenser's Imagery," *ELH*, 26 (1959), 156–170; Millar MacLure, "Nature and Art in *The Faerie Queene*," *ELH*, 28 (1961), 1–20; Ian Sowton, "Hidden Persuaders as a Means of Literary Grace: 16th-C Poetics and Rhetoric in England," *University of Toronto Quarterly*, 32 (1962), 55–69; G. Pellegrini, "Symbols and Significances," *Shakespeare Survey* 17, ed. Kenneth Muir (Cambridge: Cambridge University Press, 1964), pp. 180–187; Kenneth Myrick, *Sir Philip Sidney as a Literary Craftsman* (Lincoln: University of Nebraska Press, 1965); Veselin Kostic, "Ariosto and Spenser," *English Miscellany*, 17 (1966), 69–174; Paul J. Alpers, *The Poetry of The Faerie Queene* (Princeton, N.J.: Princeton University Press, 1967); Philip K. Wion, "The Poetic Styles of Edmund Spenser," Ph.D. dissertation, Yale University (1968); Donald M. Friedman, *Marvell's Pastoral Art* (Berkeley: University of California Press, 1970); D. M. Beach, "The Poetry of Idea: Sir Philip Sidney and the Theory of Allegory," *Texas Studies in Literature and Language*, 13 (1971), 356–389; Rawdon Wilson, "Images and Allegoremes of Time," *English Literary Renaissance*, 4 (1974), 56–82.

25. Estienne/Blount, p. 21 abbreviated and cited in the text hereafter as (E/B 21) because of the large number of quotations from this same translation. Estienne summarizes the theories and rules of Bargagli, Ammirato, Palazzi, Ruscelli, as well as Giovo, all Italian *devise* critics and collectors.

26. *Poetics*, 57b6a, tr. Allan H. Gilbert, *Literary Criticism Plato to Dryden* (New York: American Book Co., 1940), p. 99; see E. H. Gombrich, *Symbolic Images: Studies in the Art of the Renaissance* (London: Phaidon, 1972), pp. 165–168.

27. *The Lamb and the Elephant: Ideal Imitation and the Context of Renaissance Allegory* (San Marino, Calif.: The Huntington Library, 1974), p. 195 and n. 36.

28. P. 179, quoted in Jean Hagstrum, *The Sister Arts: the Tradition of Literary Pictorialism and English Poetry from Dryden to Gray* (Chicago: University of Chicago Press, 1958), p. 96 and n. 15.

29. Quoted in Praz, p. 60; Clements, p. 174; and Hagstrum, p. 95.

30. *L'Art*, 1662, p. 1 and 1684, p. 19.

31. There are these studies on Spenser and *ut pictura poesis*: Joseph B. Dallett, "Ideas of Sight in *The Faerie Queene*," *ELH*, 27 (1960), 59–75; Paul J. Alpers, *The Poetry of "The Faerie Queene*," pp. 11–14, 102–105; Frances J. Stillman, "The Visual Arts and Spenser's *The Faerie Queene*," Ph.D. disserta-

tion, The City University of New York (1971); John B. Bender, *Spenser and Literary Pictorialism* (Princeton, N.J.: Princeton University Press, 1972), pp. 10–23. General studies on the doctrine are: W. G. Howard, "*Ut Pictura Poesis*," *PMLA*, 24 (1909), 40–123; Cicely Davis, "*Ut Pictura Poesis*," *Modern Language Review*, 30 (1935), 159–169; Rensselaer W. Lee, "*Ut Pictura Poesis*," *Art Bulletin*, 22 (1940), 197–269, rpt. New York: Norton, 1967; W. H. Carter, Jr., "*Ut Pictura Poesis*: A Study of the Parallel between Painting and Poetry from Classical Times through the 17th Century," Ph.D. dissertation, Harvard University (1951); Douglas Bush, *Classical Influences in Renaissance Literature* (Cambridge, Mass.: Harvard University Press, 1952); John R. Spencer, "*Ut Rhetorica Pictura*: A Study in Quattrocento Theory of Painting," *Journal of the Warburg and Courtauld Institutes*, 20 (1957), 26–44; E. H. Gombrich, *Art and Illusion: a Study in the Psychology of Pictorial Representation* (New York: Pantheon Books, 1960), pp. 181–202; R. G. Saisselin, "*Ut Pictura Poesis*: Du Bos to Dederot," *Journal of Aesthetics and Art Criticism*, 20 (1961), 145–156; Wesley Trimpi, "The Meaning of Horace's 'Ut pictura poesis,' " *Journal of the Warburg and Courtauld Institutes*, 36 (1973), 1–34.

32. P. 62; for similar views held by the emblematists, see Clements, p. 227.

33. Hagstrum, pp. 12, 65, 9ff. That Spenser knew the works of Aristotle is common knowledge through efforts of generations of Spenserian scholars. However, it is difficult to be sure of the precise degree in which he practiced the Aristotelian imitation as explained by Hagstrum except to infer from examples such as his handling of the Graces' dance (see below). From such exercises of imitation, we know that Spenser always "assimilates" and "transcends" his models. See the three types of imitation as explained by G. S. Pigman in "Versions of Imitation in the Renaissance," *Renaissance Quarterly*, 33 (1980), 1–33; especially useful are the surveys of scholarship on imitation in nn. 1, 13, and 32.

34. See my "Spenser's Graces and Costalius' *Pegma*," *English Miscellany*, 23 (1972), 9–14 and Lila Geller, "The Acidalian Vision: Spenser's Graces in the *Faerie Queene* VI," *Review of English Studies*, new series, 23 (1972), 267–277. Since the publication of my study, I have discovered a new position of the three Graces in the anonymous *Mikrokosmos* (see p. 00 above), no. 19 "De beneficiis," showing two of the Graces coming towards the viewer on the right of the picture, one going away from him on the left (Plate 25), not in the traditional circular dance but in the traditional moral. This simply means that the last word on the Graces' dance has yet to be written, although its possible impact on Spenser remains doubtful.

35. Scholars have commented on Spenser's "inventiveness" and "originality" in the following works: Waldo F. McNeir, "Ariosto's Sospetto, Gascoigne's Suspicion, and Spenser's Malbecco," in *Festschrift für Walter Fischer* (Heidelberg, 1959), pp. 34–48; Anthony E. Friedman, "The Description of Landscape in Spenser's *Faerie Queene*: A Study of Rhetorical Tradition," Ph.D. dissertation, Columbia University (1965), on Spenser's imaginative innovations and adaptations; William Blisset, "Florimell and Marinell," *Studies in English Literature, 1500-1900*, 5 (1965), 87–104, on Spenser as a "mythmaker" in his own right; Wolfgang Clemen, *Originalität und Tradition in der englischen Dichtungsgeschichte* (München, 1978).

THOMAS P. ROCHE, JR.

Autobiographical Elements in Sidney's
Astrophil and Stella

"I am not I, pitie the tale of me."

*I*T IS my firm conviction that we all have been taking sonnet
sequences too seriously, by which I mean that we have clutched
on our reading of those massive and unwieldy packets of lyrical
desperation, with so few guideposts along the way, the destina-
tion clearly marked "no entry." That there is a man who desires
a woman and a woman who does not desire that man we all will
accept, but that is the point at which the serious clutching sets
in. After four hundred years, we still have not decided what to
make of the man's desire or of the woman's rejection. Not even
the fact that she very often is married seems to assuage our
sympathy for this young man who writes so well and who is
treated so badly. We are almost out of the delusion of "courtly
love" as an explanation of medieval love poetry, that fantastic
misreading of Ovid perpetrated by Gaston Paris in the 1890s,
solemnized for English readers by C. S. Lewis, and bowed to
by scores of scholars who accepted a god of love who jammed
the gears of sexual desire.

This essay is an addendum to my earlier essay on Sidney in
this journal, in which I tried to establish a distance between
Sidney as artist and his fictional spokesman Astrophil.[1] I still
adhere to the argument of that essay, but among the subjects I
did not treat there are the clearly autobiographical references to
Sidney's life invoked by Astrophil that pull Sidney back into the
realm of Astrophil's exaggerated rhetoric. A reading of those
autobiographical references is the subject of this essay.

I

The autobiographical references are scattered throughout the
sequence, beginning with the title *Astrophil and Stella*, in which

209

the third syllable of the poet-lover's name is not only the Greek for *love* but also the first syllable of Sidney's Christian name. The pun is repeated in the "Good brother *Philip*" of sonnet 83, fictionally a reference to the name of Stella's pet sparrow. There are references to current events and to his father's career (sonnet 30), to his own position as cupbearer to Queen Elizabeth (sonnet 70), and to the Sidney arms (sonnet 65). There is a reference to the Devereux arms, Stella's family (sonnet 13), and more important, perhaps, are the slurs on Lord Rich through the puns on his name (sonnets 9, 24, 35, 37, the latter three sometimes omitted from manuscripts and early editions).[2]

The evidence for the "identification" of Stella with Penelope Devereux, Lady Rich, has been documented for the past fifty years through the work of Hoyt Hudson, Jack Stillinger, and Ephim Fogel,[3] but that richly substantiated identification has almost always been pressed into the service of the unsupported allegation that Sidney was passionately in love with Penelope. Not until 1964, when we were moving away from the critically simplistic autobiographical interpretation of Sidney's sequence did Jean Robertson throw new fuel on the fire through her publication of the Juel-Jensen manuscript of George Gifford's *The Manner of Sir Philip Sidneyes Death*.[4] Gifford was the priest who attended Sidney during his prolonged dying, and his report reads:

> Hee [Sidney] added further I had this night a trouble in my mynde. For, examining my selfe, mee thought I had not a sure hold in Christ. After I had continued in this Perplexi- tie a while, Obserue how stranglie God did deliuer mee (For indeed it was a strange deliuerance I had). There came to my remembraunce a Vanitie wherein I had taken de- light, whereof I had not rid my selfe. It was my Ladie Rich. But I ridd my selfe of it, and presentlie my Ioy and Comfort returned within fewe howers.[5]

If Sidney in fact said something to this effect, then we might well credit him with a yen for Lady Rich at some earlier point in his life, but the statement should not be construed that his "Vanitie" about Lady Rich was an overriding passion of his life. Let us review the facts of the case.

The English nobility was unusually closely knit during the

reign of the Tudors. Sidney's mother was a Dudley. Her brother, Robert, the Earl of Leicester, was the favorite of the Queen. Another brother, Ambrose, was the Earl of Warwick. Her sister, Catherine, was the wife of Henry Hastings, third Earl of Huntingdon, who was given the guardianship of Penelope after the death of her father, the first Earl of Essex, in 1576,[6] and it was his Countess who introduced Penelope to court where Sidney first met her.[7] That is, Sidney first met Penelope under the tutelage of his aunt in 1581, at a time when the Countess, Leicester, and Sir Francis Walsingham, Sidney's friend and future father-in-law, were negotiating the marriage of Penelope to Lord Rich, which took place on 1 November 1581.[8] We do not know whether Sidney knew of the Earl of Essex's presumed interest in 1576 about the "treaty betwene Mr. *Phillip* and my Lady *Penelope*,"[9] nor of the 1582 will drawn up by his uncle Leicester suggesting that Philip be married to Penelope's younger sister Dorothy.[10] We do know that Sidney married the daughter of Sir Francis Walsingham on 23 September 1583[11] and that he publicly acknowledged his chagrin at being disinherited from his uncle's title when Leicester's marriage to the widowed mother of Penelope produced a male heir in 1581, a deprivation greater I believe than his failure to win Penelope, if he had ever tried.[12]

Of the later events of this closely knit circle Sidney could not have known after his death in 1586, but the ironies are too powerful to resist citing. In his will Sidney left his best sword to Penelope's brother, second Earl of Essex, who married Sidney's widow in 1590.[13] Leicester's son and heir from Penelope's mother predeceased the father, and Sidney's younger brother, Robert, succeeded to the title.[14] Penelope, never acknowledging Sidney's "inky tribute," went on to her open adultery with Charles Blount, Lord Mountjoy, her bearing him four children (at least one interspersed with a child fathered by her husband), her intrigues with her brother's plot in the last years of the Queen, her high position in the early years of James's reign, her disgrace after her marriage to her lover by the young priest, William Laud, and her death shortly after her marriage.[15]

None of these historical facts suggests an undying love of Sidney for Penelope. Politics more than passion is the catalyst of the historical facts, not one of which suggests that the story Sidney allows Astrophil to tell bears any relationship to the life

Sidney led. Therefore I would like to propose that Sidney's comment on Lady Rich as reported by Gifford has little or nothing to do with his life but much to do with his making her the subject of his "inky tribute." At least part of Sidney's guilt must have come from his having turned Penelope into his Stella, for the word *Vanitie* may refer to the use he made of Penelope in writing *Astrophil and Stella*. We merely assume that a woman might have been delighted to have the flattery of a sonnet sequence, but we have no evidence either positive or negative from Beatrice, Laura, or Stella. Mr. Beatrice and Mr. Laura are soothingly absent from Dante's and Petrarch's sequences, but we should consider the response of Lord Rich, so viciously satirized, so abruptly caught up in a literary caricature during the first years of his marriage. The wounded husband aside, what woman would tolerate such vehement and breathless devotion as a sonnet sequence to be circulated in print or even to a small coterie of friends? Even Emma Bovary would have boggled at the *Vanitie* that Sidney constructed. From any point of view *Astrophil and Stella* is a major *Vanitie*, a major affront to society, to family, and to the person addressed, and Sidney might well have felt estrangement from his Lord because of his *Vanitie* and because of his pride in what he had created.

Sidney's *Vanitie* may be compared to the equal concern that Chaucer felt at the end of his life:

> For oure booke seith, "Al that is writen is writen for oure doctrine," and that is myn entente. / Wherefore I biseke yow mekely, for the mercy of God, that ye preye for me that Crist have mercy on me and foryeve me my giltes; / and namely of my translacions and enditynges of worldly *vanities*, the which I revoke in my retracciouns. . . .
>
> (Italics mine).[16]

In that retraction Chaucer proceeds through every one of the poems for which we admire him today, but he is not reneging on either literature or on love. He is taking authorial responsibility for his humorously ironic treatment of love, which might lead readers to believe that he was espousing the vanities of love as depicted in his *Troilus* "and the tales of Canterbury, thilke that sownen into synne."[17] Irony is the most corruptible of literary stances, and much modern criticism has shown Chaucer to be in advance of his time on this score. The ironist with a Christian conscience is caught in a Catch-22 bind between derring-do and doing good, and both Chaucer and Sidney tried the dangerous expedient of irony, only to have their ironies believed as true by later generations, most notably our own. Both Chaucer and Sidney had scruples (or what used to be called scruples) about their literary cleverness in depicting witty immorality. We today too easily dismiss their pious concern about possible misinterpretation, but then we are too far removed from the pieties that claimed them. Their literary sprightliness, even call it "psychological depth," which we so much admire, inspired them with a fear of their own *vanitie*.

II

Sidney's scruple about "my Ladie Rich" is one face of this issue, and my attempt to discharge its value as a claim that Sidney had a lifelong passion for Penelope must be countered by equally strong claims that many of Sidney's contemporaries felt that his *Vanitie* was a compliment and honor to Lady Rich. Hudson cites the numerous documents of praise that claim Sidney's poetic use of Penelope as one of her outstanding attributes, in which she is linked to Sidney's widow (Spenser's *Astrophel*)[18] and to his daughter, the Countess of Rutland (Matthew Gwinne's sonnet),[19] and one poem that calls Penelope's son, Henry Rich, "Lord of Arcadia."[20] This praise of Penelope includes her in an extended family of the Sidneys that argues against a passionate involvement. Would not widow or orphaned daughter (to say nothing of bereaved sister) have objected to the inclusion of an earlier love in compliments to the family or to memory of beloved husband, father, brother? Or after 1590 when the sequence was just being printed and circulated publicly, what did newly married widow say to new sister-in-law about the poem to her? I cannot believe that if they spoke of dead Philip's poem, the conversation would be a sexual rivalry. On the one hand Sidney feels scruples; on the other hand the literary and court world at large understands praise of the lady. The "real-life" situation seems to be *Astrophil and Stella* turned inside out. What the poet has made Astrophil lust after in the sequence and considers a *Vanitie* at the end of his life becomes for his contemporaries and family a celebration of the lady. To me the whole business smacks of literary convention.

And that is precisely what happens in sonnet sequences that follow the publication of *Astrophil and Stella*. In 1593 Barnabe Barnes imitated the double title of Sidney's poem in his *Parthenophil and Parthenophe*, a much maligned sequence that deserves more attention than it has got. For example, Stella is the presiding deity in Barnes's Canzon 2, the subject of which is the birthday of Astrophil, probably a numerological reference to Sidney's birthday on 30 November.[21] Barnes also attempts to "overgo" various of Sidney's tactics, such as writing 109 sonnets, one more than Sidney, in imitation of what Alastair Fowler has pointed out as the Penelope game of the 108 suitors in the *Odyssey*, Sidney's 108 suitor-sonnets just missing by one the Penelope he wanted.[22] The 108 "sonnets" of the anonymous *Alcilia* of 1595 also seem to be an allusion to the Sidneyan number. I would also like to think that not coincidentally the 108th poem in *England's Helicon* (1600) is the famous Eighth Song of Sidney's sequence. The recurrence of the number 108 (or 109) in these sequences and collections suggests a clear awareness of Sidney's submerged number symbolism and its inescapable reference to Penelope Rich as a literary device. There is no reason to suppose that commiseration for Sidney's loss of Penelope was their intention.

More important is the Todd MS version of Henry Constable's sequence *Diana* because Constable knew both Sidney and Penelope.[23] Constable addresses two sonnets "To my Lady Rich,"[24] one on the birth and one on the death of "my Lady Riches daughter,"[25] one to "Mr Hilliard vpon occasion of a picture he made of my Ladie Rich," presumably the same portrait Constable carried with him to present to James VI.[26] There is also a sonnet to the Countess of Pembroke and one to the Countess of Essex "vpon occasion of the death of her first husband Sir Philip Sydney" and three to "Sir Philip Sydneyes soule."[27] Although these poems sit in close proximity to each other in the sequence, it seems almost as if the subjects had never met or heard of one another in that Constable makes no overt attempt to relate them to each other in the sequence. That Constable was well aware of the biographical connections cannot be doubted, but he nowhere mentions Sidney and

Penelope together, although he knew the *Astrophil and Stella* because his second sonnet to Penelope is an amalgam of devices used by Sidney in sonnets 13, 24, and 37, with the usual puns on the name *Rich*.[28] I think that Constable knew that there was no passionate affair between them, that *Astrophil and Stella* was an elaborate game concocted by Sidney, a fiction more brilliantly executed than by any previous English sonneteer. The reason that Constable does not relate Sidney and Penelope within his sequence is not a conspiracy of silence but a frank acknowledgment that the lives they led were greater and of more importance than the fictional account told by Astrophil.

Much later than Barnes and Constable, Alexander Craig in his *Amorose Songes, Sonnets and Elegies* (1606) writes a 108 poem sequence to eight different ladies, one of whom is named Penelope.[29] Craig, who followed James I to London in hope of preferment, begins his sequence with an epistle to Queen Anne, followed by an Epistle Generall to the eight ladies, in which he signs himself *Zeuxis*. The reference is to Cicero's story in *De inventione*, II.1–3 of Zeuxis's choosing five of the most beautiful Croatian maidens as models for a statue of Helen "because in no single case has Nature made anything perfect and finished in every part. Therefore as if she would have no bounty to lavish on the others if she gave everything to one, she bestows some advantage on one and some on another, but always joins it with some defect."[30] Even with this fictional ploy, Craig would have needed the powers of a Joseph Smith poetically to pull this off, especially considering the names he chooses: Idea, Cynthia, Lithocardia ("stony heart"), Kala ("beautiful," a loved one in the *Arcadia*), Lais (the whore in Ovid), Erantina (the "wanderer"), Pandora, and Penelope.

Penelope might be a simple classical allusion except that in the first poem addressed to her Craig identifies her as Sidney's Penelope: "If curious heades to know her name do craue, / Shee is a Lady *Rich*. . . ." Twenty years after Sidney's death, two years after Penelope had ceased to be Lady Rich even in name, Craig is invoking the literary game that Sidney invented. Despite Craig's pleas in the ten sonnets he addressed to Penelope, he could not have been in love with her any more than Sidney. He might have met her when she was part of the English delegation sent to meet Queen Anne and to escort her back to London, but we have no proof of any such meeting,[31] nor should we expect to, given the high social status of Penelope within the court world and Craig's insignificant position as poetaster trying to make the big time. His final sonnet to Penelope, "His vnwilling Farewell to PENELOPE,"plays off another well known literary line, Lord Vaux's famous, "I loathe that I did love" from *Tottel's Miscellany*.[32]

> Not that I loath, where I so long did loue,
> Thou art vnkind, and I must needs remoue.

What the unkindness was, what the love proffered, cannot be distinguished from the unkindness requited by the other ladies and the indistinguishable love proffered to each of them. Craig's deployment of these literary loves cannot be distinguished, although we might see that Idea, Cynthia and Pandora were sonnet loves in earlier sequences[33] and that Craig in his address "To the Reader," makes a clear distinction between Lais and the others: " So haue I in middest of my modest Affections, committed to the Presse my vnchast Loue to Lais, that contraries by contraries, and Vertue by Vice, more cleerely may shine."[34] Craig was obviously trying to urge his way into the tradition of the sonnet sequence, and he did so by a mincing observance of what I have called elsewhere the "negative example," by which the poet makes the poet-lover show through his skill as poet the inadequacy and selfishness of his love to the lady. Craig overgoes by eight the possibility of genuine affection and exposes the game of love sonnetry for the subterfuge it was. His inclusion of a Penelope hovers somewhere between the poetic power of Sidney's fiction and the social power that Penelope exerted in her own right. At the time Craig was writing, Penelope had already committed her adultery with Mountjoy with its attendant four offspring, had been implicated and exonerated from her brother's conspiracy against the Queen, and had contracted her scandalous marriage to Mountjoy, which had earned her dismissal from the court of James. Craig, like the other sonneteers, was merely playing out a Penelope game they had learned from Sidney.

A more important problem in the influence of Sidney's fiction on later writers occurs in the six "Astrophel" elegies contained in Spenser's *Colin Clouts Come Home Again* (1595). Jack Stillinger in his excellent article states that both Spenser's and Lodowick Bryskett's two elegies "clearly identify Stella with Sidney's wife, Frances Walsingham," adding in a footnote the challenge: "Anyone wishing to prove that Stella is always Penelope will have to explain the 'Astrophel' series."[35] I would like to take up that challenge because it bears on my views of the decorum displayed by Constable and Craig.

Of the six elegies, three, those of Spenser and Bryskett, are pastoral elegy, that of Matthew Roydon could be called domesticated pastoral, and those by Ralegh and Greville straightforward elegiac lament. If we count the "Dolefull Lay of Clorinda," attributed by some to the Countess of Pembroke, as a separate poem and not the invention of Spenser himself, it falls into the latter category of elegiac lament. Not one of the last poems mentioned makes any reference to Stella or to love.[36] In 1595 when this volume was published, Sidney had been dead for nine years, his widow married for five years to Penelope's brother, and Penelope living in open adultery with Mountjoy.[37] Several of the elegies had already been published. Bryskett's *The Mourning Muse of Thestylis* had been entered in the Stationers' Register in 1587; Roydon, Ralegh, and Greville had been published in *The Phoenix Nest* (1593). Only Spenser's poem is late, proclaiming again his neglect of Sidney's death as he had in the preface to *The Ruins of Time* (1591). But in 1595 Colin Clout had come home again, at least in print, and saw to it that these six elegies for Sidney were printed along with his fictional eclogue of praise for the court of Elizabeth, as he had observed it in his trip to England with Sir Walter Ralegh in 1589.[38] Among the ladies he chose to praise in that poem was Stella:

> Ne lesse praisworthie *Stella* do I read,
> Though nought my praises of her needed arre,
> Whom verse of noblest shepheard lately dead
> Hath prais'd and rais'd aboue each other starre.
>
> (532–535)

That Spenser is referring to the *Astrophil and Stella* cannot be doubted, nor that this Stella refers to Penelope. More important are the dedications to Ralegh for *Colin Clout* and to the Countess of Essex for *Astrophel*. The enmity between Ralegh and Essex posed a tactical problem for Spenser.[39] Ralegh's generosity in sponsoring him at court in 1589 deserved Spenser's thanks; his earlier patronage by the Dudley family in the persons of Leicester and Sidney also deserved his thanks, and therefore his dedication of the *Astrophel* elegies to Sidney's widow, now wife of Essex, must have been an attempt to bridge the gap between Ralegh and Essex. His poem had to give praise not only to Sidney's widow for the decease of her first husband but also praise to the second husband, whose sister was the Stella of whom the first husband wrote.

Regardless of the historical suppositions I am making (and we know too little about the niceties of dedications) Spenser in his poem describes the love of Astrophil for Stella:

> For one alone he cared, for one he sight,
> His lifes desire, and his deare loues delight.
>
> *Stella* the faire, the fairest star in skie,
> As faire as *Venus* or the fairest faire:
> A fairer star saw neuer liuing eie,
> Shot her sharp pointed beames through purest aire.
> Her he did loue, her he alone did honor,
> His thoughts, his rimes, his songs were all vpon her.
>
> To her he vowd the seruice of his daies,
> On her he spent the riches of his wit:
> For her he made hymnes of immortal praise,
> Of onely her he sung, he thought, he writ.
> Her, and but her of loue he worthie deemed,
> For all the rest but litle he esteemed.
>
> (53–66)[40]

This looks for all the world like a real life story seen through the looking glass of pastoral, but I would like to suggest that we observe it, like Alice, in that world in which we find ourselves as readers. Spenser seems to be describing Sidney's Astrophil himself in pursuit of Stella, in which all thoughts of reason, virtue, courtly chivalry, world events take second place to his desire for Stella: "For all the rest but litle he esteemed." That statement is true of Astrophil, but it is patently false applied to Sidney, who withdrew to Wilton when his advice about the French marriage was refused, who eagerly sought to fight for the cause of Protestantism in the Low Countries, for which he lost his life. It is also true of Astrophil that "his thoughts, his rimes, his songs were all upon her," that "On her he spent the *riches* of his wit" (italics mine), that "For her he made hymnes of immortal praise," which may sound like simple Spenserian hyperbole unless we recall the outright blasphemy of Astrophil in Song I: "To you, to you, all song of praise is due; / Only in you my song begins and endeth," of which Spenser's line, "Of onely her he sung, he thought, he writ," should surely be an imitation and a further indication that Spenser read his Astrophil ironically. Spenser seems to see the idolatry of Sidney's Astrophil: "A fairer star saw neuer liuing eie." This line could be just another example of simple Spenserian hyperbole, but we might be selling Spenser short to settle for that reading; he could be calling into question the possibility of any living eye ever seeing such a star, calling into question the rhetorical demands of Astrophil. Such a reading makes Spenser's poem more interesting, more perceptive, and insists that we consider more carefully his belated praise of Sidney.

If we read over Spenser's poem, we find many embarrassing comments if applied to Sidney, comments that apply more readily to Astrophil. Spenser's Astrophel is:

> In one thing onely fayling of the best,
> That he was not so happie as the rest.
> (11–12)

What kind of praise is that for Sidney, unless we take Spenser's pastoral metaphor seriously? He is writing about the shepherds among whom he places his Astrophel,

> That all mens hearts with secret rauishment
> He stole away, and *weetingly beguyld.*
> Ne spight it selfe that all good things doth spill,
> Found ought in him, that she could say was ill.
> (21–24; italics mine)

I think that Spenser is here speaking of Sidney's *weeting beguilement* of the reader of his sequence through the brilliance of his poetry so that spite itself could not fault him. Spenser is playing his irrepressible game of allegory, pastoral to be sure, but allegory nonetheless, doubly speaking of both Sidney and

Astrophil, Sidney and his Astrophil both subsumed into Spenser's Astrophel:

> Ne her with ydle words alone he wowed,
> And verses vaine (yet verses are not vaine)
> But with braue deeds to her sole seruice vowed,
> And bold atchieuements her did entertaine.
> For both in deeds and words he nourtred was,
> Both wise and hardie (too hardie alas).
>
> (67–72)

In this stanza Spenser takes us beyond the Sidney of *Astrophil and Stella* to the Sidney at Zutphen, whose hardy deeds ("too hardie alas") killed him. There is no mention of Low Countries or Zutphen; it is a pastoral beast that kills him:

> A cruell beast of most accursed brood
> Vpon him turnd (despeyre makes cowards stout)
> And with fell tooth accustomed to blood,
> Launched his thigh with so mischievous might
> That it both bone and muscles ryued quight.
>
> (116–120)

We are not meant to translate these images back into facts historical, although we must be aware of them. Sidney's exploits in the battle of Zutphen are being *incorporated* into Spenser's fiction of his Astrophel, and thus when Stella rushes in to transform herself into a flower with the dying Astrophel, Spenser is telling us that the Stella that Sidney created *literally* dies with the death of Sidney: "It was my Ladie Rich."

The challenge issued by Stillinger cannot be answered by reference either to Penelope or to Frances Walsingham because it is Stella whom Spenser kills off in his poem because "She likewise did *deforme* like him to be" (156), and after two stanzas of extravagant deformation on her part, Spenser concludes:

> The rest of her impatient regret,
> And piteous mone the which she for him made:
> *No toong can tell, nor any forth can set.*
> But *he* whose heart like sorrow did inuade.

> At last when paine his vitall powres had spent,
> *His* wasted life *her* weary lodge forwent.
>
> (169–174; italics mine)

Spenser's modest muse allows "No toong" to complete Astrophel's tale, even while he is in the act of completing it by allowing Astrophil a consummation and a leavetaking that Sidney did not allow, achieved in this poem through Spenser's characteristic dismissal of attention to pronominal adjectives. That they both become a flower in Ovidian manner is only to give praise to the creator, Sidney, because that Stella of whom he wrote most certainly died in his death, and they became one in a way that Astrophil could never have expected. He could tell no more lies about her, and she, still alive as Penelope, had no longer need to restrain his fantasies.

Read in this way, Spenser's poem is a compliment to Frances, Countess of Essex, to Mary, Countess of Pembroke, to Penelope Lady Rich, and to Sidney's skill as a poet. All their relationships were subsumed under Spenser's pastoral metaphor if we will allow Spenser the option of using his metaphors with intelligence in accordance with literary convention, which requires one further example from the "Astrophel" elegies to bring back Sidney's enterprize to its ultimate source in Petrarch.

In the second of Bryskett's elegies, Stella appears, again transformed, toward the end of the poem. Bryskett has been addressing women mourners in the form of classical "Nymphs and Naiades:"

> Away all griefe and sorrow from your harts:
> Alas! who now is left that like him sings?
> When shall you heare againe like harmonie?
> So sweet a sownd who to you now imparts?
> Loe where engraved by his hand yet lives
> The name of Stella, in yonder bay tree.
> Happie name, happie tree! faire may you grow,
> And spred your sacred branch, which honor gives
> To famous emperours, and poets crowne.
>
> (121–129)

In becoming a laurel, Stella here becomes another literary artifact that reaches back to the mythic subtext of Petrarch's

Canzoniere in Ovid's myth of Apollo and Daphne in Book I of the *Metamorphoses*. At the end of Apollo's unavailing race for Daphne, as she is changing into the laurel, Ovid relates:

> But even now in this new form Apollo loved her; and placing his hand upon the trunk, he felt the heart still fluttering beneath the bark. He embraced the branches as if human limbs, and pressed his lips upon the wood. But even the wood shrank from his kisses. And the god cried out to this: "Since thou canst not be my bride, thou shalt at least be my tree. *My hair, my lyre, my quiver shall always be entwined with thee, O laurel. With thee shall Roman generals wreathe their heads, when shouts of joy shall acclaim their triumph, and long processions climb the Capitol.* Thou at Augustus' portals shall stand a trusty guardian, and keep watch over the civic crown of oak which hangs between. And as my head is ever young and my locks unshorn, so do thou keep the beauty of thy leaves perpetual." Paean was done. The laurel waved her new-made branches, and seemed to move her head-like top in full consent.[41]
>
> (553–567, italics mine)

Bryskett is referring to this passage in Ovid where the Roman poet created the myth of the poet crowned with laurel. Apollo allows his love defeat at the hands of a nymph to become the victory of poets. From the time of Ovid, defeat in the race of love becomes the means of praise for both pursuer and pursued because Apollo is crowned with his transformed defeat. Bryskett's awareness of this crucial nexus of love and poetic fame records the compromise of sonneteers from Petrarch on: love defeated can become poetic victory. Daphne, Laura, or Penelope, transliterated, woven into a context of words, becomes the greater prize, unsought, unexpected in Ovid but eagerly sought and written for thereafter. Sidney as well as any other sonneteer knew that passion defeated in poetry could become praise, and thus he began his Penelope game not out of love but out of love poetry, and that is the use to which each of the later poets puts the lesson they learned from Sidney's *Astrophil and Stella*. It must be excellent poetry to turn the trick, but that is just what Sidney wrote (as we all know), and that is why neither widow, nor sister, nor Penelope, nor fellow poets, who equally well understood the conventions out of which Sidney was writing, thought a minute about the social improprieties that have consumed what I called at the beginning of this essay our over-serious attention to sonnet sequences.

III

If my argument about the essentially literary assessment of Sidney's love for Penelope by later poets is tenable, if we indeed must make a distinction between Sidney and Astrophil, between Penelope and Stella, between biography and poetry, then we must try to account for those striking acts of poetic bravado in which Sidney puts into Astrophil's voice unmistakable references to his own life. If Sidney is not writing about himself, then why introduce the reference to his father's work in Ulster (sonnet 30), the puns on the name *Rich* (sonnets 9, 24, 35, 37), the reference to his own arms (sonnet 65), to his being cup-bearer to the Queen (sonnet 70), and the address to Stella's sparrow, "Good brother Philip" (sonnet 83)? There are others, but it is not my purpose to glean a catalogue to Devereux arms (sonnet 13) or to tournaments Sidney might have participated in (sonnet 41) because I believe that Sidney was following literary convention in this respect as well as in his treatment of Penelope as Stella.

I will begin with the final line of sonnet 45, "I am not I, pitie the tale of me," which I have used as the epigraph for this essay. I suggested in my earlier essay the bawdy pun on *tale-tail* that Sidney intended for Astrophil, which is the apparently urgent subagent of his prolific outpouring in verse, a specific example of Fowler's argument that the 108 sonnets are meant to represent the 108 unruly suitors of Penelope. I follow the spurious logic of Astrophil, in which he wants to become the words he speaks in order to obtain Stella's *grace*, but I can also hear Sidney's voice crying "I am not I" because he is not describing himself but asking for an intelligent moral response to the scurrilous tale he is telling. How do we separate I from *I* and *tale* from *tail*, except in our proper discriminations of love, or as Sidney states it for Astrophil in sonnets 1 and 63, in our discriminations of grammar, rhetoric, and logic, trivial matter, to be sure, but fundamental to right reason and proper speech? Therefore Sidney with bold audacity allows Astrophil to bring

in to his tale Sidney's father's exploits in Ulster ("wherewith
my father once made it half tame") among the other grave
problems of the Elizabethan world, to make us see the ultimate
triviality of his Astrophil, to make us hear another tale than the
one Astrophil is telling. Within the ambience of such riddling
sonnets, the puns on Lord Rich's name are merely penny ante,
an in-house joke, that would have produced only a smile of
recognition. One wonders to what heights Astrophil's wit
would have been spurred had Penelope's affair with Mountjoy
occurred during Sidney's life.

Since that possibility was denied him historically and linguis-
tically, let us turn to sonnet 83, "Good brother Philip," which I
think is Astrophil's anti-sonnet response to Sidney's earnest
intention. In the same spirit of game, Sidney, who gave Astrophil his father, his arms, now gives him himself in the form of a
sparrow who has found his way to Stella's love for Astrophil to
play his foulest revenge on his creator:

> Good brother *Philip*, I have borne you long,
>   I was content you should in favour creepe,
>   While craftily you seem'd your cut to keepe,
> As though that faire soft hand did you great wrong.
> I bare (with Envie) yet I bare your song,
>   When in her necke you did *Love* ditties peepe;
>   Nay, more foole I, oft suffered you to sleepe
> In Lillies' neast, where *Love's* selfe lies along.
>   What, doth high place ambitious thoughts augment?
> Is sawcinesse reward of curtesie?
> Cannot such grace your silly selfe content,
> But you must needs with those lips billing be?
>   And through those lips drinke Nectar from that toong;
>   Leave that sir *Phip*, least off your necke be wroong.

This poem is doing something more than Skelton's *Philip
Sparrow* and Catullus 2: *Passer, deliceae meae puellae*, which is its
ultimate source. It comes in the sequence between sonnet 82, in
which Astrophil exults over the kiss he has extracted from
Stella, ending with an apology for biting her lips (never more to
do so) and Song III, a poem about Orpheus, a poet whose
singing head was torn off by "maenads fierce." Thus the sonnet
is caught between a poem that shows Astrophil in the same

situation as the sparrow (Sidney) of sonnet 83 and a poem about
Orpheus and the power of music.

> What could the Muse herself that *Orpheus* bore
> The Muse herself, for her enchanting son
> When Universal nature did lament,
> When by the rout that made the hideous roar,
> His gory visage down the stream was sent,
> Down the swift *Hebrus* to the *Lesbian* shore?
> (Lycidas, 58–63)

That neck of billing sparrow that may "off be wroong" is
followed immediately by a song about the mighty early poet
whose power of song cost him his head. I do not think that
Sidney was unaware of the connections, although unlike us he
would not have had the advantage of Milton's lines. Sidney's
own poem on Orpheus is divided by Astrophil's spurious logic
and superlative mechanical skills into three stanzas of rhetorical
porridge in which Stella's singing is likened to Orpheus's
teaching trees to sing and Amphion's power to make stones
dance into the walls of Thebes in the first stanza, in which sight
takes precedence in the second stanza, and nonsense takes over
in the third stanza:

> Knowe that small Love is quicke, and great
>   Love doth amaze:
> They are amaz'd, but you with reason armed.
> O eyes, o eares of men how are you charmed!
> (16–18)

Astrophil is off on his quest again, but Sidney in sonnet 83 is
allowing his creation Astrophil to take revenge on him for his
instructive structuring of the sequence. Sidney allows himself
to become the billing sparrow, the bird of Venus, the singing
delight that so annoys Astrophil because he preempts his own
desires. By following this sonnet with the Orpheus reference in
Song III, Sidney indicates to us the danger he foresaw in his
singing, a danger described in *The Dolefull Lay of Clorinda*,
whether written by the Countess of Pembroke or by Spenser
himself. Clorinda, speaking to the shepherd lasses, advises:

Ne euer sing the loue-layes which he made,
Who euer made such layes of loue as hee?
Ne euer read the riddles, which he sayd
Vnto your selues, to make you mery glee.
    Your mery glee is now laid all abed,
    Your mery maker now alasse is dead.
                                              (43–48)

I am assuming, of course, that the "layes of loue" include
Astrophil and Stella, which seems to me a tenable assumption in
a volume entitled *Astrophel*. If so, then what are the "riddles . . .
to make you mery glee?" They may be the conventional
"ditties" of pastoral verse, but if they are the riddling passions
of Astrophil's love for Stella, Sidney under*cutting* himself and
his poet-lover in order to create the "mery glee" of his poem,
then we may read Astrophil's reply to Sidney in sonnet 83 as
Sidney's slap at himself for the riddling intentions of his sequence:

Good brother *Philip*, I have borne you long,
    I was content you should in favour creepe,
    While craftily you seem'd your cut to keepe,
As though that faire soft hand did you great wrong.

The sexual rivalry established between Astrophil and "*Philip*" is
also the literary burden that Astrophil has borne from his
creator while *craftily* he seemed his *cut* to keep, "As though that
faire soft hand did you great wrong." This is, in fact, the story
that Sidney allows his Astro*phil* to tell, and it has become the
story of Sir Philip Sidney, to the detriment of poet and poem,
for it establishes a myth of identity that obscures the "mery
glee" of Sidney's invention. Astrophil is making as great a
misreading of good brother Philip's crafty cuts as Malvolio did
of Olivia's C's, U's, and T's, and to the same bawdy effect. If
one reads beneath the riddle of the sparrow metaphor, one can
see that the sparrow is giving the lie to Astrophil's demands on
Stella. Astrophil's complaints about good brother Philip are
precisely those that Sidney made to under*cut* the *tale-tail* of
Astrophil. Sexual and literary undercuttings are meant by
Sidney to come together, to show the insularity of Astrophil's
vision of life in general, and of Stella in particular. The refer-

ences to his father's exploits in Ulster, the coats of arms made the butt of easy, clever jokes, his own Christian name reduced to the level of a sparrow, show Sidney's awareness of the triviality he had allowed Astrophil to make of real life and of the insidiousness of the "mery glee" he had allowed himself to perpetrate.

I think that something like this explanation led Sidney to remark about the vanity, "It was my lady Rich," that vanity that came between him and his Redeemer in his dying hours. Sexual desire, although I cannot prove it, was not his "Vanitie," more than I have suggested from reading words, both of Sidney and of later poets commenting on his poem.[42] I sincerely hope that Sidney resolved his literary difficulty with his Creator, if not along the lines I have suggested, at least not in despair over one of his most triumphant creations.

Princeton University

NOTES

1. "*Astrophil and Stella*: A Radical Reading," *Spenser Studies* III, Patrick Cullen and Thomas P. Roche, Jr., eds. (Pittsburgh: University of Pittsburgh Press, 1982), pp. 139–191.

2. See note to sonnet 37 in William A. Ringler, Jr., ed., *The Poems of Sir Philip Sidney* (Oxford: At the Clarendon Press, 1962), p. 473. All quotations from Sidney are from this edition and citations from Ringler's commentary will be referred to as Ringler hereafter.

3. Hoyt H. Hudson, "Penelope Devereux as Sidney's Stella," *Huntington Library Bulletin*, 7 (1935), 89–129; Jack Stillinger, "The Biographical Problem of *Astrophel and Stella*," *Journal of English and Germanic Philology*, 59 (1960), 617–639; Ephim Fogel, "The Mythical Sorrows of Astrophel," *Studies in Literature and Language in Honour of Margaret Schlauch* (Warsaw, 1966), pp. 133–151.

4. Jean Robertson, "Sir Philip Sidney and Lady Penelope Rich," *Review of English Studies*, n.s. 15 (1964), 296–297.

5. *Ibid.*, p. 297.

6. Ringler, p. 436.

7. Ringler, p. 438.

8. Ringler, p. 438.

9. See Hudson, pp. 90–91.

10. Ringler, p. 442.

11. Ringler, p. 443.

12. Ringler, p. 441: "Camden reported that on the next tilt day Sidney bore

as his device, 'SPERAVI, thus dashed through, to shew his hope therein was dashed.' "

13. Ringler, p. 443.

14. See *DNB* entry for Robert Sidney. Hudson, p. 126, claims that it was the son of Robert, which is true, but he inherited the title from his father, not his great uncle.

15. Ringler, pp. 444–446; Hudson, p. 126. The divorce settlement between the Riches proscribed remarriage while the other was alive. Laud, who was chaplain to Mountjoy (by the time of the marriage Earl of Devonshire) kept a day of penance each 1 November, All Saints, for the illegal marriage he had performed, even when he had become Archbishop of Canterbury.

16. *The Poetical Works of Chaucer*, ed. F. N. Robinson (Cambridge, Mass.: Houghton Mifflin, 1933), p. 314.

17. *Ibid.*, p. 314.

18. Stillinger, p. 630.

19. Hudson, pp. 98–104; Stillinger, pp. 628–629.

20. Hudson, p. 107.

21. I argue the point in my forthcoming book *Petrarch and the English Sonnet Sequences*.

22. See Alastair Fowler, *Triumphal Forms* (Cambridge: Cambridge University Press, 1970), pp. 175–176 and my article in *Spenser Studies* III, pp. 139–140 and note 32.

23. The Todd MS (BL MS. Dyce 44) has been superbly edited by Joan Grundy, *The Poems of Henry Constable* (Liverpool: Liverpool University Press, 1960), p. 26.

24. Grundy, pp. 150–151.

25. Grundy, pp. 157, 170.

26. Grundy, pp. 158 and 239n.

27. Grundy, pp. 154, 155, 167–169.

28. Grundy, p. 151.

29. *The Poetical Works of Alexander Craig* (Glasgow: Printed for the Hunterian Club by R. Anderson, 1873).

30. Cicero, *De inventione*, ed. and trans. H. M. Hubbell, Loeb Classical Library (Cambridge, Mass.: Harvard University Press, 1976) p. 169.

31. See *DNB* entry for Penelope Rich, p. 1008.

32. *Tottel's Miscellany (1557–1587)*, ed. Hyder Edward Rollins, 2 vols. (Cambridge, Mass.: Harvard University Press, 1965), I, 165 (# 212). Rollins notes, II, 316–317, that stanza one is derived from Boethius, *De consolatione philosphiae*, III, meter 5.

33. John Soowtherne, *Pandora* (1584); Michael Drayton, *Ideas Mirrour* (1594); Richard Barnfield, *Cynthia* (1595).

34. Craig, p. 11.

35. Stillinger, p. 630.

36. A similar point is made in Hudson, p. 119.

37. Hudson, p. 118.

38. Hudson suggests that Ponsonbie merely added the Roydon, Ralegh, and Greville poems from *The Phoenix Nest*, p. 119, note 1.

39. See *DNB* entry for Robert Devereux, p. 876 and Ralegh, p. 638.

40. *The Works of Edmund Spenser: A Variorum Edition: The Minor Poems*, ed.

Charles Grosvenor Osgood and Henry Gibbons Lotspeich, 2 vols. (Baltimore: The Johns Hopkins University Press, 1943), I, 160. The Variorum does not include the poems of Roydon, Ralegh, and Greville, but they are reprinted in *The Complete Poetical Works of Spenser*, ed. R. E. Neil Dodge (Cambridge, Mass.: Houghton Mifflin, 1908), pp. 710–715.

41. Ovid, *Metamorphoses*, trans. Frank Justus Miller, 2 vols. (Cambridge, Mass.: Harvard University Press, 1968), I, 41–43.

42. While I cannot accept Alan Hager's skillfully wrought contention that Sidney was actually in love with Penelope, I agree with his reading of Sidney's use of the device SPERAVI and his desire to have his poem, "La cuisse rompue," sung to him on his deathbed. His phrase "corrective irony," although I am using it out of context, describes well the reasons I think Sidney introduced autobiographical elements into his sequence. Hager writes: "What Sidney has performed in these cases is a corrective irony. He creates the special effect of surprising us into going back and reevaluating aspects of what are conventionally understood to be solemn affairs. His characteristic mode of thought in his own life as well as his art seems to be a criticism of weaknesses in our conventional understandings or constructions of experience." (Alan Hager, "The Exemplary Mirage: Fabrication of Sir Philip Sidney's Biographical Image and the Sidney Reader," *ELH*, 48 (1981), 10.) I do not think that Greville was even "somewhat puzzled."

E. MALCOLM PARKINSON

Sidney's Portrayal of Mounted Combat with Lances

*W*HEN SIDNEY revised his *Arcadia*, he added to it more than a dozen chivalrous incidents. In the incomplete revised version of 1590, combat and horsemanship gradually intrude up to the time when the siege of Cecropia's castle precipitates a series of skirmishes and crucial, even deadly, contests between individual knights.[1] The heroes of Sidney's rewritten *Arcadia* participate in tournaments, fight each other in pitched battles, challenge enemies to single combat with lances, hack ferociously at each other with swords, and indulge in stylish equitation. I will analyze some of these martial episodes, limiting myself to Sidney's portrayal of combat with lances and the exercise with the lance known as running at the ring.

When he revised the *Arcadia*, Sidney brought to it a first-hand knowledge of mounted combat, for he rode in various tournaments in England. He ran as a defender in the tournament of January 22, 1581, the challenge being issued by the Earl of Arundel assisted by Sir William Drury.[2] As one of "The Four Foster Children of Desire," he participated in the triumph "The Fortress of Perfect Beauty," held in May, 1581.[3] According to the score cheques in the College of Arms, he intended in 1581 to run at tilt against Sir Henry Lee in the Accession Day Tilt, the spectacle staged each November 17 in honor of Queen Elizabeth;[4] a score cheque shows he ran at tilt in the 1584 spectacle.[5] His name appears too in the list for the tournament of December 6, 1584 between the bachelors and the married men.[6] And he may well have jousted or run at tilt in other tournaments.[7]

During Sidney's lifetime, running at tilt was popular in English tournaments. In this contest two knights charged at each other with lances along either side of a fence, the tilt, that separated the horses. The lances had blunted, or rebated, tips rather than sharp ones. If knights charged at each other without a tilt separating them, one would say the knights ran "at large" when jousting. As well as tilting, the tourney was staged in which knights fought on horseback with blunted swords.[8]

Sidney's interest in horses and horsemanship stemmed largely from his aristocratic station, but extended beyond the rough and tumble of a tournament. As a male from the upper ranks of society, he would have learned to ride at an early age.[9] Yet he seems to have striven later in life to improve his horsemanship, both by studying the art and in practicing its elements. He thought highly of the chief Italian writers such as Grisone and Corte on the manège, the art of riding, recommending them to his own brother.[10] At that time the Italian writers still dominated the literature of the manège, the English largely translating or paraphrasing their works.[11] And when spending a winter at court in Vienna, he himself tells us, he polished his own riding skills at the imperial stables with the aid of an esquire, John Pietro Pugliano, whose extravagant adulation of things equine Sidney obviously relished.[12]

To find out how Sidney, himself a jouster and exponent of fine horsemanship, portrays mounted combat, I examine first the fighting abilities of Amphialus. As part of his intricate portraiture of Amphialus, Sidney recounts his combats from the time Cecropia imprisons the princesses Pamela and Philoclea until Amphialus kills himself. Four of the combats begin with the knights on horseback wielding lances. In two others the knight fights, again on a horse, but with a sword as weapon.

In the *Arcadia* many epithets describe Amphialus. He is called "valiant" and a "noble prince."[13] Certainly he is famous: after he has fought with Zelmane, the bathing ladies, at whom he peeps surreptitiously, recognize him as their own cousin the "famous Amphialus."[14] His own page, when identifying the lost armor of his master, laments, as we would expect a loyal page to lament, that it belonged to the "best Knight living."[15] Helen too praises lavishly his "deeds of Armes" and adventures, though she speaks as a distracted lover.[16] None other than Zelmane, Pyrocles in disguise of course, acknowledges "the reputation he had, to be one of the best knights in the world" and even tells Philoclea that Amphialus "for some yeares hath universally borne the name of the best Knight in the world."[17] But Amphialus deserves more than epithets denoting fame and nobility.

Thus in one instance, the narrating voice of the *Arcadia* talks of
the "deemed invincible Amphialus," and in another says that
"the earth brought forth few matches" to his swordsmanship.[18]
We learn too that after he had fought with Musidorus, Musidorus was praised because he had "bettered the most esteemed
Knight in the world."[19] The princes Pyrocles and Musidorus,
then, knew of his abilities not only by repute, but also by
fighting with him.

What then does Sidney reveal of the martial abilities of this
knight whom Musidorus and Pyrocles considered a formidable
opponent? Do we see the skill that warranted such widespread
respect? In the mounted combats, Sidney certainly does reveal
some of that skill.[20]

In the formal joust with Argalus, everything proceeded as
expected, the horses running correctly, Amphialus and Argalus
performing the proper motions with their lances.[21] But when
the horses were close to each other, Argalus's steed "prest in
with his head," thus swinging slightly into Amphialus's path.
Amphialus, we are told, realized that if he reacted by veering off
slightly to the right, he would expose his flank and place
himself at a disadvantage.[22] He therefore chose to match the
behavior of Argalus's mount by making his own swing slightly
to the left. Since no tilt, or barrier, separated the riders,
Amphialus's daring maneuver, which prevented him from being placed at a disadvantage, resulted in the horses crashing into
each other. The two men and their steeds then fell to the
ground. Here Sidney shows how a skilled jouster reacts quickly
to the awkward behavior of a horse. After all, knights joust on
horseback, and the accomplished knight must be able to respond to equine disobedience.[23] In contrast to Argalus, Amphialus exercises such control over his own horse that he can
direct it to crash into the opposing steed, and do it so accurately
that the knights crash shoulder to shoulder exactly when the
horses smash into each other. Thus, not only does Amphialus
decide on a daring course, but also his skill in horsemanship is
equal to the demands of his tactics. Unfortunately for Amphialus, his skilled jousting does not prevent him from killing
Argalus later in their fight, and so he ends eventually jousting
with Parthenia, Argalus's outraged wife disguised as the Knight
of the Tombe.

In jousting with the Knight of the Tombe, Amphialus reacts

once more to the unexpected as he nears his opponent. Combatants often began their careers a considerable distance from each other, and thus a rider could not discern details of his opponent's bearing until he had come closer. Only when Amphialus had followed the routine of lifting his lance up from his thigh, and had set it in the rest, was he close enough to realize that the Knight of the Tombe had missed his rest, Amphialus still thinking that his opponent was a man. Since he would have seen the knight lift up his lance as he charged forward, Amphialus would have noticed nothing unusual until the knight had lowered it, attempting to set it in the rest. Because the motions would have been executed by the two riders almost in unison, when the knight missed his rest, Amphialus was probably setting his own lance snugly on the metal support. Realizing then that his opponent was fumbling with his lance, Amphialus quickly decided to hold the tip of his lance upward. He therefore did not sweep it down, which would have been the next, and automatic, action. Instead, his courtesy prompted him to ride past his opponent, the tip of his lance high in the air. Plate 26 shows a contemporary jousting harness with a rest attached to the breastplate. Sidney is suggesting that, however aristocratic, a woman seeking revenge could not don armor, get on a horse, and expect to wield a lance like a trained knight. She could not even perform the standard sequence of motions, whereas the trained knight not only could follow the sequence but also could interrupt the flow to react quickly to the unexpected. All of this Sidney packs into a few lines:[24]

> But when his staffe was in his rest, comming downe to meete with the Knight, nowe verie neere him, he perceyved the Knight had mist his rest: wherefore the curteous Amphialus woulde not let his Launce descende, but with a gallant grace, ranne over the heade of his there-in friended enemie. . . .

The contest with Phalantus illustrates the skill of Amphialus in delivering a better blow than his capable opponent. In the accepted way, both men gradually lowered their lances so that they aimed precisely at their targets just as the men clashed. Phalantus held his lance horizontally to hit Amphialus's vamplate, the metallic disc attached to the lance to protect the jouster's hand. Amphialus had aimed much higher, hitting his opponent on the gorget, the armor protecting the neck, and in this case composed of metal strips, the lames. Both lances broke.[25] Amphialus's hit, or attaint, would likely have scored better with the judges than Phalantus's. And the blow pushed Phalantus back so far that his head almost touched the horse's crupper.[26] Both men controlled their steeds perfectly, the horses running in straight lines and passing very close to each other, but without touching. After the lances had been broken and the two men continued their fight on horseback with swords, however, Amphialus's cleverer horsemanship gave him the edge over his opponent. In fact, he had chosen a twenty-year-old horse instead of a young one, knowing it was experienced and dependable. He could also rely on its strength, forfeiting the nimbleness of a younger steed. In Sidney's imaginative *Arcadia*, the skilled knight understands horses thoroughly, knowing how to choose a mount with the most appropriate combination of the elements earth, air, fire, and water for any occasion.[27]

The tragic encounter between Amphialus and the young Agenor portrays Amphialus modifying his tactics as circumstances demanded. Agenor confronted Amphialus who was riding at the head of his army. Agenor, who had his beaver up to allow him to breathe easily, ignored his captain's orders not to rush at the opposing forces, and charged at Amphialus without bothering to protect his face by lowering his beaver.[28] When Amphialus had closed in on him and had swept his lance down to aim at his head, he was close enough to recognize in his enemy a handsome youth. Immediately he dropped the tip of his lance to let it hit Agenor's vamplate:[29]

> But Amphialus launce was already come to the last of his descending line, and began to make the full point of death against the head of this young Gentleman, when Amphialus perceyving his youth and beautie, Compassion so rebated the edge of Choller, that he spared that faire nakednesse, and let his staffe fall to Agenors vamplat: so as both with brave breaking should hurtleslie have perfourmed that match. . . .

Since the vamplate was the disc attached to the lance to protect the jouster's hand, Amphialus could neutralize Agenor's lance by hitting it. If the lances were much the same length, then

Amphialus could strike the vamplate almost at the same time as
Agenor's weapon would hit him, and he therefore could throw
the lance off direction, destroying Agenor's aim. Yet, from a
distance, onlookers would think the combatants had performed
equally well, and neither man would be injured. Such was
Amphialus's strategy.

But Agenor was killed, for when Amphialus's lance broke,
the splintered end, the truncheon, struck him in the face. Here
Sidney brings to the fore what must have been one of the
greatest fears of the jouster, one Sidney himself must have lived
with when he participated in tournaments. His readers knew
well the danger of splinters penetrating a narrow visor, never
mind an open helmet; accidents did happen. For example, when
tilting against the Duke of Suffolk in 1524, Henry VIII left his
helmet open, the splintered lance entered it. Amazingly, Henry
was not injured.[30] In 1526, at another Henrician tournament, Sir
Francis Brian lost an eye because of a splintered lance.[31] For
Sidney and other Elizabethan tilters, probably the most famous
accident of all was the fatal wounding of Henry II of France in
1559 when splinters pierced one of his eyes.[32] Even in Sidney's
lifetime, jousting and tilting still exposed riders to danger, a
powerful reminder coming to Sidney in a letter from a friend in
1575 telling him that Albert Count of Hohenlohe had just been
killed with a lance while jousting at a wedding celebration.[33] It
is ironic that Sidney himself, like the brash youth Agenor, died
from a wound received in battle because he knowingly refused
to protect himself adequately. When fighting without armor to
protect his legs, Sidney was hit by a musket shot. Soon
afterwards, he died.[34] Only the wiliest and fastest of men, such
as Jacques de Lalaing, the renowned foot-combat fighter of the
fifteenth century, could afford to fight with beaver up or with a
vital part of the body exposed, and survive.[35] Plate 27 shows a
three-quarter armor from about 1575, of fine quality, suitable
for an officer. Sidney might well have been wearing armor of
this type when he was injured.[36]

From the jousts alone, and without analyzing Amphialus's
combats in which he displays his swordsmanship, we see that
Sidney has created a knight who wields his lance with style,
who reacts quickly to changing circumstances, whose arsenal of
tactics matches the severest of tests, and who can choose a horse
cleverly. When Sidney announces that a knight fights superbly,
the reader of the *Arcadia* witnesses that superbness in action.

But Sidney's anatomies of jousts dissect more than the impressive abilities of individual knights. He believes that the
perception of jousting varies with the viewpoint of the per-
ceiver. Not limiting himself to the perspective of a spectator in
the lists craning his neck to glimpse the quick clashes of
knights, he moves freely from one viewpoint to another. Here
he parts company with many literary representations of tournaments and official chronicles of court spectacles, such as Olivier
de la Marche's records for the Burgundian court.[37]

In Amphialus's combat with Phalantus, for example, the
perceptions of the spectators differed drastically from those of
the two knights.[38] Phalantus's lance penetrated Amphialus's
vamplate at the butt, or bottom, end of the lance, and passed
between his arm and his body. When the tip of the lance
appeared behind him, the spectators thought he had been
impaled on the weapon; yet he was not hurt at all. As we have
already seen, Amphialus got the better of his opponent, delivering a blow to his gorget. Thus the outcome was in Amphialus's
favor, the opposite of what the onlookers first thought. Sidney
knew chivalrous combat is not exempt from the deception of
appearance.

In another joust, the narrative is written in the first person,
Sidney placing the reader in the saddle to experience a combat
from the perspective of one, and only one, of the combatants.
Pyrocles, masquerading as Zelmane, exclaimed that when he
and Anaxius hit each other, he had never felt such a blow:[39]

> And so putting our horses into a full careere, we hit ech
> other upon the head with our Launces: I think he felte my
> blowe; for my parte (I must confesse) I never received the
> like: but I thinke though my senses were astonished, my
> minde forced them to quicken themselves, because I had
> learned of him, how little favour he is woont to show in
> any matter of advantage.

Here we see the uncertainty of Pyrocles about the effect of his
blow on his opponent. After the horses had charged past each
other and Pyrocles could not see his opponent, he knew only
that he had received a severe jolt while he supposed the other
man felt his blow. It is very unusual for a knight in literature to
talk about the effects of a blow and to describe, in the first
person, what happens to him as he prepares for the next part of

the fight. Here Sidney is drawing upon his own experience and understanding of jousting and tilting as he portrays the thoughts of a stunned knight trying desperately to recover in order to prevent his opponent, whom he knows to be ruthless, from gaining any advantage.

Or sometimes the knight's perception of his own performance can differ from that of the judge at a formal tournament. In the tournament at which Phalantus was the challenger on behalf of his mistress Artesia, the judge found it difficult to decide whether Phalantus or Clitophon performed better.[40] Both broke six lances with outstanding "skill in the hitting, & grace in the maner." Phalantus was deemed the better of the two because he broke more lances on the helmet than his opponent, and on one occasion Clitophon "had received such a blowe, that he had lost the raines of his horse, with his head well nie touching the crooper of the horse." Clitophon disagreed with the judge's decision.

In the rapid rise of a shepherd, Philisides, to fame as a jouster, Sidney reveals light-heartedly how much the assessments of spectators vary on the performance of a horseman. When asked how one of their own number became a famous tilter so quickly, the shepherds replied with a song that included the following stanza:[41]

> Me thought some staves he mist: if so, not much amisse:
> For where he most would hit, he ever yet did misse.
> One said he brake acrosse; full well it so might be.
> For never was there man more crossely crost then he.
> But most cryed, O well broke: O foole full gaily blest:
> Where failing is a shame, and breaking is his best.

Clearly, the shepherds disagreed on Philisides's skills. Some thought he missed with his lance; some argued he almost hit; others believed he did not score any of the more difficult hits; perhaps his hits were of the easiest type to score; yet most roared their approval anyway: "O well broke." Such uncertainties about a jouster's skill sound cogent, especially since the shepherds represent inexpert observers. At actual tournaments, spectators at a considerable distance from the knights would have difficulty interpreting the action. And a spectator's view of one knight would often have been obstructed by the other knight at the time of impact. Into the bargain, if we assume the horses travelled at least about sixteen mph. each, and if the tip of the lance extended roughly twelve feet beyond the body of the rider, then only about one-quarter second elapsed from the moment of impact until the knights had passed each other, not enough time for an observer always to note exactly what hits the combatants scored.[42]

If Philisides represents Sidney himself, then Sidney is light-heartedly implying that his own reputation rests partly on the inability of his admirers to discern precisely what happens when two knights clash.[43] Similar uncertainties about a jouster's skill appear in the forty-first sonnet of the "Astrophil and Stella" sequence, people variously attributing success to skilled horsemanship, the strength of the knight, chance, aristocratic ancestry, and cleverness arising from experience.[44]

Sidney also introduces deception, or cheating, into his reper-toire of knightly tactics. After the stanza on Philisides, he shows how an experienced tilter can outwit unskilled observers.[45] When tilting against Philisides, Lelius deliberately missed with his lance. The lance brushed his helmet instead of hitting it squarely. Philisides was puzzled until Lelius let him in on the secret—to redress the day's scoring. Lelius's "willing-missing" eluded the spectators, except that "skilfull eyes" would under-stand he was in complete control of where he pointed his weapon. Indeed, "he shewed more knowledge in missing, then others did in hitting."

James H. Hanford and Sara R. Watson have argued tantaliz-ingly that not only does Philisides represent Sidney himself, but also that Lelius refers to Sir Henry Lee.[46] Records exist for Lee's combats from the 1570s. Older than Sidney by twenty-one years, he was already a tilter with an established reputation when they both rode in the tournament "The Fortress of Perfect Beauty" in May, 1581, held in honor of visiting French dignitaries. Records suggest the two men might have run at tilt against each other on Accession Day, 1581; they competed against each other on Accession Day in 1584.[47]

Apparently Lee originated the tilts held annually in Eliza-beth's honor on Accession Day. At those tilts, until he retired in 1590 at the age of fifty-seven, he enjoyed a position of promi-nence as Champion to the Queen.[48] If, as has been maintained, Lelius is Sir Henry, then Sidney's mischievous wit suggests that the Queen's Champion would not have been above participating in a set of rigged courses intended to deceive onlookers. And Sidney is therefore also representing himself as a willing participant in such trickery. If Lee ever delved into the *Arcadia*, one wonders how he reacted to the attribution of "willing-missing."

For cheating to succeed in actual tournaments, it must remain undetected, and therefore will not appear in historical records. Nor would court chroniclers be anxious to include blatant violations of a chivalrous code by aristocratic contestants in public spectacles, for that code often constituted the framework conferring order on the sequence of events they recorded. Olivier de la Marche, however, does relate an instance of alleged cheating by Jacques de Lalaing. He relates that in 1452 the Count of Charolais's father, Duke Philip of Burgundy, watched the veteran Lalaing joust with his son, providing him with some formidable practice before his first tournament, to be held in Brussels. As the duke and his wife observed the first course, the count broke his lance on Lalaing's shield, while to their surprise Lalaing failed to touch his opponent at all. Probably Lalaing's tactic resembled Lelius's, for La Marche says he "courut haut," suggesting that the tip of his lance swept over his opponent. Simultaneously, Lalaing made sure the horses passed close to each other, allowing his inexperienced opponent to break his lance. Immediately suspecting that Lalaing, a first-rate jouster, deliberately missed his son, a mere novice at the sport, the duke demanded that Lalaing stop interfering. In the next course both riders broke their lances. The count went on to win the prize at the tournament in Brussels.[49] Despite the obvious similarities with the joust between the older Lelius and the younger Philisides, the difference between the incidents is what stands out: La Marche offers a spectator's interpretation whereas Sidney relates his story from the viewpoint of the jousters, as he frequently does in the *Arcadia*.

Sidney has portrayed jousts for us from a variety of viewpoints. We have followed the action as it was perceived by a judge, by skilled spectators, by unskilled spectators, and by the knights themselves. Obviously, Sidney is playing with the variation of appearance with perspective. The judge's assessment of a sequence of combats differs from that of one of the knights. The shepherds disagree over how a jouster performs.

He is also illustrating the difference between appearance and reality. Some spectators think Lelius misses his opponent by jousting poorly, whereas others realize that he misses deliberately, jousting slyly. Onlookers think a rider in danger when he is not hurt at all. Surely such a distinction occurs elsewhere in the *Arcadia*, in the disguises of the heroes. Dorus and Zelmane are princes, not what they appear to be, a shepherd and an Amazon.[50] And the same distinction operates in the deceptions staged in Cecropia's castle. Pamela does not die on the scaffolding, though the onlookers believe her to be executed.[51] Nor is it Philoclea's disembodied, lifeless head lying in a basin; she is still alive.[52] Each person's knowledge is restricted, the restriction often limiting that knowledge to an appearance that excludes awareness of the reality the appearance hides.[53] Maybe in reality Sidney's treatment of combat differs less from the rest of the *Arcadia* than appears to be the case.

Sidney's skills as rider and writer can be demonstrated further by examining two other episodes in the *Arcadia*: Musidorus running at the ring, and the "combat of cowards." In the former we admire the ideal bearing of the lance by the prince, whereas in the latter we witness a comedy combining incompetent horsemanship with cowardice. In his frequent descriptions of the handling of the lance, Sidney carefully follows equestrian practice. Although embellished with metaphors and embedded in his rich rhetoric, what Sidney expects of his horsemen coincides with what some writers on equitation and court equerries demanded of their students. The major English writers and translators during Sidney's lifetime, however, did not bother to discuss the wielding of the lance. Blundeville, Astley, Bedingfield, and Clifford ignore it when expounding the manège.[54] Sidney's fastidious standards for the ideal horseman resemble much more closely the views of the French master Salomon de la Broue. In his book *Preceptes principaux que les bons caualerisses doiuent exactemant obseruer en leurs escoles*, published in 1593–1594, he expounded his methods for training horses, his version of the elements of the manège, and his recommendations for equestrian equipment.[55] For La Broue, precise rules governed every gesture with the lance from the moment an aide handed it to the rider until he returned it unbroken or dropped the remains of the smashed instrument on the ground.[56]

I take La Broue's technique for the handling of the lance as representative of the finest style of the 1580s and 1590s. His description and accompanying diagram are closely followed by the English writer Gervase Markham in his book *Cavelarice* of 1607.[57] For running at the ring, in which the rider retrieves with his pointed lance a removable ring suspended from a post, Markham asks the horseman to picture the four lines shown in Plate 28. One goes horizontally from the butt end of the lance, held almost upright at the start of the career, to the place where the ring is suspended. This is the line along which the horse should run. The second line runs from the rider's right eye to the center of the ring itself. The eye should not deviate from this line as the horse approaches the ring. The third is a straight line from the tip of the lance to the center of the ring. The fourth is the line that the tip carves out as the horse moves. The fourth is therefore not one straight line. It is divided into three segments. The first segment is almost a horizontal line. This line is traced out while the rider spends the first third of the length of the course lifting the lance away from his thigh and extending his right arm sideways. While extending his arm sideways to its full extent, the rider gradually lowers his hand to the level of his thigh. Thus the rider is expected simultaneously to keep the tip of the lance moving in a straight line, a maneuver that unquestionably required much practice to master. In the second segment of the course, the horseman brings the lance back towards his body, setting the weapon into the rest. In the final segment, the tip of the lance is swept down smoothly to the ring.

Ideally, the motions are continuous so that they appear to be only one sweeping movement. Markham's version of La Broue's rules reveals how scrupulously Pamela recounts Musidorus running at the ring as the perfect horseman:[58]

> Wherein truely at lest my womanish eyes could not discerne, but that taking his staffe from his thigh, the descending it a little downe, the getting of it up into the rest, the letting of the point fall, and taking the ring was but all one motion, at lest (if they were divers motions) they did so stealingly slippe one into another, as the latter parte was ever in hande, before the eye could discerne the former was ended.

Now Sidney's curious statement, "the descending it a little downe," becomes clear. It represents the motion of the hand outward and, at the same time, downward. The wielding of the lance in jousting and tilting resembled the exercise of running at the ring described by Sidney. Mastery of the exercise of inserting a lance into the ring, a much smaller and therefore more difficult target to hit than an approaching knight's body, constituted excellent training for warfare, though a ring stayed stationary while an enemy moved continually. Both in England and in continental Europe, running at the ring remained a popular military exercise into the seventeenth century.[59] Plate 29, from a manual for mounted combat, illustrates the usefulness of running at the ring in honing military tactics, either to strike an opponent or to maim or kill his horse.

Since for Sidney a man ought to ride with style and grace, he almost always points out how well or how poorly contestants handle their lances.[60] The "combat of cowards" is an hilarious example. In the so-called combat, one of the horses starts forward unexpectedly, its rider Dametas, an incompetent horseman, quickly throwing away his lance and holding on firmly to the pommel of his saddle.[61] In the same comic joust, his equally incapable opponent Clinias had already placed his lance in the rest when someone hit his horse from the rear, causing it to start forward. When the wind then caught the lance, he could not control it, and rode along with the instrument pointing sideways. A strong crosswind could easily catch hold of a lance twelve or more feet long. Once a lance had rotated in the wind, a novice would have found it difficult to swing the weapon back because of its moment of inertia about the rest at the butt end. Except for his emphasis on details of the joust, Sidney here pokes fun at the incompetent horsemanship of people not from the upper ranks of society in much the same way as Robert Laneham records peasants clumsily running courses at the quintain during the entertainments for Elizabeth held in 1575 at Kenilworth Castle, the estate of Sidney's uncle, Robert Dudley, Earl of Leicester. Sidney himself stayed at his uncle's residence during the royal visit, and might have witnessed, with amusement, the local lads riding without stirrups, falling off their horses, or sometimes hitting the quintain, a revolving board, shaped like a person, to be hit with a lance;

one aspiring rider even missed the quintain with his lance, only to hit the board with his head.[62] A quintain is shown in Plate 30. Any Elizabethan who would have laughed at Laneham's account of the festivities at Kenilworth would have laughed at Sidney's "combat of cowards." Certainly Sidney's portrayal, with its authentic details of poor horsemanship, would have evoked laughter from an experienced tilter.[63]

Sidney depicts jousting authentically: an Elizabethan jouster reading the *Arcadia* would find his accounts convincing. In literary terms, I would call them verisimilar. Such sustained authenticity of detail or such continual and skillful shifting among multiple viewpoints is not found in the Burgundian records of Olivier de la Marche or in the accounts of the exploits of Jacques de Lalaing, or in Ariosto's *Orlando Furioso*, or in any of the books of *Amadis of Gaul* that I have read.[64] As for the documentation of Elizabethan tournaments found in score cheques, heraldic records, and historical accounts, none of it reveals any tactics of knights.[65] Nor do the poems of Peele or Blenerhasset help. Nor does Edmund Spenser's Neo-Platonic, allegorical poem *The Faerie Queene*, with its tournaments and numerous mounted clashes, although reflecting the annual tilts, offer the reader any insight into mounted contests. Like Blenerhasset and Peele, Spenser forces the jousting in his poem to be subservient to the outer trappings of the chivalric events.[66] Nor does Robert Parry paint a verisimilar picture of the jousting of his Black Knight.[67] Thus Sidney's combats in the *Arcadia* stand as pre-eminently revealing when they are compared with, at the very least, other English literary sources of the period.

I conclude that Sidney presents mounted combat in the *Arcadia* with great care. His descriptions have the ring of an experienced tilter, and an accuracy of detail that Elizabethans who attended tournaments, or who tilted, would recognize immediately. With a consummate artist such as Sidney, we must assume that his sustained authenticity of detail, his continual verisimilitude, reflects his own understanding of the psychology of the knight and the processes of combat, both of which he harnesses to allow the reader to see combat as it was perceived by the competing knights and their onlookers. His energetic narratives, compelling in their detailed anatomies of jousts, show that mounted combats are more than perfunctory additions to Sidney's major work of prose; they are the studied fictions of a perpetuator of chivalric spectacles.

Worcester Polytechnic Institute

NOTES

1. Sir Philip Sidney, *The Complete Prose Works of Sir Philip Sidney*, ed. A. Feuillerat, 4 vols. Vol. I: *The Countesse of Pembrokes Arcadia* (Cambridge: Cambridge University Press, 1912; rpt. 1965). In the present paper, we refer to this text, published in 1590, as *Arcadia*.

2. See William A. Ringler, Jr., ed., *The Poems of Sir Philip Sidney* (Oxford: Clarendon Press, 1962; rpt. 1967), p. 474 for tournaments in which Sidney participated, and others in which he might have ridden. For January 22, 1581, see *Honor Military and Civil (1602)*, p. 195 in Sir William Segar, *The Book of Honor and Armes (1590) and Honor Military and Civil (1602)*, with an Introduction by D. Bornstein (Delmar, New York: Scholars' Facsimiles & Reprints, 1975); *Holinshed's Chronicles of England, Scotland and Ireland*, 6 vols. (London, 1808; rpt. New York: AMS Press, 1969), IV, 434; and John Stow, *Annales, or A General Chronicle of England. Begun by John Stow: continued and Augmented with matters Foreigne and Domestique, Ancient and Moderne, unto the end of this present yeere, 1631* (London, 1631), pp. 688–689; Sydney Anglo, "Archives of the English Tournament: Score Cheques and Lists," *Journal of the Society of Archivists*, 2 (1961), 153–162 includes in his inventory a scored cheque dated January 22, 1580, for the challenge of Arundel and Drury, in the College of Arms MS. "Collection Formerly in Box 37: Now in a Portfolio."

3. *Holinshed's Chronicles*, IV, 435–445; and John Nichols, *The Progresses and Public Processions of Queen Elizabeth*, 3 vols. (London, 1823; rpt. New York: AMS Press, 1969), II, 310–329.

4. Sidney's name appears in the list of tilters on the unscored cheque Bodleian MS Ashmole 845, f. 165, quoted in Robert C. Clephan, *The Tournament: Its Periods and Phases* (London: Methuen & Co., 1919), pp. 132–133. Roy C. Strong, *The Cult of Elizabeth: Elizabethan Portraiture and Pageantry* (London: Thames and Hudson, 1977), p. 206 refers also to an identical, but undated, list in College of Arms "MS. M. 4 and 14," where the word "not" appears with Sidney's name. In spite of the implication that Sidney might not have ridden in the 1581 Accession Day Tilt, Strong, *ibid.*, p. 149 concludes he did run his courses.

5. For scored cheques of November 17, 1584 in College of Arms "Collection Formerly in Box 37: Now in Portfolio," consult Anglo, "Archives," p. 160. Part of one of the scored cheques is reproduced as Item No. 26 in *Heralds Commemorative Exhibition, 1484–1934, Held at The College of Arms* (London: printed for the Kings, Heralds & Pursuivants of Arms of England, 1936), Plate XII.

6. Ringler, *Poems*, p. 474 cites Bodleian MS. Ashmole 845, f. 168.

7. Ringler, *ibid.*, argues on the basis of William Segar, *The Book of Honor and Armes (1590)*, Nn 3, that Sidney rode in a tournament sometime between May, 1579 and March, 1580. "Sidney" also appears on a list for tilt and tourney dated 1574, a scored cheque dated 1577, and a list dated 1579 in College of Arms MS. M.4, Anglo, "Archives," p. 161.

8. Anglo, "Archives." Viscount Dillon, "Tilting in Tudor Times," *The Archaeological Journal*, 55 (1898), 296–321, 329–339; Francis H. Cripps-Day, *The History of the Tournament in England and in France* (London: Bernard Quaritch Limited, 1918); Clephan, *The Tournament*; and Sydney Anglo, *The Great Tournament Roll of Westminster* (Oxford: Clarendon Press, 1968) also describe or analyze Tudor tournaments.

9. For the interest of the English aristocracy in horsemanship, see Lawrence Stone, *The Crisis of the Aristocracy 1558–1641* (Oxford: Clarendon Press, 1965), pp. 694–695.

10. Philip Sidney to Robert Sidney, October 18, 1580, in *The Prose Works of Sir Philip Sidney*, ed. A. Feuillerat, 4 vols. (Cambridge: University Press, 1912; rpt. 1963), III, 130–133. He recommends reading "Grison Claudio" and *La gloria del cavallo*. For the argument that Sidney refers to Federico Grisone, *Gli Ordini di cavalcare* (Naples, 1550); Claudio Corte, *Il Cavallerizzo* (Venice, 1573); and Pasquel Caracciolo, *La gloria del cavallo* (Venice, 1567), see, for example, James M. Osborn, *Young Philip Sidney 1572–1577* (New Haven and London: Yale University Press, 1972), p. 81. The suggestion that Sidney is referring to Thomas Blundeville, *The Fower Chiefyst Offices Belonging to Horsemanshippe* (London, 1565), a translation of Grisone's work, is found in the anonymous review "The Art of Horsemanship," *Quarterly Review*, 183 (January 1896), 139–162. A. Forbes Sieveking, in his essay "Horsemanship, with Farriery," in *Shakespeare's England*, 2 vols., ed. Charles T. Onions (Oxford: Clarendon Press, 1916; rpt. 1932), II, 426 cites himself and Francis H. Cripps-Day as the authors of "The Art of Horsemanship."

11. Blundeville, *The Fower Chiefyst Offices*, an English rendering of Grisone, *Gli Ordini di cavalcare*; Thomas Blundeville, *The Art of Ryding and Breakinge Great Horses* (London, 1560; rpt. Amsterdam and New York: Da Capo Press and Theatrum Orbis Terrarum Ltd., 1969), which is a part of Blundeville, *The Fower Chiefyst Offices*; Claudio Corte, *The Art of Riding* (London, 1584), an English version by Thomas Bedingfield of Book II of Corte, *Il Cavallerizzo*.

12. "A Defense of Poetry," in *Miscellaneous Prose of Sir Philip Sidney*, eds. Katherine Duncan-Jones and Jan van Dorsten (Oxford: Clarendon Press, 1973), pp. 73, 186. Nicholas Morgan, *The Perfection of Horse-Manship, Drawne from Nature; Arte, and Practise* (London, 1609), B1 recto, verso, places Pugliano along with Xenophon, Berardino, Pagano, Grisone, and Corte in his list of famous foreign horsemen.

13. *Arcadia*, pp. 26, 31.

14. *Ibid.*, p. 225.

15. *Ibid.*, p. 74.

16. *Ibid.*, pp. 67–68.

17. *Ibid.*, pp. 251, 263.

18. *Ibid.*, pp. 443, 446.

19. *Ibid.*, p. 463.

20. Walter R. Davis, *A Map of Arcadia*, pp. 114–135, in Walter R. Davis and Richard A. Lanham, *Sidney's Arcadia* (New Haven and London: Yale University Press, 1965), places the combats of Amphialus in the context of the major plot of the *Arcadia*; his interpretation of the fighting in terms of love, passion, reason, order, and disorder complements, therefore, my analysis of the technical skills of the combatants.

21. Sidney uses the words lance, spear, staff, and stave, interchanging them freely; Claude Blair, *European and American Arms* (London: B. T. Batsford Ltd., 1962), pp. 27–28, discusses the evolution of the lance and the terms used to describe the weapon.

22. We assume that the knights approach left arm to left arm, and that lances are held in the right hand, the standard procedure at tournaments: Dillon, "Tilting," p. 303, and Sydney Anglo, "Financial and Heraldic Records of the English Tournament," *Journal of the Society of Archivists*, 2 (April 1962), 192.

23. *Arcadia*, p. 423. Sidney's detailed correlation of the coloring of Argalus's steed with its behavior agrees with Grisone's equine psychology as presented by Blundeville, *The Art of Ryding and Breakinge Greate Horses*, Book I, Ai–Aiiii. Argalus's horse is described as "hot," and "of a firie sorrell, with blacke feete, and blacke list on his back." The bright chestnut coloring implied that the element fire probably predominated in the animal, and that it therefore had a choleric temperament and was hot. The blackness of the feet and the black stripe on its back would have improved its temperament somewhat. But the absence of a white mark on a horse of such coloring indicated an animal of two minds, one that would not behave consistently, so it is not surprising that the horse twisted its head to the left during the joust.

24. *Arcadia*, p. 446.

25. *Ibid.*, p. 416.

26. Sidney does not mention what rules the judges followed at the joust. However, according to the rules of John Tiptoft, Earl of Worcester, which seem to have been commonly used in Elizabethan England, hits, or attaints, to the body scored lower than attaints to the area of the head. Anglo, *Great Tournament Roll*, pp. 108–109, reproduces Tiptoft's ordinances, his version being taken from College of Arms MS. M. 6, f. 56–57. Segar, *Honor Military and Civil (1602)*, pp. 188–190, prints a version of the rules. For a brief discussion of the adoption of the rules in England, see Anglo, "Archives," p. 155.

Frequently in tournaments a higher hit merited a higher score, as in the rules for jousts and tournaments in Naples, quoted by Segar, *ibid.*, p. 187: "He that on horsebacke directeth his Launce at the head, is more to be praised, then he that toucheth lower. For the higher the Launce hitteth, the greater is the Runners commendation." See also Antoine de Pluvinel, *L'instruction du Roy; Reitkunst* (Frankfurt am Main, 1628), p. 122, and Cripps-Day, *History of the Tournament, passim.* Also in the Neapolitan rules, the bearing of the rider in the saddle is carefully assessed, and in much more detail than in Tiptoft's rules. Thus, being forced back until he almost lay along the horse's crupper might well have counted against Phalantus. Segar, *ibid.*, pp. 187–188.

27. By choosing a well-shaped brown bay steed, Amphialus rode an

animal of better temperament for combat than the milk-white horse of
Phalantus. Blundeville, *The Art of Ryding and Breakinge Greate Horses*, Book I,
Ai–Av.

28. *Arcadia*, pp. 386–387.

29. *Ibid.*, 387.

30. Edward Hall, *The Union of the Two Noble and Illustrious Families of
Lancastre and York*, ed. Sir Henry Ellis (London, 1809), p. 674.

31. *Ibid.*, pp. 707–708.

32. Segar, *Honor Military and Civil (1602)*, pp. 171–172.

33. Jean Lobbet to Sidney, November 22, 1575, quoted in Osborn, *Young
Philip Sidney*, p. 385. For a succinct discussion of accidents in tournaments,
see August Demmin, *Die Kriegswaffen in Ihren Geschichtlichen Entwickelungen
von den Ältesten Zeiten bis auf die Gegenwart* (Leipzig, 1893), pp. 90–92.

34. Roger Howell, *Sir Philip Sidney: The Shepherd Knight* (Boston and
Toronto: Little, Brown and Company, 1968), pp. 255–263.

35. "Le livre des faits du bon chevalier messire Jacques de Lalaing," in
George Chastellain, *Oeuvres*, ed. M. le baron Kervyn de Lettenhove, vol. 8:
Oeuvres diverses (Geneva: Slatkine Reprints, 1971), pp. 1–259. See also
Viscount Dillon, "Barriers and Foot Combats," *The Archaeological Journal*, 61
(1904), 276–308.

36. James G. Mann, "Recollections of the Wilton Armoury," *The Connois-
seur*, 104 (July 1939), 10–16 sets the three-quarter suit JWHA 427 in the
context of the armory of the Pembroke family. Claude Blair, *European
Armour circa 1066 to circa 1700* (London: B. T. Batsford Ltd., 1958), p. 144
discusses cavalry armor at the end of the sixteenth century.

37. *Mémoires d'Olivier de la Marche*, Henri Beaune and G. D'Arbaumont,
eds., 4 vols. (Paris: Société de l'histoire de France, 1883–1888). Malcolm G.
A. Vale, *War and Chivalry* (Athens, Georgia: University of Georgia Press,
1981), pp. 63–87 contains a fine assessment of Burgundian tournaments.

38. *Arcadia*, p. 416.

39. *Ibid.*, p. 270.

40. *Arcadia*, pp. 108–109. Sidney offers no details about the scoring
method used at the tournament, though the judge's decision would be
consistent with a combination of Tiptoft's rules and the Neapolitan rules for
accidents and various contingencies not covered by Tiptoft, in Segar, *Honor
Military and Civil (1602)*, pp. 187–190. In the same tournament, Phalantus
later lost to another knight when his girths broke and he and his saddle
crashed to the ground (*Arcadia*, p. 111); such a contingency is discussed, with
an example from an actual Neapolitan tournament, the loser being the person
who was unhorsed, in Segar, *ibid*.

41. *Arcadia*, p. 285. Ringler comments on the stanza in *Poems*, p. 492.

42. According to Charles J. Ffoulkes, *Inventory and Survey of the Armories of
the Tower of London* (London: H.M.S.O., 1916), 2: 233, the Tower possessed
79 lance staves of the sixteenth and seventeenth centuries, the average length
of which was 12 ft. 6 in.

43. On the traditional identification of Philisides as Sidney see, for example, Frances A. Yates, "Elizabethan Chivalry: The Romance of the Accession
Day Tilts," *Journal of the Warburg and Courtauld Institutes*, 20 (1957), 4–25,
which is reprinted in *Astraea: the imperial theme in the sixteenth century* (London
and Boston: Routledge & Kegan Paul, 1975), pp. 88–111.

44. Ringler, *Poems*, p. 185.

45. *Arcadia*, pp. 284–286. Of all the combats in the *Arcadia*, only in this one does Sidney state explicitly that the opponents run at tilt, and therefore with a barrier between them. Sidney's own experience in spectacles was acquired mainly at the tilt rather than in jousting without a barrier, if the surviving records of his participation in tournaments reflect accurately his career as a knight.

Despite Sidney's European travels, especially in the German states, in Saxony and at the Emperor's court, I detect no traces in the *Arcadia* of any forms of combat peculiar to that part of Europe in the sixteenth century. For jousting in Saxony, consult *Der Sächsischen Kürfursten Turnierbücher in ihren hervorragendsten darstellungen auf vierzig tafeln*, ed. Erich Haenel (Frankfurt am Main: Heinrich Keller, 1910). The bewildering variety of jousts and tilts practiced early in the century at the court of Maximilian I are depicted in *Freydal*, ed. Quirin von Leitner (Vienna, 1880–1882) and Hans Burgmair, *The Triumphs of the Emperor Maximilian*, ed. Alfred Asplund (London: Holbein Society, 1873). See also Clephan, *The Tournament*, pp. 85–110.

46. James H. Hanford and Sara R. Watson, "Personal Allegory in the Arcadia: Philisides and Lelius," *Modern Philology*, 32 (1934), 1–10; also Yates, *Astraea*, pp. 88–111.

47. Edmund K. Chambers, *Sir Henry Lee* (Oxford: Clarendon Press, 1936); also footnotes 2–5 above. Sir Henry's horsemanship and skill with the lance had astonished Champany, on an ambassadorial mission in 1576 from the Low Countries, leading him to exclaim in one of his dispatches that Lee was "the most accomplished Caualiero" he had ever seen. Segar, *Honor Military and Civil (1602)*, p. 200, and Chambers, *Lee*, pp. 134–135, 269. For illustrations of Lee's Greenwich armor, see *An Almain Armourer's Album. Selections from an Original MS. in Victoria and Albert Museum, South Kensington*, with Introduction and Notes by Viscount Dillon (London: W. Griggs, 1905), Plates XV–XX. For Greenwich armor, including tilting harnesses of the type used in England during Lee's and Sidney's tournament days, see *Exhibition of Armour Made in the Royal Workshops at Greenwich. Tower of London 22nd May – 29th September 1951*, with a Forward by Sir James Mann (London: H.M.S.O., 1951). The evolution of tournament armor is assessed in Claude Blair, *European Armour*, pp. 156–169.

48. Segar, *Honor Military and Civil (1602)*, pp. 197–200, and Sara R. Watson, "The Queen's Champion," *Western Reserve University Bulletin*, 34 (1931), 65–89.

49. *Mémoires d'Olivier de la Marche*, II, 214–215. The incident, though a violation of the behavior expected of Lalaing, enhances the standing of the count, for it implies he needs no bending of chivalrous strictures to emerge as a man worthy to succeed his father as a duke of Burgundy.

50. Walter Davis, *Idea and Act in Elizabethan Fiction* (Princeton, N.J.: Princeton University Press, 1969), pp. 45–53 discusses roles and disguises; Mark Rose, "Sidney's Waspish Woman," *Review of English Studies*, new series, 15 (1964), 353–363.

51. *Arcadia*, pp. 476–477.

52. *Ibid.*, pp. 482–483.

53. Rodney Delasanta, *The Epic Voice* (The Hague and Paris: Mouton, 1967), pp. 61–81.

54. Blundeville, *The Arte of Ryding and Breakinge Greate Horses,* and *The Fower Chiefyst Offices*; John Astley, *The Art of Riding* (London, 1584; rpt. Amsterdam and New York: Da Capo Press, 1968); Claudio Corte, *The Art of Riding* (London, 1584), an English version by Thomas Bedingfield of the second book of Corte, *Il Cavalerizzo*; Christopher Clifford, *The Schoole of Horsemanship* (London, 1585).

55. Salomon de la Broue, *Preceptes principaux que les bons caualerisses doiuent exactement obseruer en leurs escoles, tant pour bien dresser les cheuaux aux exercices de la guerre & de la carriere que pour les bien emboucher* (La Rochelle: 1593–1594). Later editions were published as *Le caualerice francois,* 2nd ed. (Paris, 1602–1608), and 3rd ed. (Paris, 1620).

56. La Broue, *Preceptes principaux,* Book I, pp. 122–126.

57. Gervase Markham, *Cavelarice or The English Horseman* (London, 1607), Book II, pp. 244–254; 2nd ed. (London, 1617). He does not discuss the handling of the lance in his earlier work, *A Discource of Horsmanshippe* (London, 1593).

58. *Arcadia,* pp. 178–179.

59. John Cruso, *Militarie Instructions for the Cavalrie* (Cambridge, 1632; rpt. Amsterdam and New York: Theatrum Orbis Terrarum Ltd. and Da Capo Press, 1968), pp. 36–37; Johann J. Wallhausen, *Ritterkunst* with a foreword by W. Hummelberger (Frankfurt am Main, 1616; rpt. Graz: Akademische Druck—u. Verlangsanstalt, 1969), pp. 89–91; Antoine de Pluvinel, *L'instruction du Roy*; *Reitkunst* (Frankfurt am Main, 1628), pp. 100 ff; Henry G. Webb, *Elizabethan Military Science* (Madison, Milwaukee, and London: University of Wisconsin Press, 1965), pp. 114–116 examines the use of the lance by cavalry in the Elizabethan period.

60. Ideally, two knights should begin their careers together and perform their motions with their lances simultaneously. Phalantus and Amphialus exhibited the perfect technique as they were about to clash. "Together they set spurres to their horses, together took their launces from their thighes, conveied them up into their restes together, together let them sink downward; so as it was a delectable sight, in a dangerous effect," *Arcadia,* p. 416. Pluvinel, *L'instruction du Roy,* pp. 121–122 mentions this requirement explicitly for tilting, partly to ensure that the knights meet at the center of the lists, opposite the royal family and other important spectators. He also recommends that a lance point precisely toward its target by the time two knights are only twenty paces apart.

61. *Arcadia,* pp. 432–433.

62. John Nichols, *The Progresses and Public Processions of Queen Elizabeth,* I, 441–446; for Sidney's stay at Kenilworth, see Osborn, *Young Philip Sidney,* pp. 325–343.

63. Robert N. Reeves III, *The Ridiculous to the Delightful: Comic Characters in Sidney's New "Arcadia"* (Cambridge, Mass.: Harvard University Press, 1974) discusses Sidney's theory of comedy, and analyzes, along with other examples, the "combat of cowards," though Reeves merely mentions the jousting buffoonery of the two aspiring horsemen, and concentrates on the combat after they are thrown from their mounts.

64. *Mémoires d'Olivier de la Marche*; "Le livre des faits du bon chevalier messire Jacques de Lalaing"; Ludovico Ariosto, *Orlando Furioso,* 2 vols., trans.

Barbara Reynolds (Harmondsworth, England: Penguin Books, 1975–1977); *"Amadis of Gaul," A Novel of Chivalry of the 14th Century Presumably First Written in Spanish. Revised and Reworked by Garci Rodriguez de Montalvo prior to 1505.* Books I–IV, trans. Edwin B. Place and Herbert C. Behm (Lexington, Kentucky: University Press of Kentucky, 1974–1975).

65. Anglo, "Archives," and "Records"; *Holinshed's Chronicles.*

66. Thomas Blenerhasset, *A Revelation of the True Minerva*, with an Introduction and a Bibliographical Note by G. W. Bennett (1581; rpt. Delmar, New York: Scholar's Facsimiles & Reprints, 1978) depicts the heraldry and symbolism of English tilting. Green's poems, "Polyhymnia" and "Anglorum Feriae," deal with the Accession Day Tilts of 1590 and 1595 respectively; they are included in *The Dramatic and Poetical Works of Robert Greene and George Peele*, ed. A. Dyce (London and New York: Routledge, Warne, and Routledge, 1861), pp. 569–573, 595–598. Though combat throughout *The Faerie Queene* in *Spenser: Poetical Works* (London: Oxford University Press, 1912; reprint ed., 1969) is not verisimilar, Spenser and Sidney do agree on the boundaries of chivalrous fighting: neither in Spenser's poem nor in the *Arcadia* does anyone hold a firearm or shoot a cannon. Gunpowder weaponry is acceptable only in metaphors and similes, not as a martial instrument for a knight: *The Faerie Queene*, I. vii. 13, IV. ii. 16, V. x. 34–35; *Arcadia*, pp. 396, 423.

67. Robert Parry, *Moderatus, The most delectable & famous Historie of the Black Knight* (London, 1595; University Microfilms no. 17117, carton 580).

JEFFREY L. SPEAR

"The Gardin of Prosérpina This Hight": Ruskin's Application of Spenser and Horizons of Reception

*I*N THE first introduction to *The Faerie Queene*, the letter to Sir Walter Raleigh, Spenser directed the reader's understanding "to wel-head of the History, that from thence gathering the whole intention of the conceit, ye may as in a handful gripe al the discourse, which otherwise may happily seem tedious and confused."[1] The poet thus set the pattern for hosts of commentators who have, rhetorically, taken his place and expanded his letter into volumes that would establish sources, intentions, and most probable, even definitive, meanings. My own concern, however, is with the reception of Spenser's text, not its genesis. Writing as a Victorianist rather than a Renaissance scholar, I am less interested in the final clarification of what might, whether through dark conceit or mere passage of time, seem unhappily tedious and confused, than with the Victorian reading of Spenser, specifically how he was read in the 1850s by John Ruskin.

Ruskin appears frequently enough in the *Variorum* Spenser, as a foil in critical works, and as a shade in the textual underworld of the scholar's footnote, to justify a reconsideration of his views for their own sake. But I also advance my understanding of Ruskin's Spenser as a specific instance of a more general approach to literary history, an approach that acknowledges the historicity of interpretation as well as creation and, consequently, emphasizes the history of reception as well as that of production. If the life of a literary work is not the product of its autonomous existence, but rather of an interaction between the work and its readers then, as Hans Robert Jauss argues:

the historical coherence of works among themselves must be seen in the interrelations of production and reception.

. . . Literature and art only obtain a history that has the
character of a process when the succession of works is
mediated not only through the producing subject but also
through the consuming subject—through the interaction
of author and public. . . . If the history of literature is
viewed in this way within the horizon of a dialogue
between a work and audience that forms a continuity, the
opposition between its aesthetic and its historical aspects is
also continuously mediated. Thus the thread from the past
appearance to the present experience of literature, which
historicism had cut, is tied back together."[2]

Jauss, taking his premises from the philosophical hermeneutics of Hans-Georg Gadamer, in effect proposes a middle way
between literary interpretation based on traditional hermeneutics (the attempt to objectively establish at least an approxima-
tion of an intentional, univocal meaning, the significance of
which would be open to critical debate) and the mode of
analysis that effectively substitutes the creativity of the reader
for that of the author producing not interpretation in the
conventional sense, but what might be called, after the muse of
lyric poetry, euterpretation. According to Gadamer's ontology,
interpretation is a fusion of horizons, a mediation between past
and present that preserves the reference of the text but sacrifices
any claim to objective, a-historical understanding. All readings
reflect their time and place and are self-applicative, that is,
revelations of the reader as well as of the text.

Recovery of the effective history of a literary work, the
history of its readings, necessarily involves the interpretation of
commentary. The critic of critics who would establish the
earlier understanding of a text is himself engaged in a dialogue
with his forebears. If his aim is understanding and interpretation rather than the history of "error," then the historical
horizon manifest in a critical text must be respected. Indeed, the
greater the aesthetic aspect in the earlier criticism, the stronger
the literary or fictive element, the closer the interpretive task
comes to the reading of a work of art. Moreover, where the
Jaussian reading of an aesthetic work demands an awareness of
two horizons, that of the text and of the present reader, the
attempt to establish the way in which a work was read in an
earlier period involves a three way relationship: the subject text

to that of the earlier reader, the earlier reader's text to the modern reader, and the subject text to the modern reader, for the contemporary reading of the subject text will be part of the horizon of the modern critic and color his understanding of his predecessors.

It would be all but impossible for the modern interpreter of a major author to do full justice to his forebears among criticism's mighty dead without making them his subject. Thus Ruskin generally appears in Spenser criticism as the anticipator of a modern view, more often than not a view with which the writer takes issue. Not surprisingly, he appears in different works as the proponent of opposing points of view. In Rosemary Freeman's *Companion for Readers of "The Faerie Queene,"* for example, Ruskin appears as the opponent of system; that is, of her book by book, theme by theme, progress through the poem. She quotes as evidence Ruskin's analogy between the creation of artificial connections and the practice of the old women of Pomona who tie cherries to their sticks for transport in false imitation of the natural bough when all that really matters is the proper cultivation, picking and choosing of them.[3] The citation would be more effective were Ruskin making reference to Spenser or his critics rather than to that volume of his own *Modern Painters* he was forced to subtitle "Of Many Things," but the point is nonetheless plausible given the scattering of Spenser quotation in his work. Paul Alpers, on the other hand, gives Ruskin the credit that most Ruskin scholars would cheerfully accept on his behalf for producing "one of the first reactions against the romantic tendency to dismiss or minimize Spenser's allegory." But we have, it seems, only been drawn from Scylla to Charybdis, for Alpers goes on to accuse Ruskin of over-systematizing, of giving the characters and settings consistent symbolic identifications so that, while the fiction is less real than abstract ideas, the fiction yet provides "both the terms and the syntax of the translation. 'What happens' poetically is taken to be identical with, or at least determined by, 'what happens' fictionally."[4] Alpers's Ruskin is thus the spiritual father of the over-allegorizers he attacks in *The Poetry of "The Faerie Queene,"* those who search for a foolish consistency in a poem stressing rhetorical effect that produces psychological affect for a moral end.

I have no comment to make upon the validity of Alpers's

method for reading Spenser, nor do I contend that what he has to say about Ruskin is completely groundless. In 1852 Ruskin did assert the priority of symbolic over allegorical imagery and over personification, associating the symbolic mode with the truths of the Bible contained in image and action and allegory with the weakening of divine truth by abstraction into systems of virtues and vices. Not until 1856, when Ruskin was on the verge of abandoning Evangelicalism, would his work sustain George Landow's claim that "Ruskin does not oppose allegory and symbolism to each other, for he holds that allegory, an imaginative mode, forms one kind of symbolism and not a lesser replacement for it."[5]

The problem here is not that Freeman and Alpers say contradictory things about Ruskin, for each has a case, but that they treat him as though he were part of the institution to which they—and we—belong, an institution that demands of, and addresses to, its members new, and preferably original, interpretations of literary texts. *The Stones of Venice* (1851–53), however, is not the same kind of book as Professor Berger's *The Allegorical Temper*, nor is its two and a half page appendix on "The Theology of *The Faerie Queene*," upon which Alpers bases his objections, the equivalent of Frank Kermode's essay on "The Cave of Mammon." It was addressed to a general audience and belongs to a different genre from those works with which Alpers disputes according to the customs of our profession, and the interpretive mode Ruskin employs in it differs as well. The historical and linguistic gap between our world and Spenser's is obvious and much discussed. That between our world and Ruskin's is more narrow but no less real, and there is a genuine historical distance from, or, if you prefer, alterity to, his text as it confronts the modern reader.

As an Evangelical, Ruskin was raised on the literal interpretation of the Bible with its attendant figural extensions into typological and prophetic truth (as opposed to allegorical fiction). But allegory supplemented revelation from childhood. As one of the few books permitted on the Sabbath, *The Pilgrim's Progress* left an indelible mark. John James Ruskin's readings from Spenser formed one of his son's earliest literary memories, and in his early maturity Ruskin came to think Dante the greatest poet since Homer. As his Evangelical dogmatism faded, Ruskin increasingly blurred the never entirely hard line between the typological and the allegorical in his own work. Ruskin's parents had intended him for the church, and he brought to his reading of literature and of visual art the pattern of Protestant exegetics.

Of the three divisions of Protestant hermeneutics, understanding, interpretation, and application, he, like an Evangelical preacher, placed heavy emphasis upon the last. Ruskin had ample precedent for this stance. In his letter to Raleigh, Spenser gave as his general purpose "To fashion a gentleman or noble person in vertuous and gentle discipline,"[6] and so teach his reader by example rather than by rule. Milton found Spenser not only "sage and serious," but "a better teacher than Scotus and Aquinas."[7] The applicative element largely gives way to an aesthetic interpretation in the nineteenth century, Ruskin being an exception to the trend. And while there have been twentieth-century readings stressing application (C. S. Lewis, arguing against what he saw as aesthetic trivialization of Spenser, contended that "to read him is to grow in mental health"[8]), most twentieth-century criticism has stressed understanding and interpretation over application. Some contemporary approaches would place more emphasis upon a form of application, but even in these days of "reader-response criticism" an article explaining how the example of The Redcrosse Knight, or Sir Guyon, or Britomart, had made the reader more holy, or temperate, or chaste would raise a few eyebrows—if, indeed, it found a publisher.

The Spenser who appears in *The Stones of Venice* and *Modern Painters* is not Hazlitt's "poet of our waking dreams,"[9] but Milton's teacher, an "historical poet" both in the sense of Spenser's letter to Raleigh and for the special place Ruskin assigns him in the history of Protestant iconography. *The Stones of Venice* itself is not a work of either art or literary criticism in the modern sense, but a gargantuan outgrowth of travel literature—a blend of the Murray guidebook, imaginative travel in time through movement in space as practiced by Byron and such lesser lights as Samuel Rogers in his poem *Italy*, an architectural treatise, and a lay sermon. Ruskin proposes to teach his audience how to read architecture while treating its history and, by extension, that of its creators, according to a pattern of type and fulfillment. He sees in the fate of Venice the completion of that of biblical Tyre and a warning to the modern sea kingdom of England unless she can learn—from John Ruskin of course—to read those messages in the stones of Venice that the Venetians themselves forgot when with the coming of the Renaissance they whored after strange gods.

Though less sectarian than *The Seven Lamps of Architecture* (1847), *The Stones of Venice* still seeks to break the link in the popular mind between Catholicism or the English High Church and ecclesiastical, particularly medieval, art. By proving such art to be not narrowly Roman Catholic but broadly Christian, Ruskin could restore to contemporary British Protestantism eyes needlessly torn out by Puritan iconoclasm. While this may seem more of a seventeenth- than nineteenth-century argument, it was in fact a topical issue. Eighteen fifty was the year in which Pope Pius IX decreed that the Catholic hierarchy would be reestablished in England, stirring cries of "No Popery" as vehement as those of earlier centuries. The proper reading of stones Ruskin equates with the reading of stanzas, which returns us to Spenser and his first appearance in *The Stones* as a source of comparison for images of the months carved on the archivolt of the central doorway of St. Mark's, figures, Ruskin says, "employed in the avocations usually attributed to them throughout the whole compass of the Middle Ages, in Northern architecture and manuscript calendars, and at last versified by Spenser."[10]

Ruskin begins with January carrying home a noble tree—not the usual Janus figure, but one given by Spenser as well: "Numbd with holding all the day / An hatchet keene, with which he felled wood" (10.317). February seated warming himself contrasts with Spenser's figure pruning trees (Plate 31).

March, always in Italy "representative of the military power of the place and period; and thus, at Venice, having the winged Lion painted on his shield. . . . Sometimes, also, he is reaping . . .; and by Spenser, who exactly marks the junction of mediaeval and classical feeling, his military and agricultural functions are united, while also, in the Latin manner, he is made the first of the months:

> 'First sturdy March, with brows full sternly bent,
> And armed strongly, rode upon a Ram,
> The same which over Hellespontus swam;
> Yet in his hand a spade he also hent,

And in a bag all sorts of seeds ysame,
Which on the earth he strowed as he went.' "

(10.317-318)

As a transitional figure Spenser brings this iconography into the English Protestant tradition and thus completes the movement suggested by the chart of parallel images Ruskin places at the end of this series (Fig. 1) tracing the customary iconography of the seasons from medieval Italy through France into the north and the fifteenth century.

Spenser next appears in Ruskin's analysis of the Ducal Palace, particularly the sequence of capitals between the three main sculptural groups, oldest to newest, seaside to Square, the Vine Angle (Drunkenness of Noah), to the Fig Angle (Adam and Eve), to the Judgment Angle (Solomon). At this point Ruskin both praises the poetry of Dante (giving a short scheme of the *Divine Comedy*) and the power of Spenser, while designating the genre of their poetry a lesser kind. Ruskin assumes that his readers will know particular descriptions and episodes of *The Faerie Queene* and makes reference to such set pieces as the description of Despair without quotation. What he does not assume, however, is familiarity with what he terms Spenser's complex, unfinished system. He refers readers to his Appendix on the "theology" of Book One not as a complete explication of the allegory but as a model for their own future inquiry.

The Appendix (reprinted below) essentially gives in narrative form the schematic outline of the book as James Nohrnberg diagrams it in *The Analogy of The Faerie Queene*.[11] Even at his most schematic, however, Ruskin's interpretive bias is clear. He gives the capture of Truth by Sans Loy both a biblical antecedent and a contemporary application. Sans Loy is "the 'unrighteousness,' or 'adikia,' of St. Paul; and his bearing of Truth away captive is a type of those 'who hold the truth in unrighteousness' " [Romans 1:18]—those who use the truth for personal advantage "as is the case with so many of the popular leaders of the present day" (11.252). That the Redcrosse Knight should sleep by the fountain after his escape from the House of Pride, Ruskin refers directly, without concern for immediate sources, to what he takes to be its type. The Knight is "exposed to drowsiness and feebleness of watch; as, after Peter's boast, came Peter's sleeping, from weakness of the flesh, and then, last

	St. MARK'S.	MS. French. Late 13th Century.	MS. French. Late 13th Century.	MS. French. Late 13th Century.	MS. French. Early 14th Century.	MS. English. Early 14th Century.	MS. Flemish. 15th Century.
JANUARY	Carrying wood.	Janus feasting.	Janus feasting	Drinking and stirring fire.	Warming feet.	Janus feasting.	Feasting.
FEBRUARY	Warming feet.	Warming feet.	Warming feet.	Pruning.	Bearing candles,	Warming feet.	Warming hands.
MARCH	Going to war.	Pruning.	Pruning.	Striking with axe.	Pruning.	Carrying candles.	Reaping.
APRIL	Carrying sheep.	Gathering flowers.	Gathering flowers.	Gathering flowers.	Gathering flowers.	Pruning.	Gathering flowers.
MAY	Crowned with flowers.	Riding (f.).	Riding (f.).	Playing on violin.	Riding (f.).	Riding (f.).	Riding with lady on pillion.
JUNE	Reaping.	Mowing.	Mowing.	Gathering large red flowers.	Carrying (fagots?)	Carrying fagots.	Sheep-shearing.
JULY	Mowing.	Reaping.	Reaping.	Mowing.	Mowing.	Mowing.	Mowing.
AUGUST	Asleep.	Threshing.	Gathering grapes.	Reaping.	Reaping.	Reaping.	Reaping.
SEPTEMBER	Carrying grapes.	Sowing.	Sowing.	Drinking wine.	Threshing.	Threshing.	Sowing.
OCTOBER	Digging.	Gathering grapes.	Beating oak.	Sowing.	Sowing.	Sowing.	Beating oak.
NOVEMBER	Catching birds.	Beating oak.	Killing swine.	Killing swine.	Killing swine.	Killing swine.	Pressing (grapes?)
DECEMBER	Killing swine.	Killing swine.	Baking.	Killing oxen.	Baking.	Baking.	Killing swine.

FIGURE 1. "The employment of the months from some Northern manuscripts" (10. 322).

of all, Peter's fall" (11.253): the triumph of Orgoglio (11.253). Characters that do not obviously fit the pattern are not forced in but are, like the Dwarf, left in the fiction, or simply left out.

The main text proceeds thematically capital to capital, with literary parallels in imagery and idea drawn primarily from Spenser, and visual parallels primarily from Giotto's Arena Chapel frescoes. Discussing the capitals and their poetic and painted analogues, Ruskin chooses to interpret details and discrete images as expressive of divine truths much as an Evangelical preacher isolates scriptural texts. I will reproduce a few examples that demonstrate the method and bear on what follows.

Plate 32: Discord, here all but lost in the blackness of Venetian air pollution, but even in Ruskin's day needing the inscription to assure us of her meaning—*Discorida sum, discordans.* "She is the Atë of Spenser; 'mother of debate,' " an identification Ruskin will later expand upon.

> Her face most fowle and filthy was to see,
> With squinted eyes contrarie wayes intended;
> And loathly mouth, unmeete a mouth to bee,
> That nought but gall and venim comprehended
> And wicked wordes that God and man offended.
>   (10.390)

Temperance bearing a pitcher of water and a cup perpetuates the common confusion between temperance and mere abstinence (as opposed to gluttony). For Ruskin, Greek temperance is the true cardinal virtue moderating all the passions, and is so represented by Giotto (Plate 33), a bridle on her lips and a sword in her hand that she binds to its scabbard. For Giotto her opposite is anger, Ira, a woman tearing open her dress (Plate 34), the same representation we find on the fourth side of the tenth capital (Plate 35). It seems strange, says Ruskin, with what to his reader seems clear application to himself as much as to his times, "that neither Giotto nor Spenser should have given any representation of the *restrained* Anger, which is infinitely the most terrible; both of them make *him* [my emphasis] violent" (10.403).

Returning to temperance, Ruskin sees in Sir Guyon the restraint of Giotto mingled with sternness. After an admiring reference to the opposition between moral temperance and the desire for various intemperances expressed by the image of the paired horses in Plato's *Phaedrus*, he notes that:

> Temperance in the mediaeval systems is generally opposed by Anger, or by Folly, or Gluttony: but her proper opposite is Spenser's Acrasia, the principal enemy of Sir Guyon, at whose gates we find the subordinate vice "Excesse," as the introduction to Intemperance; a graceful and feminine image, necessary to illustrate the more dangerous forms of subtle intemperance, as opposed to the brutal "Gluttony" in the first book. She presses grapes into a cup, because of the words of St. Paul, " 'Be not drunk with wine, wherein is excess'; but always delicately.
>
>> 'Into her cup her scruzd with dantie breach
>> Of her fine fingers, without fowle empeach,
>> That so faire winepresse made the wine more sweet.' "
>>   (10. 396)

Ruskin is a true son of the English Puritan tradition, and no one is more wary of sensual temptation than he. But he does not therefore assume that the reader should be warned of the evils of Excesse or even of Acrasia herself by any surface clue that would guard the reader against the temptations to which Sir Guyon is exposed. The danger lies in the very attractiveness of Acrasia's realm. Ruskin does not distinguish, as we tend to do, between the moral and the psychological, and he believes in the positive power of the reflexive, self-restraining will, in the denial of desire. Approaching Spenser with this set of mind, there is no conflict between moral determination and surface seductiveness, between the lure of the Bower of Bliss and its pitiless destruction. Ruskin does not feel the contradiction that suggests even to so sympathetic a reader of Spenser's surfaces as Paul Alpers "that he is wanting in self-knowledge."[12] Rather Ruskin points back to a set of mind that could find in Sir Guyon's action a felt necessity.

Charity as depicted on the ninth capital (Plate 36) is mere loaf giving, far inferior to Giotto's image (Plate 37):

> distinguished from all the other virtues by having a circular glory round her head, and a cross of fire; she is crowned

with flowers, presents with her right hand a vase of corn and fruit, and with her left receives treasure from Christ, who appears above her, to provide her with the means of continual offices of beneficence, while she tramples under foot the treasures of the earth.

(10.397)

Ruskin's economic writings, which stressed the need for society to guarantee provision of the necessities of life to all unless they prove themselves unworthy, were in good measure an application of this prime Christian virtue to a capitalist England that he, like Carlyle, saw devoted to Mammon.

Luxury (Plate 38) with her mirror and bared breast the opposite of Chastity, evokes the obvious comparison to the figure mounted on a goat in the House of Pride, but that parallel is not sufficient for Ruskin whose Evangelical (and personal) bias emphasizes the danger of sensual temptation. Consequently he imports Cupid from Book Three as a figure of terror, giving an anticipation in embryo of Erwin Panofsky's essay on "Blind Cupid."[13]

Spenser, who has been so often noticed as furnishing the exactly intermediate type of conception between the mediaeval and the Renaissance, indeed represents Cupid under the ancient form of a beautiful winged god, and riding a lion, but still no plaything of the Graces, but full of terror:

"With that the darts which his right hand did straine
Full dreadfully he shooke, and all did quake,
And clapt on hye his coloured wingës twaine,
That all his many it afraide did make."

His *many*, that is to say, his company; and observe what a company it is. . . .

"Unquiet Care, and fond Unthriftyhead,
Lewd Losse of Time, and Sorrow seeming dead,
Inconstant Chaunge, . . .
Vile poverty, and lastly Death with infamy."

Compare these two pictures of Cupid with the Love-god of the Renaissance, as he is represented to this day, con-

fused with angels, in every faded form of ornament and
allegory, in our furniture, our literature, and our minds.

(10.401)

Finally Envy with serpentine cap and girdle, a dragon on her
lap (Plate 39), is augmented by Giotto's Envy, grasping, back-
biting and covetous (Plate 40), which became for Ruskin the
image of capitalist competition as opposed to Christian cooperation. To the serpentine imagery of the Ducal Palace and
Giotto, Spenser adds "the idea of fury, in the wolf on which he
rides, with that of corruption on his lips, and of discolouration
or distortion in the whole mind:

'Malicious Envy rode
Upon a ravenous wolfe, and still did chaw
Between his cankred teeth a venomous tode
That all the poison ran about his jaw. . . .' "

(10.406)

By 1856 Ruskin was willing to call creative allegory genu-
inely symbolical. In addition he transferred the category in
which he chose to discuss the description of Envy from allegory
to the grotesque, making it an example of that noble grotesque
art that arises from the contemplation of terrible things or evil
in general. Ruskin lists seven characteristics that can be abstracted from Spenser's description of Envy, but the imagery
now has clear priority over the abstractions, the affective power
of the verse over the narrative, which has little bearing on this
mode of analysis. "All noble grotesques are concentrations of
this kind, and the noblest convey truths which nothing else
could convey; . . . which no mere utterance of the symbolized
truth would have possessed, but which belongs to the effort of
the mind to unweave the riddle, or to the sense it has of there
being an infinite power and meaning in the thing seen, beyond
all that is apparent therein . . ." (*Modern Painters III*, 5.133).
Spenser's language is now the equivalent of Scripture, specifically of Jeremiah's seething pot the face thereof to the north
where an evil shall break forth upon the inhabitants of the land
(Jer. 1:13, 14). The power of the great artist to turn moral
abstraction into the equivalent of experience for the reader
implicit in the discussion of Temperance in *The Stones of Venice*

is here made explicit and deliberately extended from the Bible into secular literature.

The Ruskin we have seen so far is less an interpreter of Spenser's allegory than a pioneer in the study of comparative iconography or literary pictorialism, and it is in this area that Ruskin's texts cross most frequently and richly the interests of modern scholarship and criticism. His citation of Jeremiah takes us to our last stage in the consideration of Ruskin's application of Spenser, a stage that is less interpretation of Spenser than a curious continuation of his tradition.

In 1860 Ruskin concluded *Modern Painters* and published his direct attack upon the ethos of Victorian capitalism, *Unto This Last*. The nature of that attack he presents in the guise of art criticism in his transformation of Turner's painting of *The Goddess of Discord Choosing the Apple of Contention in the Garden of the Hesperides* into a prophecy of what Ruskin warned against in *The Stones of Venice*: the denial of Christian charity; the consequent assumption of a satanic god (Plate 41), Ruskin's reading of the Turner painting is an example of his own syncretic myth-making and allegorizing. Turner's monster proves the product of a whole demonic Genesis, a "begat" of dragons, pages of them, from Hesiod and Euripides through Dante, whose introduction of Plutus provides the caption for Ruskin's loving copy (Plate 42), and whose sea dragon "gathered the air up with retractile claws," to Milton's Mammon, the least erect of those that fell.

Discord, Ruskin says, comes to Turner by way of the Eris of Homer and Virgil and what he considers to be Spenser's confusion between Eris, or Discord, and Atë, Error, her daughter according to Hesiod. But the lines he quotes here are not those cited to illustrate the *Discordia sum, discordans* capital, but those emphasizing her doubleness and distortion (Book IV, canto i, 27-29), all of which Ruskin's Turner follows while adding as his own final touch her inability even to choose between the proffered apples. But the Greek Hesperid garden was splendid, a Hesperid Aeglé or brightness last seen, according to the mythopoesis of Ruskin's art history, in the Venetian sunset of Giorgione's art. Turner's garden is dark, and the darkness derives from the garden in the cave of Mammon: "The gardin of Prosérpina this hight" where "eke that famous golden apple grew, / The which among the gods false Atë threw"

(7.407). Hence comes the darkness of the stream, a Cyrene fountain become Cocytus, and the diseased nature of the tree that Turner shows broken by the weight of its own fruit.

I conclude with a portion of Ruskin's own peroration to this chapter of *Modern Painters V* with its syncretic mythology, its last allusion to Spenser's allegory, and its application to Victorian England.

> In each city and country of past time, the master-minds had to declare the chief worship which lay at the nation's heart; to define it; adorn it; show the range and authority of it. Thus in Athens, we have the triumph of Pallas; and in Venice the Assumption of the Virgin; here, in England is our great spiritual fact for ever interpreted to us—the Assumption of the Dragon. . . . The fairy English Queen once thought to command the waves, but it is the sea-dragon now who commands her valleys; of old the Angel of the Sea ministered to them, but now the Serpent of the Sea; where once flowed their clear springs now spreads the black Cocytus pool; and the fair blooming of the Hesperid meadows fades into ashes beneath the Nereid's Guard.
>
> (7.408)

New York University

APPENDIX

2. [VOL. X. p. 383 *n*.] THEOLOGY OF SPENSER

The following analysis of the first book of the *Faërie Queene* may be interesting to readers who have been in the habit of reading the noble poem too hastily to connect its parts completely together, and may perhaps induce them to more careful study of the rest of the poem.

The Redcrosse Knight is Holiness,—the "Pietas" of St. Mark's, the "Devotio" of Orcagna, [See Vol. X. p. 385.]—meaning, I think, in general, Reverence and Godly Fear.

This Virtue, in the opening of the book, has Truth (or Una) at its side, but presently enters the Wandering Wood, and encounters the serpent Error; that is to say, Error in her universal form, the first enemy of Reverence and Holiness; and more especially Error as founded on learning; for when Holiness strangles her,

"Her vomit *full of bookes and papers was,*
With loathly frogs and toades, which eyes did lacke."

Having vanquished this first open and palpable form of Error, as Reverence and Religion must always vanquish it, the Knight encounters Hypocrisy, or Archimagus: Holiness cannot detect Hypocrisy, but believes him, and goes home with him; whereupon, Hypocrisy succeeds in separating Holiness from Truth; and the Knight (Holiness) and Lady (Truth) go forth separately from the house of Archimagus.

Now observe; the moment Godly Fear, or Holiness, is separated from Truth, he meets Infidelity, or the Knight Sans Foy; Infidelity having False-hood, or Duessa, riding behind him. The instant the Redcrosse Knight is aware of the attack of Infidelity, he

"Gan fairly couch his speare, and towards ride."

He vanquishes and slays Infidelity; but is deceived by his companion, Falsehood, and takes her for his lady: thus showing the condition of Religion, when, after being attacked by Doubt, and remaining victorious, it is never-theless seduced, by any form of Falsehood, to pay reverence where it ought not. This, then, is the first fortune of Godly Fear separated from Truth. The poet then returns to Truth, separated from Godly Fear. She is immediately attended by a lion, or Violence, which makes her dreaded wherever she comes; and when she enters the mart of superstition, this Lion tears Kirkra-pine in pieces: showing how Truth, separated from Godliness, does indeed put an end to the abuses of superstition, but does so violently and desperately. She then meets again with Hypocrisy, whom she mistakes for her own lord, or Godly Fear, and travels a little way under his guardianship (Hypocrisy thus not unfrequently appearing to defend the Truth), until they are both met by Lawlessness, or the Knight Sans Loy, whom Hypocrisy cannot resist. Law-lessness overthrows Hypocrisy, and seizes upon Truth, first slaying her lion attendant: showing that the first aim of licence is to destroy the force and authority of Truth. Sans Loy then takes Truth captive, and bears her away. Now this Lawlessness is the "unrighteousness," or "adikia," of St. Paul; and his bearing Truth away captive is a type of those "who hold the truth in unrighteousness,"[Romans i. 18.]—that is to say, generally, of men who, knowing what is true, make the truth give way to their own purposes, or use it only to forward them, as is the case with so many of the popular leaders of the present day. Una is then delivered from Sans Loy by the satyrs, to show that nature, in the end, must work out the deliverance of the truth, although, where it has been captive to Lawlessness, that deliverance can only be obtained through Savageness, and a return to barbarism. Una is then taken from among the satyrs by Satyrane, the son of a satyr and a "lady myld, fair Thyamis" (typifying the early steps of renewed civilization, and its rough and hardy character, "nousled up in life and manners wilde"), who meeting again with Sans Loy, enters instantly into rough and prolonged combat with him: showing how the early organization of a hardy nation must be wrought out through much discouragement from Lawlessness. This contest the poet leaving for the time undecided, returns to trace the adventures of the

Redcrosse Knight, or Godly Fear, who, having vanquished Infidelity, presently is led by Falsehood to the house of Pride: thus showing how religion,
separated from truth, is first tempted by doubts of God, and then by the pride
of life. The description of this house of Pride is one of the most elaborate and
noble pieces in the poem; and here we begin to get at the proposed system of
Virtues and Vices. For Pride, as Queen, has six other vices yoked in her
chariot; namely, first, Idleness, then Gluttony, Lust, Avarice, Envy, and
Anger, all driven on by "Sathan, with a smarting whip in hand." From these
lower vices and their company, Godly Fear, though lodging in the house of
Pride, holds aloof; but he is challenged, and has a hard battle to fight with Sans
Joy, the brother of Sans Foy: showing, that though he has conquered
Infidelity, and does not give himself up to the allurements of Pride, he is yet
exposed, so long as he dwells in her house, to distress of mind and loss of his
accustomed rejoicing before God. He, however, having partly conquered
Despondency, or Sans Joy, Falsehood goes down to Hades, in order to obtain
drugs to maintain the power or life of Despondency; but, meantime, the
Knight leaves the house of Pride: Falsehood pursues and overtakes him, and
finds him by a fountain side, of which the waters are

> "Dull and slow,
> And all that drinke thereof do faint and feeble grow."

Of which the meaning is, that Godly Fear, after passing through the house of
Pride, is exposed to drowsiness and feebleness of watch; as, after Peter's
boast, came Peter's sleeping, from weakness of the flesh, and then, last of all,
Peter's fall. And so it follows, for the Redcrosse Knight, being overcome with
faintness by drinking of the fountain, is thereupon attacked by the giant
Orgoglio, overcome, and thrown by him into a dungeon. This Orgoglio is
Orgueil, or Carnal Pride; not the pride of life, spiritual and subtle, but the
common and vulgar pride in the power of this world: and his throwing the
Redcrosse Knight into a dungeon is a type of the captivity of true religion
under the temporal power of corrupt churches, more especially of the Church
of Rome; and of its gradually wasting away in unknown places, while Carnal
Pride has the pre-eminence over all things. That Spenser means especially the
pride of the Papacy, is shown by the 16th stanza of the book; for there the
giant Orgoglio is said to have taken Duessa, or Falsehood, for his "deare,"
and to have set upon her head a triple crown, and endowed her with royal
majesty, and made her to ride upon a seven-headed beast.

In the meantime, the dwarf, the attendant of the Redcrosse Knight, takes
his arms, and finding Una, tells her of the captivity of her lord. Una, in the
midst of her mourning, meets Prince Arthur, in whom, as Spenser himself
tells us, is set forth generally Magnificence; but who, as is shown by the
choice of the hero's name, is more especially the magnificence, or literally,
"great doing," of the kingdom of England. This power of England, going
forth with Truth, attacks Orgoglio, or the Pride of Papacy, slays him; strips
Duessa, or Falsehood, naked; and liberates the Redcrosse Knight. The magnificent and well-known description of Despair [See Vol. X. p. 391.] follows,
by whom the Redcrosse Knight is hard bested, on account of his past errors

and captivity, and is only saved by Truth, who, perceiving him to be still feeble, brings him to the house of Coelia, called, in the argument of the canto, Holiness, but properly, Heavenly Grace, the mother of the Virtues. Her "three daughters, well upbrought," are Faith, Hope, and Charity. Her porter is Humility; because Humility opens the door of Heavenly Grace. Zeal and Reverence are her chamberlains, introducing the new-comers to her presence; her groom, or servant, is Obedience; and her physician, Patience. Under the commands of Charity, the matron Mercy rules over her hospital, under whose care the Knight is healed of his sickness; and it is to be especially noticed how much importance Spenser, though never ceasing to chastise all hypocrisies and mere observances of form, attaches to true and faithful *penance* in effecting this cure. Having his strength restored to him, the Knight is trusted to the guidance of Mercy, who, leading him forth by a narrow and thorny way, first instructs him in the seven works of Mercy, and then leads him to the hill of Heavenly Contemplation; whence, having a sight of the New Jerusalem, as Christian of the Delectable Mountains, he goes forth to the final victory over Satan, the old serpent, with which the book closes.

NOTES

This paper was presented at the session sponsored by the Spenser Society at the 1982 MLA Convention.

1. The Letter to Raleigh, *The Fairie Queene*, T. P. Roche, Jr., ed. (New Haven, Conn.: Yale University Press, 1978), p. 18.

2. *Toward an Aesthetic of Reception*, Timothy Bahti, tr. (Minneapolis: University of Minnesota Press, 1982), pp. 15, 19.

3. *Companion* (Berkeley: University of California Press, 1970) p. 11.

4. *The Poetry of "The Faerie Queene"* (Princeton, N.J.: Princeton University Press, 1967), p. 4.

5. *The Aesthetic and Critical Theories of John Ruskin* (Princeton, N.J.: Princeton University Press, 1971), p. 329.

6. *The Faerie Queene*, p. 16.

7. *Areopagitica, John Milton: Complete Poems and Major Prose*, Merritt Y. Hughes, ed. (New York: Odyssey Press, 1957), pp. 728–729.

8. *The Allegory of Love* (Oxford: Clarendon Press, 1936), p. 359.

9. "On Chaucer and Spenser," *Lectures on the English Poets, The Collected Works of William Hazlitt*, 21 vols., A. R. Waller and Arnold Grover, eds. (London: J. M. Dent, 1902), V, 44.

10. *The Stones of Venice* (1851–53), *The Works of John Ruskin*, Library Edition, 39 vols. E. T. Cook and Alexander Wedderburn, eds. (London: George Allen, 1903–1912), X, 315; hereafter cited in the text by volume and page number. All quotations from Spenser to follow are from Ruskin's text. While the distinctions Ruskin draws between medieval and Renaissance capitals generally holds, the carvings now in place are copies.

11. *The Analogy . . .* (Princeton, N.J.: Princeton University Press, 1976), p. 202.

12. *The Poetry of the Faerie Queene*, p. 306.

13. *Studies in Iconology* (New York: Harper, 1962, reprint of the 1939 edition), pp. 95–128.

14. For a discussion of the "self-evidencing" power of the Bible and its influence on the way Ruskin read, see my "Ruskin as a Prejudiced Reader," *ELH*, 49 (1982), 73–98.

Illustrations

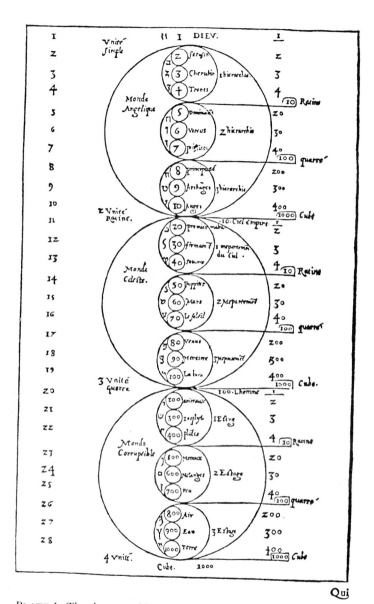

PLATE 1. The three worlds according to Pico: Angelic, Celestial, and Corruptible. From the Introduction by Nicholas Le Fevre de la Boderie to *L'Harmonie du monde diuisée en trois cantiques, par François Georges . . . plus L'Heptaple de Iean Picus Comte de la Mirande* (Paris, 1579), sig. e6ᵛ. Courtesy of The British Library.

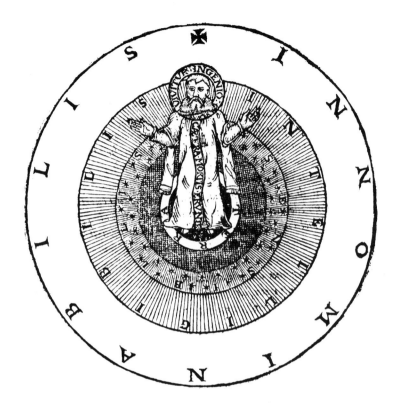

Argumentum Libri ſecundi.

*P Er metam apprehenſionis ſublimata mens humana, & propè
ſummitatem lucibilis pyramidis locata, eius beneficio lucis,
diſtinctè iam videt lumen in omnibus intelligibilibus ſenſibili-
buſq̃, quod antea confuſè tantùm apprehenderat, Ideas, Ange-
los, actus puros, ſimul ac naturales infra ſe cernens, de cernens de-
monſtrans, haud aliter atq̃ is qui per multos gradus preſſuſq̃
difficultæ caẜuuucu montis in duo lauer ẜictẜitẜ ꝟ ſẜ ꝟ al-
titudine, vno conſpectu omnem ad cacumen montis methodum
vndiq̃ dirigentem clara luce intuetur, è praſenti vt lucet figura.*

PLATE 2. The three worlds after Reuchlin: Sensible, Intelligible, and
Unnamable. From Everard Digby, *Theoria Analytica Viam ad Monar-
chiam Scientiarum Demonstrans . . . In Tres Libros Digesta* (London: Henry
Bynneman, 1579), p. 48. Courtesy of The Huntington Library.

PLATE 3. Charity. Printer's device from the title page of *L'Orlando furioso di M. Lodovico Ariosto con . . . allegorie, & annotatione di M. Tomaso Porcacchi* (Venice: Domenico Farri, 1594). Courtesy of The Folger Shakespeare Library.

| Ex Chao triplici Mundus triplex per Amorem vel Amoris triplicem faciem eſt fabricatus. | 1 Mens angelica {Informis / Formata} 2 Anima mundi {Informis / Formata} 3 Corpus mundi {Informis / Formata} | Ita ſemu tuo côſe quuntur iuxta Platonem | Chaos 1. / Mundus 1. / Chaos 2. / Mundus 2. / Chaos 3. / Mundus 3 | Iuxta partitio-nê ante dictâ & nouenariam | Chaos eſſent. ſimp. / Progreſſus eſſent. ſimp. / Status eſſent. ſimp. / Chaos eſſent. protenſi. / Progreſ. eſſent. proteſi. / Status eſſent. protenſi. / Chaos eſſent. abſolut. / Progreſ.eſſent. abſolut. / Status eſſentiæ abſolutę vel circularis. |

Iunge his demum gradus Vniuerſi totidem, & Amoris ſpecies, habebis ſanè ſyſtema pulcherrimum & planè muſicum, quod interuallis iunctum imparibus, ſed tamen pro rata portione diſtinctis, acuta cum grauibus temperans, varios æquabiliter concentus efficit; etſi illum aures non capiant noſtræ, quippe ad ſublunares turbines, affectuumque procellas varias, velut ad Nili Catadupa obſurdeſcentes.

Mundi Symphonia pulcherrima.

VNIVERSI MVSICA INTRA AMORIS
Circulum comprehenſa.

Pulchrè itaque & diuinorum operum, & circularis in amore progreſſus, & totius denique concentus in vniuerſo muſica ratio, ſenario numero ſic exprimêda eſt, vt in ſeptenarium finiat. Cuius apud Philonem cæterosque Platonicos laudes ſunt innumerabiles, vtque vel idem in nouenarium vel in ternarium; rurſus &. hinc in vnitatem vnicam reducatur. Nam & triangulus
        N   Iſopleuros

Senarius numerus vniuerſi in xta Platonem.

PLATE 4. The three worlds according to Ficino: Angelic Mind, World Soul, and World Body. From Cornelius Gemma, *De Arte Cyclognomica, Libri III* (Antwerp, 1569), p. 97. Courtesy of The Bodleian Library.

dicio esse potuisset, & sapientiæ maioris, & ingentis, quod Deus in
creaturas insumeret impendij. Quare cum artifex ipsum DeiVer-
bum hæc vellet ostentare, animal quoddam vnum ex vtraque natura, visibili, scilicet, & inuisibili, nempe Hominem fabricat, corpore quidem à materia, quæ iam antè suppetebat, accepto; vita verò
per ipsum indita, quam rationalem animam nûcupamus. Hunc cô-
positum, vt alium quendam Mundum in re tenui magnum, in terris constituit, vt mixtum quendam adoratorem, visibilis quidem
creaturæ inspectorem, intelligibilis autem cultorem. Deus igitur
cum Verbo suo & Spiritu sancto, quæ Tria vnum sunt Deus vnus
omnipotens, Tres condidit mundos, angelicum, materialem, &
humanum; intelligibilem, scilicet, corporeum, & mistum.

Mundus { Angelicus,   Materialis,   Humanus,
         { Intelligibilis, Corporeus,   Mixtus.

Omne autem quod creatum est, aut est extremum, aut medium;
si extremum, intellectus est, aut angelicus, aut humanus; si medium, est sensibilis creatura, posterior Angelis, Homine prior creata.
Angelicus intellectus est esse omnium, & vniuersalis omnium a-
ctus: sicut enim à materia abiunctus est; ita & sine specie intelligit,
nouitque omnia, non per ipsa omnia, neque per ipsorum omnium
species, sed simpliciter, & per se, intuitu & contemplatione sui
esse, antequam omnia fiant. Humanus intellectus est omnium posse,
& vniuersalis omnium potentia. Et quæcumque intra vtrumque
intellectum relinquuntur, sunt omnia secundum substantiam ex
actu & potentia. Intellectus enim angelicus est, vt simplex omniũ
actus: humanus, vt simplex & vniuersalis omnium potẽtia. Quid-
quid verò superest, sensibile est, & eorum medium, ex actu & potentia. Fit igitur vt omnia sint tantum Tria, duo videlicet, extre-
mi intellectus, quorum vterque est omnia: & reliqua omnia, quæ
vtriusque intellectus medio claudũtur. Et eorum quodlibet est quod-

PLATE 5. Man as "middle" of three worlds. From Pietro
Bongo, *Numerorum Mysteria* (Paris, 1618), p. 111.
Courtesy of The Huntington Library.

Lib·X   Fo·LXXIII·

D I V I N V S finiti: certã habêtes
aut re aut cogitatio
ne dyametrũ:multi
tudine tamen & nu
mero entiũ reperiũ-
tur infiniti.diuinus
autem mundus e di
uerso cũ sit magni-
tudine infinitus: nõ
modo multitudin e:
sed etiam vnitate en
tis finitus & vnic us
esse declaratur.

Intellectualis

Sensibilismundus.

Vnde sit: vt rite cũ **X.**
cti definiãt deũ esse
spherã:cuius centrũ
est vbiq̃ & circunfe
rétia nusq̃. quando
quidem in quolibet
inferiorum mũdorũ
est vbiq̃ accipere di

Caelestis

ulnitatis diuiniq̃ mundi cétrum: quinimmo & quilibet
eorum est diuini mundi centrum. Circunferentiam au
tem eiusdem nusq̃ reperire liceat.

Qz in quinto & vigesimo numero:qui quintus
quadratus est toti⁹vniuersi scala ab imo ad sum
mum consũmatur.   Cap.V. Ĺ

Vm sint(vtdiximus)in vniuerso quattuor mũ
di: sensibilis cœlestis: intelligibilis: diuinus:
sibi inuicem recta succedentes seq̃ circũplecté
tes: omnis illorum pecculiaris distinctio:ab imo ad sum
mum contendens: numerum quintum supra vigesimũ
(qui quintus quadratus est)adimplere'reperitur.   **II.**
Nam sensibilis mundus:quatenitas quædam est elemẽ
                   k.

PLATE 6. Hierarchy of worlds from Charles de Bouelles,
Physicorum Elementorum . . . Libri Decem (Paris, 1512),
fol. 73. Courtesy of The Bodleian Library.

PLATE 7. Man as microcosm of the three worlds. From Jean Thenaud, *L'Introduction en la Cabale*. Geneva, Bibliothèque publique et universitaire, MS fr. 167, fol. 24ᵛ. Courtesy of the Bibliothèque publique et universitaire, Geneva.

In Archetypo	Pater	שדי Sadai Filius	Spūs ſctūs	Nomē dei trium literarum Tres perſonæ in diuinis
In mundo intelleĉtuali.	Suprema Innocentes	Media Martyres	Infima Cōfeſſores.	Tres hierarchiæ angelorum Tres gradus beatorum
In mundo cœleſti	Mobilia Cardines Diurnus	Fixa Succedentes Noĉturnus	Cōmunia Cadentes Particeps	Tres quaterniones ſignorũ. Tres quaterniones domorũ Tres domini triplicitatum.
In mundo elementali	Simplicia	Compoſita	Decōpoſita	Tres gradus elementorum.
In minore mundo	Caput ĩ quo uiget itelleĉtus reſpondēs mundo intelleĉtuali.	Peĉtus, ubi cor ſedes uitæ, reſpondēs mũdo cæleſti.	Vēter, ubi gi gnitiua uirtus mēbraꝗ genitalia, rĩ ſpondens mũdo ele mentali	Tres partes reſpondentes triplici mundo
In mundo infernali	Aleĉto Minos Malefici	Megera Aeacus Apoſtatæ	Cteſiphone Rhadamātᵒ Infideles	Tres furiæ infernales Tres iudices infernales Tres gradus damnatorũm.

PLATE 8. Triadic correspondences from Heinrich Cornelius Agrippa, *De Occulta Philosophia Libri Tres* (n.p., 1533), fol. 107.

158　　*DE NVM. III.*

Mundus $\begin{cases} Terra, & Sol, & Firmamentum: \\ Elementum, & Planeta, & Stella fixa: \end{cases}$ $\begin{cases} Proportio- \\ nabilia. \end{cases}$

Homo $\begin{cases} Venter, & Cor, & Cerebrum: \\ Ima pars, & Medium, Suprema pars. \end{cases}$

*Secundum distinctionem mundi angelici, cælestis, & elementa-
ris, sunt in humano corpore tres partes, ita disclusæ & separatæ,
vt tribus mundi partibus proportione respondeant. Prima quidem
& suprema, caput; secunda quæ à collo ad vmbilicum protenditur;
tertia quæ ab vmbilico extenditur ad pedes: est in capite cerebrum
fons cognitionis: est in pectore cor, fons motus vitæ & caloris:
sunt in postrema parte genitalia membra, principium generationis. Sic & in mundo, suprema pars, quæ est mundus Angelicus
seu intellectualis, est fons cognitionis, quia facta est illa natura ad
intelligendum: pars media, quæ est cælum principium vitæ motus & caloris, in qua Sol veluti cor in pectore dominatur: est infra Lunam, quod omnibus notum, generationis principium & cor-
ruptionis. Vide quam aptè Tres maioris & minoris mundi partes
inuicem congruant.*

	Supremus,	*Medius,*	*Infimus:*
Mundus	*Intellectualis,*	*Cælestis,*	*Sublunaris:*
	Angelus,	*Sol,*	*Elementum:*
	Cognitio,	*Vita & calor,*	*Generatio:*
Homo	*Caput,*	*Pectus,*	*Postrema pars ventris:*
	Cerebrum,	*Cor,*	*Genitalia:*
	Suprema,	*Media,*	*Infima.*

Proportionabilia

TRINITAS in Artifice.

Nic. Cuf.
excit. li. 8.
Sanctus. *Ars oritur de exercitio artificis, & est artificium in arte, vt Pa-
ter in Filio: & ars in artificio, vt Filius in Patre: hoc autem quod
conseruat operātem in opere, est delectatio, quæ est hoc bonum quod
procedit ex exercitio & arte. Tres igitur caussas ex artificiato
deprehendimus, scilicet, efficientem, formalem, & finalem, &*

PLATE 9. Table of correspondences from Pietro Bongo,
Numerorum Mysteria (Paris, 1618), p. 158. Courtesy of
The Huntington Library.

L

In ignibus	Sol	Ignis	Cor
Proprietates	Maturitas	Decoctio	Digestio
In animabus	Vegetariua	Sensitiua	Rationalis
In intellectû	Diuina	Angelicus	Humanus
Insapientia	Diuina	Angelica	Humana
In mundo	Sol	Luna	Terra
In magnitudine	Longitudo	Latitudo	Profunditas
Rursum	Linea	Superficies	Corpus
In numeris	Linearis	Planus	Solidus
In eruditione	Conceptus	Vox	Scriptura
In luminosis	Sol	Mior planeta	Stella
In aspectu solis	Oriens	Occidens	Meridies
In motu aquarum	Fons	Fluuius	Mare
In angulis	Obtusus	Acutus	Rectus
In hois positione	Iacere	Sedere	Stare
In motibus	Augmentatio	Alteratio	Latio
Proprietates	Quantitas	Qualitas	Locus
Infantis status	In vtero	In natiuitate	Post natiuitatem
In etate hominis	Infans	Puer	Vir
In partu animi	Sensibile	Imaginabile	Rationale
In sensibus	Imaginatio	Auditus	Visus
In abiectioribus	Olfactus	Gustus	Tactus
In obiectis	Odor	Lux	Scriptura
In intellectualibus	Mens	Intellectus	Ratio
In syllogismis	Maior extremitas	Minor	Medium
In syllogismis	Prima figura	Secunda	Tertia
In syllogismis	Maior Propositio	Minor	Conclusio

Deus	Intellectus	Memoria	Voluntas	1
Angel⁹	Intellectus	Memoria	Voluntas	2
Homo	Intellectus	Memoria	Voluntas	3

Omne etenim quod consumatum est & perfectum: est ex necessitate trinû. Sapientia autem perfecta est/ trinitas perfecta est: ideoqɜ et sapientia trina & trinitas trina reperitur.

Trinitas in deo	Pater	Filius	Spiritus
Trinitas i hoie	Adam	Eua	Abel
Expressiones	A nullo	Ab vno	Abvtroqɜ
Trinitas anime	Intellect⁹	Memoria	Voluntas
In arbore	Folium	Flos	Fructus
In nube	Pluuia	Nix	Grando
In animali	Os	Stomach⁹	Cor
Proprietates	Assumens	Recipiens	Digerens
In mundo	Intellectual	Celestis	Sensibilis
In corpore	Os	Neruus	Caro
In scientijs	Sermociales	Reales	Naturales
In plantis	Arbor	Frutex	Herba
In sole	Lux	Lumem	Vmbra
In luua	Coniuctio	Medium.	Oppositio
In circulo	Centrum	Dyameter	Circuferena

t ij

PLATE 10. Triadic correspondences from Charles de Bouelles, *Liber de Sapientie,* in *Liber de Intellectu* (Paris, 1510), fols. 136–136ᵛ. Courtesy of The Folger Shakespeare Library.

PLATE 11. Necessity and the Three Fates, "all sitting round about /
The direfull distaffe standing in the mid." From Vincenzo Cartari,
Le imagini de i dei de gli antichi (Venice, 1592), p. 246. Courtesy
of the Alderman Library, University of Virginia.

PLATE 12. Cosmic harmony according to Plato, with Necessity and the Three Fates in center. Engraving by Agostino Caracci, after a design by Bernardo Buontalenti for the first *Intermezzo* at the Ufizzi theater, May 2, 1589. Courtesy of the Courtauld Institute.

PLATE 13. Necessity and the Three Fates. Watercolor design for the first
Intermezzo by Bernardo Buontalenti. Courtesy of the
Bibliteca Nazionale Centrale, Florence.

PLATE 14. Necessity with the Three Fates as spinners. From Jean Thenaud, *L'Introduction en la Cabale*. Geneva, Bibliothèque publique et universitaire, MS fr. 167, fol. 74ᵛ. Courtesy of the Bibliothèque publique et universitaire, Geneva.

152   ## Theoriæ Analyticæ

seipso luminis cōparationem & supraſupremi radiationem, quod referente Sidonio tam illuſtre regnum, tam luminoſum eſt imperium, vt eius æterno curriculo vaſtiſſimi orbis, nulla vnquam ætas finē ſit allatura. Huic cōcinit heroicus Poëta hunc in modū,

Non alium videre patres,aliumúe nepotes
Aſpicient: deus eſt,qui non mutatur in æuo.

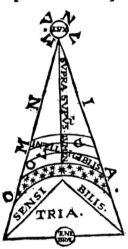

Ad ſe recurrit immēſi Oceani inſtar, attrahēs fluctus:vnitas in triade,triades in Pyramide, cuius ſummitas eſt vnitas lucis,effluxus per triadem ignis, baſis,cubus perfectionis,ſtatuens fundamēſq, vtraq, in ſoliditate ſua : ex ſe producens tāquam principia, continens in perfectione figuræ Pyramidalis ſummam aſcenſionem, ad ima rerum fundamenta , intimaq, penetralia permeans, quæ eſt lux in abyſſo micans,& Pyramis in ſummo perfectionis, quam

repreſentat ignis apud mundum ſenſibilem & elementarem, quamq, nobis Philolaus ſignificauit his verbis : Atq, deus ipſe non eſt lux creata , ſed lucibilis autor omnis luminis. Quare Pyramidem abſolutiſſimam & retractiſſimam à triangula baſi ſe erigentem ,ſignificat , & ſimiliter igneum vigorem, in diuina mundi incomparabilis triade contentum : cuius erectio, vnitas ſignificat , punctum erectum, duo latera & baſin vtriuſq, quæ eſt vnitas ipſa in ſummitate erecta ſuperlucens his omnibus,& vnitas eorum per quam hæc tria ſimul ſunt quatuor & vnum: quod occultè olim ſymbolizauit Pythagoras aſſerendo principium vniuerſorum eſſe infinitum , vnum, & duo : infinitudinem deum,vnitatis formam: alteritatis,materiam primum initium ſtatuens?

PLATE 15. Diagram of the three worlds from the center chapter of Everard Digby, *Theoria Analytica Viam ad Monarchiam Scientiarum Demonstrans . . . In Tres Libros Digesta* (London: Henry Bynneman, 1579), p. 152. Courtesy of The Huntington Library.

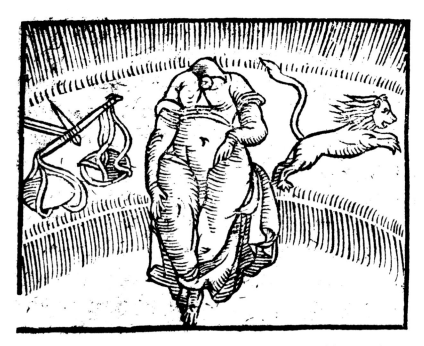

PLATE 16. "Astraea," from Valeriano, *Hieroglyphica* (Frankfurt, 1614),
p. 748. Courtesy of the Edinburgh University Library.

PLATE 17. "Nemesis," from Alciati, *Emblematum liber* (Augsburg, 1531), sig. A7. Courtesy of The British Library.

PLATE 18. IN SENATUM BONI PRINCIPIS, from Alciati, *Emblematum liber*
(Augsburg, 1531), sig. D1. Courtesy of The British Library.

PLATE 19. NEC VERBO NEC FACTO QUENQUAM LAEDENDUM, from
Alciati, *Emblematum liber* (Antwerp, 1581), p. 128.
Courtesy of The British Library.

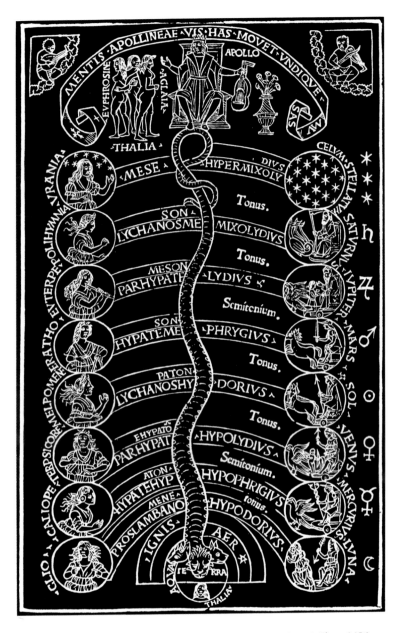

PLATE 20. The frontispiece of Gafori's *Practica musicae*, Milan, 1496.

Improbitas solet esse sibi justissima merces,
Auctor es interitus sic Basilisce tibi.

INTER

PLATE 21. Joachim Camerarius, *Symbolorum & Emblematum,* vol. 4 (Nurem-
berg, 1604), no. 79, "NOXA NOCENTI," reproduced from the
1634 edition. Courtesy of The Princeton University Library.

PLATE 22, Figure 1. Nicolas Reusner, *Emblemata* (Frankfurt am Main, 1581), book 2, no. 23, "Incerta pro certis amplecti stultum," reproduced from the microfiche copy of the Inter Documentation Co., Zug, Switzerland, based on that in the National Art Library.

PLATE 22, Figure 2. Andrea Alciati, *Emblematum liber* (Augsburg, 1531), fol. D6, "ALIUS PECCAT. ALIUS PLECTITUR." Courtesy of The Princeton University Library.

IN FERTILITATEM SIBI IPSI DAMNOSAM.

PLATE 23, Figure 1. Andrea Alciati, *Emblematum liber* (Augsburg, 1531), fol. B8v, "IN FERTILITATEM SIBI IPSI DAMNOSAM." Courtesy of The Princeton University Library.

IN OCCASIONEM

PLATE 23, Figure 2. Andrea Alciati, *Emblematum liber* (Augsburg, 1531), fol. A8, "IN OCCASIONEM." Courtesy of The Princeton University Library.

298

In occaſionem.   **181**

To my *Kinſman*. M. GEFFREY WHITNEY.

PLATE 24. Geffrey Whitney, *A Choice of Emblemes* (Leyden, 1586),
p. 181, "In occasionem." Courtesy of The
Princeton University Library.

Des Benefices.

Heb. 13.

Ne mettez en oubli la beneficence & communication:
Car Dieu prend plaisir à tels sacrifices.

PLATE 25. *MIKROKOSMOS Parvus Mundus* (Antwerp, 1579), no. 19,
"DE BENEFICIIS," reproduced from the 1680 French edition.
Courtesy of The Princeton University Library.

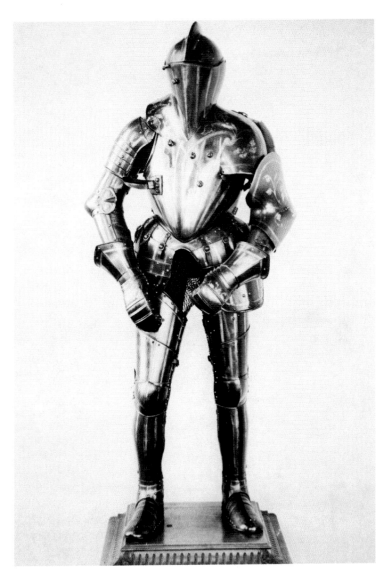

PLATE 26. A French jousting harness of the 1580s. The rest for the lance is on the right-hand side of the breastplate. When in armor for a tournament, a knight could not see the rest when he placed the lance in it. JWHA 428. Stephen V. Grancsay, *Catalogue of Armor: The John Woodman Higgins Armory* (Worcester, Mass.: Privately printed by Davis Press, Inc., 1961), p. 90. Photo courtesy of Higgins Armory Museum, Worcester, Massachusetts.

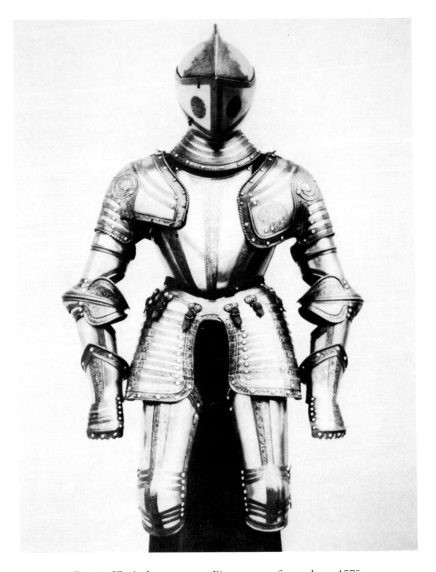

PLATE 27. A three-quarter Pisan armor from about 1575, of fine quality. This suit comes from the Wilton armory of Sidney's relatives by marriage, the Pembroke family. Sidney might well have been wearing armor similar to this when he was shot, though perhaps with a burgonet replacing the close-helmet. JWHA 427. Stephen V. Grancsay, *Catalogue of Armor: The John Woodman Higgins Armory,* pp. 84–85. Photo courtesy of Higgins Armory Museum, Worcester, Massachusetts.

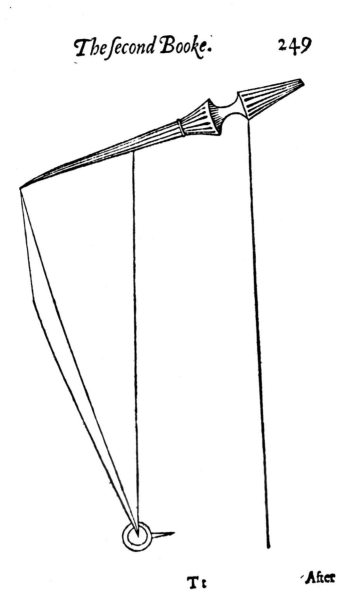

T t   **After**

PLATE 28. Gervase Markham's diagram of the four lines a horseman should picture when he is about to run at the ring. The first, or bottom, line, runs from the butt of the lance horizontally to a point below the ring. The second runs from the rider's right eye to the ring itself. The third goes from the tip of the lance directly to the ring. The fourth, or top line, is made up of three segments and is the path traced out by the tip of the lance as the rider approaches the ring.

    Markham's analysis of the motion of the lance follows that of the French writer on horsemanship, Salomon de la Broue. Gervase Markham, *Cavelarice or the English Horseman* (London, 1607), Book II, p. 249. The Beinecke Rare Book and Manuscript Library, Yale University.

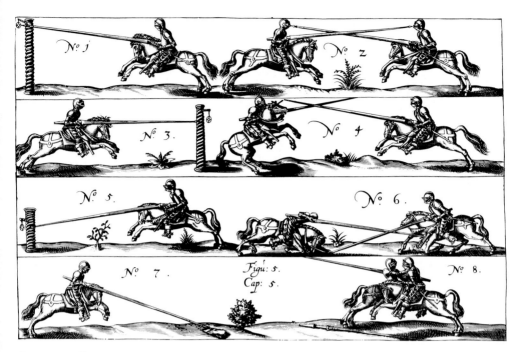

PLATE 29. Illustrations showing how running at the ring served as practice for combat. The lance was held in the same position for running at a ring suspended at eye-level and for striking an opponent on the head or neck (Nos. 1–2). Holding the lance horizontally was practice for killing a horse by hitting it directly on the forehead (Nos. 3–4). Running at a ring close to the ground was equivalent to piercing a horse's breast (Nos. 5–6). A cavalryman could also lift objects off the ground (No. 7) or drop his weapon in order to grab his opponent bodily (No. 8). From Johann J. Wallhausen, *Ritterkunst* (Frankfurt am Main, 1616; reprint ed., Graz: Akademische Druck—u. Verlagsanstalt, 1969), Figure 5.

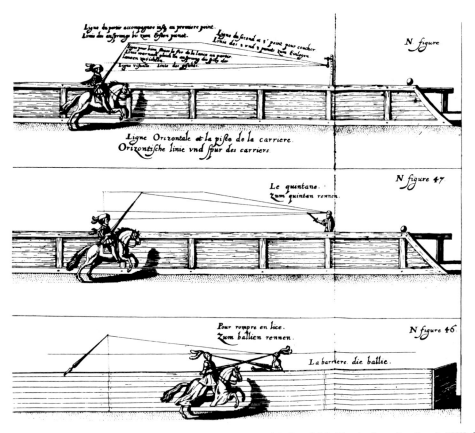

PLATE 30. Part of a plate from the treatise on horsemanship in which Pluvinel teaches Louis XIII the manège and the fine points of riding. The top illustration of the three shows the geometry of the motion of the lance in "running at the ring." The center illustration depicts the quintain, a revolvable mannequin, and the bottom one, two knights tilting. Pluvinel's magnificently illustrated treatise first appeared as *Maneige royal* (Paris, 1623). The plate shown here is taken from the bilingual French and German edition. Antoine de Pluvinel, *L'instruction du Roy; Reitkunst* (Frankfurt am Main, 1628), from Figure 37. The Beinecke Rare Book and Manuscript Library, Yale University.

PLATE 31. February, archivolt, St. Mark's.

PLATE 32. Discord, capital, Ducal Palace.

PLATE 33. Temperance, Giotto, Arena Chapel.

PLATE 34. Ire, Giotto, Arena Chapel.

PLATE 35. Ire, capital, Ducal Palace.

312

PLATE 36. Charity, capital, Ducal Palace.

PLATE 37. Charity, Giotto, Arena Chapel.

PLATE 38. Luxury, capital, Ducal Palace.

PLATE 39. Envy. capital, Ducal Palace.

PLATE 40. Envy, Giotto, Arena Chapel.

PLATE 41. J. M. W. Turner, *The Goddess of Discord Choosing the Apple of Contention in the Garden of the Hesperides.*

318

PLATE 42. Ruskin after Turner, *Quivi Trovammo*, (7. illustration 78).

Index

Contents of Previous Volumes